THE OUTSIDER

THE OUTSIDER

A History of the Goalkeeper

JONATHAN WILSON

This edition first published in Great Britain in 2012 by
Orion Books
an imprint of the Orion Publishing Group Ltd
Orion House, 5 Upper St Martin's Lane,
London WC2H 9EA
An Hachette UK Company

1 3 5 7 9 10 8 6 4 2

A CIP catalogue record for this book is available
from the British Library.

ISBN: 978 1 4091 2319 4

Typeset by Input Data Services Ltd, Bridgwater, Somerset

Printed and bound by CPI Group (UK) Ltd, Croydon, CR0 4YY

The Orion Publishing Group's policy is to use papers that are natural,
renewable and recyclable and made from wood grown in sustainable
forests. The logging and manufacturing processes are expected to conform
to the environmental regulations of the country of origin.

Every effort has been made to fulfil requirements with regard to
reproducing copyright material. The author and publisher will
be glad to rectify any omissions at the earliest opportunity.

www.orionbooks.co.uk

CONTENTS

ACKNOWLEDGEMENTS

All books are to a large extent collaborations. There's one name on the cover but a multitude of people behind that whose contributions deserve recognition and to whom I am extremely grateful. The willingness of so many people to offer their assistance so readily has been humbling.

In Cameroon, thanks to Willie Niba for his help in arranging interviews and translating, to Théophile Abega and Jean Manga-Onguené for their hospitality, to Jean-Paul Akono and Robert Atah for going out of their way to give me lifts, and to Adjutant Kwang for his driving and general air of authority. Thanks to Ian Hawkey for nudging me, however inadvertently, towards the story of Bob Mensah in Cape Coast (sadly that Peter Crouch to Mysterious Dwarfs transfer still hasn't come off) and to Silas Akowuah at the archive of the *Daily Graphic* in Accra. Thanks in Ghana also to Yao, for not getting lost too often and only starting to sing right at the end of the trip.

In Brazil, thanks to Tim Vickery and Arturo Hartmann for arranging interviews and interpreting and to Cassiano Gobbet and Rodrigo Orihuela for their hospitality and advice. In Argentina, thanks to Sebastian Garcia, Joel Richards and Araceli Alemán for information and assistance with translation. For their work with logistics, research and translation, thanks in Serbia to Vladimir Novak, in Hungary to Sandor Láczkó, in Poland to Maciej Iwanski, in Romania to Emanuel Roşu, in Ukraine to Taras Hordiyenko and Oleksandr Sereda and in Russia to Igor Rabiner, Ivan Kalashnikov and Vladimir Soldatkin.

Thanks to James Horncastle for all his help in researching

Italian goalkeeping, to Richard Jolly for his work in the north-west and to Alex Jackson and Sally Hawley from the National Football Museum for sharing their knowledge of football before the First World War.

Thanks to all at the British Library at St Pancras and the British Newspaper Library at Colindale and to the dozens of people who gave up their time to be interviewed.

Thanks also to Jon Adams, Philippe Auclair, Sheridan Bird, Duncan Castles, Dan Colasimone, James Corbett, Michael Cox, Miguel Delaney, Gavin Hamilton, Uli Hesse, Raphael Honigstein, Graham Hunter, Juliet Jacques, Sam Kelly, Simon Kuper, Sid Lowe, Musa Okwonga, Ed Malyon, Gabriele Marcotti, Kevin McCarra, Scott Murray, Paul Myers, Lars Sivertsen, Rob Smyth, Grant Wahl and David Winner for offering guidance, advice and various nuggets of information.

Thanks to my agent, David Luxton, my editor, Ian Preece, my copy editor, John English, and to Jillian Young and Alan Samson at Orion.

And thanks, particularly, to Kat Petersen, for her patience, support, eagle-eyed assessment of the text and generally for putting me right.

'... in disgrace with fortune and men's eyes,
I all alone beweep my outcast state ...'

William Shakespeare, Sonnet IXXX, 1-2

PROLOGUE

My greatest sporting moment? That's easy. It was the final minute of a school hockey match against Whickham, the only side in the North East who could touch us. It was 0-0 and they had a short corner. The ball was pushed out, two defenders charged and the ball was stopped for their centre-half, who was called Robson and was in the England youth squad. He shaped to strike the ball but in the end decided to flick it. As he did so, the thought went through my mind that he was outside the D. I remember thinking, as the ball rose to my right, that I ought at least to dive for it even if he were outside the D. Everything seemed to be happening very slowly. I even remember wondering what the rule was if he had shot from outside the D and the ball glanced in off my stick. Looking through the grille of the helmet, I could see the red airtex sleeve of my shirt, my fat white glove, and the black and blue of my stick. I could also see the ball, its trajectory taking it a little above the stick. Apparently having all the time in the world, I moved my wrist, angling the stick to intercept the ball. The intersection of post and bar came abruptly into view and, about six inches in front of the top corner of the net, the ball slapped into the meat of the stick. I glanced down – and again I remember the mental process clearly – and was shocked at how high up I was, and immediately concerned by how much it was going to hurt when I hit the ground.

It didn't; one of the few advantages of being a hockey keeper is that the entire front of your body is covered in two inches of stiff foam. I could see the ball spinning loose and, for a split second, nobody seemed to be moving towards it. In that moment there was a glorious stillness, a silence. It was a sensation I'd never had before and one that I've only had once since – when I took a diving catch at short midwicket to end a stubborn ninth-wicket partnership as the Oxfordshire village for whom I was playing won a low-scoring match against the BBC. That time, as I saw the ball slap into my left palm, I even thought, *This is just like that game against Whickham*, before landing on a painful combination of shoulder and hip.

Two instances, twelve years apart. For somebody who has played some kind of sport on average at least once a week for thirty years, it doesn't seem much, but at least I've felt it. I'm sure proper sportspeople regularly get that sensation of time slowing down, of being utterly in control. As the Ajax coach David Endt put it, 'The seconds of the greats last longer than those of normal people.' There is evidence to suggest the memory of control is false, that it is an invention of the brain to explain a reflex reaction that begins in the muscles themselves. Wherever it originates, that sensation of control over fractional changes happening extraordinarily quickly seems to lie at the heart of sporting excellence.

The very best must have it most of the time. That first occasion, I thought it might be a perpetual state, that I might, through practice, have attained some level at which time and my reflexes were in harmony. I even expounded at what must have been deeply tedious length on the possibility that night on the minibus to York for a Latin lecture. Nobody cared. I was like the hobbits returning to the Shire to find everybody too wrapped up in their own mundane lives to care about my adventures. But who knew what heights I could scale? If I could claw a flick from an England midfielder away from the top corner, then what was to stop me making the England squad?

The next game we played was the following week, away at Hall Cross School in Doncaster. I hadn't had much to do when, shortly before half-time, their forward turned in a crowded D and shot. I was unsighted, but threw myself down, thinking my prone body would provide a barrier. It would have done, but he mishit it dreadfully and the ball slithered through the tiny space between my feet and the post. We went on to lose 4–0 and, by a generous estimate, two of the other three goals were my fault. On the bus back, I was exiled to the front seat next to the teacher. That was my dreams of greatness over. It was also the end for me as a goalkeeper. It was never quite the same after that.

I played on that season but by the time I got to university, after a year of teaching in a Tibetan monastery and washing dishes in a Sunderland pub, I decided I didn't fancy having the ball pinged at me at speeds that left bruising even through the padding for the occasional fleeting moment of glory that nobody cared about and the certainty that, sooner or later, you'd have a game bad enough that you wouldn't be able to stop thinking about it for – well, it's nineteen years since the Hall Cross game and it still niggles.

I've gone in goal every now and again for Barnes Beavers, the team I play for in the Surrey League, when they've been really desperate. On one magnificently hung-over occasion against Wanderers at Battersea Park, I had one of those games where the ball hits you whatever you do. Then, ten minutes from time, with a heroic goalless draw in sight, I was beaten by an own goal, stiff-limbed, silver-haired, fortysomething Roger diverting a right-wing cross in at the near post as I edged out to clear. I've never gone back in goal since: it's just too cruel, too frustrating.

Maybe that's why goalkeepers tend to be reflective types, prone to introversion, trying, perhaps, to rationalise why such unfair things happen to such undeserving people. The question, I suppose, is whether gloomy prognosticators are drawn to goal-keeping or whether goalkeeping makes them like that.

Again, cause and effect are hard to align, but goalkeepers tend to be individuals, not necessarily intellectuals, but at the very least people who think for themselves. Generally speaking, goal-keepers make for better interviews than other players. Perhaps that's why when, on the very rare occasions literature considers football, it concerns itself so disproportionately with goalkeep-ers. One of the most popular fictional detectives of the eighties, for instance, was Duffy, a cynical bisexual ex-policeman created by Dan Kavanagh, the pseudonym of Julian Barnes, himself an occasional goalkeeper. His 1985 novel *Putting the Boot In* is also one of the few novels to deal realistically with the world of football, in those days a grim, violent place of ersatz glamour in which hooliganism is rife and neo-fascist gangs hand out pamphlets at the turnstiles. Duffy, at least at the start of the novel, is more concerned by another threat: that of AIDS. A fastidious man anyway, he spends hours checking his skin for the brown marks he believes indicate infection while fretting about incubation periods.

Duffy is also a Sunday league footballer, an anxious outsider in the brusque, overtly masculine world of the park game. He is, naturally, a goalkeeper. The opening section of *Putting the Boot In* follows Duffy's thoughts during a match, introducing the case – that of a player for the third-division London side 'Athletic' who has had his Achilles deliberately snapped in a car park – as he worries about 'that speedy little ginge' on the wing, who has the beating of the full-back.

Like other keepers, Duffy 'worried about playing badly, and losing, and letting the side down, and getting kicked, and facing penalties, and getting called a wally'. But his worrying went deeper than that.

> One of the reasons he liked goalkeeping – and one of the reasons he worried – was that he liked things neat. He liked the neat box of the penalty area; he liked the way it marked out his territory, his manor. Everything that happens inside this box is *your* responsibility, Duffy; he felt like some young copper being given his first beat. He also liked the way everything in his manor had corners; the penalty area, the goal area, the woodwork; even the netting was made in squares. He liked these right-angles; they reassured him. The only thing on his patch that didn't have corners was the penalty spot. A great big round chalky mess, as if some enormous pigeon up above had decided to unload right into the middle of his manor: *splat.*

He is neurotic and he hates penalties, evoking – whether by design or not – the most famous serious film about football, *The Goalkeeper's Fear of the Penalty*, directed by Wim Wenders. That film, and the Peter Handke novel it's based on, set the template for the goalkeeper – or, at least, the goalkeeper as he is perceived in wider culture, a perception that may or may not be accurate.

This is a book about goalkeepers and goalkeeping, about goal-keeping as it manifests itself on the pitch but also about how goalkeepers are represented culturally, from the haplessness represented in the British films *Kes* and *Gregory's Girl* to the hero-ism of the Soviet musical *Vratar*. Although there is some discus-sion of technical and tactical aspects of the position, this is not a coaching manual; rather it's about how the goalkeeper and the perception of goalkeepers have changed over time and from country to country. It's about the relationship between an indi-vidual and the team and about how sport reflects and reacts to the political culture of its time. It's not an encyclopaedia of goal-keeping – some very fine goalkeepers don't feature or are men-tioned only in passing; it's about those who have most shaped or challenged our perceptions of what it is to be a goalkeeper.

I: THE BRINGER OF FAMINE

Today, the goalkeeper seems eternal. It feels natural that a team should be made of ten plus one, that behind the outfielders scurrying in their 4-4-2 or 4-2-3-1 or strikerless 4-3-3 there should be an unspoken other, his place so taken for granted that nobody even bothers to refer to it when discussing formations. That, though, is a relatively modern phenomenon. When the game that would evolve into football began with the foundation of the Football Association in 1863, there was no such thing as a goalkeeper in the modern sense.

Early football – in Britain at least – was all about dribbling and scoring goals, and very little to do with organising means of stopping them. None of the many mid-nineteenth-century attempts at a set of unified rules – that is, developing a football code that could bring together in the same game sportsmen from different public schools, all of whom had their own way of playing what they termed 'football' – makes reference to a goalkeeper. The first match played under the rules of the FA was contested by Barnes and Richmond. It finished in a goalless draw, despite both sides taking to the field with two backs and nine forwards, the usual formation of the age. Under the early rules, any player could handle the ball by taking a 'Fair Catch', which permitted them a free-kick if, immediately after catching the ball, they made an impression in the pitch with their boot. Running with the ball in both hands or scoring with a throw, though, was not permitted.

In that, the FA was merely following centuries of tradition. The rules drawn up at Shrewsbury School in 1858 and the Sheffield Rules of 1857 both allow for 'fair catches' but make no reference to goalkeepers, while the 1887 Harrow Rules, which clearly reflect the game as it had been played at the school for some time, allowed 'handling' but only to take a clean catch, at which the player had to shout 'yards'. If he did so, he was entitled to move three yards in any direction without being challenged.

None of the various games that claim to have been the forerunner of football features a lone player who hung back. Most seem to have allowed all of their players to handle or catch the ball, although only some allowed it to be carried, and all seem to have been weighted in favour of attacking rather than defending (even if in some variants goals were scored only a couple of times a century).

Yet, few and insignificant as they may have been, there were defenders, from whom the goalkeeper must be seen to have evolved. In *phaininda* and *harpastum*, the ancient Greek and Roman games, for instance – which used a small ball and had far more in common with the Cornish variant of hurling than football – slower players were positioned at the back in what the physician and philosopher Galen termed the '*locus stantium*' – 'the position of the standing players'.

Our knowledge of both games is limited but by the late sixteenth century another ball game that, it's logical to assume, had its origins in *harpastum* had grown in popularity in Italy and particularly in Florence: *calcio*. From the rules set down by the Florentine nobleman Giovanni de' Bardi, it's known that teams consisted of twenty-seven players which, according to the *Vocabolario della Crusca*, published in 1612, were laid out as '15 *innanzi o corridori, 5 sconciatori, 4 datori innanzi, 3 datori e dietro*' – a 15-5-4-3 formation, but no goalkeeper – although, in a game in which everybody was permitted to handle the ball, all defenders were in a sense goalkeepers.

Before there could be goalkeepers, of course, there had to be goals, and there was very little consensus in early football as to what that meant. In *calcio*, for instance, the goal at each end spanned the entire width of the pitch. The British tradition, the direct antecedent of modern football, seems generally to have preferred a smaller, demarcated area at either end.

In his 1801 book *Sports and Pastime of the People of England*, for instance, Joseph Strutt described a game in Yorkshire. 'When a match at football is made an equal number of competitors take the field and stand between two goals placed at a distance of eighty or one hundred yards from each other,' he wrote. 'The goal is usually made of two sticks driven into the ground about two or three feet apart.' No need then, with a goal that slender, for anybody to be designated to stand between the posts. The Eton Wall Game, similarly, played on a pitch 120 yards long by 6 yards wide, had goals so small – a door at one end and a marked portion of an elm tree at the other – that to designate a specialist goalkeeper from the eighteen- or twenty-man sides was pointless.

Gradually, through the nineteenth century, there grew an awareness that those who defended deep were performing a particular role, even if it were one that tended not to be much respected. In Roman times it may have been the slowest players who played at the back, but in the Victorian school defenders were those perceived as lacking not physically so much as morally. In *Football at Westminster School*, H. C. Benham writes of games that featured goals about twelve yards wide, the space between conveniently located trees at either end of the pitch. 'The small boys, the duffers, and the funk-sticks were the goalkeepers, twelve or fifteen at each end, and were spread out across this wide space,' he said. 'If any fellow who was playing out showed any sign of "funk" or failed to play up, he was packed off into the goal at once, not for that day, but as a lasting degradation. On the other hand, if any goalkeeper made a good save of a goal, he was called for immediately to play out, and thenceforth he played out always.' There's a basic logical flaw there, of course, in that as soon as somebody proved themselves good at goalkeeping they ceased to be a goalkeeper but, more than that, there was a stigma attached to playing in goal, one that, in Britain at least, appears to linger still beneath the surface.

All schools had their own rules that depended largely on the pitch available, but the idea of multiple goalkeepers seems to have been common. *The Book of Rugby School* includes a chapter seemingly written by W. H. Arnold, brother of the headmaster Thomas, that was almost certainly source material for the famous match described by Thomas Hughes in *Tom Brown's Schooldays*. In it, he details a team of forty members of the Sixth playing against 460 others, of whom 260 play in goal.

The thankless task of being a goalkeeper was clear. In his *Recollections of Schooldays at Harrow*, Reverend H. J. Torre describes how, 'It fell to the lot of the small boys to keep "base" or goal, which was uncommonly cold work, and when the rush came they generally found themselves on their backs in the mud. The headmaster Christopher Wordsworth (1836–44) stipulated that no more than four boys could '"keep base" at any one time and for no more than thirty minutes'.

If anything, the position was even more dangerous at Charterhouse, where football was played not on a grass field, but on a cloister twelve feet wide and seventy yards long. Again, defending or keeping goal was left to the fags. 'The ball very soon got into one of the buttresses, when a terrific squash would be the result, some fifty or sixty boys huddled together, vigorously "rouging", kicking and shoving to extricate the ball,' wrote E. P. Eardley-Wilmot and E. C. Streatfield in *Charterhouse Old and New*.

> A skilful player, feeling that he had the ball in front of his legs, would patiently bide his time, until, perceiving an opportunity, he would dexterously work out the ball and rush wildly with it down Cloisters towards the coveted goal. The squash would then dissolve and go in pursuit. Now was the time for the pluck and judgement of the fags to be tried.
>
> To prevent the ball getting in amongst them at the goal, one of the foremost fags would rush out and engage the onset of the dribbling foe, generally to be sent spinning head over heels for five yards along the stones. It served a purpose, however, for it not only gave his side time to come up, but also his fellow Fags encouragement to show a close and firm front. If the boy with the ball happened to be well backed up by his own house, they would launch themselves right into the

middle of the Fags, when a terrific scrimmage would ensue. The Fags would strive their utmost to prevent the ball being driven through, and hammer away with fists at hands grasping the corners of the wall to obtain a better purchase for shoving. One of those scrimmages sometimes lasted for three quarters of an hour. Shins would be kicked black and blue; jackets and other articles of clothing almost torn to shreds; and Fags trampled underfoot.

As the century approached its midpoint, there came a greater uniformity as to the number of players per side and the size of the goals. In his *History of British Football*, Percy M. Young presents anecdotal evidence that eleven-a-side football was common at Harrow in the 1830s, but the first concrete report of the eleven-a-side game came in 1841 as *Bell's Life* magazine noted that the Field Game (which, although not exactly football, was clearly closely related to it) had been contested at Eton between two eleven-man sides.

The size of the goals was even more variable than the size of the pitch. An eleven-a-side match between Eton and Harrow in 1862, for instance, featured 'bases' twelve feet apart and twenty feet high. The notion of a goal that could reasonably be defended by one man evidently had no currency. The first FA laws, drawn up in 1863, stipulated the goals should be twenty-four feet across (as it remains), but made clear that a goal was scored when the ball passed 'over the space between the goal-posts'; there was no restriction as to height.

After lobbying from the Sheffield club, the foremost of those northern bodies whose version of football had grown up outside the framework of the public schools, the law was changed in 1866 so the maximum height of the goal was set at eight feet and marked by a tape; the dimensions haven't changed since. Sheffield had wanted a crossbar, and the FA eventually saw the advantages, legalising crossbars in 1875 and making them compulsory in 1882.

That there was a desire to impose a maximum height makes sense. The northern game is far less well-documented than that of the public schools but it appears that for some time before the unified law-making in the 1860s at least some variants of the game featured a version of a goalkeeper. 'The goalkeeper,' the Sheffield rules of 1857 stated, 'is that player on the defending side who, for the time being, is nearest to his own goal.' It sounds, in other words, like the last-man-back rule often applied in casual kickabouts.

In the public schools, though, the earliest reference to a goalkeeper comes in an account of a game between Uppingham School and Old Boys in the school magazine on 15 December 1865.

> After some interval the Old Boys obtained a goal. This advantage they seemed determined to keep. The goal keeping of Rawnsley [W. F. Rawnsley, 1845–1927, who was a page at Tennyson's wedding; his younger brother, Canon H. D. Rawnsley, was one of the founders of the National Trust] for our opponents was in excellent style; not so that of the school which was loose and defective in generalship ... the ball was kept in close proximity to the old boys' goal and, but alas, it evinced a decided repugnance to the space between the two posts.
>
> Meanwhile the minutes were getting very precious and still the old boys were that envious goal ahead. 'Two minutes more,' cried the umpire. Now for a last effort. The school led gallantly by [C.] Childs was becoming eager and furious. Rawnsley was cool and observant at the goal. No ball passed his ubiquitous hands and feet. Could nothing be done? Was there no pluck left to deserve and win success? Yes. A sudden rush, a flying ball, a desperate charge, feet well together, enemy after enemy passed, Childs demonstrating the well-known proverb, the 'right foot in the right place', Rawnsley's eye deceived and quickness frustrated and the goal was won.

What is noticeable is the change in tone. Here, the goalkeeper is heroic, far from the 'funk-stick' of twenty years earlier, which suggests a growing appreciation of the importance of his role.

In *A Century of Soccer*, Terence Delaney speculated that it was in 1865 that one of the backs began to be designated as a 'goal-keeper', with the ten outfielders comprising a 'goal-cover', a 'back' and eight forwards.

Only in 1871, though, did the laws finally make reference to a 'goalkeeper' as the one player who 'shall be at liberty to use his hands for the protection of his goal'; he was, effectively, a back who had dropped deeper and deeper to become something else, one who retained the privilege of handling – in his own half – after it was stripped from every other player. Initially he was allowed to handle anywhere on the field; only in 1887 was that privilege curtailed. 'The Committee,' the FA *Memorandum for the Guidance of Umpires and Referees* read, 'does not consider a goalkeeper to be in *defence* of his goal when he is in his opponents' half of the ground, therefore a goalkeeper is prohibited from using his hands in his opponents' half.' It wouldn't be until 1912 that the goalkeeper was limited to handling in his own box only – although in practice he left his line so rarely, and players were so generally static in their positions, that was probably not such a striking difference from the modern game as it may sound; in fact as soon as goalkeepers did start to try to take advantage, the law was changed.

By the 1870s, then, the role of the goalkeeper was accepted. 'The formation of a team as a rule,' Charles W. Alcock, the first secretary of the FA, the inventor of the FA Cup and the principal motivator behind the first international fixture, wrote, 'was to provide for seven forwards and only four players to cover the three lines of the defence. The last line was, of course, the goal-keeper, and in front of him was only one full-back, who had again before him but two half-backs, to check the rushes of the opposite forwards.'

And so was born the goalkeeper, that curious figure, both part of the team and somehow different. He was not, though, that different, wearing the same strip as his team-mates until 1909, and it was not uncommon for outfield players to take a turn in goal when required, or to become specialist goalkeepers later in their careers.

Major Sir Arthur Francis Mandarin, for instance, was renowned as a full-back for Royal Engineers, the club he founded, and also played in goal for Old Etonians. When the two sides met in the 1875 FA Cup final, he decided not to play for either. Two years later, Wanderers found themselves without a goalkeeper for the FA Cup final against Oxford University, an indication, perhaps, of the lack of seriousness attached to the position – or at least the lack of a sense that it was a specialised position. Lord Arthur Fitzgerald Kinnaird, celebrated as a red-bearded hard man and one of the foremost names of Victorian football, although more usually a half, volunteered for the role. Early on, Evelyn Waddington tried a shot from long range which Kinnaird seemed to have dealt with, gathering the ball cleanly, only then to step back over the goal line. Oxford appealed for the goal, and the umpires gave it. Wanderers went on to equal-ise and won the game in extra-time, but Kinnaird couldn't bear the embarrassment and petitioned the FA to expunge his own goal from the records. Remarkably, they agreed, and although the goal has now been reinstated, for over 100 years the final was officially listed as having finished 2–0.

Perhaps the oddity of the goalkeeper, the reluctance to embrace the position or install him as something unique, the suspicion with which he was so often viewed, is only natural. In *Only the Goalkeeper to Beat*, Francis Hodgson, an amateur goalkeeper him-self and one who argues the keeper's corner with remarkable vehemence, points out that the goalkeeper is a 'spoilsport', the one man on the pitch who 'is there to do his utmost to prevent the very thing that everybody present wants to occur ... At root, he is an anti-footballer. By being devoted to the prevention of goals he is set against the core of football.' But it goes deeper than that.

Most anthropologists agree that football, like the majority of sports, began as a quasi-religious rite. As Young summarises in his history of British football, the game had its origins as 'the dark gods of fertility were served through the ceremonies of ball-play. Thus the ball was driven towards the goal – the sanctified landmark of tree or stream. The ball, the emblem of the sun, was carried home as a guarantee of good fortune.' The annual Shrove Tuesday game in Ashbourne, Derbyshire, for instance, Young says, 'enshrines the ancient invocations to the deities of earth, and air, and water'.

In many fertility rites, W. B. Johnson pointed out in a piece in the *Contemporary Review* in 1929, a disc-shaped or globular object is used to represent the sun and is hung in trees or buried among crops to symbolise the arrival of the sun to stimulate growth. In some Irish villages, Johnson says, gold and silver balls representing the sun and moon were paraded on May Day, while Native Americans in Oklahoma played a version of football to celebrate the harvest, aligning the pitch from east to west to evoke the passage of the sun (frustratingly, he doesn't specify which of the ninety-one Native American tribes in Oklahoma enacted the ritual). The traditional mob football of England follows a similar pattern: the goal was often a tree, while certain games, such as that at Scone, required the ball to be placed repeatedly in a hole in the ground (a symbolic burial) for a 'goal' to be scored. According to F. K. Robinson in his *Glossary of Words used in the Neighbourhood of Whitby*, it was believed there was a correlation between a farmer's performance in the Shrove Tuesday game at Whitby and his performance at the following harvest, while in Normandy it was thought that the winning side in the Shrove Tuesday game would enjoy a better yield of cider apples than the losing side. As Maurice Marples demonstrates in his history of football, there are countless examples of societies in which it was believed that good crops depended on good management of the symbolic ball.

E. K. Chambers sets out a slightly different variant of the rite in *The Medieval Stage*, arguing that the ball represents not the sun but the head of a sacrificial beast. Either way, the ramifications for the goalkeeper remain the same. If football represents an elaborate fertility rite in which the gods were served by forcing the ball into or against the sanctified landmark – by scoring a goal – then logically the role of the goalkeeper – who only, of course, emerged much later – was an aberration; he was the man whose job was to stop the rite being fulfilled, to prevent the symbolic sun completing its journey. If the knowledge of those primal rites lies deep in the psyche of the game, then the goalkeeper is a symbolic prophylactic, the destroyer of harvests, the bringer of famine.

That is one reason why the figure of the goalkeeper should evoke unease, but its origins are submerged in the game's past, understood, if it is understood at all, only subconsciously. There is, of course, a much more obvious incongruity about the keeper's role, which is that he will have least to do when his side has played best and will be at his best only when the rest of the side has in some way failed. He is like the lifeguard or the fireman, to be thanked in times of crisis even as everybody wonders why the crisis arose in the first place.

Perhaps Ted Ditchburn, the former Tottenham goalkeeper, captured that inevitability of disregard best in his almost elegiac contribution to the 1951 collection *My Greatest Game*. 'I pass on to the occasions when a keeper can really shine,' he wrote.

And unfortunately for your own team, these periods come when your side is usually having a bad game so that you are given plenty to do. No keeper can really get warmed up unless he is worked hard. To make one or two good saves a match is most goalkeepers' usual habit, but to give such a show as will have the crowd roaring and yelling, the poor keeper has to be subjected to a rain of shots and a storm of attacks. This is a sad state of affairs, I must confess, for it assumes you won't shine unless your side is overrun; and though it is possible to finish on the winning side when you have given a brilliant display, more often than not you are bound to finish on the losing end.

Ditchburn was at least speaking in a time in which goalkeeper was a recognised position and his unique, if unsettling, role accepted. In was only in the late 1870s and early 1880s, though, that the goalkeeper was really acknowledged as a significant member of the side. Typically, it was another of the players who began life as outfielders who began the process of making the position respectable.

James McAulay, who would be the first to be accorded the title 'the Prince of Goalkeepers', was highly enough regarded as a centre-forward to make his international debut in the position. He scored for Dumbarton in the 1881 Scottish Cup final, which they lost 2–1 (and then 3–1 when the game was replayed following a protest) and played at centre-forward in the final the following year as Dumbarton lost to the same opposition. Dumbarton's goalkeeper John Kennedy, who played in both those finals, then suffered a catastrophic loss of form, prompting McAulay to take his place. He was in goal as Dumbarton won the 1883 Scottish Cup final against Vale of Leven and went on to win a further eight Scottish caps as a keeper before his work as an engineer forced him to move to Burma in 1887. 'It was as a goalkeeper that his greatness was revealed on taking up the position,' a piece marking his emigration in the *Glasgow Herald* insisted. 'Intrepid, cool to the point of nonchalance and maker of innumerable saves with hands and feet.'

The impression McAulay made was clear from the 1887 book *Athletics and Football*, written by Montague Shearman, the founder of the Amateur Athletics Association and later a judge. 'Perhaps the most important position on the whole field is that of the goalkeeper,' he wrote, in radical contrast to what had gone before. 'He must have a cool head, a quick eye and hand, and the longer reach he has with his arms the better. Although, too, he has only to defend the space between the posts, and all his work has to be done between the posts or within a few yards of them, he must be ready to display the greatest possible activity within his limited circle ...'

Shearman may have gone further than others, but he was reflecting a general trend. By the mid-1880s, the goalkeeper was respected enough that companies began to manufacture specialist equipment for him. Geo. G. Bussey of Peckham, manufacturers of 'gymnastic apparatus and every requisite for British sports and indoor and outdoor games', for instance, advertised goalkeepers' gloves in its catalogue alongside 'shin guards', 'football ear guards', 'ankle guards', 'football players' bags' and 'football belts'. They were available in either 'buff leather and black rubber' for 5/- a pair or, if you wanted to splash out, 'white leather and red leather' for 5/9. From the illustration, they look remarkably modern – more modern, in fact, than the cotton and dimpled rubber available in the 1970s. The backs, presumably the leather part, are ventilated and resemble a driving glove, while the fronts, the rubber part, are two-tone, four fingers in one colour and the thumb and lower part of the hand another. Shearman went on:

> It is sometimes little short of marvellous to see goalkeepers like Arthur, of the Blackburn Rovers, or McAulay, the Scottish international, stop shot after shot in rapid succession, turning from side to side without ever losing presence of mind or balance of body. The goalkeepers of today have no easy task when the forwards have learnt to pass to one another in the jaws of the goal; and the best that can be said of modern goalkeepers is that they have proved themselves equal to the task. Doubtless players in this position were as plucky and as resolute in the days when Kirkpatrick kept goal for more than half an hour to the end of a match while one arm was hanging broken from his shoulder; but the modern players have better tactics to contend with and are equally successful in their defence.

Kirkpatrick was one of the great figures of early football. Sir James Kirkpatrick, eighth baronet of Closeburn, Dumfriesshire, was private secretary to Lord George Hamilton, first Lord of the Admiralty, and goalkeeper and captain of Scotland when they faced England at The Oval in 1870. Some regard that fixture as the first international but as the Scotland team was drawn only from those living in London, it is not accorded full international status. A regular for Wanderers and his county, the *Football Annual* for 1875 described him as 'a goalkeeper [who] is always excellent and Surrey owes much to him in that position' while the 1879 edition said that he was 'a very useful goalkeeper; fields well, and does not lose his head'.

Although he played fifty-eight games in eleven seasons for the club, he was rarely available for FA Cup ties. He did, though, umpire the first FA Cup final, in 1872, and played in every round in 1877–78 as Wanderers reached the final against Royal Engineers. It was that game that sealed his legend. Sometime in the second half – Shearman's suggestion that more than half an hour remained is challenged by Derek Warsop in his 2004 book on the early FA Cup finals; he reckons fifteen minutes from time more likely – Kirkpatrick made a save in a goal-line skirmish, breaking his arm in the process. With no substitutes available he refused to go off or even swap positions with another player and wander about on the wing, insisting on playing on, ensuring Wanderers won 3–1, their last FA Cup final success and Kirkpatrick's swansong for the club.

The Arthur to whom Shearman refers, meanwhile, is Herby Arthur, a seven-time England international who won three FA Cups with Blackburn Rovers between 1884 and 1886. Whatever his talents between the posts, though, Arthur is probably most often recalled these days for his role in the first major instance of corruption in football. In 1898, in a piece in *Football News*, a goalkeeper spoke of an incident that had occurred a few years earlier. Although he wrote anonymously, he said that he was an England international, that he had played for a club from Lancashire starting with B and that the incident had happened before a Cup semi-final while training in 'a town noted for its cutlery'. He claimed that ten days before the game, he received a letter 'asking my terms to throw the match away'. He reported the issue to the club secretary and thought little more about it.

A couple of days later, he was walking through the town when he bumped into 'a sporting publican'. The goalkeeper was an abstainer but 'he would have me go into a wayside public house to drink success to the result and after drinking a lemonade my mind was a complete blank'. When he came round he was in a small room 'in the company of two powerful-looking men'. Through the window he could see only rough moorland.

When they left him, locking the door, the goalkeeper took out his 'strong pocket-knife' and chiselled away at the mortar of the window until he could take it out and make his escape.

Hearing the noise of a train in the darkness, he headed for the sound until he came upon a small station. Once there, he roused the stationmaster and was given a sofa to sleep on. The following morning, the goalkeeper sent a telegram to the club secretary who came to collect him, at which point one of the kidnappers appeared. The stationmaster overpowered him and, in a panic, he confessed the plot. The centre-forward had been nobbled and the second-choice goalkeeper was injured; the publican had made a sizeable bet on B— losing; all he needed effectively to guarantee the result was to put the first-choice keeper out of the picture as well. Faced with the evidence, the publican owned up, fled B—, paying £20 to charity and £10 to the club for expenses. The goalkeeper urged the club to take pity on the centre-forward, who of course went on to play brilliantly as the club won both semi-final and final.

The story, it must be said, doesn't sound overly convincing – in fact, it reads more like one of Enid Blyton's less plausible tales than a genuine account of danger and skulduggery – while the attempts at anonymity are laughably transparent. Only two clubs starting with B had won the FA Cup by 1898: Blackburn Olympic in 1883 and Blackburn Rovers in 1884, 1885, 1886, 1890 and 1891. Only one England goalkeeper played for any of those sides: Herby Arthur. The only question then, if the story is taken at face value, is to which of the three finals in which he played he was referring. A best guess would be 1885, when Blackburn beat Old Carthusians 5–1 in the semi-final in Nottingham, or 1886 when they beat Swifts 2–1 in Derby; it makes sense to have trained in Sheffield (assuming that is the cutlery town referred to) for games in the east Midlands; less so for a match in Birmingham, which is where they played their 1884 semi-final.

Whether true or not, the anecdote highlights the other problem with goalkeepers, the other reason why they so often evoked mistrust: they were seen as corruptible. If you were going to fix a game and were only going to pay off one player, then of course it would be the goalkeeper. Who, after all, has more direct influence on whether goals are scored or not? Who really understands the art enough to know whether a moment's hesitation in coming for a cross, a fumbled catch or a delayed dive is bad play or foul play? Goalkeepers have always been targets for the fixers.

Long before his confession, Arthur had gained notoriety for an incident in a game against Burnley in December 1891. In dreadful conditions, Burnley led 3–0 by half-time, despite Arthur's attempts to kid the referee that the third of the goals had gone narrowly wide by scooping it back onto the pitch from the outside of the net and shaping to take a goal-kick. Blackburn offered to concede the game, but Burnley insisted on playing on, something Blackburn were so reluctant to do that four of their players hung around in the dressing room and missed the restart. Joseph Lofthouse of Blackburn and Alexander Stewart of Burnley then clashed and were both sent off, at which the rest of the Blackburn team decided to join them in leaving the field.

The rest of the Blackburn team, that is, apart from Arthur, who stayed out in the cold and the rain to take on Burnley alone. 'The affair,' Rambler wrote in the *Lancashire Evening Express*, 'was not totally void of the comical … The referee blew his whistle for play to proceed, and Burnley threw the ball in from the touchline, that being where the row had occurred. Arthur ran towards his goal surrounded by opponents, and I wondered what he would do. When within a few yards of the mouth he stopped and, turning coolly, appealed for offside. Roars of laughter greeted him from all quarters of the pitch.' The referee, a Mr Clegg, gave the free-kick, which Arthur, highlighting the absurdity of it all, rolled into his own net, at which the game was abandoned. The FA suspended Lofthouse and Stewart and introduced new legislation banning players from leaving the pitch without the referee's permission.

What is more generally significant about Shearman's account of the position, though, is the fact there is no mention of diving: he seemed to think the most admirable thing was for a goalkeeper to keep his balance. Perhaps understandably it took time for the goalkeeper, having at last been invented, to start doing goal-keeperly things like flinging himself about in his goalmouth. That Kennedy, the man McAulay replaced in goal at Dumbarton, was nicknamed 'Diver' seems relevant in that regard; he, pre-sumably, did dive, but it was considered so unusual that it was something that defined him.

The great Austrian journalist Willy Meisl, himself a goal-keeper of some repute, wrote in his 1956 book *Soccer Revolution* that the first time he saw goalkeepers deliberately diving for balls was in 1899. 'In that year,' he said, 'the first English pro-fessionals came over [to Austria], Southampton FC. They beat the Viennese city XI 6–0 and their goalkeeper, [Jack] Robinson, showed for the first time how to tackle low shots by flying through the air with the greatest of ease.' As a result, that type of save was known in Austria – in the first half of the twent-ieth century at least – as a Robinsonade. 'After the match,' Meisl went on, 'Robinson gave an exhibition. His goal was bombarded simultaneously with six balls and he saved most of the shots.'

Meisl's book was written in response to England's 'decline and fall' as a football nation – as he put it – something ham-mered home by the 6–3 defeat to Hungary in 1953, the first defeat England had suffered at home to continental opposition. The goalkeeper of that side, Gyula Grosics, who was widely con-sidered a pioneer of leaving his line and his box, also credited Robinson as one of the two principal models for continental Europeans. 'It was Moon of the Corinthians, Robinson, and many other world-famous English goalkeepers who had been the pioneers of this art and they showed the way for all Europe's goalkeepers,' he wrote. 'The fact that the Hungarians were good pupils has been amply proved by them and can be measured in the achievements of their goalies. Let me just mention the names of Ferenc Zsák and Ferenc Plattkó from among my excel-lent predecessors, who have not only mastered the motion style of English goalies but had developed it to some extent.'

Moon never toured, so he can have been known purely by his reputation. 'The standard of goalkeeping [in the 1880s] ...'

F. N. S. Creek wrote in his *History of the Corinthian Football Club*, 'was generally poor, especially on wet grounds, when long shots frequently "slipped through the goalkeeper's fingers." The one exception to this rule was W. R. Moon ... Moon was originally a full-back; but once when the Casuals were playing against Cambridge, they were a goalkeeper short and Moon kept goal to such good purpose that Cambridge did not score and England's future goalkeeper was discovered.'

Jack Robinson himself wrote a lengthy article in Gibson and Pickford's four-volume 1905 history *Association Football and the Men who Made It*, outlining what he considered the key attributes of the goalkeeper. The first decade of the twentieth century saw a number of similar pieces on the theory of football, as the sport gained enough credibility to be discussed and analysed with a measure of seriousness.

Like many of the other guides to goalkeeping, Robinson began by discussing size:

> They say a good *big* horse is better than a good *little* horse. A lot of these sayings are only half true. The one I have quoted does not hold true for football. I know several good *big* goalkeepers at the present time who, in my opinion, would have to yield the palm to the good *little* goalkeeper of Middlesbrough, [Tim] Williamson. Nevertheless, the old Latin saying *in medio stat virtus* sums up my views as to the height of the good custodian. It goes without saying that the little man is at a big disadvantage in dealing with high shots. On the other hand, the over-tall man finds great difficulty in stopping the 'daisy-croppers'. I know one goalkeeper who is positively brilliant in dealing with shots sent in at any height above his knees, yet he has given away as many as five goals in a match because the opposing forwards had for their motto, 'Keep them low.' The ideal height to my mind for a goalkeeper is five feet nine to five feet eleven inches.

The argument remains relevant today, even if the perceived ideal height of the goalkeeper has increased.

'You must in addition,' Robinson went on, 'be robust. I know from only too painful personal experience that the man in goal must be a compound of steel and gutta percha. You may be a weakling in other positions on the field and yet dodge damage, but in goal you are waiting for it and expecting it all the time – and you get it not infrequently.'

He lists other attributes – good eyesight, good and rapid judgement, 'courage and pluck' – and then adds intuition, something on which he expounds at length.

Whilst you are not actually defending, do not mope about like a sore-footed bear. Regard your opponents and study them. You note the tricks that the left-wingers or the right-wingers play, the tactics they adopt to beat your halves, to which man does the centre-forward mostly play, and the hundred and one little happenings which the game produces. Your judgement pieces these little things together, and forms a verdict as to what the result of a certain set of contingencies would be. But all this judgement and piecing together of things is simply the building up, unconsciously, of intuition, and intuition comes to your rescue when judgement would be slow-footed. You read of goalkeepers hypnotising the opposing forwards; in fact I have myself been credited with a certain mesmeric influence in that direction. The forward is blamed for shooting, as if spell-bound, right into the hands of the goalkeeper. Do not blame hypnotism for such a result. It was only intuitive knowledge on the part of the custodian. He knew that the ball would come in a certain way, and he was there to meet it.

While he may have been scornful of the notion of 'hypnotism', Robinson was superstitious, insisting on having a nail hammered into the back of every goalframe and hanging his watch from it. What he was advocating, which in essence is the practice of anticipation developed a few years earlier by the Morton and Scotland goalkeeper Harry Rennie, is something that was part of a far wider trend: the goalkeeper began as part of the team, as one of the backs, and then was segregated from them; Robinson, though, insists that the goalkeeper should not regard himself as cut off from the rest of the game, should not merely be a figure standing apart, reacting when the ball comes to him.

Robinson also advocated a careful diet. 'Eat well,' he wrote, 'but never be gluttonous. Don't spend your time and money in the many light-refreshment rooms which flourish in our towns, to the ruination of many a good digestion. Sweets, ices, pastry and other such rubbish are not natural foods and indulgence in eating them is bound to clog the muscles and produce shortness of wind.' That said, he himself loved rice pudding and would insist 'no pudding, no points' if there was ever a suggestion he should forgo his favourite pre-match meal. On one occasion when he did, he leaked eleven against Sunderland.

Moderation may have been the key for Robinson, but it was the last thing associated with the most famous goalkeeper of the era, William 'Fatty' Foulke, a man whose heft created a legend that still endures. 'A goalkeeper,' the Woolwich Arsenal keeper James Ashcroft wrote, 'must not carry too much flesh. The great Foulke may be instanced as an argument against my contention, but it must be remembered that the old Sheffield United man is a law unto himself. Take a thousand men of Foulke's bulk and you would not find one to compare with him for a moment in the matter of rapid agility and rapid action.'

Actually, Foulke was not quite unique. He had his precursor in the – considerable – form of Mordecai Sherwin, a wicketkeeper for Nottinghamshire in the summer and a goalkeeper for Notts County in the winter. He was 5'9" and almost 17st, but in the *Athletic News* James Catton described him as being 'very nimble, as quick a custodian as he was a wicket-keeper'. In one game, the Blackburn Rovers outside-right Joseph Lofthouse – although 'sturdy and skilful' – decided to prove a point against Sherwin. 'He charged him, and rebounded. Sherwin said, "Young man, you'll hurt yourself if you do that again." Undeterred, Lofthouse returned to the attack, but Sherwin stepped aside with the alacrity of a dancer, and the Lancashire lad found out how hard was the goalpost and how sharp its edge.'

It was Foulke, though, who came to define the extra-large keeper. Born in April 1874, the illegitimate son of Mary Ann Foulke, he was brought up by his grandparents in Blackwell in Derbyshire and, as most in the area did, started his working life down the pit. He played in goal for Blackwell and got his break in a friendly against Derby County, in which he excelled and, mistiming a punch, smacked the Derby forward John Goodall in the face, knocking out his two front teeth.

Derby offered him a contract but, acting on the advice of his brother, who insisted playing hard to get would secure a bigger wage, Foulkes turned them down. Sure enough, having been alerted to Foulke's talent by a referee who'd officiated in another Blackwell game, Sheffield United approached him, offering Foulke £5 as a signing-on fee and Blackwell £1 for each day that remained of the season. As he left the room where Foulke had signed the contract, Sheffield United's representative Joseph Tomlinson passed Derby officials returning with an improved offer.

Turning professional did nothing to curb Foulke's appetite. In 1896 he weighed 14st 12lb; by 1899 he weighed 19st 8lb; by 1902 it was 22st 8lb; by the end of his career he was said to be up to 28st. Photographs show his transformation from strapping 6'4" athlete to an otherworldly roundness; in black-and-white shots, his striped Sheffield United shirt worn with voluminous shorts makes it appear as though he were wearing dungarees, like some grotesquely oversized Tweedledum. In its report on the 1899 FA Cup final, in which Sheffield United beat Derby 4–1 at Crystal Palace, the *Sheffield and Rotherham Independent* detailed 'the ripple of amused wonder as Londoners surveyed the dimensions of the United Mammoth as he stalked majestically to his place between the goalposts'.

Foulke may not have been especially mobile, but he was blessed with sharp reflexes and great power, being able to punch and throw the ball further than most players could kick it. He was also a charismatic eccentric, loved by crowds for his unpredictability and the sense he gave that he didn't take football all that seriously. He did seem to take himself relatively seriously, though, and after that final, as he collected his medal from the Leader of the House of Commons, A. J. Balfour, who was soon to become Prime Minister, he told him that he didn't think he was up to the job.

Hilarity and controversy followed him around, adding to his legend. In February 1897, for instance, on a weekend on which neither side had an official fixture, Sheffield United played Sheffield Wednesday in a friendly at Bramall Lane, a game that drew a crowd of around 6,000. Just after half-time, the *Sheffield Daily Telegraph* reported, 'Brush sent in a long, dropping shot, which went straight for goal, and Foulke jumped up to clear. He missed the ball and caught the crossbar, snapping it clean in two.' Foulke was left sprawled on the ground, tangled in the netting. 'Another bar had to be requisitioned,' the report went on, '... to the great delight of the crowd, who indulged in sarcastic remarks about the carpentering efforts ... The first bar which was brought proved too short, and a second had to be brought which was fixed up amid loud cheers.'

Two years later, at the time of the Boer War, Sheffield United played against a touring team of black South Africans. Bored with the lack of action in his own half, Foulke charged forward and scored twice. And in a game against Chelsea in 1905, after it had been decided that the colour of his shirt clashed with that of the home team, he came out wrapped in a white bath towel. 'Nobody is fonder of fun or "divvlement" than I am,' he said in an interview with the *London Evening News* in 1907.

I don't mind admitting that I think I had as much as most men during my football career. To my mind almost the best time for a joke is after the team has lost.

When we'd won I was as ready to go to sleep in the railway carriage as anybody. All was peace and comfort then! But when we lost I made it my business to be a clown. Once when we were very disappointed I begged some black stuff from the engine-driver and rubbed it over my face. There I was sitting on the table and playing some silly game, with the team all around me, laughing like kiddies at a Punch and Judy show, when some grumpy committeeman looked in. Ask the old team if a bit of Little Willie's foolery didn't help to chirp 'em up before a big match.

Foulke, though, also had a temper. Once in a railway carriage, he was tucking in to some bread and cheese with a Spanish onion when a curate, sitting opposite him, tried to make conversation. 'My friend, I see that you are an epicure,' he said. Foulke looked stunned, and replied, 'Oh, am I? Then you're a —' 'The final word,' *Athletic News* reported, 'was more unparliamentary than that which Mr Bernard Shaw employed once in *Pygmalion and Galatea*.'

Foulke presumably simply hadn't understood, for at other times he was happy to make light of his eating. At Chelsea, for example, he once ate his own breakfast and that of each of his team-mates before they'd come down from their rooms. 'I don't care what you call me,' he said unapologetically, 'as long as you don't call me late for dinner.'

A larger-than-life joker he may have been, but Foulke's short fuse got him into trouble. In 1897, for instance, in a game against Everton that Sheffield United won 4–1, he was accused of bundling over Laurie Bell, the Everton centre-forward, rubbing his face in the mud, then hauling him up when the trainer came on. He insisted he'd accidentally fallen on top of Bell and, fearing the force of the impact might have killed him, he picked him up 'as tenderly as a baby'.

The controversies kept coming. In September a year later, in a game at Trent Bridge, he lashed out at a Notts County winger, prompting a pitch invasion that held up the game for several minutes. The following month, he was involved in a clash with the Liverpool centre-forward George Allan who had, supposedly, declared before the game that he intended to 'knock Foulke into the back of the net'. Irritated by his constant physicality, Foulke finally snapped when Allan charged him as he cleared a shot from Tom Robertson. According to the *Liverpool Football Echo*, 'the big man, losing his temper, seized Allan illegitimately and turned him upside down,' planting him headfirst in the mud. The referee awarded Liverpool a penalty. Andrew McCowie scored to equalise and Liverpool went on to win. Foulke and Allan, meanwhile, at least if the media of the time are to be believed, conducted a protracted feud that added an edge to games between Sheffield United and Liverpool. Foulke claimed it was blown out of proportion, even insisting that Allan had tumbled over him and the fact he'd finished face down in the mud had been an accident.

Perhaps the most notorious incident came after the 1902 FA Cup final. Sheffield United led Southampton 1–0 when, in the closing seconds, Harry Wood broke through to equalise. He looked offside, but after consultation with his linesman, the referee Tom Kirkham decided the ball had come off a United player and Wood was thus onside. United were disgusted, as were their fans, and as the players left the field there was a kerfuffle as police tried to create a path for them to reach the dressing rooms.

Lord Kinnaird, by then the president of the FA, gave a speech in which he singled out Foulke for praise. As he was doing so, though, at least according to legend, Foulke was stalking naked round the dressing rooms, hunting the referee. Kirkham, the story goes, had taken precautionary action by locking himself in a broom cupboard and escaped only as a crowd of onlookers, including the secretary of the FA, pulled Foulke away. Given that Kirkham happily refereed the replay a week later, though, the anecdote is probably, at the very least, embellished.

Yet there was still ill-feeling. James Catton, who went by the pen-name 'Tityrus' and was one of the great early sportswriters, found the Sheffield United defender Peter Boyle waiting for him, demanding to know if he'd blamed him for Southampton's equaliser. Catton admitted he had. Boyle raised his fists. 'Just at the crisis …' Catton wrote, 'who should step out of his cubicle, or dressing-box, but good Master Foulke, 19st 7lb of perfect nakedness. He looked down at me, and with his lusty voice and a smile which would have set a Quaker's meeting in a roar, said: "I'm your man for a fight. You're just about my weight. As I was under

5ft and scaled less that 11st in the Turkish Bath, the reader can imagine this sally was the restorative of good humour.' A Billy Barnes winner eleven minutes from time gave Sheffield United a 2–1 win.

Foulke admitted that he felt his size made him a target. 'You might have thought,' he said, 'that forwards would steer clear of such a big chap. Some did, but others seemed to get wild when they couldn't get the ball into the goal and I suffered a lot through kicks administered when the referee wasn't looking.'

His size also tends to obscure what a good goalkeeper he must have been. Foulke played only once for England, in a 4–0 win over Wales in 1897, a game in which he had few opportunities to show what he was capable of, but in 1896–97 Sheffield United conceded only twenty-nine goals in thirty games, and the following season only thirty-one, the lowest and third-lowest tallies recorded in the decade after the league was expanded from twelve teams to sixteen.

As Foulke's form began to waver as he passed thirty, Sheffield United in 1905 accepted a £50 offer from Chelsea, then of the Second Division. Foulke soon became a celebrity in the capital, his attendance at music-hall events being announced from the stage as the social invitations flooded in. His popularity and impact on the wider culture are undoubtable. At around the time of his move to Chelsea, the Amalgamated Press started producing football stories for its weekly boys' papers. Some of the most popular ones were written by A.S. Hardy, the pen name of Arthur Joseph Steffens, who clearly drew on contemporary figures for his fiction. The first team he wrote about, in his most popular football tales, was called the Blue Crusaders; it doesn't take much unravelling to work out who the inspiration was for their goalkeeper, the large, jovial but quick-tempered William Fowke.

Foulke was also an inspiration behind Stiffy the Goalkeeper, a music-hall figure played by Harry Weldon who was the most popular fictional footballer before the First World War. He first appeared at the Palace Theatre, Manchester, in December 1906 as part of a sketch called 'The Football Match' written by the impresario Fred Karno – the man credited with inventing the custard-pie-in-the-face-gag – and his writing partner Fred Kitchen. 'An attempt to bribe certain members to lose the match is afoot,' an early review explained, 'and the attempt is watched by a detective, who bears no resemblance to any detective ever seen at Scotland Yard, and whose idea of finding out the delinquents is to watch the action closely from the fragrant precincts of the smoke-room. The chief person to be bribed is Stiffy, the goal-keeper, whose integrity, however, in spite of his many oddities of conduct, is proof against temptation. What his prowess may be on the field does not really matter; it is enough for the audience that his true vocation is that of a comedian and the extent of his fitness for the stage is demonstrated with ample effect by Mr Harry Weldon.'

This was the goalkeeper as the player most vulnerable to corruption, but Stiffy's character soon grew. Weldon was an Everton fan and he and Karno began to introduce real-life elements as Stiffy's character outgrew the regular sketch. 'Stiffy was a character study – full of burlesque, perhaps, but never satirical,' the critic Hannen Swaffer wrote. 'A lesser comedian than Harry Weldon would have failed to have realised the character and, instead of applauding, the gods would have hissed.'

Stiffy, as John Harding notes in Issue Seven of *The Blizzard*, was far from a heroic figure, often doing little other than eat and drink. 'Stiffy's Song' captures perfectly his ludicrous, hapless persona:

> Hark to the shouting, Stiffy is the man they're cheering.
> Stiffy is the best goalkeeper that ever let a ball go through.
> They said this morning that by a hundred goals they'd beat me
> But they didn't know the man they had to deal with
> 'Cos we only lost by forty-two.

Yet for all he would mock them, Stiffy won a great following among footballers, who would take seats in the front rows at performances. Then came the ultimate seal of approval: Foulke donated a pair of his shorts for Weldon to wear on stage. Stiffy, perhaps, was the first significant cultural representation of the goalkeeper and his character, which was portrayed as preposterous, gluttonous and corruptible. It was not an auspicious start.

As his fame increased, Foulke became increasingly temperamental, walking off the pitch if he felt his defenders weren't giving their all, and engaging in regular physical confrontations with forwards, many of whom found themselves picked up and dumped on the ground. Nonetheless, in his first season at Chelsea, he kept nine clean sheets in a row and also saved ten penalties, perhaps in part because of his trick of positioning a ball-boy either side of him behind the goal to create the illusion that the goal was even more filled than it actually was. Chelsea, though, missed out on promotion and Foulke was sold on to Bradford City.

There the manager, Peter O'Rourke, would make him collect his wages via a narrow gate as though to mock his bulk. Foulke lasted just a season before retiring in 1907 at the age of thirty-three. He suffered rheumatism and, having spent much of what he'd earned, he was reduced to making a paltry living on the beach at Blackpool, charging holidaymakers a penny to test themselves against him from the penalty spot. Legend has it that he contracted pneumonia while doing so – and it is true that he may have contracted pneumonia from a chill caught after he was caught in a downpour at Sheffield races – but the prime cause of his death was another job he took on. He became landlord of the Duke Inn on Matilda Street in Sheffield and began drinking to excess. He died on 1 May 1916, the week compulsory conscription was introduced, of cirrhosis of the liver and a fatty heart. He was forty-two.

Penury – often leading to premature death – was a common theme of the early keepers. It was Brian Clough's mentor Harry Storer who noted that football was a game in which nobody ever said thank you, but football was an ungrateful game from the beginning. James Trainer was arguably the most talented goalkeeper of the 1880s, but he seemed always suspicious of the sport. He worked as a coach-builder in Wrexham before finally being persuaded, aged nineteen, to turn out for his local club.

His ability was obvious, but within a year he was facing a ban from the game after a fierce FA Cup tie against Oswestry in which he was alleged to have insulted the referee. The Football Association expelled Wrexham from the competition and called on the club to discipline Trainer but, before they could, he had accepted an offer of 30/- a week during the season and 13/- during the summer to play for Great Lever in Lancashire. Two seasons later Bolton offered 50/-, gave him a £5 signing-on fee and packed him and his girlfriend off to the Isle of Man until the start of the 1885–86 season. Great Lever were not impressed. 'I hope when he's coming home his boat will go down,' said their chairman, 'and everybody will be saved except-ing him.'

Trainer's boat survived the curse, and he spent two seasons at Bolton before so impressing the great Preston North End in a friendly (in which, puzzlingly, he conceded twelve) that they signed him, describing him as being 'safe as a sandbag'. Trainer thus became Preston's goalkeeper for the 1888–89 season, and let in only fifteen goals in twenty-two matches as they went unbeaten in clinching the inaugural league title. He went on to win twenty caps for Wales and later became a director of Bolton. Like so many goalkeepers, though, there was a shadow across his soul. He separated from his wife, with whom he had ten children, in 1904, and became involved in a business enterprise putting on football exhibitions at London Olympia. When that failed, he was banned by the FA and he spent his final days hang-ing around the team hotel before Wales internationals, trying to scrounge money. He died in poverty in 1915, aged fifty-two.

Probably the greatest pre-war goalkeeper of them all also died horribly young the following year, not in poverty, but amid the chaos of the Somme. Leigh Richmond Roose wasn't just a fine goalkeeper; he redefined the position, both in terms of how it was regarded and in how it was played.

The early goalkeepers were caught in a paradoxical position. On the one hand, they were subject to repeated physical assault, virtually unprotected by the laws of the game.

'There was at Eton,' Gibson and Pickford wrote of the early nineteenth-century game,

> a most delicious regulation that read as follows: 'Should a player fall on the ball or crawl on his hands and knees with the ball between his legs, the umpire must, if possible, force him to rise, or break the "bully" or "rouge".' What a picture might be drawn of an old-style player, filled with a burning zeal to pierce the enemy's lines and a fine disregard of danger, crawling painfully along with the ball between his legs, the prey to numerous kicks and plunges, and resisting with his utmost strength not only the unlawful attempts of the opponents to upset him, but also the rule-sanctioned prowess of the umpire, whose limitations are so aptly described by the phrase 'if possible'. A Foulke or a [Jack] Hillman, given the law under such conditions, would have been a formidable engine of attack, while there is no modern referee whose size and power would in the least avail him to force an athletic nineteen-stone player to rise. The crawling method has often been adopted by goalkeepers of later days, and it is on record how [Ned] Doig, a champion of the Sunderland club, in a great match, so held the ball on the confines of his goal, and resisting successfully all the efforts of the trained band of antagonists to rob him of it for some minutes, finally rolled with it to the side of the goalpost and safely delivered himself of his responsibilities by pushing it over the goal line.

Yet at the same time they carried the same connotations of inadequacy present in Galen's reference to the slow men of the defence and Benham's to the funk-sticks of Westminster. Goalkeeping, implicitly, was for those without the pluck or the wherewithal to play outfield. In that, they didn't always help themselves. Having noted – quite rationally – the need for a 'steely nerve', the Woolwich Arsenal goalkeeper James Ashcroft wrote in J. A. McWeeney's 1906 *Football Guide, or How to Play Soccer* that the goalkeeper 'must stand very frequently on damp grass, shivering with cold and inviting an onslaught from pneumonia or the influenza fiend. If you are constitutionally strong you can laugh at damp, colds in the head and rheumatic twinges.' It seems an extraordinary thing to worry about: yes, watch out for flying boots and stray elbows but, most of all, make sure you wrap up warm: there is something sickly, almost contemptible, in Ashcroft's words. Roose stopped all that: people accused him of many things, but weakness wasn't one of them.

Born on 26 November 1877, the fourth son of a preacher in Holt, north Wales, Roose moved to Aberystwyth when he was seventeen to study medicine. He became goalkeeper for the university side and was noted from the off for his willingness to leave his goal, acting almost as an auxiliary defender, something that simply hadn't happened since a defender had become a goalkeeper in the 1860s. As his Sunderland team-mate George Holley would later put it, 'He was the mould from which all others were created.'

Roose also developed a habit of bouncing the ball up to the halfway line – which meant evading the challenges of opposing forwards that would have been far more robust, far more akin to rugby, than anything in the modern game – and launching kicks at the opponent's goal, taking advantage of the rule that allowed him to handle the ball anywhere in his own half. This was the goalkeeper getting his own back: it was as late as 1892 that the rule had been changed to allow players to charge the goalkeeper only 'in the act of playing the ball or while obstructing an opponent'; before that he was seen as fair game with or without the ball, almost as though, because he could handle, he was regarded as a rugby player and so subject to rugby's rules.

'Charging the goalkeeper was a definite form of attack,' wrote F. N. S. Creek in his history of the Corinthian club, 'and was permissible so long as the chargers were onside when the ball was last kicked. In consequence, we learn that "from a fine middle by Bambridge, Prail got a capital goal, Dewhurst having previously disposed of the goalkeeper." Some teams, notably Preston North End, made full use of this licence. A half-back, carefully judging the time to pass, would kick the ball in the air in the direction of the goalkeeper who would at once be attacked by two of the inside-forwards, while the third would attempt to slip past the backs and shoot into the empty goal. Corner kicks were even more serious, for the goalkeeper, while side-stepping (and occasionally "flooring") two forwards, he was still expected to get the ball away. For this reason, many goals were scored from "scrimmages" and as there were then no nets, many too were the doubtful ones.'

That physicality perhaps explains why goalkeepers fell into two broad characters: the stoics who quietly absorbed the punishment, and the extroverts. Roose was very definitely in the latter category. That sense of danger perhaps also explains why goalkeepers, acutely aware of the dangers of their profession, were so superstitious. The great Liverpool keeper Elisha Scott, for instance, would arrive two hours before matches started, change alone, bounce a ball against a wall for an hour and then, whatever the weather, minutes before kick-off put on two additional shirts and an extra pair of socks. Ashcroft referred to Scott as 'one of the immortals'. 'Somewhat roughly hewn from granite, Scott held no charm for the aesthete,' he wrote. 'He was of iron will. In the obstinate tradition of his province he held fast to a single conviction – that the enemy should not breach his defences. They rarely did. Often it was England, or Wales, or Scotland, against Scott. Come what may he held them off. And at Liverpool it was the same. A player of the old order, honest in endeavour and ever prepared for immolation in the single cause, Scott abjured fine habits and unfitting ambitions, cheap publicity and popular acclaim, and was all concentration.'

There were others, though, who delighted in the publicity, who enjoyed making the game all about them – and it was that tradition that Roose followed. 'Happy' Jack Hillman of Burnley and Manchester City, for instance, once won a £5 bet that he could keep a clean sheet with one arm tied behind his back. Albert Iremonger, at 6'6" believed to be the tallest player to have played league football before the First World War, was a born controversialist. In 1912, playing for Notts Country against Arsenal, he wasted time by sitting on the ball. The referee tried to persuade him to move, eventually becoming so frustrated he threatened him with a firework. When Iremonger still refused to shift, the game was abandoned. He would regularly argue with match officials, and his obstreperousness led to his departure from Notts County in 1925 after 564 appearances. He joined Lincoln aged forty-two and, when they were awarded a penalty in one of his first appearances, he insisted on taking it. He took a huge run, smacked it against the bar so hard that it rebounded to the halfway line and in his attempts to recover ended up thrashing the ball into his own net.

Roose, albeit in a less high-profile way, became a significant attraction for the Aberystwyth university eleven, running onto the field with an arm raised to acknowledge the crowd then pacing out his goal muttering under his breath, as though reciting a mantra, as part of his pre-kick-off ritual. More and more fans came to watch the university side, an unprecedented number of them women drawn by Roose's charisma and good looks.

After the sale of Jack Jones to Liverpool, Aberystwyth Town needed a new goalkeeper, and they turned to Roose in autumn 1898. He impressed, and stayed on for a year after completing his studies. So quickly did his reputation grow that, in February 1900, he was making his debut for the national team against Ireland in a Home International at Llandudno. Wales won 2–0, but the game was most notable for a challenge Roose made midway through the second half when he bundled Harry O'Reilly into touch, knocking him unconscious as he did so. This was a goalkeeper charging back, doing to another what had been done to him on dozens of occasions. Yet controversial as the incident was, the referee didn't even give a free-kick.

That season was the most successful in Aberystwyth's history, as they won a treble of Towyn Cup, South Wales Cup and Welsh Cup. Roose, though, felt constricted in a small provincial town and moved to London, where he became an assistant at King's College Hospital and started playing for London Welsh. The pattern of Aberystwyth was repeated: attendances soared, his reputation grew and he became a regular for Wales. Several clubs tried to sign him, but Roose was reluctant to turn professional, which would have meant giving up his medical career.

A solution was found the following summer by Stoke City, who offered him an amateur contract, agreeing to allow him to remain in London, paying for first-class travel, luxury hotels and extras such as suits, shoes and help with his rent. Roose was a professional in all but name and the FA's laws on amateurism were stretched to the limit.

Those weren't the only boundaries he pushed. Roose was a showman to his core. He would arrange for a hansom cab to meet him off the Euston train at Stoke station and would then drive it himself at top speed, with a train of fans and admirers in pursuit.

For a medical man, he was oddly superstitious. 'Roose is one of the cleanest custodians we have,' an article in *Cricket and Football Field* noted, 'but he apparently is a trifle superstitious about his football garments, for he seldom seems to trouble his charwoman with them.' For Wales games and key matches for Stoke, he would wear his old Aberystwyth Town top, unwashed since the Welsh Cup final win over Druids.

He chatted to the crowd, which increased his popularity at the Victoria Ground, but made him a target at away matches. He was hit by a coin at Bramall Lane after commenting that Sheffield United 'would have to do considerably better than that' to beat him; at Manchester City, he performed the sort of wobbly legs routine Bruce Grobbelaar would later make famous before saving a penalty, then turned to the crowd with a broad grin on his face, prompting an irate fan to hurl an apple at him.

A goalkeeper, Roose said, 'need not set out to keep goal on the usual stereotype lines. He is at liberty to cultivate originality and, more often than not, if he has a variety of methods in his clearances and means of getting rid of the ball, he will confound and puzzle the attacking forwards. Let a goalkeeper be success-ful in his clearances, and great will be his triumph. Let him fail, and oblivion will be his portion.' Occasionally he did fail – being caught in possession outside his box against Sheffield Wednesday, for instance, leaving the opposing centre-forward with an open goal – but he was generally so successful that his team-mates were quick to forgive. 'He plays like no other custodian in the land dares to play,' said the defender Sam Ashworth. 'That's why he is the man that he is.'

Stoke narrowly avoided relegation that season but the repayments on a loan taken out to fund ground redevelopment carried them into financial difficulty. That in turn led the club to trim Roose's expense account. Against Derby County on the final day of the 1903–04 season, Roose chased out of his box and misjudged the bounce of the ball, falling over and gifting Steve Bloomer a goal. Frustrated and disillusioned, as he took the train back to London that night, Roose decided he would quit league football and – at last – begin the medical degree he had postponed for three years. He wrote letters to Stoke and the Football Association of Wales informing them of his retirement, but it was only that August, as *Athletic News* published its season preview, that the news became widely known.

By the November, though, Roose was missing his football. Still wanting to maintain his medical studies, he started seeking clubs who would accept a London-based amateur. When Everton lost Bill Scott to a shoulder injury just as his understudy George Kitchen went down with flu, Roose had his chance and agreed to play for them until Scott recovered. He made his debut against Sunderland and, his lack of match practice perhaps showing, fumbled a cross with five minutes remaining to gift Arthur Bridgett a winner. Ahead of the next game, at home to Derby, he spent quarter of an hour before kick-off shaking hands with fans and apologising for his mistake. That enhanced his standing, and he augmented it further by playing well and hauling himself up onto the bar and sitting on it during a break while a player received treatment for an injury. Against Stoke he saved a penalty in a 4–1 win, and such was his form that Roose was asked to stay on even after Scott's recovery.

Everton lost in the semi-final of the FA Cup and finished second in the league that year, achievements in which Roose had played a significant part. He fell out with the manager, William C. Cuff, though, having made a complaint about the fixture pile-up at the end of the season and, when he was dropped for the final game of the season, he refused to travel. That was the end of his time at Everton and come the following September he was turning out for Stoke again, making his second debut in a 3–0 win over Notts County. 'There is not his equal for smartness in getting down to a low shot apparently well out of reach,' the match report in *Athletic News* affirmed.

By mid-November, with Stoke third in the table, the *Daily Mail* named Roose in their World XI to face a team from another planet. 'Few men exhibit their personality so vividly in their play as L. R. Roose,' wrote a reporter from the *Bristol Times*. 'You cannot spend five minutes in his company without being impressed by his vivacity, his boldness, his knowledge of men and things – a clever man undoubtedly, but entirely unrestrained in word or action. He rarely stands listlessly by the goalpost even when the ball is at the other end of the enclosure, but is ever following the play keenly and closely. Directly his charge is threatened, he is on the move. He thinks nothing of dashing out ten or fifteen yards, even when his backs have as good a chance of clearing as he makes for himself. He will also rush along the touchline, field the ball and get in a kick too, to keep the game going briskly.' The description is telling of the general style of goalkeeping at the time: clearly a lot of goal-keepers did hang around by their goalposts, while the notion of a keeper coming out ten or fifteen yards was evidently shocking.

Roose helped Wales win the Home Championship for the first time, but at Stoke things were going less well. As the club ran out of money, he had to renegotiate his deal. Stoke, having been relegated, released details of a 'London-based player' who had filed an expenses claim for a dog-sitter despite him not having a dog, presumably in an attempt to rein in Roose's demands. Not surprisingly, he was furious and relations with the club became distinctly frosty. Although he began the 1907–08 season at the Victoria Ground, a move was inevitable. When Sunderland offered him a contract, he had little hesitation in accepting.

He enjoyed two seasons on Wearside, where he continued to leave his goal and his penalty area whenever possible. 'The law states that any custodian is free to run over half of the field of play before ridding themselves of the ball,' he said. 'This not only helps to puzzle the attacking forwards, but to build the foundations for swift, incisive counter-attacking play. Why then do so few make use of it?' The answer, George Holley suggested, was that 'he was the only one who could kick or throw a ball that accurately over long distances, giving himself time to return to his goal without fear of conceding.'

Even then, it did occasionally go wrong, as for instance when the Sheffield United goalkeeper Ernest Needham scored against him with a clearance that sailed over his head. Roose, though, never let his occasional errors bother him. He bought a drink for Needham that night and continued to showboat. In tipping a shot over the bar against Aston Villa, his hands came into contact with the bar, so he grabbed on and flipped himself up to sit on his goalframe and take the applause. Against Woolwich Arsenal, he saved a shot with his chest, brought the ball down on to his foot and performed some keepie-uppies before clearing.

Off the pitch, his life remained just as flamboyant and he had a fling with the music-hall star Marie Lloyd. That increased his fame yet further, but in November 1910, Roose fractured his wrist in a game against Newcastle, something that effectively signalled the end of his career. He drifted on through a handful of clubs – Celtic, Port Vale, Huddersfield Town, Aston Villa and Arsenal – but he never recaptured his former level of ability. The hammer blow came in 1912, when his style of goalkeeping was effectively abolished. Two members of the Rules Review Committee had seen a game Roose had played for Sunderland in London and felt he'd ruined it as a spectacle by bouncing the ball to halfway at every opportunity, so breaking up the chance of creative play; from the start of the 1912–13 season goalkeepers were restricted to handling in their own box.

Roose retired and committed to medicine, confining himself to one-off games for villages and Beat the Goalie contests at public events. He became a popular after-dinner speaker and then, when war was declared in 1914, he signed up. His family thought he'd been killed in Gallipoli in 1915, but in 2007 the true story emerged after some remarkable research by the journalist Spencer Vignes in writing his biography of Roose, *Lost in France*.

A chance remark from the sports cartoonist Tom Webster that he'd played cricket with Roose in Egypt after the evacuation from Gallipoli had always puzzled the family. Their attempts to track him down yielded only the suggestion that he'd joined the Royal Fusiliers in 1916, but no Roose appeared in their records. Vignes, though, uncovered what was presumably a clerical error (although it is possible Roose was trying to disguise his true identity): there was no Roose, but there was a Leigh Richmond Rouse. Immediately, the truth became clear.

Roose was awarded the Military Cross on 28 August 1916 and promoted to Lance Corporal for his actions in a battle at Agny, in which he'd been left with burned clothes and damaged lungs by a flame-thrower attack but had refused medical attention and had continued to fight. On 13 November he was involved in an attack near Gueudecourt, on the Somme. An artillery barrage was supposed to have cleared German positions but had neglected a machine gun post on the left flank. The Fusiliers had no chance, the majority of them cut down within a few minutes of the attack being launched. A Sergeant Quinnell reported seeing Roose in a crater, but whether dead, wounded or taking cover, he couldn't say. His body was never found.

2: THE THREE-AND-A-HALF INCARNATIONS OF LEV YASHIN

In the world of goalkeeping, one name stands above all others: Lev Yashin. Whether he was the best ever is open to debate, but he was certainly the most vaunted and he remains the most iconic goalkeeper there has ever been. Undemonstrative and unyielding, clad in the all-black kit that earned him the nickname of the Black Panther (or the Black Spider, depending which country he happened to be in), he became, to a western audience, the essence of minimalist Soviet chic. Back home, he was a national hero, understated, diligent and brave. 'Everything that Yashin did was of the highest order,' said his great English contemporary Gordon Banks. 'He made great saves, could take crosses and knew his angles. He was also a real gentleman. In the 1966 World Cup he made a save at the feet of a guy who nearly took his head off. The first thing he did was get up and make sure the fella who'd just clattered him was all right.'

Yashin lacked the flamboyance of many of the greats – and was openly scathing of the excesses of his sometime international team-mate Eduard Streltsov – but he was undoubtedly charismatic. His name remains synonymous with great goalkeeping: any goalkeeper who keeps 100 clean sheets in the Russian league is said to have joined the Yashin Club, while Fifa presents the best goalkeeper at each World Cup with the Lev Yashin Award. And, like any idol, he casts a shadow that isn't necessarily healthy: just as any promising young all-rounder in English cricket is automatically dubbed the new Botham, so any promising young goalkeeper in Russia will be hailed as the next Yashin, as though his genius must be reincarnated in every generation.

No nation idolises its goalkeepers as Russia does. Such things are difficult to quantify but anecdotal evidence at least suggests that whereas most British schoolchildren start out wanting to be the player up front scoring the goals and collecting the glory, in Russia they want to be the enigmatic figure at the back, the one in the different coloured shirt. The status of Yashin, of course, contributed to that phenomenon: Billy Casper may not have ended up playing up front in a Russian version of *Kes*, but there's no doubt that Brian Glover's PE teacher would have reached for the black number one shirt rather than the red number nine of Bobby Charlton.

Except, shockingly, Yashin's jersey wasn't black. 'It was a very dark blue – a woollen jersey with a number one sewn on the back,' his widow, Valentina Timofeevna Yashina, revealed. 'I suppose at the time all goalkeepers wore a dark kit. In 2000, when I received the award for Goalkeeper of the Century on Lev's behalf, Sepp Maier said, "Before all goalkeepers wore black so you couldn't have mixed them up with anybody else. Now, they're red, yellow, blue – like parrots."

'Lev always played in that colour. In twenty years he changed it two or three times when he wore holes into the sleeves. Then he'd take one of the same design. Pitches, especially in spring and autumn, were muddy, and on a dark uniform this dirt was not so noticeable. When he brought home his kit, the whole bath became black and filled with sawdust – penalty areas were covered with it so goalkeepers didn't sink into the slush.'

He wouldn't change even in the warmest weather. 'It stopped him getting hurt,' Valentina explained. 'And he'd always wear quilted trunks underneath. He got angry with his team-mates who didn't do that. "I'm telling you," he'd say, "you can't play without it. You could hurt your thighs. Bruises are guaranteed, muscles will tear and then you'll be afraid of going down the next time. And how can you play in goal if you're afraid?"'

Valentina still has a fridge Yashin was given because of his status as a footballer but – remarkably – she doesn't have any of the fabled dark jerseys. 'In those days you had to give everything back,' she told the journalist Igor Rabiner. 'Even after Lev had played in his farewell game in 1971 Dinamo sent him an order to return the kit – and even the gloves that he'd personally sewn up when they were torn. We laughed about it, but he gathered everything up and returned everything. He didn't keep a single Dinamo jersey. It was the same story every year: at the end of the season I'd wash all his kit so we could return it looking good.

'He kept only one jersey and that was a yellow number thirteen, not a black number one, from when he kept a clean sheet for the Rest of the World against England in London in the famous game the whole planet saw. Nobody wanted to wear thirteen but Lev said, "Okay, give it to me – I don't care." He had a great game and afterwards regarded thirteen as a lucky number for him.'

The other item of kit for which Yashin became famous was his cap. He would even at times, if he were dealing with a high cross, take the cap off, head the ball away, and then return the cap to his head. 'That happened a lot,' Valentina said, 'but only when there was nobody around. At that time penalty areas weren't as crowded as they are now. The first time he did it, he came into the dressing room and hung his head, thinking [the Dinamo coach Mikhail] Yakushin would criticise him because he could be sly and biting. But he said nothing. Lev asked, "Is something wrong?"

'"No, everything's fine," Yakushin replied. "But you have to take the cap off." That time he'd headed the ball with his cap on. Fans liked it a lot and they'd always react with a storm of cheers. A few more times he headed the ball without the cap but he stopped doing it as the game became faster and tougher.'

In the Soviet Union, of course, the individuality and separateness of the goalkeeper had specific connotations. It's tempting to believe that, in a society that demanded uniformity, playing in goal was a rare opportunity to express individuality, to stand apart from the collective, and to imagine that aspect of the position was what made it so attractive in a Communist society. Perhaps that was part of the allure but Yashin was no dissident and the elevated position of goalkeeping in the Russian psyche predates the 1917 revolution.

In his autobiography *Speak, Memory*, Vladimir Nabokov, who was born into a family of minor nobility in St Petersburg in 1899 and fled Russia after the Revolution, wrote of having been 'crazy about goalkeeping' as a young man. Football, in fact, seems to have been one of the few things he remembers clearly about his time studying at Cambridge immediately after the First World War. There were the 'bright, bracing days' when he would make 'a lucky save', feeling 'its protracted tingle' in his palms, but there were also the games under 'dismal skies' when 'the goal area [was] a mass of black mud, the ball as greasy as a plum pudding', when the mists would gather and 'the dilapidated rooks' would caw in 'a leafless elm', and he 'would fumble badly'.

In his preference for the position, Nabokov saw himself as typical of his nation. He wrote:

In Russia and the Latin countries, that gallant art has always been surrounded with a halo of singular glamour. Aloof, solitary, impassive, the crack goalie is followed in the streets by entranced small boys. He vies with the matador and the flying ace as an object of thrilled adulation. His sweater, his peaked cap, his kneeguards, the gloves protruding from the hip pocket of his shorts, set him apart from the rest of the team. He is the lone eagle, the man of mystery, the last defender. Photographers, reverently bending one knee, snap him in the act of making a spectacular dive across the goalmouth to deflect with his fingers a low lightning-like shot and the stadium roars in approval as he remains for a moment or two lying full length where he fell, his goal still intact.

The English mentality, Nabokov felt, was unconducive to goalkeeping. 'The national dread of showing off,' he asserted, 'and a too grim preoccupation with solid teamwork were not conducive to the development of the goalie's eccentric art.' With that in mind, it's perhaps not insignificant that so many of the gifted early British goalkeepers were notably, even wilfully, odd.

That Russian love of the goalkeeper was demonstrated by the success of *Vratar*, a 1937 musical-comedy film directed by

Semyon Timoshenko and starring the Russian matinee idol Grigori Pluzhnik as Anton Kandidov, a boy who worked stacking watermelons onto a cart and became so adept at catching those that fell that he was noticed by a scout and called up to play in goal for an unnamed Russian team. The climax of the film came when, having made a series of fine saves against a touring Basque side, he ran the length of the field to score a last-minute winner. Just in case anybody hadn't worked out the political message, the most famous song of the film contained the lines,

> *Hey, keeper, prepare for the fight*
> *You are a sentry in the goal.*
> *Imagine there is a border behind you.*

The film was based on Leo Kassil's 1936 novel *Vratar Respubliki*, which was a much darker work than the musical. In the book, the huge 'spontaneous' Kandidov joined a commune called Gidraer to play in goal for their football team, but then left to join the more prestigious Magneto team before they went on a tour of Europe. There he was corrupted by his new friends and foreign influences and on his return Magneto lost to Gidraer 'because of their lack of cohesion and, most importantly, because of Kandidov's rashly individualistic decision to leave his goalposts at a decisive moment in the game,' as Keith A. Livers put it in an essay in *The Russian Review*. Mortified, Kandidov then went through a period of soul-searching and almost killed himself by accidentally leaving the gas on, but was ultimately reunited with Gidraer. It's essentially a Communist take on the Prodigal Son: again the political message is clear and again it seems significant that it is the goalkeeper who is cast out, the one left alone, needing to be reintegrated to earn his redemption.

Vratar Respubliki wasn't the first Russian novel to deal with football. The climax of Yury Olesha's novel *Zavist* (*Envy*) comes at a football match between a Soviet team and a German team. The hero of the game is the goalkeeper Volodya Makarov, whose shirt is torn to shreds by his efforts to withstand the German attack as they play with a strong wind in the first half. 'Volodya grabbed the ball in a sort of flight, when this seemed mathematically impossible ... The referee threw his whistle into his lips on the run, prepared to whistle the score. Volodya did not catch the ball – he plucked it from the line of flight and, as if violating physics, subjected himself to the stunning effect of indignant forces. He flew up together with the ball, whirling, literally getting screwed onto it: he clasped the ball with his whole body – knees, stomach and chin, throwing his weight onto the velocity of the ball, as they throw rags to put out a flare-up. The intercepted velocity of the ball threw Volodya sidewards two metres; he fell in the form of a coloured paper bomb.'

While the German star Getzke, a forward, is portrayed as a selfish individualist, Volodya is already the committed team man Kandidov must learn to become in Kassil's novel. 'Volodya was a professional sportsman – the other was a professional player. Important to Volodya was the general course of the game, the overall victory, the outcome – Getzke strove only to show his own skill.' Elsewhere, Volodya is portrayed as the ideal modern Soviet – the novel as a whole is concerned with the relationship of individuals to society and exposes flaws in both Communist and bourgeois models; he is an individual who strives his utmost for the team. Being discrete from his team-mates, of course, the goalkeeper is the ideal position for the loner; he neither has to cover for others or have others cover him and yet his effort, his sacrifice, his talent is directed to achieving what is best for the collective. The goalkeeper, perhaps, provides a model for the idiosyncratic individual, for the artist, in a socialist system.

What is most remarkable about *Vratar*, though, is what happened to Mykola Trusevych, the Ukrainian goalkeeper on whom Kandidov was at least partially based. Tall and dark-haired, he was recognised as one of the best goalkeepers in the USSR in the thirties as a national championship was established. He began his career in Odessa with Pischevik, joined Dynamo Odessa in 1929 and then, in 1935, Dynamo Kyiv, the team of the local secret police. That year, as Kassil was preparing his novel, Dynamo toured France and struggled against more experienced opposition. Trusevych was second choice behind Anton Idzkovskyi, who fell ill just before a match against Red Star Olympic of Paris. Red Star were expected to win easily but, called upon unexpectedly, Trusevych performed brilliantly in a 6–1 win – although without scoring any goals himself.

He returned a hero, his reputation amplified by the sharpness of his dress and his good humour, even if it was undercut by an occasionally quick temper. After beating a touring Turkish team 9–1, for instance, he attempted to ease the embarrassment of the visitors by performing what became known as 'the Dance of the Goalkeeper', mimicking his on-pitch movements and repeatedly falling forwards and then springing up off his hands at the last moment.

In *Vratar*, art had, to an extent, imitated life; after the Nazi invasion in 1941, Trusevych took the central metaphor of the novel and made it flesh. Many Ukrainians, seeing the invasion as a way of shaking off the Soviet yoke, collaborated with the Germans; Trusevych, though, was a committed Communist and, after smuggling his Jewish wife and daughter to Odessa, fought with the resistance. He was shot in the leg shortly before Kyiv fell and, captured in the encirclement, was imprisoned in the camp at Darnytsya before being released after signing an oath of allegiance. It seems he returned to his apartment to find it destroyed and so was forced to live on the streets, tormented by grief for his city and by guilt for having submitted to German rule. A few months later, as he walked past a cafe, he was spotted by a bakery manager called Josef Kordyk.

Plump and pink-skinned, Kordyk was a Moravian Czech who had fought for Germany during the First World War and, initially forbidden to return home by the Soviet authorities, was stranded in Ukraine after the Armistice in 1918. As he struggled to find a role, football became his major pleasure and he became a keen supporter of Dynamo. Although he married and had a daughter, which is presumably why he opted to stay after the prohibition on his return home was lifted, he seems to have felt resentful towards the Soviets; for him, the invasion was an opportunity. Lying that he'd been born in Austria, he claimed

Volksdeutsch status and was placed in charge of a bakery.

Kordyk recognised Trusevych and rushed out of the cafe to speak to him. After listening to his story, he offered him work and a place to sleep at the bakery. As he discovered that other former players were suffering similar difficulties, he found them work as well.

Keen to normalise life in the city, the Germans decided in spring 1942 to allow football to be played again. Having a significant number of former Dynamo players working for him, it was natural for Kordyk to launch a team, which became known as Start. Trusevych was initially opposed to the idea of playing in the Germans' tournament but was persuaded that a successful side could become a rallying point for the opposition, a conviction strengthened by the chance discovery of a batch of red (and so symbolically Communist) shirts.

Start beat all before them, thrashing a Hungarian garrison team 6–2 and a Romanian side 11–0. As their reputation spread, they began to draw large crowds. On Friday 17 July 1942 there came the first sign of unease on the part of the authorities as PGS, a German garrison side, were beaten 6–0. *Novo Ukrainski Slovo*, for the first time, carried a match report by 'RD', which attempted to excuse the defeat by making clear a lack of training on the part of PGS, blaming the Romanian referee and a bumpy pitch and criticising Start for being offside ten times to the Germans' none.

Two days later, Start won 5–1 against MSG, a Hungarian garrison side, but one with former professional players who took training seriously. RD's report this time focused on the fact that the Hungarians had lost a man to injury early on and so had played the majority of the game with only ten men. The following week they played a rematch, seemingly organised by the Hungarian captain. Start raced into a 3–0 lead before being pegged back to 3–2. All the indications are of a great sporting contest, with the Hungarians generous in their praise of Start after the game.

The same day, Flakelf, a Luftwaffe side featuring a number of former professionals, played Rukh, a team of Ukrainian nationalists broadly sympathetic to the new regime, in what was fairly evidently a training game before they took on Start to re-establish the superiority of the Germans over the Slavic *Untermensch*.

On 28 July, in response to the fall of Rostov-na-Donu, Stalin issued Order no. 227, known as 'Not one step backwards': 'Panicmongers and cowards must be destroyed on the spot. The retreat mentality must be decisively eliminated. Army commanders who have allowed voluntary abandonment of their positions must be removed and sent for immediate trial by military tribunal.' It was circulated by resistance groups within Kyiv and must surely have been seen by the former footballers at the bakery.

Start played Flakelf on Thursday 6 August. Despite an increased German presence in the stands, the crowd at the Zenit Stadium was smaller than usual, presumably because it was a weekday. Start won 5–1 but there was no report in the *Novo Ukrainski Slovo* and further details are difficult to come by. The next day, posters began to appear in Kyiv advertising a rematch for Sunday 9 August billed, in German and Russian, as 'FOOTBALL REVENGE'.

This time, the stadium was packed and, this time, there was a determination on the part of the Germans that Flakelf would not lose. Penetrating the layers of myth that the game has generated since is all but impossible, but it does seem that the referee was a German, even if claims he was a balding SS officer who spoke fluent Russian may be an embellishment. It's said that he warned the Start players to give the Nazi salute before kick-off, something they ignored, instead clapping hands to hearts and shouting '*FizcultHura!*', the traditional shout of Soviet sportsmen. The term is an abbreviation of 'Physical Culture, Hurrah!', although the '*Hura!*' is a far more aggressive term than its English equivalent and would be shouted by Soviet troops on their way into battle.

Whether even that incident really happened is debatable and piecing together the narrative of the match is even harder. When the war ended the Soviet authorities initially seem to have tried to pretend the game didn't happen at all, concerned that Dynamo players should have been involved in something that could have been construed as collaboration. Then the game became a propaganda tool, which meant the Communist Party pushed one version of the tale and disaffected Ukrainian nationalists another. By the mid-nineties, when sports historians finally began sifting through the evidence, most eye-witnesses were dead and many of those who weren't had had their memories contorted by the various 'official' versions.

So, this is little more than a best guess at how the game went. It seems Flakelf were more aggressive than they had been in the first game and that several bad challenges went unchecked, particularly on Trusevych. They took the lead but Start came back and by half-time led 3–1. That much seems widely accepted.

At half-time, Start supposedly received two visits to their dressing room, one from another player, a nationalist and collaborator, the other from the referee. Both warned of the severe consequences if Start went on to win. Trusevych, it's said, gave a rousing speech, urging his team-mates to ignore the threat. The early part of the second half is the most confusing, but what is generally agreed upon is that four goals were shared (the order is disputed), so Start led 5–3 with four minutes remaining when their youthful full-back Oleksiy Klymenko ran from deep, rounded the goalkeeper, took the ball to the goal line and hoofed it not into the net but back into play. Aware of the humiliation, the referee stopped the game early. There were scuffles between Germans and Ukrainians in the crowd, German dignitaries were jostled on the way to their vehicles and soldiers set their dogs loose to try to clear the crowd.

One version of the story had the Start players being machine-gunned on the pitch but that certainly did not happen. In fact, the next Sunday they played Rukh, a nationalist side, and beat them 8–0. In the week that followed that match, the players were called one by one into the office at the bakery and arrested. They were taken to Gestapo headquarters on Korolenko Street and interrogated to try to make them confess to being saboteurs or thieves. None broke and, with the exception of the winger

Mykola Korotkykh, the players were moved to the Siretz prison camp near Baba Yar, the ravine where thousands of Jews had been massacred in 1941. Korotkykh had been an active officer in the NKVD, the forerunner to the KGB, ten years earlier and, when that was discovered, he was subjected to far harsher treatment than the others, dying after twenty days of torture.

Prisoners at Siretz, restricted to a diet of 150–200g of bread a day, usually served with a soup made of acorns, were used as slave labourers. When one attempted to escape, his entire workdetail of eighteen was shot. Fitter than most, the players survived the worst of the winter until, on 23 February 1943, the anniversary of the foundation of the Red Army, the resistance launched a series of bomb attacks on German targets, destroying a factory that repaired motorised sleighs.

A reprisal came the following day. At roll call, the prisoners were lined up in ranks. Every third man was beaten to the ground and shot. Ivan Kuzmenko, who had scored at least one and possibly two in the second game against Flakelf, was the first player to be killed. Klymenko was the second. Trusevych, his heroism far surpassing that of Kandidov, was the third and last.

The story has spawned various fictional imitations, the most notable of them, to a western audience at least, being *Escape to Victory*, which was itself based on the Hungarian director Zoltán Fábri's 1962 film *Két félidő a pokolban* (*Two Half-times in Hell*). Weirdly – and surely not entirely honestly – a version of the story was co-opted by the Russian poet Yevgeny Yevtushenko in an essay on his relationship with sport in *Sports Illustrated* in 1966. Like Albert Camus, Yevtushenko saw football as a metaphor. 'Allegorical verses,' he wrote, 'are like dribbling and feinting at football, a ruse to lead the defenders astray so that you can kick the ball into the rival's goal.' He too played football regularly, initially with 'a bundle of rags' or 'a tin can', but later with 'the real thing, made of leather'.

'I would play truant from school to meet my friends on some empty lot,' he wrote, 'and we would play for hours at a time, until we were exhausted. The goals were usually constructed from a pile of school briefcases, the exercise books lying idle within.' Invariably, Yevtushenko would play in goal and he insisted a great future had been foreseen for him in the position until, at the age of sixteen, he had his first verses published and committed himself full-time to poetry.

He describes in some detail a game 'against the team from Maryina Roshcha, a suburb of Moscow famous for its roughnecks. Our opponents were solidly built guys with low foreheads and modish haircuts. They were impressively tattooed with sayings like "Never forget mother" and "Death to the Nazis" as well as pictures of grinning skulls and bearded mermaids. On their bodies our opponents bore, as proudly as if they were decorations, the scars of numberless battles.' They were known as the Destroyers and rumour suggested they carried knives in their socks.

'We played on a large vacant lot behind a vodka distillery, where we had made ourselves goals out of rusty rails,' Yevtushenko recalled. 'Several hundred spectators assembled, among them the Maryina Roshcha fans, who could be distinguished by their grim conspiratorial air. This claque was headed by a one-eyed fellow of about thirty, known as Billy Bones. He was a rag-and-bone man by trade, but by inclination he was a drunkard and bandit.'

As expected, the Destroyers played with great violence. Yevtushenko's team's centre-forward and main defender both sustained injuries and so, inevitably, did the goalkeeper before carrying on bravely. Yevtushenko continues his account:

As the end of the game neared, all our players were covered with bruises and scars. However, there had been no score. The Destroyers were almost mad with rage. In a tense moment one of our defenders was foolish enough to stop the ball with his hand. This led to the most alarming moment possible for a goalkeeper – a penalty kick. The captain of the Destroyers spun the ball around in his hands, slapped it on its sides, spat upon it and put it on the penalty spot. I got myself ready.

At that very moment Billy Bones made an imperious sign to his henchmen with his fingers, and I felt a sharp blow on my face, then another, then a third. The fans of the Destroyers were shooting small stones at me from slingshots. The whole thing was happening in the best Latin American fashion. I was half blind from the pain and could see practically nothing beyond the ball sitting there motionless. Maybe that helped me.

The captain of the Destroyers put on his fiercest expression, ran up and shot. I don't know how it happened, but the ball came into my hands. Billy Bones looked furious. The captain of the Destroyers came up to me with a sweet smile on his face and put out his hand to congratulate me. I was a little surprised at such a miraculous transformation in character of the Destroyers but, in the simplicity of my heart, I stretched out my hand in response. Then, continuing to smile just as sweetly, the captain of the Destroyers, unseen by the people standing nearby, painfully squeezed my hand until it crunched and then twisted it a little, at the same time trying to kick the ball out of my other hand with his foot.

That would have been heroic enough and, perhaps, believable but Yevtushenko went on:

At that point I went into some kind of trance as a result of my just fury. I tore myself away and rushed forward with the ball, keeping it at my feet. I jumped over the outstretched legs of opponents trying to trip me. A piece of my shirt remained behind in the hands of one of the Destroyers who had vainly attempted to slow me down by whatever means he could. I was peppered from slingshots, but I no longer felt pain. Finally, having covered the whole field, I weaved past the Destroyer goalkeeper as well. But, out of a feeling of sadistic vengeance, I did not shoot the goal immediately. I stopped the ball on the goal line and turned around so that my back was to it and I was facing the Destroyers, who were rushing toward me with contorted, tense faces. I stood as if at attention, bowed my head slightly and, still hit by the slingshots, waited. When the Destroyers were upon me I lightly pushed the ball into the net with my heel. The referee's whistle sounded, proclaiming the end of the match, and our victory.

The Destroyers surrounded Yevtushenko, knocked him to the ground and drew their knives only for Billy Bones, apparently overcome by the goalkeeper's courage, to persuade them to leave him be. This was the end of *Vratar* and the end of the Death Match replayed and as such it's hard not to avoid the conclusion that Yevtushenko has overegged his pudding, merging fiction with fact. Even so, it's telling how pervasive the trope of the heroic goalkeeper was in the USSR.

Vratar prepared the stage for Yashin, but before his emergence there was a true-life precursor, a goalkeeper many still insist was the best Russia has ever produced, a goalkeeper whose grasp on the position at Dinamo Moscow almost led Yashin to quit football and commit himself to ice-hockey: Alexei Khomich.

He was serving with the army in Iran during the Second World War when his goalkeeping ability first became apparent. Although only 5'8" in height – short for a goalkeeper even in those days – he had a prodigious leap that led officers to nickname him 'Tiger'. A natural athlete, Khomich was also a proficient gymnast, swimmer and diver and played volleyball and chess to a decent level. He was an uncompromising self-improver dedicated to training but also to thinking about the game, developing new ways of throwing the ball out from the back.

He was twenty-five by the time he made his debut for Dinamo, but soon became recognised as the best goalkeeper in the country. Although he is commonly described as having been reserved, almost to the point of introversion, he had a certain charm and became a cult figure on Dinamo's 1945 tour of Britain, despite a gaffe at the reception to welcome the team to London. Confused by a film about Lord Nelson's lover that was enjoying great popularity in Moscow at the time, he began his speech with the words, 'Ladies and Hamiltons ...' His goal-keeping ability impressed as well. 'He's always on the move, very agile, hard to beat,' said the then-Chelsea manager Billy Birrell.

So revered was Khomich that when Rangers toured Russia in the early sixties the *Daily Express* asked the journalist James Sanderson to interview him. After a desultory effort to track him down, Sanderson pocketed Khomich's fee himself and made up the column, after which he was terrorised for weeks by telephone calls from Rangers players pretending to be Soviet officials threatening legal action over the misrepresentation of a comrade. By then Khomich had long since been supplanted, both in the Dinamo team and the public's affections, by Yashin.

Born in 1929, nine years after Khomich, Yashin lost his mother to tuberculosis when he was six. Germany invaded the USSR five years later, meaning he had to combine his schooling with helping the war effort, working alongside his father at a factory that made parts for aeroplanes at the Krasny Bogatyr (Red Hero) military enterprise in the village of Tushino near Moscow. From the start, the generosity and humility for which he'd become noted were apparent – at least according to Valentina. 'The second wife of his father told me that, during the war, little Lyova [a diminutive of Lev] would bring to their home a boy called Izya, who lived with a large family in some nearby barracks. Lev told her that they had nothing to eat and so his father and stepmother always fed him. Once he took off his sweater and gave it to Izya, telling his parents, "There are many children in their family and they have nothing to wear."'

Not that Yashin's family was particularly well off. In fact the poor quality of the food he ate at the time gave him a gastric ulcer and when he was sixteen he had to spend time in a health resort on the Black Sea. 'Tough training didn't help,' said Valentina, 'particularly given that Lev worked like the damned. In his whole career he wasn't late for a single training session. He was always punctual and he demanded the same from others. After every training session he would stay in the goal and ask somebody to have a number of shots at him. I watched that once and I couldn't ever watch it again. There were thirty or forty of the hardest shots that my husband took to his stomach. It seemed to me his whole abdominal cavity was being punched out. Lev told me that his abdominal muscles were very strong and that he caught the ball with his hands so it didn't touch his stomach. I saw, though, that it did.

'After some win I met Yakushin in the Savoy restaurant. Mikhail Iosifovich [that is, Yakushin] called me over and asked if Lev had complained about him. I said no and asked what had happened. "I suppose he was injured," Yakushin said. "He said during the training before the game that he had stomach pain and couldn't dive but I asked him to do it once. He got back up with difficulty and returned to the dressing room at snail's pace. But the next day he jumped and dived as usual ..."

'He had stomach aches permanently – and finally he died from stomach cancer. Because he had a very high level of acidity, he always carried in his pocket bicarbonate of soda. And water if possible. His heartburn was so strong that if he didn't have the water with him he couldn't rely on having time to find a cup of water and dissolve a teaspoon of soda in it. Sometimes he poured soda from a paper bag into his palm and put it straight in his mouth and then looked round desperately for some liquid to take it with.'

It was only in 1944, when football began again in Moscow after a three-year hiatus, that Yashin started to take the game seriously, trying out for the factory team. Contrary to national stereotype, he wasn't desperate to play in goal. 'Like all kids in Moscow, I'd started to kick the ball about in the streets,' he said. 'My first memories are of those crazy games. I would have loved to have played as a striker because I loved scoring goals but because of my height and my leap I was destined to be a goalkeeper. The bosses of the team imposed that decision upon me.'

Called up for his military service in 1947, Yashin was deployed in Moscow where, having shown early promise in his new position, he began playing in the city council championship for the Dinamo Sports Society. In July 1949 he was spotted by Arkady

Chernyshev, later a world-renowned ice-hockey coach, who invited him to join the youth section of the central team of Dinamo. That autumn, Dinamo's youth side produced a great upset as they beat Dinamo's senior team – including Khomich – 1–0 in the semi-final of the Moscow Cup. Yashin's performance caught the eye and, the following March, he was promoted to the senior squad for a tour to the Caucasus, initially as back-up for Khomich and his usual reserve, Walter Sanaya.

He was given his chance in a friendly against Traktor Stalingrad (now Rotor Volgograd) in 1950, but it could hardly have gone worse as he was involved in the sort of mix-up that can haunt goalkeepers for the rest of their careers. A strong wind carried a long clearance from the opposing keeper into his box. Yashin came to claim it but, his eyes on the ball, he didn't see the defender Yevgeny Averyanov racing to head clear. The two collided, both went down, and the ball bounced on into the net. Yashin later recalled lying on the ground and seeing illustrious team-mates such as Konstantin Beskov and Vasily Kartsev laughing at him. 'I heard them asking where on earth they'd found this goalkeeper,' he said.

His first official match, on 2 July that year, hardly went any better. Dinamo led Spartak 1–0 with quarter of an hour remaining when Khomich was injured. On came Yashin and, with three minutes left, Alexey Paramonov launched a looping cross into the box. Yashin came for it and again he collided with a defender – Vsevolod Blinkov this time – gifting Nikolai Parshin a tap-in to make it 1–1. His gaffe in the friendly in Volograd had gone largely unnoticed but this one was painfully high profile. After the game, a general in the NKVD burst into the dressing room and demanded that 'this idiot be cleaned from the team'.

Dinamo's coaches ignored him but their confidence in Yashin's ability looked misplaced when he was given a third opportunity, away against Dinamo Tbilisi, that autumn. Dinamo Moscow won 5–4, but Yashin conceded four in a ten-minute spell that seemed to have brought an end to his career. He didn't play again that season, or the next, or the one after that. Yashin himself, though, remained patient, training assiduously and doing all he could to make sure that if a fourth opportunity came his way, he would not let it pass. 'If I'd told them during that spell that I wanted to leave, I don't think they'd have spent much time trying to persuade me not to,' he said. 'But I couldn't imagine a life without football. I continued to work hard and, to my surprise, they didn't get rid of me.'

It helped that he was proving so useful as a net-minder in the ice-hockey section of the club, demonstrating both sharp reflexes and developing his sense of angles and positioning. He was part of the Dinamo side that won the USSR Cup in 1953 and was named in the USSR's squad for the 1954 World Championship. He rejected the invitation, though, deciding that it was impossible to play two sports at the highest level. The timing was critical.

His spring supposedly gone, Khomich left the club in 1953, joining Spartak Minsk before embarking on a career as a sports photographer that took him to the 1970, 1974 and 1978 World Cups. Suddenly Yashin had another chance. This time, he took it. He played thirteen league games that season and helped Dinamo to the Cup, although he didn't complete the final, suffering a second-half injury and having to be substituted. Faced with a choice between football and hockey, he chose football but had Khomich held on a year longer, the decision could easily have fallen the other way.

Khomich had won two league titles but Dinamo's golden age coincided with Yashin's first consistent run in the first team. Between 1954 and 1959, they won the Soviet title four times and were twice runners-up. He was still, though, a controversial figure. He may have later come to seem the model of po-faced probity, but he was sent off in the Soviet Cup final in 1955 after striking the CSKA forward Vladimir Agapov; his temper bubbled always just beneath the surface. Dinamo went on to lose 2–1, and Yashin was widely blamed. The Dinamo club newspaper carried a cartoon of the goalkeeper in boxing gloves with the caption, 'The Cup would undoubtedly have been ours ... but for Comrade Yashin.'

Still, he was by then an established star, having been called up to the national team in 1954 for their first game in over two years. The side had been disbanded after a politically embarrassing reverse against Yugoslavia in the 1952 Olympics, so defeat in their first game after reformation was unthinkable – even if their opponents were Sweden, who had just finished third at the World Cup. The USSR, though, produced one of their greatest performances, cruising to a 7–0 victory.

By the end of the year, Yashin was the USSR's undisputed number one and within two seasons he was attracting worldwide acclaim. He was in great form in the 1956 Olympics in Melbourne, letting in just two goals in four games and producing a match-winning performance in the final against Yugoslavia. As the returning Soviet team made the long journey by train from Vladivostok, where their ship had docked, to Moscow, it was Yashin the fans flocked to see, and he was awarded the Order of the Red Labour Banner by the Party. Later that year he came fifth in *France Football*'s poll for European Player of the Year.

Yashin was just as impressive at the 1958 World Cup and then, in 1960, came more silverware as the USSR lifted the inaugural European Championship. The report in *France Football* praised Yashin's 'extraordinary precision' in the semi-final win over Czechoslovakia while Yugoslavia were beaten in the final, their headline claimed, because of 'the brio of Yashin and the head of Ponedelnik'. Yashin, the report went on, 'proved he is surely the best goalkeeper in the world'. *L'Équipe* was just as impressed, highlighting Yashin's 'class and vigilance' in keeping out two efforts from Bora Kostić and describing him as 'equally the master of his eighteen-yard box and sharp between the posts'. His charges from his goal, though, caused concern. 'His audacity, though, almost cost him dear,' the report said, detailing how he was nearly caught out by a second-half lob from Dragoslav Šekularac and he had to backpedal quickly to turn the ball away. 'His clearances,' an analysis of the Soviet side noted, 'especially with his hands, were a sensation.'

The only negative was that his famous cap was stolen in the pitch invasion that followed the final whistle. 'Thousands of people ran onto the pitch,' said Valentina. 'At that time they weren't as well organised with security as now. In the chaos, a fan took the cap from Lev's head and ran away. The crowd was so huge that it was impossible to find him. Lev said that he looked around but couldn't see anybody with the cap. The newspapers later wrote that French police found the cap after the game and gave it back to Lev, but that's a lie. It disappeared for ever.'

Yashin's performances earned further individual recognition as he was awarded the Order of Lenin (Highest Class). It wasn't just that he was successful, though: Yashin was one of the small group of elite goalkeepers of the age who continued the process of reinterpreting the goalkeeper's role, seeing the value in commanding his box and the space beyond. He would regularly leave his box to make clearances and became noted both for his physical courage and his heading ability. He had been inspired, he said, by seeing Apostol Sokolov, Bulgaria's goalkeeper when they toured the USSR in 1952. 'That blond devil played high up and blocked any forward who might get behind the defence,' he explained. 'It was something completely new to me, but I followed his example.' Properly harnessed, what in his first two games had been seen as reckless charges to the ball became accepted as a virtue and, as he grew in confidence and authority, he began to command his defence in a way that would seem natural to modern goalkeepers but which was unusual at the time.

All careers, no matter how garlanded, have their dark moments, and goalkeepers are probably particularly susceptible to slumps in confidence. Yashin's most difficult time came at the 1962 World Cup. He kept a clean sheet as the USSR beat Yugoslavia 2–0 in their opening game and they were 4–1 up in their second against Colombia when Marcos Coll scored direct from a corner after sixty-eight minutes, with the defender Givi Chokheli almost ushering the ball over the line. Chokheli explained that he had misheard Yashin's shout of '*Igray!*' ("Play!") as '*Igrayu!*' ('I play!'), but that did little to calm the goalkeeper, who gave him a firm slap on the backside. With the Soviets rattled, Colombia hit back, and scored twice more to force an improbable draw.

In that regard, Yashin perhaps suffered from his reluctance to criticise his team-mates. 'He hated gossips, never blamed anyone or said spiteful things, and he was reticent in general,' Valentina said. 'Sometimes I would ask, "Why does this player give all the passes to the opponent?" and he would make a helpless gesture. "He just isn't able to! He doesn't see the pitch!" It was his favourite saying: "He doesn't see the pitch," and he transferred it from football to regular life.'

Victory over an injury-depleted Uruguay meant the USSR topped their group, setting up a quarter-final against the hosts, Chile. Yashin was surprised at his near post by a Leonel Sánchez free-kick from wide on the right and then, after Igor Chislenko had equalised, he was beaten by a long-range drive from Eladio Rojas. Valentin Ivanov had given the ball away cheaply in the build-up but it was Yashin who took the blame, despite the fact that the angled shot flew only a foot or so inside the post. 'There was only one Soviet journalist there, from the APN news agency,' Yashin said. 'He knew nothing about football and he made me the scapegoat. When I came back to the USSR I was welcomed as the person responsible for our defeat. I was so angry I thought about giving it up.'

Valentina remembers the hostility that greeted her husband even at home games. 'The crowd whistled and shouted many things,' she said. 'It happened for two or three games. There was no television in Russia at the time and so all anybody knew was from that APN journalist. Because of him, everybody thought, "Yashin lost the World Cup." Our windows were broken twice but I don't know if that is connected. There was a street lamp under our window, so maybe some hooligans threw stones at it and hit the windows instead. And people wrote unspeakable things about him in the dust on our car.'

Given the standards he had set before the tournament, it's hard to understand the fury of the feeling against Yashin even if he had, for once, been at fault, perhaps underlining just how precarious a goalkeeper's reputation is. 'It happens not only in football,' Valentina went on. 'We are the same in everything. If something goes wrong, somebody must be blamed. The top bosses wanted to escape punishment so they passed the blame on to Yashin.'

France Football also suggested it might be time for him to retire, but whether he was to blame or not, Yashin decided to carry on. 'He knew, as any human does, periods of great doubt, uncertainty and weakness,' said Yakushin, 'but the feeling of personal responsibility for the team generated his courageous, strong nature.' For a while he didn't train, but the Dinamo coach Alexander Ponomarev was supportive and told Yashin to leave Russia for a while to go fishing. When he came back he trained with the reserve side and didn't make his return to the first team until the following season.

It was emphatically the right decision: 1963 was probably his greatest season. In twenty-seven league matches he conceded just six goals and he added to his international reputation with an excellent performance for a Rest of the World XI against England at Wembley in a game to mark the centenary of the Football Association, a match that persuaded Konstantin Beskov, the Russia coach, to restore him to the national team. The following year, after saving a penalty from Sandro Mazzola in a European Championship qualifier against Italy – one of around 150 penalty saves he made in his career – Yashin was named European Player of the Year, so far the only goalkeeper to be so honoured.

He was superb again at the 1966 World Cup, particularly in the quarter-final victory over Hungary at Roker Park and, although he retired from the national team in 1967, he was included in the USSR squad for the 1970 World Cup in Mexico, where he served as a reserve goalkeeper and general adviser. Even nearing his fortieth birthday, he was in fine form domestically, letting in only one goal for Dinamo in his first ten games that season. He retired shortly after returning from Mexico, playing his final league game on 30 August 1970, twenty years and fifty-nine days after he had played his first. In football, statistics rarely tell the full story but some are so startling that they bear retelling. Yashin's career for Dinamo Moscow and for the USSR comprised 438 games. Both sides were successful but only moderately so and yet he managed a total of 209 clean sheets. In other words, he was unbeaten in 48 per cent of the games in which he played.

Yashin pulled on the dark jersey again the following May as he was granted a ceremonial farewell with a friendly between a World XI, including Gerd Müller, Dragan Dzajić and Hristo Bonev, and a side made up of the teams of the Dinamo association. Appropriately, he was unbeaten when he was substituted to emotional applause seven minutes into the second half. He worked as a director at Dinamo Moscow, but most of his retirement was spent fishing. 'I can think of no better way to relax,' he said, 'than out on a lake or a marsh with a rod in my hand.' His bravery, though, had taken its toll. Regular blows to the legs had done internal damage and, after falling ill while with the Soviet veterans team in Budapest in 1984, Yashin had his right leg amputated. A heavy smoking habit only worsened his condition and he died in 1990, six months after his sixtieth birthday. His legacy, though, lives on.

There were the precursors to Yashin and then there were the successors: Rinat Dasaev was the Yashin of the eighties and is probably second only to him in the pantheon of Russian goalkeeping. Born in Astrakhan in southern Russia in 1957, he is almost certainly the greatest Tatar footballer there has ever been, having played in three World Cups, taken bronze at the 1980 Olympics and finished as runner-up at Euro 88. He was capped 91 times between 1979 and 1990; only Oleh Blokhin played more games for the USSR.

Dasaev rates the 2–1 defeat to Brazil in the group stage of the 1982 World Cup and the 1–0 win over the Netherlands in the group stage at Euro 88 (the Dutch then beat the Soviets 2–0 in the final) as his greatest ever games. '82 was the first World Cup for me,' he said. 'I have a DVD and watch it from time to time. I remember every individual moment of this game and I still think if I'd used one hand and not two I'd have been able to stop both goals.'

Dasaev was also a key player in the great Spartak Moscow team of the late seventies and eighties that took two league titles playing a fast attractive style based on close passing and the interchange of players. Six times named Soviet goalkeeper of the year, he became known as 'the Iron Curtain', but after the collapse of Communism he was one of the first players to take advantage of the opportunities of free movement, joining Sevilla in 1990 for a fee of around £1.5m. 'When I joined Sevilla, I was thirty-one,' he said, 'but I felt like a teenager because I couldn't explain what I wanted or what I wanted other players to do. I kept myself away from the team. That was the consequence of my lack of linguistic skills.'

Nearing the end of his career, Dasaev disappointed in Spain. He had shown uncharacteristic signs of fallibility during Italia 90 and regularly found himself the fourth foreigner in an age when only three were permitted in Spanish football. His contract expired in 1994, after which he chose to remain in Spain, despite having no obvious means of finding work. 'My wife is from Seville and we have lots of friends there,' he said. 'I go there often. Seville is a second Motherland for me. It's a place I belong to.' For several years, Dasaev seemed to have disappeared, until the newspaper *Komsomolskaya Pravda* tracked him down, living, they said, in poverty. He was persuaded to go back to Russia, where he was welcomed as a returning hero.

He found the country changed beyond recognition. 'I did not witness what was happening here,' he said of the radical changes that followed *perestroika*. 'I was lucky. I had left by then. I was calling my friends from Spain and they told me to stay there, not to come back. That was good advice. When I came back after ten years in Spain I had another challenge; I had to learn Russian again because I'd spent ten years speaking only in Spanish. I had to spend a while thinking what I wanted to say. It took me time as well to get accustomed to the new reality in this country. I left one country and I came back to another one, absolutely, in terms of politics, so I had to once again start my life from scratch.'

Dasaev seems to have mixed feelings about the old system, recognising that his position as a leading footballer meant his experience of life under Communism was very different to that of many of his compatriots. 'I talk not only on my own behalf, but also on the behalf of other big athletes who represented the Soviet Union,' he said. 'A kind of pressure existed but it was not so difficult or so heavy that you suffered. For we football players the fact that the USSR was a closed country wasn't a reality because we were travelling often. We lived a different USSR to others. The issue was that we were not able to leave the country to play for other clubs. That was forbidden. Don't forget that we grew up in the USSR and we were part of this society.

'We were an integral part of the Soviet lifestyle. I am often asked when was better, in Soviet times or now? From the point of view of football, it's true that we were not paid such big wages as players are paid now, but the money we were getting at that time was more than enough for us to enjoy our life – I'm talking about athletes. There was no problem with buying an apartment or a car, and the prices were so low that the money we were getting was enough to guarantee a very high standard of lifestyle. Now guys are getting a lot of money but they have to spend a lot of money.' And perhaps the attitude to goalkeepers changed as well; in the new society, individuals sought the fame and glory of goals rather than the self-sacrificing independence of the goalkeeper.

After working for a time as an assistant coach with the national team, Dasaev went on to run a coaching academy at the Luzhniki.

The man who was earmarked as the next incarnation was Mikhail Yeremin. He was eighteen when he made his debut for CSKA Moscow in 1986, was a key figure as the USSR won the European Under-21 championship in 1990 and was called up to the national team for a friendly against Romania in 1990. In 1991 he was part of the dynamic CSKA side that beat Torpedo Moscow to win the Soviet Cup and would go on to win the last Soviet league title. Driving home after the final, though, a tyre burst on Yeremin's car. He lost control and crashed into a bus, and died from his injuries a week later.

And so the mantle passed on. Sergei Ovchinnikov was the next New Yashin, even if his brashness and David

Seaman-style ponytail suggested a markedly different personality. Ovchinnikov's talent swiftly emerged at school – where he first acquired the nickname 'Boss' – and he was accepted into the youth system at Dinamo Moscow, the club at which Yashin made his name. He left to join Lokomotiv Moscow in 1991, and after six years there, moved to Portugal where he played for Benfica, Alverca and Porto before returning to Loko in 2002. It is a commonplace that Russians don't travel well but Ovchinnikov had clearly learned in Portugal. When he left, he was brilliant but erratic; on his return he was brilliant and consistent, keeping a Russian record twenty clean sheets as Loko won the first title in their history. 'The situation at Loko with Ovchinnikov now,' the former Loko forward Valentin Bubukin said, 'is like it was at Dinamo with Yashin.'

Except, that is, for Ovchinnikov's temper. Yashin had been fiery but had learned to control his emotions; Ovchinnikov never did. 'The keeper should be aggressive,' he said. 'He should shout, take command, fight for his team-mates. It becomes a part of your image. You do it on purpose to put pressure on the referees and to get the opposition off balance. But don't think I am the same in everyday life.' That aggression, though, had a tendency to spill over. In 2003 he was suspended for five games after chasing a Zenit St Petersburg coach he claimed had insulted Loko. 'The thing that irritates me most in people is when they disrespect Loko,' he says. 'When they say bad things about my club it is the same as a personal insult.'

Although there were claims in 2000 that he had vowed never to play for the national team again after being left on the bench for a friendly in Germany, it was largely his desire to play himself into the World Cup team that prompted his return from Portugal. He won two successive Russian Goalkeeper of the Year awards to go with the two he had won in his first stint at Loko, but a red card for handling outside his area against Portugal in Euro 2004 effectively ended his international career. Having won only thirty-five caps, the feeling is that, gifted as he was, he never quite lived up to the hype. As if to prove Russian goalkeepers can never escape the *Vratar* template, Ovchinnikov worked as an adviser on a recent Ukrainian film about the Death Match, training the actor playing the Trusevych character.

After Yeremin and Ovchinnikov, there came Igor Akinfeev. He was born in Vidnoye, just outside Moscow, in 1986. His father was a driver and his mother a nursery-school teacher but his grandfather had been a goalkeeper in the Soviet second flight. 'He knew a coach in the CSKA youth system and that's why they put me there when I was four years old,' Akinfeev said. 'I think there's nobody loves CSKA more than me.'

Akinfeev was sixteen when he made his debut for CSKA, saving a penalty in a 2–0 win over Krylya Sovetov. '[Veniamin] Mandrykin got an injury,' he remembered. 'I was very nervous, afraid as to how the other players would receive me. I shut myself in a room in our camp. I didn't speak to anybody. But in the evening we had a training session, so I had to go out. But the guys greeted me and after that first game I took a load of beer to the sauna to celebrate.'

He doesn't seem the anxious sort, as CSKA's goalkeeping coach Vyacheslav Chanov, a former goalkeeper Akinfeev refers to as his 'life-coach', acknowledged. 'He's got courage,' he said. 'He doesn't get nervous. His main strength is his confidence, which transmits itself to his team-mates. It's very rare for him to make a mistake in positioning.' Akinfeev went on to make thirteen league appearances in that 2003 season as CSKA won their first league title since the break-up of the USSR. The following year he established himself as CSKA's first choice. He was named Russian goalkeeper of the year and, the season after that, CSKA became the first Russian side to win a European trophy, beating Sporting 3–1 in the Uefa Cup final at the Portuguese side's home ground in Lisbon.

Although he too has a volatile temperament – as demonstrated by the five-game ban he collected for smacking Krylya Sovetov's Serbian midfielder Ognjen Koroman who had, seemingly unintentionally, kicked the ball at him while celebrating a goal – Akinfeev has matured into a gentle, reflective, almost melancholic figure. Back in 2005 he was contemplating a move abroad although, it must be said, without much enthusiasm. He is a Russian and there is perhaps no nation that feels so strongly the tie to home. 'From her own people Russia elicits a helpless worship of belonging,' Colin Thubron observes in *Among the Russians*. 'She contains them with the elemental despotism of an earth mother, and they feel for her the supplicant's tormented tenderness.'

For Akinfeev, that bond is strengthened by his Orthodox faith. 'When I have spare time,' he said when I first interviewed him in 2006, 'I try to go to church. I just light a candle ... and then I feel easiness within my soul. I can't imagine myself in the colours of any team but CSKA but if you get the chance to leave for a prestigious club, you must take it. Maybe not now, but certainly by the time I'm twenty-five. In Russia, when you turn thirty everybody forgets about you. There are great actors who were famous across the whole country who die in poverty and oblivion.'

By the time he was twenty-five, though, Akinfeev was still unsure about a move. 'Ask me if I want to leave CSKA and I'll say "no",' he said. Others believe he has to leave if he is to advance. 'He was the best among the youngsters when he began his career,' Dasaev said. 'He was very promising, but as of today he is probably not delivering. I think he is not growing the way he has to if he is to become the best. For several seasons, he was progressing and now he is not. Probably it's time for him to leave and move abroad. Unless he does so he will stagnate.'

Akinfeev agrees, intellectually at least; emotionally, though, he remains tied to Russia. 'I understand that every player needs to progress and you can progress only with better teams,' he said. 'So I'd never leave for, say, Aston Villa or Fiorentina. I've heard that Arsenal and Manchester United had some interest in me. If some day I found out it was true then I'd start to think a lot. These are very strong teams but I love CSKA and I love Russia as well. I like Russian people – they are my people. I like Russian nature, especially birch trees. I believe in God and like to walk by Orthodox churches. Obviously, I can't get enough of that in Europe. Even two weeks of training camps in Europe makes me sad.'

In that, perhaps, he is typical. Countless Russian players have spoken of intense homesickness when moving to foreign clubs – Yegor Titov said he used to get nauseous sitting on a plane waiting to leave Moscow – something that seems to go deeper than the usual issues of footballers adapting to a new environment. Even his linking of nature and the Orthodox faith, in fact, is typical, something Thubron makes clear in his discussion of the Russian preference for the *eleousa* representations of the Virgin Mary in icons which emphasise her maternal rather than her reginal qualities. 'The image of motherhood plucks a profound chord in the Russia soul,' he wrote. 'It pervades Soviet nationalism with its mystical invocation of Rodina, the motherland, and reaches back, it seems, to a time long before Christianity, when a primordial Great Mother ruled these pagan woods and plains. This mother was faceless, perhaps nameless: an all-engendering womb. Through the animistic worship of her nature – trees, pools, fire, stones – she enveloped her worshippers with a passive omnipotence.'

Akinfeev is also typically Russian, of course, in being a goalkeeper, and is keenly aware of his heritage. 'I consider myself part of Russian goalkeeping tradition but I can't really say that I was taught the same things Yashin, Khomich and Dasaev used to do,' he said. 'Yes, Yashin was "king of the penalty box" but nowadays every goalkeeper has to act that way. The modern game has become faster and sometimes it's necessary to play with your legs instead of hands, like Dasaev did, but I don't do that because of him personally. It's just faster. But I have respect for every great Russian goalkeeper and am proud to be a part of this tradition.'

The tradition, though, is changing: in a world in which individualism is the norm – often rampantly so – the position of goalkeeper perhaps no longer offers a release. Football is now a wholly global game so while Akinfeev respects the tradition of the commanding loners of Soviet Russia, his model came from the opposite side of Europe: Spain, and specifically Valencia. 'Santiago Cañizares was my childhood hero,' Akinfeev said. 'Not that I've adopted his goalkeeping style, but we are similar in some ways: we both like to play solidly. When you're calm, your net is safe. Football is a simple game and if you're playing in a spectacular way then you're minimising your chances to keep your net safe. Why jump and dive to the top corner if you can just make two steps and catch the ball firmly? When I saw René Higuita's famous "scorpion kick" I said, "This guy is nuts! He's lucky he hasn't broken his spine." That style of goalkeeping is obviously not for me. By the time Cañizares had finished his career, I'd stopped watching goalkeepers play. Chanov keeps telling me that every goalkeeper needs to concentrate on his own style.'

At 6'1", Akinfeev is not tall for a goalkeeper by today's standards but where he does fit a modern template of goalkeeping is in his ability to pass the ball. He proudly cites the former national coach Guus Hiddink's line from his time as Russia coach that 'Aki can deliver a good long ball' – not in the sense of being able to kick the ball a long way, but in terms of the accuracy of his passing. 'He always said that I can start an attack,' Akinfeev said. 'At Euro 2008 he asked central defenders to pass to me when they see no unmarked player. I can pass for a sixty-seventy-metre distance. I love it, I must admit. So I do it very often.'

That tournament marked Akinfeev's return after a serious knee injury suffered in May 2007. It affected him deeply. 'The most important thing for every man, not only football players, is to have a core,' he said. 'I had a dreadful injury. I needed to lie on my back for a month after the operation and was told not to move onto my side. Full rehabilitation took six months but I felt the pain for about a year more. When I watched CSKA play, I cried because I couldn't help my team. My parents and friends were very supportive but no one can really take this pain away. I had to do it myself – and I did. But people in Russia tend to forget that Akinfeev had that injury and could return to the same level of play. There isn't much appreciation here. Good words are mostly coming from foreigners.'

Whether he ever did truly regain his form is debatable. Certainly towards the end of 2009, it became apparent that he was conceding a lot of goals through his legs. The former USSR international Anzar Kavazashvili suggested it was a technical issue related to the speed at which he advanced from his goal; Akinfeev responded by altering his starting position, playing always a little further out from goal so he didn't have so much ground to cover to close forwards down. He coupled that with a change of studs that appeared to have solved the specific problem, even if doubts remained as to whether he had ever quite delivered on that early promise.

And, then, in August 2011, he damaged the same ligaments in the same knee having landed awkwardly following a needless late challenge from the Spartak forward Welliton, who was banned for six games for the foul, reduced to three on appeal. At twenty-five, Akinfeev had won a half century of caps and had played over 200 times for CSKA; he looked set to break records for longevity if nothing else. The worry is that, after two years of battling to recover after the first injury, he never quite recovers fully after the second and so, even if he is as gifted as his three illustrious predecessors, he is stuck forever halfway up the pantheon.

Yashin's shadow is a long one.

3: A BANK CLERK IN FLANNELS

Other cultures may have seen the goalkeeper as a heroic individual, increasingly so as football spread in the years between the wars, but in Britain he has always been regarded as an outsider, often socially or physically awkward. Bill Naughton's classic 1961 children's book *The Goalkeeper's Revenge* sets out the stereotype in its first paragraph. 'Sim Dalt [the goalkeeper of the title] had two long, loose arms, spindly legs, a bony face with gleaming brown eyes, and, from the age of twelve, was reckoned to be a bit touched in the head.'

He performed marvels for his school team but when an inspector found Sim's 'scholastic ability' to be of 'a low order' he was sent to the local 'special school'. His teacher wanted him to carry on playing, but his team-mates objected to the thought of 'a cracky school lad' turning out with them. Replacing him, the captain thought, shouldn't be a problem. '"They're ten a penny," grunted Bob. "Especially daft 'uns."' Bob became a professional for the local side while Sim ended up as the star attraction at a 'Beat the Goalie' stand at an amusement arcade. There he had his revenge, first saving three penalties from Bob, so winning a hefty bet and then making enough money to buy the club and terminate Bob's contract. He may have triumphed in the end but the underlying message was clear enough: goalkeepers were weird, cunning and different. And to be cunning or clever, as the Hungarian humourist Georg Mikes makes clear in *How to Be English*, was the most suspicious trait of all, particularly in British football.

Sim Dalt is just one in a long line of goalkeeping misfits. In *Soccer Special*, for instance, written by Michael Hardcastle, probably the most prolific writer of sports fiction for children Britain has produced, the protagonist Miles is unable to play football after a series of childhood illnesses. He instead watches local youth matches, writing them up for a magazine he produces, until one day he is cajoled into playing in goal after the regular keeper suffers an accident. Typically, he excels. A number of tropes pull together here: the goalkeeper is an odd, sickly outsider; the goalkeeper is an intellectual who prefers to write than to play; and goalkeeper is a position any random passer-by might be able to play, as though goalkeeping were some kind of natural gift (or affliction) rather than a skill to be learned and practised.

In *Jossy's Giants*, the BBC children's serial scripted by the late darts commentator Sid Waddell and screened in 1986 and 1987, the goalkeeper, Harvey McGuinn, is a thin, awkward, brooding presence. In the first episode, Jossy, who eventually takes over as coach of the Glipton Grasshoppers, dispatches Tracey Gaunt, the girl who hangs around the club, to distract the opposition goalkeeper. The implication is obvious: he is so unused to the attentions of girls that he dare not pass up the opportunity to talk to one even while the game is still going on.

Advertisers, not surprisingly, picked up the stereotype. The notion of the 'Weetabix dive', the grinning, hapless geek diving way over the ball, reverberated long after the early eighties advert that had spawned it; it somehow clicked with the general perception of what goalkeepers were like even though English goalkeeping at the time was going through a golden period.

An explanation for the more general British distrust of goalkeeping isn't too difficult to find. If, as Nabokov argued, the showmanship necessary for a goalkeeper to assert himself is alien to the British psyche, then what reward does goalkeeping offer? Forwards, at least, have the tally of goals scored by which to achieve a measure of self-validation. In his 1944 book *Soccer, The Ace of Games*, Alec Whitcher suggests the issue began at school.

Rightly or wrongly, what seemed to happen in a boy's early days of soccer was that he was left to his own devices, without the control of any master, who was normally occupied with the seniors. Consequently what followed was that the weakest and most nervous boys were invariably consigned to goalkeeping, whether they liked it or not. The less aggressive found themselves full-backs, and after a good argument the half-backs and forwards generally sorted themselves out. I believe I am right in asserting that the stronger lads always fancied themselves as forwards, and so the weaker section continued to play in the first position allotted to them, or change at their peril ... Now why do boys give preference to forward play? It may be for various reasons, for instance, to be up in the middle of the field of play where they can take part both in attack and midfield defence, or, and which is more probable, they love to experience the superiority of scoring a goal ... Coming back to the poor goalkeeper, you would say, if my arguments held, that there would never be any good goalkeepers. This, therefore, requires clarifying ... But I am sure I am right in saying there are fewer candidates for goal, which is not surprising when on a cold day, and not being under pressure, the lad nearly perishes in spite of his endeavours to keep warm; his excitement and participation in the game are spasmodic.

There were exceptions, though, and great goalkeepers did emerge from the British system between the world wars. Arguably the greatest of them, although it is true that his tragic end means he is judged on potential as much as on achievement, was Celtic's John Thomson. Scottish goalkeeping would later become as tired a comedy staple as mothers-in-law and British Rail sandwiches, but in the inter-war years there was little to separate the English and Scottish traditions. As Hugh Taylor wrote in his section on Thomson in *The Masters of Scottish Football*, in the Scotland of the age, 'there was little time for drama and histrionics'. The extravagant keeper, he said, had as much chance of success as 'a bank clerk who went to work in a sports jacket and flannels'. Thomson, though, was different. 'Perhaps it was his essential niceness,' Taylor wrote. 'Perhaps it was his youthful eagerness. More likely, it was because, despite his agility, his new ideas, his spectacular leaps, everyone realised no more reliable goalkeeper could have been found anywhere in the world.'

Thomson's career was tragically brief, his death at twenty-two prompting one of the first great outpourings of public grief for a lost sportsman. Although he had won only four caps, he was already considered one of the finest goalkeepers Scotland had ever produced. 'He was not just a goalkeeper,' said the Celtic centre-forward Jimmy McGrory, 'he was a great natural athlete. He was not big but he had a magnificently developed body with all the grace and litheness of an Olympic gymnast. He had not big hands but he had neat hands and I have never seen hands that were safer in clutching a ball.'

Celtic's chief scout, Steve Callaghan, had been taken by Thomson while at a game in Fife to watch the other goalkeeper. He was puzzled, though, that his name had not been mentioned to him before. When he approached him, he found out why: Thomson's mother had had a dream that her son would be severely injured playing in goal and had determined that she would never allow him to sign professional forms. Callaghan realised, though, that if he let Thomson leave the ground he would never recruit him, so he persuaded him there and then, the contract being signed against a lamp-post.

His first game, away against Dundee in 1927, brought a dire error as he fumbled a Willie Cook cross but Celtic won 2–1 and the incident was largely forgotten, except by Thomson himself who seemed thereafter to devote himself to even the simplest catch with extreme focus. 'His hands,' Taylor said, 'were those of a surgeon, fine but powerful.'

There are countless stories of the saves he made, and he seems to have been adept at changing the direction of a dive mid-air, something he did both against Peerie Cunningham of Kilmarnock and in an international against England at Hampden in 1931 when he pushed away a deflected shot from

Gordon Hodgson. Playing for the Scottish League against the English League at Birmingham in November 1928, he made a save and was still grounded as the ball fell for the Leicester inside-forward Ernie Hine, who 'hit the shot full on his instep', as John Rafferty described it in *The Great Ones*. 'Thomson was still on his knees as the ball streaked towards the goal, directed to slip under the crossbar and lodge in the roof of the net. And then with a great gymnast's leap John Thomson rose and in a blur of action his body arched and his arms stretched and his fingers reached the ball and its path was bent and it rose to clear the crossbar.'

He was just as impressive in the same inter-league fixture the following year. 'The goal that day,' wrote Rafferty, 'was a concert platform for him and on it he received modestly the adulation due a virtuoso. The performance was climaxed by a flourish that did not matter except to show his abundant talent. The English centre-forward burst through after a running pass but not before the referee had whistled offside. He was furious with frustration and, as John Thomson came out to retrieve the ball for the free-kick the centre-forward lashed at it. Straight at the goalkeeper it flew rising over his head but he, without breaking his leisurely walking stride, reached up, held the ball and continued his walk and placed it for the free-kick. The non-chalance of the action did not hide the skill of the clutch and the cheering and applause must have been the greatest ever for a non-save.'

His fateful, final game came on 5 September 1931. It was against Rangers, a match that highlighted the oddity that, at a time when Celtic's players and support were almost entirely Catholic, he was a Protestant. In a previous Old Firm game, he'd complained to his team-mate Jimmy McGrory about an oppo-nent who'd repeatedly called him a 'papish bastard'. McGrory told him not to worry; he got called that every week. 'It's all right for you,' Thomson is supposed to have replied. 'You are one.'

The first half was dull. Match reports spoke of a sense of boredom; observers yearned for anything to break the tedium, but when it was punctuated, it was in the most tragic way. Five minutes after half-time, Jimmy Fleming laid the Rangers striker Sam English clean through with just the goalkeeper to beat. Thomson was famed for his bravery, though, and had suffered a broken jaw and damaged ribs making a save against Airdrie in February the previous year. He hurled himself at English's feet, his head colliding with the forward's knee. English limped away as Thomson lay unconscious.

As Celtic fans cheered the save and Rangers fans jeered at the prone keeper, only English seemed to realised how serious the situation was. He waved urgently for assistance while Davie Meiklejohn, the Rangers captain, quietened the home fans. As the severity of Thomson's condition became apparent, a hush fell over the ground. Margaret Finlay, Thomson's fiancée, with whom he was planning to open a gentleman's outfitters, broke down in tears as she saw his limp body carried off the ground. A report in *The Scotsman* suggested Thomson sat up and looked back to his goalmouth as he was stretchered off, although that seems implausible. He died at 9.25 that night of a depressed fracture of the skull.

Fans from both sides of the divide were united in grief. In Bridgeton, traffic was stopped by pedestrians walking past a floral tribute in the window of a Rangers supporters' club. So many tried to get into his memorial service at the Trinity Congregational Church that the Celtic right-half Peter Wilson, who was supposed to read a lesson, was locked out and police had to intervene to avoid a crush. Tens of thousands gathered at Queen Street station to see the coffin off on its journey back to Thomson's home village of Cardenden in Fife. Hundreds of unemployed workers walked the fifty-five miles, sleeping on the Crags, a group of hills near Auchterderran. The local pits in Fife were closed for the day, and the streets were packed to see six Celtic players carry the coffin to Bowhill cemetery.

Difference seemed to haunt the goalkeeper. Even if he didn't fall into penury, if he survived the war and managed to avoid tragedy on the pitch, there was still something about him that encouraged others to project ideologies upon him, to transform him into a tragic hero. 'He wears the number one on his back,' the Uruguayan poet and political thinker Eduardo Galeano wrote. 'The first to be paid? No; the first to pay. It's always the keeper's fault. And if it isn't, he still gets blamed. When any player commits a foul, he's the one who gets punished: they leave him there in the immensity of the empty net, abandoned to face his executioner alone.' In Britain, the tendency was to focus on the haplessness of the keeper; elsewhere it was the valour that was emphasised.

Ferenc Plattkó, born in 1898, for instance, was one of the first great goalkeepers from continental Europe. He played for a number of clubs in Budapest and Vienna and was a player-coach with KAFK from the Serbian city of Kula. His break-through came in two friendlies MTK of Budapest played against Barcelona. Both finished goalless draws and Barcelona were impressed enough to sign him. He helped them to their first league title and three cups.

His performance in the 1928 Copa del Rey final against Real Sociedad led to him becoming the subject of an odd poem by the Spanish poet Rafael Alberti. Although Plattkó's own politics were never explicit, Alberti's sympathies are clear as he makes reference to the '*camisetas reales*' ['royal shirts'] and '*las doradas insignias*' ['golden emblems'] of Sociedad: this, for him, is a team of the monarchy – by then propped up by the dictator Miguel Primo de Rivera – taking on a team of Catalan Republicans. As a punishment for booing the national anthem, fans had been banned from Barcelona games for three months before the final so there was an understandable mood of tension around the stadium in Santander.

Plattkó, though, 'the goalkeeper in the dust', was implacable. Alberti saw him as the game's hero, describing him as 'the blond bear', and in his version of events the Hungarian, displaced and alienated, regained a sense of identity by backing a just cause and keeping a clean sheet in a 1–0 win. In reality, the game was drawn 1–1, although Barcelona eventually won after a second replay.

What Alberti didn't mention, although it was surely implicit, was the contrast he saw between Plattkó and the man he had replaced at Barcelona, Ricardo Zamora. According to Galeano, 'for twenty years he was the best goalkeeper in the world' and it is after Zamora that La Liga's annual goalkeeping award is named.

Born in a poor suburb of Barcelona in 1901 to Spanish parents – and thus considered an immigrant to Catalunya – Zamora played pelota until seeing a game of football in 1914, at which he decided to switch on the grounds that 'the ball was so much bigger I thought it would be much easier'. He rapidly took to the new game, making his debut for Espanyol at sixteen. He won a Catalan championship in 1918 but the following year, apparently after an argument with a director, he moved to Barcelona, where his habitual attire of flat cap and white polo-neck jumper became as legendary as his willingness to hurl himself at the feet of onrushing forwards. 'Over the years,' wrote Galeano, 'the image of Zamora in those clothes became famous. He sowed panic among strikers. If they looked his way, they were lost: with Zamora in goal, the net would shrink and the posts would lose themselves in the distance.'

After three years in which he won three Catalan titles and two Copas del Rey, made his international debut at the 1920 Olympics and gained the nickname 'the Divine One', Zamora returned to his first club – some say for money to pay off his debts, others simply that he felt more at home there. Whichever is true, it's certainly the case that he felt uncomfortable at a club that celebrated its non-Spanishness and, as Phil Ball says in *White Storm*, one of the reasons for Zamora's enduring popularity among Real Madrid fans is that, by joining them in 1930, he proved himself no *catalanista*, whatever Barcelona's attempts to claim him for themselves.

By the end of the twenties, Espanyol had a team to match the one Zamora had left a decade earlier. They won another Catalan championship in 1928–29 and, crucially for Zamora, reached the final of the Copa del Rey. Because of the amount of rain that fell on Valencia that day, the game became known as the *final del agua*. Zamora excelled as Espanyol won 2–1 and Santiago Bernabéu, who had become one of Real's three directors two years earlier, was smitten, recognising in his talent and charisma the sort of player who could elevate his club to the levels he envisaged.

It wouldn't be until October 1930 that he signed him, but when he did, it provoked a storm of interest. When Zamora arrived in Madrid by train, he had to give a speech on the platform as though he were some visiting statesman. Others might have been daunted, but Zamora was a natural performer and announced he had come to somewhere that 'the spectators understand their football.' Although he insisted he still had 'many friends in Barcelona' you wonder how many were ostracised by the implication that, when it came to football, they didn't really get it. Jacinto Quincoces, the great defender who signed for Real Madrid from Deportivo Alavés the following year, commented that at the time Zamora was 'more famous than Garbo and better looking'. Four years later, when Niceto Zamora, a Liberal politician who happened to share his name, was sworn in as Spanish president, Stalin is supposed to have remarked, 'Ah, that goalkeeper!'

Zamora was Real Madrid's first big star, joining them at a time when Barça and Athletic Bilbao were more successful clubs. Signing him was Bernabéu's first major decision as manager and the furore his move created was almost as significant as what he did on the pitch. He made his debut in the regional championship against Rácing de Madrid and for the next game, against Atlético de Madrid, so many fans descended on Chamartín that mounted police had to be deployed to clear the crush.

In the second half, Zamora dived at the feet of Buiría, took a blow to the head, and collapsed motionless on the ground. He was carried off, and didn't return until the eighth game of the season. In the first seven Real Madrid conceded seventeen goals; in the remaining eleven they let in only ten, but they still finished only sixth. The next season, after the signings of the defenders Quincoces and Errasti Ciriaco and the forward Luis Regueiro, and with Zamora in superb form, they went unbeaten for the entire eighteen-game campaign, conceding only fifteen goals as they won La Liga for the first time. They retained the title the following year and won the cup the year after that; nobody doubted what a key part Zamora had played in their success. He also made forty-six appearances for Spain and was voted the best goalkeeper at the World Cup in Italy in 1934, despite missing the second round replay in which Spain were eliminated by the hosts because of a blow he took to the throat from Angelo Schiavo.

By 1935–36, the political situation was worsening. In May 1936, Athletic Bilbao, pride of the Basque country, won the league while Real Madrid and Barcelona reached the cup final. A month later, the Civil War began: this was perhaps the *clásico* to end them all. The designation of Barcelona as republican and of Real Madrid as pro-fascist was a simplification – and Real Madrid only became Franco's side after Bernabéu had ascended to the presidency in the mid-forties – but still, it was clear where the broad political fault lines lay.

The final was held in Valencia which, at the time, was generally pro-Barcelona. As a result, Zamora faced a hostile crowd, their mood only worsened by comments he had made suggesting Barcelona had abandoned him. He was struck, before kick-off, by a bottle thrown from the stands, but seemed unfazed. Goals from Eugenio and Lecue gave Real a 2–0 lead inside twelve minutes, but Josep Escolá pulled one back for Barcelona before half-time. Real's defence seemed to be holding out when, with three minutes remaining, the Barça forward Martin Ventorlá broke down the shaded right side of the pitch. He nutmegged Quincoces and slipped the ball inside to Escolá. His strike was low and hard, and seemed to be heading just inside Zamora's left-hand post. The keeper dived, sending up a great cloud of dust from the dry surface. Many assumed the ball must have gone in but as the dust cleared, Zamora emerged, standing impassively with the ball in his arms. A photograph taken from just behind the goal showed him plunging down to his left, the ball striking his outstretched arm just before his body hit the ground. The still, frankly, makes it look a slightly ungainly save, nothing out of the ordinary, but it is probably the most famous save in Spanish history – helped in that regard, of course, by the fact it won the cup.

It was the last trophy Zamora won as a player. A few months later, newspapers reported that he had been found dead in a roadside ditch in the Mocloa district of Madrid, his body studded with bullets. At the time, Zamora's politics were still open to debate, and the fact that he'd been awarded the Order of the Republic by the national president, Niceto Zamora, led many to believe he was sympathetic to the leftist cause. That made it conceivable that he might have been murdered by the Nationalists, but the right preferred to paint him as a heroic victim of the Reds. As it was, he was neither, because he wasn't dead at all. As communities held memorial services for him, Zamora was arrested by militiamen and taken to the Modelo prison. He could easily have been executed, but instead he entertained his captors with tales of his playing days and penalty competitions, eventually managing to escape to Nice, where he met up with the centre-forward Josep Samitier, another who had left Barcelona for Real Madrid. When football resumed after the Civil War, Zamora took charge of Atlético Aviación (as Atlético Madrid were known between 1939 and 1947). Made up of top players from the army and air force, they won the first two post-Civil War league titles.

What Zamora actually believed was never clear. 'First and foremost,' he always said when pressed on Catalunya's claims to nationhood, 'I am a Spaniard.' His politics may have been unclear, but his charisma and his talent were not.

Yet even Zamora couldn't escape the suspicion and ridicule of Britain. The English may have distrusted their own goalkeepers, but they found foreign ones preposterous. A Spain side featuring Zamora had become the first foreign team to beat England, winning 4–3 in Madrid in 1929, but that gained them little respect for a return game in London two years later. Zamora became a figure of fun for the British press as it emerged that he was unsettled by the Spanish federation's refusal to let partners travel, his wife being not merely his talisman, but also his food-taster. As the players took the field at Highbury, the England forward Dixie Dean asked the band to play something Spanish. They responded with the march from Bizet's *Carmen* at which, according to Dean's biographer John Keith, 'Zamora, to the dumbstruck reaction of spectators, responded by goose-stepping to his goal and bowing to the crowd. He then proceeded to leap acrobatically around his goalmouth during the kick-in to produce a series of grossly over-spectacular saves. And while this was going on Dean turned to his Everton and England teammate Charlie Gee and bet his six pounds international fee that they'd put more than five goals past Zamora, a wager Charlie accepted.' Zamora went on to have what was perhaps the worst game of his international career, and England won 7–1. The message was seemingly clear: Britain remained the centre of the football world and there was nothing worth learning from abroad.

The difference was that foreign goalkeepers could alleviate the spasmodic nature of their involvement by making sure what they did do was as spectacular as possible. Britain, of course, frowned upon needless extravagance, something clear from John Macadam's description of the Italian goalkeeper Aldo Olivieri.

Olivieri was regarded by the Italian crowds as well as by himself as pretty nearly the whole show. British crowds have a way of concentrating behind the home team's goal because they feel that, since the object in the game is to score goals, it is there that they will see most of the play. A continental crowd huddles also behind the goal, but for an entirely different reason – to watch the goalkeeper. The continental goalkeeper is more than a player in the side. He is the supreme artist in the side, the epitome of all athletic prowess. The forwards, the half-backs, the backs can play as they will and they will get appreciation according to their deserts. If the goalkeeper fails for any reason to put up a spectacular show the afternoon is wasted.

Any football match on the continent is a melodrama with two main parts – one for each goalkeeper … It is necessary to understand this to understand Olivieri and his tribe and the distance between them and the phlegmatic, position-finding, safety-first British goalkeepers whose job is to protect their goal and not in the least to thrill and entertain the crowd.

Olivieri was hailed by the national coach Vittorio Pozzo as the greatest goalkeeper of the age and was nicknamed '*Ercolino Semprimpiedi*', the 'always-standing Hercules', by the great Italian journalist Gianni Brera, yet Macadam's tone swiftly turned to mockery as he describes the efficient understatement of 'Dawson, Swift, Merrick, Williams' and contrasts it with Olivieri's effervescence. 'There will be leaps that bring his head above the level of the crossbar,' he wrote. 'There will be pounces on balls that are yards away from him. There will be gesticulations and shouts. There will be Douglas Fairbanks snr, Errol Flynn, Joe Louis and the Early Christian Martyrs all rolled into one magnificent goalkeeper. The fact that it has nothing whatever to do with football will be the least of anybody's worry.'

The first sport in which Olivieri, who was born near Verona in 1910, showed an interest was cycling but after struggling in his first mountain race, he accepted his friends' request that he should play in goal for the local team in a youth tournament. 'I conceded four goals on my debut, then I went to watch how the other goalkeepers trained and followed their example,' he said. 'At the end of the tournament my team finished second and they gave me the silver medal as best goalkeeper.' He was constantly looking to improve, watching ballerinas to develop his foot movement.

He was signed by Hellas Verona in 1929 then moved to Padova in 1933. There he fractured his skull in a collision with a forward in a friendly against Fiumana. After life-saving surgery, he went through seven months of recuperation before, against his doctor's advice, resuming his career. His 'hole in the head', as he called it, blighted him throughout his life. He suffered headaches and showed an unusual sensitivity to the weather. 'At training camp, when I was at Torino, I'd go up to my team-mates and say, "Wear long studs. It'll rain this afternoon."

'They would say, "Come on, Aldo, it's sunny."

'"It'll rain," I'd say. "It'll rain. My head says so." And often it'd rain.'

It was after a move to Lucchese, under the tutelage of the great Hungarian coach Ernő Egri Erbstein, who died in the Superga air crash, that Olivieri came to prominence. Both goalkeeper and coach moved to Torino in 1938 after the World Cup, a tournament in which Olivieri was at his very best, producing a series of exceptional performances as Italy retained the title. In Italy's first game, a 2–1 extra-time win over Norway, Olivieri made one save so good, denying Knut Brynildsen when he was clean through, that the Norway centre-forward made the referee stop play so he could shake the goalkeeper's hand. Probably his best game, though, came against France in the quarter-final and, when Italy celebrated beating Hungary in the final with a reception at the Palazzo Venezia in Rome, Mussolini made straight for Oliveri, patting him on the back and saying, 'I know that you were the hero. You saved Italy.'

It was in a game in Amsterdam that Macadam saw Olivieri, 'cloth cap on head, white shorts very short, knees grimly bandaged'. After an extravagant warm-up, though, he was barely involved. The only time the ball 'came anywhere near Olivieri it was pushed back to him, for kindness's sake, by his own centre-half. Even at that, although a child in a go-cart could have stopped the ball by swinging his dummy-teat at it, Olivieri met the ball with a cry of exultation, executed his leap and his panther pounce, clutched, bounced and punted as if he had just saved the whole side from disaster.'

The stereotype lingered. Brian Glanville was – by some way – the most cosmopolitan British football journalist of the age, living and working for several years in Italy. Yet in his novel *Goalkeepers Are Different*, published in 1971, his protagonist, Ronnie Blake, is struck by the performance of the Italian goalkeeper he faces at a youth tournament in Nice: 'The way their keeper strutted about his own penalty area, you'd have thought he owned it, honestly. He wasn't a bad goalkeeper, either, he was acrobatic, but my goodness, the way he made things look hard when they could have been easy. Balls that I'd have strolled across to and practically picked up, he'd be positioning himself not so he could take them easy, but so that he *had* to dive for them. And the crowd loved it, that was the other thing that amazed me, because you would have thought they'd have seen through it; to me, it was all so obvious. But no; they'd cheer him like anything when he made one of his flashy saves.'

Now of course, that isn't Glanville speaking in his own voice; it's him speaking as Ronnie – as is highlighted by the use of 'easy' rather than the grammatically correct 'easily' – and it's fairly clear that at times he is consciously exposing, perhaps even having a little fun with, the blinkered self-certainty of the English professional. (In that regard, the back-cover blurb from Peter Shilton, who comes across as painfully lacking in self-awareness in his own autobiography, seems like a devastating metatextual joke: 'I never thought anybody would understand a young goalkeeper's problems so well,' he said.) But still, even if Glanville is mocking the British disregard for 'continental' flashiness, the passage at the very least highlights that there was a perceived difference in style between British and Italian goalkeeping.

That difference was perhaps best summed up by the great Morton goalkeeper Harry Rennie in an interview in the *Daily Record* when he was asked to respond to Hugo Meisl's suggestion that Britain led continental Europe in every respect but goal-keeping. 'If it is true,' he said, 'it can only be because the Latin temperament is more suitable for orthodox or goal-line keeping which necessitates acrobatic displays. As a thoroughbred Scotsman, my mental make-up would never allow me to suffer such a loss of dignity as I thought would be suffered by a descent to acrobatics ... I always thought that this would be a descent to mere animalism. Hence, I resorted to strategic fielding, sometimes far advanced from goal; and I would advise our young Scottish goalkeepers to develop that style of play, as I think goal-line goalkeeping is a game far, far beneath their great Scottish inheritance.'

Yet to most, Italian goalkeeping was far from ridiculous. Olivieri was a great and he wasn't even the first great Italian goalkeeper. The tradition – a proud one that stretches through the likes of Dino Zoff, Walter Zenga and Francesco Toldo to Gianluigi Buffon – was founded by Giovanni De Prà. He is one of the early romantic heroes of Italian football, thanks in part to the fact that he played for the outstanding Genoa side of the 1920s. The footballing section of Genoa Cricket and Football Club, the first in Italy, was founded by James Richardson Spensley in 1897 and the English links were maintained by William Garbutt, the pipe-smoking manager who is the reason Italian coaches are still addressed as 'Mister'. Between 1898 and 1924, Genoa won nine *scudetti*, including six of the first seven to be contested, but never achieved the tenth that would allow them to wear a commemorative star on their shirts, at least in part because the Fascist regime had an interest in Bologna breaking the north-western monopoly that dominated the game at the time. Nor, by unfortunate timing, have Genoa ever been able to wear the *scudetto* patch on their shirts; the shield in the colours of the *tricolore* worn by the reigning champions was introduced a year after their last success.

Along with the defender Renzo De Vecchi, nicknamed the 'Son of God', De Prà is the most famous player from that Genoa side of the twenties, so revered that one of the major roads approaching the Marassi stadium is named after him. 'When I entered the Luigi Ferraris [the other name for the Marassi] as a boy,' Buffon wrote in a preface to a biography of De Prà, 'I dreamed with my eyes wide open of one day becoming the new De Prà ... to interpret a fascinating role as a goalkeeper and be a reference for everyone. A legend.'

De Prà first came to national attention in 1920 playing for the Genovese side SPES against the Italy national team, who were preparing for a game against France. SPES surprisingly won and, at the final whistle, his team-mates and fans surrounded De Prà to embrace him. He joined Genoa a year later and, in his first season, conceded only thirteen goals in twenty-eight games in the regular campaign before his side lost to Pro Vercelli in the two-legged play-off for the title.

Like many of the early keepers, De Prà wasn't tall – only around 5'7" – but he was muscular and had a large pair of hands. His positional sense was said to be good, although he occasionally misjudged crosses or the timing of runs to close down forwards. In pre-season in 1922, Garbutt used his connections in England to arrange a friendly against Liverpool. De Prà made a point of introducing himself to the Liverpool keeper Elisha Scott and trained with him, something he credited with making him a much better goalkeeper from a technical point of view. Genoa went on to win the league that season, becoming the first Italian side to pass undefeated through an entire campaign. The following summer, they went on a tour of South America and lost only 2–1 to the Uruguay national team that would win Olympic gold a year later.

De Prà made his international debut in 1924, and his legendary status was secured later that year in a game against a Spain side featuring Zamora. The Italian keeper was caught by Luis Zabala, stretching into a challenge after the ball had got away from him as he dribbled into the box. De Prà was left in obvious pain but played on. Moments later, he caught an elbow across the back of the head from José Samitier. Legend has it that De Prà played on for the last seventy minutes with his arm in a sling but, while there seems little truth in that tale, he certainly was bloodied and bruised when he made a decisive save from José Maria Laca in the closing minute to protect a 0–0 draw. De Prà, having shaken hands warmly with Zamora at the final whistle, was sent to hospital, and reported feeling pain all over his body, waking at dawn in a cold sweat. 'The boy showed a lot of courage,' Pozzo, who had returned to prepare the national side for the 1924 Olympics, said after visiting him in hospital. 'I've never seen so many illegal blows in a friendly. Giovanni has to rest for a long while but they've assured me that none of his vital organs have been compromised.'

La Gazzetta dello Sport hailed De Prà for a heroic performance and Guerin Sportivo went a step further, organising a collection to which so many readers contributed that the newspaper was able to buy him a gold medal and a stopwatch. De Prà returned in time to play in the Paris Olympics, a tournament the Italians took so seriously that domestic football was suspended for its duration. Italy faced Spain in their first game at the Stade de Colombes and De Prà again came in for rough treatment, taking a knee in the chest from Samitier. Italy again defended bravely and, this time, they nicked a win thanks to an 84th-minute own goal from Pedro Vallana and a last-minute goal-line clearance from Adolfo Baloncieri. This time the handshake with Zamora was rather less convincing. Italy beat Luxembourg in the next round but went out 2–0 to Switzerland in the quarter-final. 'De Prà played at a level commensurate with his hunger,' reported *La Gazzetta dello Sport*. 'The two goals conceded weren't saveable. They were scored from three feet away.'

Shortly after the Italy squad had returned home, Pozzo resigned, stricken with grief after the death of his wife. De Prà, meanwhile, secured his second successive championship medal as Genoa, on the anniversary of their foundation, won their ninth *scudetto*. It was the last title they would ever win. Bologna claimed the title in 1925 after the *Partita Infinita*, the never-ending game. It took five matches to settle the Lega Nord play-off between Genoa and Bologna, the latter eventually winning 2–0 after being reduced to nine men. 'We were taken to a little village outside of Milan,' De Prà said many years later. 'Even today I still don't know where we played. Thousands of squaddies were lined up around the pitch in black shirts: they told us that it was for public order. They spoke in clear *romagnolo* [the dialect from the Bologna region]. The result was 2–0 but it was a huge joke.'

Fascism was changing Italian football as Mussolini's government drew up plans for a new national and professional league structure. De Prà instead chose to remain amateur – which meant he couldn't be forced to leave Genoa for another club. By 1926, Juventus were entering their first golden age and, as an era came to an end, Garbutt quit Genoa for the newly founded Roma, leaving Renzo De Vecchi to succeed him as coach. Even as Genoa's form slid, De Prà held off the challenge of Juve's

Gianpiero Combi to remain Italy's first choice at the 1928 Olympics. Italy again beat Spain, this time without Zamora, on their way to the semi-final, where they lost 3–2 to the eventual champions Uruguay. Italy then thrashed Egypt 11–3 to win bronze, but it wasn't until 1971 that De Prà was given his bronze medal, punished for remaining amateur and for asking if his wife, whom he had married shortly before the tournament, could travel with him to Amsterdam as a sort of honeymoon.

He retired in 1933, playing his final match on the fortieth anniversary of Genoa's foundation and receiving a long ovation on his way off the pitch. For the previous seven years he had been working for his father-in-law, who owned a company that sold office furniture. He kept the job for the rest of his life. De Prà died in 1979. He had requested in his will that his bronze Olympic medal be buried near the right goalpost at the Gradinata Nord end of the Marassi. His wish was granted, but when the stadium was refurbished ahead of Italia 90, the medal went missing.

De Prà was succeeded in the Italy goal by Gianpiero Combi, one of the pillars of the Juventus side that dominated Italian football from the mid-twenties to the mid-thirties, winning six *scudetti* between 1926 and 1935, the last five of them in a row. Along with the full-backs Virginio Rosetta and Umberto Caligaris, Combi formed what was considered the best defence in the history of Italian football. 'It was an unconquerable trio,' said Pozzo, by then in a break from football and no more than an interested observer. 'Rossetta was all technique and study, Caligaris all aggression and quickness. Combi epitomised the gifts of both players and integrated them perfectly.'

A little under six feet tall, Combi was a muscular figure known as '*Fusetta*', which means 'firecracker' in the Piemontese dialect. He was noted for the explosiveness of his dives and for his courage in flinging himself into dangerous situations. He suffered for his bravery: he played with three cracked ribs in a game against Modena; he played with a fractured coccyx against Cremonese and rather than go off, leant against the post until an opponent's attack called for his intervention. He admitted his willingness to risk and then endure pain was born not of fearlessness but out of a deeper terror: that he would lose his place. That insecurity seems very typical of goalkeepers in general; in Combi it was so extreme that he played at times with jaundice, broken wrists and broken fingers.

Combi had initially presented himself for a trial at Torino but they rejected him. 'He's full of good intentions,' one of their directors said, 'but he doesn't have the fabric to be a footballer.' So Combi went to Juventus, telling them he was so desperate to play, he'd even have a go on the left wing. He signed for them in 1918 and made his debut four years later against Pro Vercelli. It could hardly have gone worse. Played on a mudbath in a torrential downpour, Juventus lost 7–1. He recovered from that setback to become a regular but his Italy debut, against Hungary in Budapest in 1924 as he replaced the injured De Prà, went similarly badly as he again shipped seven.

Combi almost gave up football that season. He represented the commercial side of the Combi family liquor distillery and considered leaving Italy for the USA to sell vermouth. Juventus persuaded him to stay and he returned to the national side. His redemption for that early disaster came with the part he played in some of Italy's landmark wins – the 7–0 demolition of France in 1925 and the 2–0 victory over Germany in Frankfurt in 1930.

Having seen off the threat of De Prà, Combi then had to compete with the Internazionale goalkeeper Carlo Ceresoli for the national shirt. Younger and in better form, Ceresoli seemed Pozzo's preferred choice in the build-up to the 1934 World Cup as Combi struggled to regain his fitness after a back injury. Twelve days before the tournament began, though, Ceresoli fractured his left arm. Combi seized his opportunity. 'In less than two weeks he managed to get back into perfect form,' said Pozzo, who had returned to the national manager's job in 1929. 'He trained ten, twelve hours a day. This backbreaking preparation allowed him to face the games of the tournament in an exemplary way. Italy's victory at the 1934 World Cup depended greatly on his spectacular saves.'

Like most of the keepers who played under Pozzo, who

preferred the *metodo* system – that is, a 2-3-2-3 formation with two full-backs, a centre-half who combined defensive work with creative play, two wing-halves, two inside-forwards, a centre-forward and two wingers, Combi preferred to stay on his line and rely on his reflexes rather than being proactive and coming for crosses. He was, like many of the great Italians – in the eyes of their journalists and coaches if not in Macadam's – a minimalist, respected for his acuity rather than his flamboyance – at least in terms of his goalkeeping.

Off the pitch he was noted for his impeccably combed, flowing hair – his two years of military service aside – and loved to wander, sumptuously dressed, around Turin's Piazza San Carlo with one of his Great Danes, usually flanked by beautiful women. Very aware of his good looks, Combi was quick to volunteer when, during his military service, the commander of the regiment asked if anybody would pose for the sculptor Alloatti. He later commissioned a bronze of himself to stand in the bar he owned on the corner of Via Roma and Piazza Castello.

Combi decided to leave the sport on a high, retiring immediately after the World Cup, despite being only thirty-one. He became a director at Juventus and died at just fifty-three, having had a heart attack while driving on the coastal road between San Remo and Imperia.

Olivieri, then, was fitting in to a tradition, probably the third great Italian keeper. By 1934, goalkeepers were respected enough in Italy, their emotions sufficiently contemplated, to be regarded as tragic figures. The poem 'Goal', having been taught in schools for many years, is the best known of the collection *Five Poems for the Game of Football* by Umberto Saba:

> The keeper, fallen in a last futile
> Defence, hides his face against
> The ground, not to see the bitter sight.
> His team-mate, kneeling to his right,
> Touches, tells him to get up, but
> Finds his eyes are full of tears.

The crowd – one with frenzy – overflows
Onto the pitch, flocks round the scorer
Mobbed, hugged by the other boys.
Few moments ever bring such joys
To those consumed with hate and love
Beneath these empty skies

In the far goalmouth, unbeaten,
The other keeper stays put. But
His soul refuses to be left alone.
In rapture, his arms are thrown
Up to blow kisses across the field.
This party – he says – is my party too.

Saba was the nom de plume of the poet and novelist Umberto Poli. He was born to a Jewish mother and an Italian father in Trieste in 1883, the fact he shares his birthplace with the great coach Nereo Rocco seeming, to Italians at least, to give his words additional resonance. He was brought up by a Slovenian nanny and seems to have spent his childhood torn between her cheeriness and the severity of his mother, while all the time yearning for a father he didn't meet until he was twenty. As the essayist and novelist Tim Parks pointed out on *The Book Show* on ABC radio in 2007, Saba 'was always torn: torn between four languages – Italian, German, Slav and Triestine dialect – between the Hebrew and Christian religions, Austria and Italy, homosexuality and heterosexuality, and finally between his real name Umberto Poli, and the pseudonym he chose for his poetry, Saba, the Hebrew word for bread.'

The scene in the stadium presents a similar division, between triumph and despair, while the goalkeeper of the team that has scored (and the implication is it is a late winner) is seen as an oddly isolated figure, having to, as Parks put it, 'hug himself because there is no one else to hug, who does somersaults and blows kisses, who isn't enjoying the pleasures of touching his companions but wants to convince himself and everybody else that he is part of the party ... Waving his arms, jumping up and down, at once happy, but frustrated to be so remote. If it's not hard to see Saba's identification with the beaten keeper and his consoling team-mate, it's even easier to see how close he is, as artist, to the man who celebrates alone, looks on from a distance and rejoices.'

There is, of course, more to it than that. By focusing on a small village team, Saba was making a political statement in refusing to write about the national side that had just won the World Cup and was being hailed across the country as representing the glory of Mussolini's Italy. Four years later, as the Race Laws were passed, Saba fled for Paris, returning to hide in friends' apartments in Trieste and Florence during the war. In another poem, he wrote of the pleasure of being 'a few shivering spectators united like last men on a mountain top ...' , standing apart from the masses. The dangers of the crowd and mob mentality, perhaps, are alluded to in the phrase '*unita ebrezza*' – collective intoxication – in 'Goal'. 'From the beginning,' Parks said,

> the poem has used the kind of vocabulary and images that suggests parallels with the heroes ... of antiquity, while at the same time never pretending that this is more than a game of football. Here Saba admits that those participating, players and spectators alike, are 'consumed by hate and by love'. He acknowledges, that is, and this is something that few sports commentators have the courage to do, that football brings into play the most negative as well as the most positive emotions. Saba places hate before love. The goal is a beautiful moment for the winners, because their hate as well as their love is gratified. Fortunately football remains a frame where these emotions can achieve expression without anyone having to die. Even the bungling keeper will be allowed to live and play again.

It wasn't just Italy that was establishing a fine tradition of goal-keeping as the art spread between the wars. Plattkó was one of a fine quadrumvirate from the Danubian school, along with František Planička of Czechoslovakia, Rudi Hiden of Austria and

Franjo Glaser of Yugoslavia. The international football statisti-cians IFFHS voted Planička the ninth best goalkeeper of the twentieth century – behind only Zamora in the inter-war period – and he embodies many of the traits of the era. At 5'7" the Cat of Prague, as he was nicknamed, wasn't tall, but he was agile and, most of all, he was brave, something he demonstrated most notably by playing on with a broken arm against Brazil in the 1938 World Cup. He captained the national team to the quarter-final in France, and was named goalkeeper of the tournament, having led his side to the final four years earlier.

Photographs show him as a squat, muscular man in a white roll-neck with the Czechoslovak badge, a white eagle on a red field, covering most of his chest. Planička amassed 969 games for Slavia Prague, winning twelve league titles and the Mitropa Cup (an early international club competition for teams from central Europe). The last of those league titles came in 1937, although Slavia were leading the Czechoslovak championship in 1939 when war forced the national league to be abandoned. In 1994, when Planička was presented with a sporting merit award on the occasion of his ninetieth birthday, Slavia still hadn't won the league again. He said in his acceptance speech that his one remaining wish was that Slavia should win the championship once more before his death. Two years later they did; Planička died two months after their triumph.

Rudi Hiden, born in 1909, was a sixteen-year-old baker's apprentice when he was given his debut by Grazer AK, moving to Wiener AC for 500 Schillinge two years later. He developed a reputation for bravery – as most contemporary goalkeepers did – and was noted for his skill in punching crosses clear and his willingness to clatter into opposing forwards. He earned his first cap at nineteen, but the coach, Hugo Meisl, preferred Franz Friedrich of Admira Wien, and didn't select him again until 1930. His third match was against England, the oppo-nent Meisl most respected and was most desperate to beat. A string of excellent reflex saves earned Austria a goalless draw. So impressive was he that a number of English clubs tried to sign him. Arsenal prevailed, thanks in large part to the fact their manager, Herbert Chapman, was good friends with Meisl, but the transfer fell through when Hiden was refused a work permit.

He played in the 5–0 defeat of Scotland in May 1931 that signalled the birth of the Wunderteam, and he attracted further admiration in the glorious 4–3 defeat to England at Stamford Bridge in December 1932 that sounded the first serious warnings that English football was being surpassed by football in continental Europe. Two months later, Austria beat France 4–0 in Paris. The president of Racing Club, Jean-Bernard Levy, promptly offered him a contract and, when a transfer of 80,000 francs was agreed, Hiden moved to Paris, ending his international career but for one game for France in 1940. He won a league title and three Coupes de France with Racing but his successes on the field masked a troubled personal life.

Whether continental goalkeepers were needlessly flamboyant or not, a disproportionate number of them seem to have been good-looking ladies' men, as though the position drew those seeking glamour. Even in Graz he had been an idol of female fans, and with the Wunderteam he was nicknamed '*Beau*'. He loved the high life and, in Paris, was persuaded to invest in a bar. It failed and he was left to make a living in beat-the-goalie contests at a circus, his narrative following the same arc as Sim Dalt's, but in the other direction. He became a journeyman coach in the lower leagues in Italy before returning to Austria in 1967. He opened a hotel by Wörthersee, but that went as badly as his Parisian bar. By then he was suffering from cancer. He had his right leg amputated in 1972 and died the following year, poor and forgotten.

Not Danubian but also from the central European belt and also with a terribly unhappy strand to his story was Franjo Glaser, 'Iron Fist' as he was nicknamed. He was only fifteen when he started playing for his hometown side Hajduk Sarajevo and seventeen when he joined Slavija Osijek in 1930. Tall, strong and with fine reflexes, he gained a reputation as an expert at saving penalties. A move to BSK of Belgrade in 1933 brought two Yugoslav championships and a call-up to the national team.

But then, after the second of those titles in 1936, he was found guilty of manslaughter after a boy was drowned in an incident on the River Sava, which meets the Danube in Belgrade. Glaser escaped prison and stayed for a year more but he was tormented by memories of the accident and left for Zagreb and HŠK Gradanski. There he recovered his form, won another Yugoslav championship in 1940 and then a Croatian title in 1943 after the German invasion had made a national league competition impossible. In total he played 623 games for Gradanski before departing after the war for Partizan, where he won the title again in 1947, becoming the only man to win Yugoslav championships on both sides of the war.

A little further north, Heinrich Stuhlfauth was hailed as Zamora's equal, playing for FC Nürnberg as they won five German championships in the twenties. 'Stuhlfauth stood in his goal like an archangel,' said the journalist Peter Lugensland, 'and no forward dared even to come near to this fearless colossus with the result that an attack on the Nürnberg goal wasn't even considered by any forward ... Heine had such a strong goalkick that quite a few cheeky little forwards would have been shot across the pitch if they hadn't got themselves to safety in time.'

Stuhlfauth originally wanted to be a cyclist but his parents banned him from the sport believing riding a bike caused consumption. He turned to football, where his huge hands – 'hands like toilet-lids' as the Nuremberg phrase of the time had it – proved a great advantage once he had abandoned ideas of playing as a forward and gone in goal. 'What Heine got between his paws he never let go of,' a profile in *Kicker* put it.

He was far from an orthodox keeper, though. He didn't like diving, particularly not to his right, and he refused to hurl himself at the feet of opponents. 'I have always avoided collisions,' he said. 'In the whole twenty years of my active playing time I was never injured so seriously that I couldn't play from one Sunday to the next. I am of the opinion that a footballer who plays intelligently and is in control of his body in every situation will rarely be injured ... A good goalkeeper does not throw himself about. Whenever I was forced to make crash landings and panther-like jumps I always asked myself what I had done wrong.'

That didn't mean Stulhfauth was reluctant to leave his line, though; far from it. He specialised in the '*Fußabwehr*' – literally the 'foot-clearance' or 'foot-defence' – often being described as 'a third defender' in the 2-3-5 system that prevailed in Germany at the time. Here he describes his technique:

> I have almost always defended with my feet. When there was still time I would bend over and pick up the ball ... To leave the goal at the right moment is a talent you're born with. Sometimes it depends on fractions of seconds to be at the ball ahead of the opponent. From the stands it often seems as though it were an error when I ran out. The opponent can easily be two or three metres away from the ball and the goal-keeper fifteen. If the goalkeeper can judge the distance cor-rectly, he will get to the ball more quickly because the ball comes towards the goalkeeper while the opponent has to run after it. When I ran out of my goal I was successful ninety-five per cent of the time and five per cent I came too late. When my defenders noticed that I ran out one of them immediately went into goal to take my place. I often ran twenty or thirty metres towards the ball and nullified the attack by kicking away the ball. I would recommend for every goalkeeper to play in his club's lower teams as a striker because a goal-keeper should also experience the game on the pitch. Before I went into goal, in my youth, I played as a left winger for a few years.

Nor was his refusal to dive at the feet of forwards the result of cowardice. According to Carl Riegel, who succeeded him in the Nürnberg goal, Stuhlfauth 'looked as intimidating as a bouncer in a night club, when he stood with his full width and his height of 1.84m (6'½") in front of his goal and his flat cap pulled jaun-tily on his head'.

He wasn't always fearless, though. In 1922 Nürnberg toured

Spain and in Seville found themselves staying in the same hotel as Lloyd George. Stuhlfauth tagged on the end of an official prime ministerial tour of Seville cathedral, sneaking in as the guide led the party into a dark side room and opened a sarcophagus to reveal the embalmed corpse of Ferdinand III. 'It wasn't deathly pale but when I looked at it I did feel a shiver down my spine … I've never been afraid of the living but you can occasionally be scared of the dead.'

Between 8 July 1918 and 5 February 1922, Nürnberg played 104 league games without defeat, scoring 480 goals and conceding just 47. Stuhlfauth's finest game, though, came away to Italy in 1929, the match that earned him the nickname 'the Hero of Turin'. In front of 80,000 fans, Stuhlfauth was inspired. 'God himself stood in the goal,' one Italian paper said. It was goalless at half-time, when the Italian team manager asked Stuhlfauth to change out of his familiar grey jumper, claiming it made him invisible. A red jumper was found, but Stuhlfauth said it was unthinkable to change. Eventually the Italians backed down and Stuhlfauth maintained his superb form as Germany won 2–1. 'That's never happened before,' he said. 'I was jumping around like greased lightning. There was hardly a second when I didn't have the ball. Often I felt in my goal as though it were me alone against eleven Italians.'

Stuhlfauth wasn't the only goalkeeper beginning to leave the comfort of his line. So too did the Brazilian Jaguaré, a true one-off who vies with the Argentinians Ángel Bossio and Juan Botasso and the Uruguayan Andrés Mazali to be called the first great South American goalkeeper. Bossio was an elegant keeper nicknamed 'the Elastic Marvel' who favoured neat collars and played for Talleres and River Plate, while Botasso was a floppy-haired aesthete who sported a white jumper and knee pads in the style of Zamora and played for Quilmes and Racing. Mazali was an outstanding all-round sportsman who won the South American 400m hurdles championship in 1920 and lifted the Uruguayan basketball championship with Olympia in 1923. He conceded just twenty-nine goals in three seasons as Nacional, won a hat-trick of titles between 1922 and 1924 and was part of the side that won Olympic football gold in Paris later that year, delighting crowds with the wit and invention of their play. Not only did they score twenty goals in five games; they conceded only two. Four years later, Mazali took gold again as Uruguay retained their title in Amsterdam, beating an Argentina team featuring Bossio in the final.

They should have met again in 1930 in the inaugural World Cup final but, a few days before the tournament's opening game, Mazali broke a curfew to spend the evening with his wife, and was dropped. In came Quique Ballestero and Mazali never played for his country again. Bossio, meanwhile, having played well in the group stage while captaining the Argentinians, was mysteriously dropped for Botasso before the semi-final. As Combi had realised, the goalkeeper's position was a precarious one.

It was Jaguaré, though, by force of personality as much as anything else, who stands out among the early South American keepers. Born in Rio de Janeiro in 1905, Jaguaré had no formal education and was working as a stevedore when he was spotted by Espanhol playing a game in his local neighbourhood of Saúde. He had to learn how to write his name so he could sign team-sheets but once he had done so he soon established himself and was snapped up by Vasco da Gama. There, always wearing a white nautical cap, he won a state championship in 1929 and played three times in unofficial games for the national side. His love of pranks, which included bouncing the ball off opposing forwards' heads, brought him great popularity. In 1931 Vasco undertook a tour of Spain and Portugal, playing twelve matches of which they won eight. Jaguaré clearly impressed, as he and the centre-half Fausto dos Santos were both offered terms by Barcelona. The rules at that time prevented foreigners from playing in official matches so, although Jaguaré played around a dozen friendly games, drawing the nickname *Araña Negra* (Black Spider), he couldn't play in the league unless he became a Spanish citizen. Despite significant financial inducements, both he and Dos Santos refused to do so. Dos Santos moved to Switzerland, while Jaguaré returned to Brazil.

There he began turning up at Vasco training sessions wearing gloves he'd brought from Europe, the earliest example of goalkeepers wearing gloves in South America. Vasco, though, distrusted him after his dabble with professionalism in Europe and so he ended up playing for *combinados*, essentially travelling sides patched together to play exhibition games. Eventually, he was signed by the São Paulo side Corinthians but when they signed José Hungarês, the first foreigner ever to join the club (he was a Hungarian, and the name he went by a nickname – 'Hungarian Joe' to give an English equivalent; his real name was József Lengyel), it was clear his days there were numbered.

A solution was offered by Fernando Giudicelli, a gifted midfielder who had played for Brazil in the 1930 World Cup before turning professional in Europe. An itinerant career took him to Torino, the Zurich side Young Fellows and Bordeaux, while he also acted as an agent, helping Brazilian amateurs find clubs in Europe. Giudicelli insisted he could find clubs in Italy for both Jaguaré and the defender Vianinha. By the time their ship had crossed the Atlantic, though, the second Italo-Abyssinian War had broken out, so the three decided to stay in Portugal, all of them joining Sporting. None lasted very long, although Jaguaré did win the city championship before being ousted by João Azevedo, who won seven league titles in his decade and a half at the club. He moved on to France, joining Olympique de Marseille in summer 1936.

That Marseille team was arguably the first great multinational side, featuring as it did the Algerians Manu Aznar, Abdelkader Ben Bouali and Mario Zatelli, the Moroccan forward Larbi Ben Barek and the Hungarian forward Vilmos Kohut, coached by József Eisenhoffer from Hungary. In Jaguaré's debut season they won the first league title in OM's history, finishing second in each of the two following seasons and winning the cup in 1938. During those three years, 'El Jaguar', as he was nicknamed, became famed for his white cap, which he would often throw at opposing penalty-takers, and for his habit of urging opposing forwards to shoot as they bore down on his goal, yelling '*Chuta! Chuta!*' Probably his finest game came against Sète in 1938 when he converted a penalty, becoming the first Marseille goalkeeper to score, and then saved two penalties himself in a 1–1 draw.

Jaguaré left Marseille in 1939 for reasons that have never been satisfactorily explained, although it may be he saw the war coming. He paused briefly in Portugal, playing nine games for Académico, before returning to Brazil. He joined São Cristavão, a small club from the north of Rio, but his best days were clearly behind him and, as his form disintegrated, so his consumption of alcohol increased. As his money ran out, he returned to work as a stevedore. On the docks, though, his tales of playing football in Europe were met with incredulity and, frustrated that he was seen as a fantasist, he left Rio. For a while he disappeared, but Jaguaré resurfaced in Santo Anastácio, a small town in the hinterland of the state of São Paulo. In August 1946 he was arrested. Exactly what for remains unclear, but he sustained a blow to the head either in a fracas with police or later in his cell, and died as a result, being buried in a pauper's grave.

4: THE SWEEPER-KEEPER

It was, of course, absurd hyperbole for those marketing Hungary's visit to Wembley in 1953 to bill it as 'The Match of the Century' and would have been even had the caveat 'so far' been added. Yet with hindsight England's 6–3 defeat stands as an indelible landmark, as arguably the most significant game in English football history, the moment at which Wembley was shaken by a fusillade of uncomfortable truths that continue to reverberate. Most of the reaction, understandably, focused on Hungary's tactical fluidity, their use of a deep-lying number nine and their vastly superior technique. Almost overlooked was the role played by their goalkeeper, Gyula Grosics.

There was a moment late in the first half with the score at 4–2 when Jimmy Dickinson launched a long ball forward for Stan Mortensen. Grosics charged out to the edge of his box and, with impeccable timing, volleyed the ball clear. 'Unorthodox but effective,' said an uncertain Kenneth Wolstenholme in commentary, seemingly not quite sure whether he should approve of this sort of thing. It was characteristic of Grosics's style of goalkeeping, a style that, as Brian Glanville noted, was integral to the way Hungary played. Grosics, he wrote, 'never hesitated to dash out of his penalty area, thus frequently becoming the extra full-back. Since his timing was generally shrewd, the effect was to decrease to some extent the burden placed on the rest of the defence by the advanced position of the inside-forwards.' Football is a holistic game: a change at one end of the pitch can have a radical impact elsewhere. A team with a goalkeeper who is comfortable leaving his goal and sweeping up behind his defence can play with a higher line than others or, more relevantly to Grosics's era, can link up with the attack, knowing that the space left behind the defensive line will at least in part be occupied by the advancing keeper.

Grosics was a charismatic if eccentric figure, somebody of natural charm who readily fitted the idiosyncratic stereotype of the keeper. A loner who preferred to play chess than to drink and watch Westerns with the rest of the squad, he was prone to intense bouts of nerves and was such a hypochondriac he would wear a red beret during training sessions because he believed it brought him relief from a brain disease. In that game at Wembley, he insisted on being substituted with nine minutes remaining because of an injury supposedly sustained around quarter of an hour earlier. It hadn't been causing him notice-able trouble and the reaction of the Dutch referee Leo Horn sug-gested he was sceptical. The suspicion was that he was gripped by anxiety. Hungary led 6–3, and were poised to become the first non-British side to beat England at Wembley; although there was nothing to suggest England were about to launch a late fightback, perhaps the possibility that they might and that he might be blamed was enough to lead him to seek the sanctu-ary of the bench.

Then again, perhaps that fear was justified given what happened in the aftermath of the World Cup final the fol-lowing year. Hungary, unbeaten in almost four years, were widely expected to win and raced into a 2–0 lead against West Germany. But, on a muddy pitch that restricted their passing game, Hungary were overhauled, with Grosics at fault for the equaliser as he flapped at a Fritz Walter corner, allowing Helmut Rahn to volley in.

Grosics had been arrested in 1949 for attempting illegally to leave the country, and felt he was always under suspicion. 'I was born into a religious family, and that wasn't a good sign at all at that time,' he explained. 'I never made any secret of what I thought about the government. My family – especially my mother – had intended that I should be a Catholic priest. I was raised in that spirit, and that was one of the reasons I was not trusted.' After the World Cup final, Grosics was exiled to house arrest in the mining town of Tatabánya. Every week, a large black car would pull up at his door to take him off for interrogation.

Not surprisingly, Grosics played his part in the 1956 Uprising. He was there by the statue of St Imre on Gellért Hill when troops again opened fire on demonstrators and subsequently allowed his house to be used as an arsenal by rebels. 'I had a lot of problems getting rid of the arms afterwards,' he said. 'Fortunately I had a good friend in the army, a captain, who came in a small truck and took the weapons and grenades away. That was my small contribution.'

In Britain, Grosics was perceived as a great innovator, the inventor of a new style of goalkeeping. The contrast with Gil Merrick, England's goalkeeper in that fateful game at Wembley, could hardly have been more obvious. Merrick, Peter Chapman wrote in *The Goalkeeper's History of Britain*, was 'the model of post-war man', with the sleeves of his sweater neatly rolled up, his receding brilliantined hair and his neat moustache. He had been a PT instructor in the war and gave an air of unflappable self-assurance. He handled the ball calmly and precisely and even the Anglophile Austrian journalist Willy Meisl, in the fabled programme notes in which he predicted England's capitulation to Hungary, indirectly praised his 'unspectacular anticipation' while casting him, all too accurately, in the role of Horatius on the bridge, facing down the Etruscan hordes single-handed. But he was of the old school, a reactive goalkeeper as opposed to the proactivity of Grosics.

Grosics, though, denied he was a pioneer. He wrote extensively on the subject in *The Gillette Book of Football and Cricket*, published in 1963, acknowledging that he was renowned for 'running out of the goal to meet an oncoming attacker or, in other words, playing the role of a fourth back ...' The term perhaps requires a little explanation: Hungary at the time played with a line of three defenders, with József Zakariás sitting deep in midfield (the formation would probably today be described as a 3-2-1-4). Even more confusingly, whereas in England the central of the three defenders was referred to as a 'centre-half' and the outer two players as 'full-backs', in Hungary all three were called 'full-backs'.

'Harmony between the full-backs and the goalkeeper is of the greatest importance,' Grosics wrote, outlining how vital it was for the goalkeeper to be considered not an addendum to the team but a part of it.

A basic condition of efficient team work between the four players is the thorough knowledge of each other's style of play. For this purpose, there must be frequent talks between the goalkeepers and the full-backs at which the reasons for a successful or unsuccessful sortie from the goal can be analysed and suitable preparations made for adapting themselves to the style of play of the next opponent's forward line. As a result of such talks, a style of play can be developed whereby a full-back can judge merely by the position of the ball whether the goalkeeper will leave the goal for handling or kicking the ball or not. At a time like this, a full-back under normal circumstances tries to slow down the running opponent player's tempo. The other full-back would keep a lookout for a possible rebound which he can then kick back into the field.

As to the practicalities of when the keeper should feel emboldened to leave his goal, Grosics is rather vaguer, admitting it depends on circumstance and advising little more than decisiveness. 'It is a frequent mistake for goalkeepers to start out of the goal and then change their minds and stop halfway,' he wrote. 'Such hesitation gives the forward the necessary time for assessing his chance and acting. However, if the goalkeeper runs out to meet the attacker without stopping, he can embarrass him even if his timing is bad. But the most dangerous situation of all is for a goalkeeper to start backing off after having left his goal.'

There is, Grosics said, no fixed rule for when a goalkeeper should leave his goal. Rather he should rely on 'adequate football sense, experience, close attention, speed and resolution'. Oddly, given how noted he was for his sallies forward, he insisted a goalkeeper 'should only do this if there is no other choice because such a move on his part always entails risks'.

The key, of course, is 'a sense of position' and that meant not hanging around on the goal line waiting for the ball. 'In the course of all the matches I ever played, I only stood actually on the goal line on the rarest of occasions, when the opponent's line of attack literally pinned me to the goal,' he wrote. 'I would like to stress that a sortie can only be successful if the goalkeeper follows the whole of the game with the closest attention and does not relent for a single moment. He should follow the course of the ball even if the game swings over to the opponent's half of the ground and as soon as the ball returns over the half line, he must stand ready to interfere at any emergency.'

And then there were technical considerations. 'I have only hurled myself before the feet of an attacker if there was absolutely no other solution. In such cases I have always tried to shut off the angle of approach before the attacker and execute my dive in the simplest and quickest possible way. I have always tried to "glide" into the line of shooting so as to avoid the possibility of the ball slipping across under me.'

For Grosics, the goalkeeper was already a figure integrated with the rest of the team. 'The goalkeeper must have a lot of training as a field-player, too,' he concluded, 'in order to be able to fill the role of a fourth back.'

To understand why Grosics was considered such a radical in Britain at the time, it's necessary only to look at the following chapter in the *Gillette* book, which was written by the Arsenal and Wales goalkeeper Jack Kelsey. Although he says a goalkeeper should 'never be afraid of coming out of the penalty area and booting the ball', his emphasis is wholly different to that of Grosics. Rather than talking about the goalkeeper as a fourth defender, he was more concerned with practical advice, suggesting goalkeepers should play tennis, table-tennis and squash to improve agility and reflexes and advocating 'string gloves' in wet conditions.

His real obsession, though, was angles, which is indicative of the fact that his style of goalkeeping was far less proactive than that of Grosics; he preferred to react to shots than to charge out and prevent anybody unleashing a strike at his goal, as he explained:

> If a forward is about to shoot from the edge of the penalty area and the goalkeeper stands in the middle of his goal and on the goal line, it means he has four yards to cover between himself and each upright. The chances are that if it is a well-placed shot just inside an upright he will fail to reach it. If, on the other hand, he moves forward about four yards, he has now cut down the target area to about two yards either side of him. But always remember … don't come too far out because the pace of the shot will beat you.
>
> Try this experiment that I used to use in my very early days in the game for which a wooden stake and about fifty yards of string is necessary. Take one end of the string and tie it to an upright. Place the stake in the ground at any point on the edge of the penalty area, pass the string round the stake and tie the loose end to the other upright. The string, then, represents the two uprights, and if the goalkeeper takes up a position on the goal line between the two lines of string and then moves forward towards the stake, he will find the most suitable angle where he will be in a position to deal with any shot that comes within the string lines. An important point about moving out of goal towards an advancing forward is that the man with the ball, noticing the goalkeeper advancing, may well try to lob the ball over his head.

It's perhaps not the clearest description: essentially if the keeper can touch the string to both sides of him, he can reach a shot that is on target (curl notwithstanding); by frequent practice and moving the stake, Kelsey was able to condition himself almost always to take up a position whereby he would be able to touch the string on both sides.

And so were set out the terms for goalkeeping's most enduring tactical debate: was it better for the keeper to be proactive, to attempt to stifle moves before they resulted in a shot and risk occasionally looking a little silly, or was it better for him to be conservative and reliable, staying back, saving what he could, and leaving his defenders to get on with the business of defending?

What is odd is that, having been just another player for so long, the goalkeeper, once marked out as being different both in terms of his duties and his shirt, so quickly became detached from the other outfielders, something that seems to have been a psychological issue as much as a technical one.

On Christmas Day 1937, for instance, with half an hour of Charlton Athletic's away game at Chelsea remaining, a heavy fog descended, making further play impossible. The respective managers walked onto the pitch and called their players off, accepting that the game had to be abandoned. Twenty-one players joined them back in the dressing room, but even as the 40,000 crowd dispersed, Charlton's keeper, Sam Bartram, was left standing alone on the edge of his penalty area. He wrote about the incident in his autobiography:

'The boys must be giving the Pensioners quite the hammer,' I thought smugly, as I stamped my feet for warmth. Quite obviously, however, we were not getting the ball in the net, for no players were coming back to line up, as they would have done following a goal. Time passed, and I made several advances towards the edge of the penalty area, peering through the murk which was getting thicker every minute. Still I could see nothing. The Chelsea defence was clearly being run off its feet.

After a long time a figure loomed out of the curtain of fog in front of me. It was a policeman, and he gaped at me incredulously. 'What on earth are you doing here?' he gasped. 'The game was stopped a quarter of an hour ago. The field's completely empty.'

And when I groped my way to the dressing-room the rest of the Charlton team, already out of the bath, were convulsed with laughter.

The whole incident was played for laughs – 'PHANTOMS AT STAMFORD BRIDGE – GAME ABANDONED WITH BARTRAM MISSING' read the headline of the *Woolwich Gazette* – but it highlights a more troubling truth about the goalkeeper's position as an outsider that has endured. At least in the English-speaking world, he is not part of the team. He is the player who can be forgotten, left behind.

In *Escape to Victory*, the (ersatz) goalkeeper ends up being the hero, the pivotal moment of drama being not Pelé's overhead kick, but the last-minute penalty saved by Robert Hatch, the swaggering US POW played by Sylvester Stallone. Even there, though, the goalkeeper's difference, his expendability, is made clear.

Hatch initially escapes alone, flees to Paris and makes contact with the Resistance. He's recaptured and put in the cooler. John Colby, the captain of the Allied team played by Michael Caine, has to find a way of incorporating him into the team and decides he could probably cope as a goalkeeper. In part that's because of the hand-to-eye co-ordination he's developed playing US sports, but it's also because, as a goalkeeper, he would not disrupt the team unit.

Colby begs Major von Steiner (Max von Sydow) to release him on the grounds that he's the only goalkeeper they have after Tony Lewis, the regular keeper, broke his arm in training. Von Steiner, supposedly a former international himself and the epitome of the 'good German', agrees. There's just one problem: Lewis hasn't broken his arm at all. As Colby explains the plan, though, Lewis (played, oddly, by the Ipswich Town left-winger Kevin O'Callaghan, while Ipswich's keeper, Laurie Sivell, played in goal for Germany) volunteers to have his arm broken, uttering the gut-wrenching line, 'Make it a clean break, skipper,' as he lies his arm across a gap between the slats of a dressing-room bench.

He's never seen again. In the moment of Hatch's penalty save, as the jubilant French crowd pours onto the pitch and Colby's side escapes into the Parisian afternoon, Lewis languishes in his camp in Germany, awaiting who knows what reprisals at the hands of the Gestapo. And nobody, not the players, probably not even the viewer, gives him a second thought: he's only a goalkeeper, barely part of the team at all, for all his courage and self-sacrifice.

The process of reintegrating the goalkeeper with the rest of the team began with the man who took James McAulay's mantle as the great Scottish goalkeeper: Harry Rennie. Like so many of the early keepers, McAulay included, he began as an outfielder, playing as a half-back for the Junior sides Volunteers, Bellgrove Ramblers and Greenock West End. He earned a callup to a Scotland Junior International side and then a move to Morton, at the time a Division Two side. Only in 1897, when he was twenty-three, did he become a goalkeeper and the first true theorist of the position.

Rennie pioneered the practice of marking the goal area so that he knew always where his posts were, he trained by diving on hard boards for half an hour a day to toughen himself (the strange thuds and groans this produced leading to a rumour that Cappielow, Morton's ground, was haunted). Long before Jack Kelsey, he became obsessed by angles, and if he were not the first goalkeeper to start closing a forward down, he was certainly the first master of the art. When the game kicked off, he would walk forwards to his penalty spot, something so shocking that when he first did it the crowd behind the goal thought he was going to attack the referee and shouted encouragement. He would then move forward and back, and from side to side, according to the position of play on the field.

He made a point of studying how players kicked the ball, trying to determine whether they were shooting, crossing or passing and so being able to anticipate where the ball was going. These were radical concepts at the time, and not wholly accepted, but they made Rennie a good enough keeper that he earned a move first to Heart of Midlothian and then to Hibernian, whom in 1903 he helped to their first league title. He won a total of thirteen caps before, after brief stints at Rangers and Kilmarnock, retiring in 1910. His influence lived on, though, as he became one of the earliest specialist goalkeeping coaches, mentoring a number of young keepers.

Although Jimmy Cowan, a regular for Morton and the Scotland national side in the forties, took on Rennie's ideas, he was unusual. The majority of his pupils were resistant. 'Mostly,' wrote John Macadam, one of the early greats of sports reporting, 'they prefer the death-defying last-minute saves that keep the fans clustered behind their goals.' Fitting the general trend of British football, they eschewed sustained and difficult thought in favour of the haphazardly spectacular: the *Roy of the Rovers* principle, as traced by Scott Murray in Issue Zero of *The Blizzard* (although one that contradicts Vladimir Nabokov's theory to explain the dearth of good British goalkeepers).

Rennie, of course, had the advantage Leigh Richmond Roose had for the bulk of his career – the ability to handle anywhere in his own half. Once goalkeepers were restricted to their own box in 1912 it interrupted that process of reintegration. The penalty area, initially, as the name suggests, merely the zone in which fouls would result in penalties rather than free-kicks, suddenly became a virtual cell for the keeper, his participation psychologically circumscribed, partly by the knowledge that the advantage he enjoyed over other players only existed within the box and partly by the fact that goalkeepers making an error outside the box would be ridiculed: miss a cross and you'd made a mistake; come charging out of your area and miss a through-ball and you'd fallen prey to the most stereotypical curse of the goalkeeper – craziness.

The process of reintegration began in eastern Europe, and it's tempting to wonder whether the breaking down of the divide between the goalkeeper and the rest was a natural function of a society that distrusted difference. Grosics, after all, could hardly have been more idiosyncratic and yet he came as close as any goalkeeper in eight decades to being just another player.

The process was carried on in Bulgaria by Apostol Sokolov who, like Grosics, was pretty much as far from the typical Communist drudge as it was possible to get. His father had been the personal telegrapher to Tsar Boris III and so his son spent his earliest weeks swaddled in cast-off royal diapers. The sense of specialness never really left him. It wasn't just that he began playing outside his box, advancing to deny forwards running on to through-balls and distributing like a sweeper, though; he was also noted for his superb positioning and his smart reflexes. Perhaps his greatest moment came in the 1947 Bulgarian Cup final when, with Levski leading Botev Plovdiv by a single goal, he made a brilliant penalty save in the last minute to secure a second consecutive double. Fate was rather less kind to him in the final minute of the Championship play-off the following year when a shot from Nako Chakmokov found its way via his hands and the post into the net to give CSKA a 4–3 aggregate victory. He later succumbed to alcoholism but his talents were beyond question.

Sokolov's son, Georgi, went on to become the youngest ever Bulgaria international, but his greatest legacy probably stemmed from his performances for his country on a tour of the USSR in 1952, when his sustained excellence convinced Lev Yashin that this new style of goalkeeping represented the future. What Grosics had begun, Yashin continued.

It was at Ajax in the sixties, though, that the goalkeeper was formally integrated into the main body of the side again, then that the incremental evolution reached a tipping point. Rinus Michels's conception of the game was based around the manipulation of space. The effective playing area had to be made as large as possible when in possession and as small as possible when the opposition had the ball. That meant the defence pushing high up the pitch, squeezing the play with an aggressive offside trap, so there could often be forty or fifty yards of space between the back line and the goal they were defending. That, potentially, represented a significant weakness: even if an opponent who had the ball was rapidly put under pressure, it required no accuracy to chip a ball into the unoccupied area for a forward to run on to. What was necessary was for the goalkeeper himself to advance, sweeping up speculative balls over the top. That meant the through-ball behind the defensive line had to be more precisely weighted, which was difficult enough to pull off even without the hard press denying the player in possesssion of the ball time to measure his pass. 'If everybody moves forward,' Johan Cruyff explained, 'you need an extra defender, so the goalkeeper has to be able to play as well.'

Heinz Stuy was Ajax's keeper for each of their three European Cup wins between 1971 and 1973, his ability to sweep behind the back four keeping him in the side despite a habit of dropping crosses as though they'd just come out of a deep fat fryer that earned him the nickname '*Heinz Kroket*'. He never played for the national team, though, and so holds the curious distinction of being the player to have won the most major trophies without winning an international cap. Instead Michels used Jan Jongbloed, the FC Amsterdam keeper who was a close friend of Cruyff, for the Netherlands. He too was far from outstanding in the terms of a conventional goalkeeper, and was only 5'10", but made up for his deficiencies in his reading of the game. With the Dutch – Cruyff and his number fourteen aside – allocating squad numbers in alphabetical order, Jongbloed wore the number eight shirt at the 1974 World Cup, retaining it in Argentina four years later, something that seemed to emphasise that he was just another player.

Even as late as 1981, while acknowledging that Jongbloed, by then forty, was realistically too old to play for the national side, Cruyff suggested he had something to offer. 'I still think Jan is always incredible value for a team,' he said. 'You can never take away a person's vision and goalkeeping at a high level is largely a question of vision.' That seems an astonishing statement: not reflexes or authority or positioning, but 'vision' – and it's particularly so given Cruyff apparently means vision not in the sense of being able to anticipate but of being able to initiate attacks.

To an extent, of course, it is probably just Cruyff being provocative but his insistence that a goalkeeper should sweep was absolute as he revealed in the same interview when discussing the Ajax goalkeeper Piet Schrijvers, himself by then thirty-four and so the sort of old dog to whom new tricks didn't come naturally. 'I said to Piet: we play attacking football at Ajax, so you shouldn't stay on your line,' Cruyff explained. 'You should try to find your position around the edge of the area. Then you have continuously to give directions and six or seven times you'll need to run out fast to make a save. Above all, you have to learn that the great fear of goalkeepers that they will be beaten by a ball lobbed over their head from the halfway line is not based in reality. If he plays like that, in the interests of the team, then it doesn't matter … if once in a while he doesn't save a high ball.'

That last point, of course, is fundamental. Goalkeeping, like so much else in football – and beyond – is about balance. The times when goalkeepers are lobbed from long range – David Seaman conceding to Nayim in the 1994 Cup-Winners' Cup final, Roy Carroll being lobbed by Pedro Mendes at Old Trafford in 2005 (when the goal wasn't given despite the ball being several feet over the line), David Beckham chipping Neil Sullivan from the halfway line in 1996, Real Sociedad's Iñigo Martínez beating Athletic's Gorka Irazoiz from inside his own half in the Basque derby in 2011 – stick in the mind, but they do so because they are comparatively rare. Essentially, if an opponent wants to start trying sixty-yard chips, it makes sense for the defensive team to let them. The problem is that when a player does get one right, the goalkeeper tends to look pretty silly.

It could perhaps be argued that Seaman was slow to move his feet, and he was a goalkeeper whose one weakness was his occasional leaden-footedness – as was seen for instance in Ronald Koeman's dinked free-kick for the Netherlands against England in a World Cup qualifier in Rotterdam in 1993 – but there was nothing wrong with his starting position. Real Zaragoza had the ball on halfway with seconds remaining: from Arsenal's point of view a wildly speculative lob that was likely to cede possession was far preferable to a measured cross towards a centre-forward; it's just that, on this occasion, it went in. Seaman was ridiculed for that for the rest of his career; Cruyff's point is that a goalkeeper has to risk that sort of humiliation because, in a far less eye-catching way, he prevents far more goals than he concedes by taking up an advanced position.

When Cruyff took over as Ajax coach in 1985, he was a man

determined to impose his philosophy. He set out the team in a 3-4-3 shape, and insisted his goalkeeper should be, as Simon Kuper put it, 'an outfield player in gloves'. Cruyff was probably too idealistic, his three years back at Ajax failing to yield a league title. He did, though, win two Dutch Cups as well as inspiring success in the 1987 Cup-Winners' Cup, ending a fourteen-year European drought. After that final, in which Marco van Basten's goal saw off Lokomotive Leipzig, Cruyff insisted his most important player was the goalkeeper, Stanley Menzo.

Usually goalkeepers are praised only when they've made save after save; here Cruyff was referring to Menzo's distribution, the way he initiated attacks. Born in Paramaribo, the capital of Surinam, Menzo was nineteen when he joined Ajax from the amateur club AVV Zeeburgia in 1980. He had a spell on loan at Haarlem but became a regular at Ajax a year before Cruyff's return. In Menzo, Cruyff found somebody who was ideal for his conception of the game, a player who read the game well and could pass the ball at pace. 'Menzo is a footballing keeper who plays as part of the team,' Fritz Barend and Henk van Dorp explained in *Ajax, Barcelona, Cruyff*. 'He is not allowed to wait statically on his goal line but has to play a long way from his goal ... If Menzo was stuck on his line, he would be much less active than when he plays with the whole team. Performing as a partial outfielder, Menzo gives Ajax half an extra player on the field against their opponents ... The philosophy behind this and the need for it is part of Ajax's attacking football. When Ajax defend in their own half, the keeper can stay in his goal. But Ajax attack and a keeper like Menzo is not a luxury but a necessity.'

Cruyff brought in the former Volendam goalkeeper Frans Hoek to coach Menzo, and the two formed a close bond, working on positioning and concluding that, for the Ajax style of play, the goalkeeper's base position should be several yards ahead of where most keepers stood. 'We have to make sure Menzo can get the ball into play as quickly as possible,' the centre-back Roland Spelbos explained. 'That's why you hardly ever see Menzo taking his time in possession. When he has the ball, he throws it to the

(top) A 1904 illustration of Stoke City's Leigh Richmond Roose, who redefined goalkeeping in the early twentieth century (*PA Images*).

(right) Bill 'Fatty' Foulke in his time at Chelsea when his weight was said to have reached 28st (*PA Images*).

(below) Liverpool's Northern Irish keeper Elisha Scott saves a penalty in an FA Cup tie against Arsenal in 1923 (*Getty Images*).

Perhaps the greatest of them all, Lev Yashin relaxing fishing (left) . . . and making a typically committed punch for Dinamo Moscow (above). And the latest in the great Russian tradition, Igor Akinfeev (*Getty Images*).

Two of the interwar greats, Italy's Gianpiero Combi and Czechoslovakia's František Plànička, shake hands before the 1934 World Cup final (*Getty Images*).

Rudi Hiden, the goalkeeper of the Wunderteam, arrives back in Vienna from Paris to the delight of autograph hunters (*Getty Images*).

(above) A warmly dressed Ricardo Zamora takes a cross in an international against Czechoslovakia on 1 January 1930 (*PA Images*).

(right) The great German goalkeeper Heinrich Stuhlfauth in his trademark grey jumper and flat cap (*PA Images*).

Hypochondriac, loner, dissident and arguably the first sweeper keeper, Gyula Grosics of Hungary, seen here in the 6–3 victory over England at Wembley in 1953 (*PA Images*).

Argentina's Ubaldo Fillol, wearing the alphabetically assigned squad number 7, in action against Brazil in the 1982 World Cup (*PA Images*).

Los Locos: René Higuita performs his
scorpion kick for Colombia against
England at Wembley (above, *PA Images*);
José Luis Chilavert celebrates a goal
for Paraguay against Bolivia (centre, *PA
Images*); and Mexico's Jorge Campos in
one of the kits he designed himself (right,
Getty Images).

Edwin van der Sar, the first modern sweeper keeper, tips the ball onto the bar against Russia in the Euro 2008 quarter-final (*PA Images*).

man furthest away from him. Sometimes you can cut out four opponents that way.'

Menzo played only six times for the Netherlands, partly because he always seemed nervous in the national shirt and partly because he had Hans van Breukelen ahead of him. He retained his place at Ajax under Louis van Gaal, but after an error in the 1992 Uefa Cup final, he was replaced by Edwin van der Sar, the goalkeeper who took the notion of the sweeper-keeper to new heights.

The emergence of Van der Sar coincided with the introduc-tion of the backpass law. It had been common for teams seeking to slow the game down to pass the ball back to their goalkeeper who, able to hold it and immune from charging, was effectively inviolable. A general rethink about the laws of the game had been prompted by the negativity of the 1990 World Cup, and in particular one passage of play in the group match between the Republic of Ireland and Egypt in which the Irish keeper Packie Bonner held the ball for almost six minutes without releasing it.

A gangling 6'6" with a wry sense of humour, it's hard to believe Van der Sar was ever anything but a goalkeeper but he is one of the many outfield converts. 'When I started playing I was a defender,' he explained. 'One day the goalkeeper wasn't there and the coach said, "You're the tallest. You can go in goal." That happens a lot with goalkeepers – or you're shit and you end up in goal.'

Van der Sar, of course, was an excellent goalkeeper in the tra-ditional ways: he commanded his box, was confident in dealing with crosses and, if he made relatively few spectacular saves, it was largely because his positioning was so good he didn't need to. At Ajax, he worked with Hoek and became the first player to operate as a genuine sweeper, rather than being merely a goal-keeper who was good with his feet. 'When the opposition put pressure on the defenders, they played the ball back to you, and you looked for a team-mate who was available to play it to,' he explained. 'If there was no option and someone was pressuring, it was just played forward, but you were always looking to keep possession.'

The perfect example of the theory in practice, perhaps, came in Euro 96 in the Netherlands' group game against Switzerland at Villa Park. The Dutch led 1–0 with eleven minutes remaining but the Swiss were threatening. Then Van der Sar caught a cross, advanced a couple of paces and sent a long drop-kick downfield to Dennis Bergkamp, who added the second. Here was the goalkeeper not merely as goal-stopper but as goal-maker.

Having won four Dutch titles and the 1995 Champions League, as well as being named European Goalkeeper of the Year in 1995 and Dutch Goalkeeper of the Year on four occasions, Van der Sar moved to Juventus in 1999. There, he found the role of the goalkeeper far more restricted. 'In Italy it was more about shot-stopping, making sure you don't concede, and you'd rather not have too many balls in defence because that's too risky – just kick it up front and take it from there.'

Juventus won nothing but the InterToto in his two seasons there and, while Van der Sar was far from a disaster, it was clear his days as first choice were over when Juve broke the transfer record for a goalkeeper, spending £32m to sign Gianluigi Buffon from Parma. He spent four years at Fulham, before a glorious conclusion to his career at Manchester United, with whom he won four Premier League titles and the 2008 Champions League. Fourteen years after he had first won the accolade, he was named European Goalkeeper of the Year again in 2009.

For the best teams, those that rarely find themselves under sustained pressure, he is convinced the sweeper-keeper is the most effective option – provided the rest of the team is equipped to play with a high offside line. 'It's the best way to play, but not for every team,' he said.

> If your defenders aren't quick, it's not a good thing to defend too high up the pitch, because if the opposition have a fast striker, every ball's over the top and they're gone. You have to look at the quality of your back four and keeper, and take it from there. If your back four moves ten yards forward, you have to move ten yards forward with them, make sure you

get the little through-balls and kick the ball away or keep possession.

'It's important to be able to use your feet. If your team-mates know you can play, they feel more comfortable with you behind them. They know if they're in trouble they can play the ball back and it's not going to be a wild kick up front or out but that you can keep possession for them and play the ball forward ... I remember when the backpass rule was announced and the next day we started practising not using hands any more, with defenders helping. When the ball was played back they were going wide, and we got three or four opportunities to pass to them, to the left, to the middle or to the right, or the long one ... Nowadays keepers have to be able to do that.

Hoek, meanwhile, followed the well-trodden path from Ajax to Barcelona, where he worked under Louis van Gaal and pursued the same theory he had at Ajax. In *A Life Too Short*, his biography of the tragic German goalkeeper Robert Enke, Ronald Reng details how Enke struggled to adapt to Hoek's demands. He had begun his career with Carl Zeiss Jena and then Borussia Mönchengladbach before moving to Benfica at the age of twenty-one. 'During his time at Benfica,' Reng wrote, 'Robert had gone to great pains to train himself to move his standing position to six or seven yards in front of the goal line.'

That he was a top-class goalkeeper from a technical point of view nobody doubted. Victor Valdés was twenty when Enke arrived at Barcelona. Enke hated flashiness and did everything he could not to milk a save, yet Valdés still insisted he 'rolled ... aesthetically'. This he sees as characteristic of the German style of goalkeeping: 'German goalkeepers fall much better than Spanish goalkeepers after a save,' he told Reng. 'We Spaniards just drop to the ground like a lump of meat ... the Germans roll.'

For Hoek, though, rolling well and standing six or seven yards off the line weren't enough. '"Robert, you're standing too far back!" ... "Robert, you've got to take the ball with your left foot!" ... "Robert, that was another poor pass. Concentrate harder on your feet!"' Enke's rival for the goalkeeping position was Roberto Bonano. 'The coaches were always telling us about Edwin van der Sar,' the Argentinian said. 'Van der Sar does this, and Van der Sar does that.'

A pre-season game against Parma in Amsterdam showed how difficult Enke was finding it to adjust. 'In slow-paced training matches he coped well with the big distance between a Barça goalkeeper and the defence,' Hoek told Reng. 'But in matches at competition speed, he still had difficulties with our very particular form of positional play. It was obvious that he had excellent reflexes on the goal line, but the question no one could answer was: how long would it take him to get used to the Barça style?'

For the next warm-up game, Van Gaal turned to Valdés, whose importance in starting Barça's attacks has taken the ideal of the sweeper-keeper to new levels. Sometimes that can go wrong, as it did for example, in the league *clásico* at the Bernabéu in 2011–12 when his misplaced pass gifted Karim Benzema the opening goal in the first minute. What was notable then, though, was that he didn't panic; he didn't start taking the easy option and belting the ball long when it came to him. He kept playing the way Barcelona always play, passing the ball out from the back. In truth, he *had* to keep playing like that because Barcelona couldn't function any other way. It would be absurd to expect their collection of 5'7" geniuses to start leaping for high balls. He is the sweeper-keeper not as an optional extra, not as a useful extra defender to be called upon every now and again, but as an essential part of the team.

His base position isn't even in his penalty area; rather he patrols just outside the box, allowing Barça to operate with a high line. Valdés may not make the spectacular saves some other goalkeepers do but, as Graham Hunter points out in *Barça: The Making of the Greatest Team in the World*, he is 'unfazed by opposition breakaways and the eyeball-to-eyeball winner-takes-all contests'. He is exceptional in one-on-one situations, something he showed, for instance, in the first two Nou Camp *clasicós* of Pep Guardiola's reign. Barcelona won both, but only because Valdés had acted decisively in thwarting a number of Real Madrid counter-attacks.

*

In England, the first sweeper-keeper was Liverpool's Tommy Lawrence, who was nicknamed 'the Flying Pig' because of his physique and willingness to fling himself at forwards who had broken through. Born in Ayrshire in 1940, Lawrence moved with his family to Lancashire as a child. He was initially a mid-fielder and played as such for Warrington Schoolboys. He ended up in goal after the regular keeper was injured during a game and was good enough to stay on in the position; two months later, he was spotted by a scout from Liverpool. That experience as an outfielder, though, would come in useful as Bill Shankly redefined what was to be expected from a goalkeeper.

'We played five-a-side in training,' Lawrence explained. 'We had ten outfield players so they played five-a-side and I was the odd man out so I played in a five-a-side team that went unbeaten for ten years with Bill Shankly, Bob Paisley, Joe Fagan and Reuben Bennett [that is, the coaching staff]. I played at the back in that team and they noticed we were losing far fewer goals than we would have done if I played a few yards further back.'

That was enough to convince Shankly to advance Lawrence in eleven-a-side games as well, although the keeper was initially dubious. 'I really was surprised,' he said. 'I was called in to his office and saw all my five-a-side team there – Bill, Bob, Joe and Reuben. At first I didn't fancy it. The first game we did it we lost to Manchester United. Then the first game we played in front of the Kop, they were shouting, "Get back in your goal." It was quite nerve-racking.

'If the defence was on the half-way line, I was on the edge of the eighteen-yard box. I could come out of the penalty area and bring people down. I didn't get my name taken once. I remember after a game at Chelsea that Brian Glanville wrote that he had never seen a team with eleven outfield players.'

In 1965–66, as Liverpool won the league, they conceded just thirty-four goals. After the 1966 Charity Shield, in which Liverpool beat Everton 1–0, the Manchester City manager Joe Mercer commented that, 'He comes so far off his line he plays like a defender.' The next season they conceded forty-seven, then forty, then an astonishing twenty-four, a tally they repeated in 1970–71.

'Ray Clemence then started playing the same way in the reserves,' Lawrence explained. 'The reserve team played the same way so if anyone got injured, the reserve player came in and played the same way. When Ray took over, he took the record down from twenty-four to sixteen [in 1978–79].'

Lawrence made the odd mistake; he remembers, for instance, being chipped in a game against Sheffield Wednesday, but the theory was that those risks were worth it for the more general benefit. Others soon realised how effective the style could be. 'It really caught on,' Lawrence said. 'It was an easy way to work. We played quite square and one of the centre-backs has got to be very quick. But so did their players because of where I was, if they put a ball over the top, I could be there to kick it before they got there from the halfway line.'

The debate reached its apogee in Argentina, where the tendency to theorise saw the differing styles of Hugo Gatti and Ubaldo Fillol, both of them born in the province of Buenos Aires, both heroes of Buenos Aires clubs, as representing two opposing schools of goalkeeping. Fillol, born in 1950, was the reliable conservative who stayed on his line and saved what he could; Gatti, six years his senior, was the extrovert risk-taker, the proactive goalkeeper who charged from his goal to try to check attacks before they had resulted in a shot on goal. 'We have two completely different styles,' explained Gatti. 'Fillol is a goal-goalkeeper who has difficulties coming too far out. He's all reflexes, but I live the game. I play it. I go out far to stop the play. I'm sure some of the goals I let in, he wouldn't; and that many shots I save, he wouldn't. The controversy is pointless; we just each do our own thing.'

Fillol may eventually have sought sanctuary on his goal line but for most of his childhood he was an outfielder. 'Before I made the decision to become a goalkeeper, I loved just playing football in my hometown of San Miguel del Monte,' he said.

I loved going to play on those dirt pitches. When there was a striker missing, I'd play as a striker. If we needed a midfielder, I'd do it. I'd play as a defender too or even a goalkeeper. My first decision was just to play football. I adored the game – still do.

'There's a club called San Miguel in my home town and that was my first club. On Saturdays we had two matches, the *tercera* and the *cuarta* [literally 'third' and 'fourth'; essentially youth sides]. The *cuarta* would play first and I was a goalkeeper for our team. Right after that match, I'd get the number five shirt and play in midfield for the *tercera*. So I would play two matches every Saturday and I was effectively a midfielder and a goalkeeper.

'It was when I went to Quilmes [a team based to the southeast of Buenos Aires] when I was thirteen years old that I had to make a decision. They asked me before my trial and I didn't hesitate and I told them, "I'm a goalkeeper." They tried me as a goalkeeper but if they wanted to try me as a midfielder, maybe I would have ended up as a midfielder instead. Before that, it was just enjoying football in any position I had to play. I took that decision because my passion was to play football and I saw I had some natural abilities. I was agile. It all started there for me.

He moved on to Racing in 1972 and a year later to River Plate.

Gatti was also initially an outfielder – a forward – and he later insisted that that had given him an insight into how strikers think and play. Only when he was sixteen and saw Amadeo Carrizo playing for River did he seriously consider goalkeeping as a career. Two years later he joined the Buenos Aires side Atlanta, then in the sixth tier of Argentinian football. After thirty-eight games there he joined Carrizo at River. Carrizo would be a major influence.

So, weirdly, was the sun. Gatti, perhaps because of his extravagance, his need always to be on the move and be proactive, seemed to diminish in damp weather. He was at his best, as the Uruguayan radio commentator Fioravanti put it, when 'the blond Phoebus was shining in the sideral firmament'.

After stints with Gimnasia y Esgrima La Plata and Unión Santa Fe, Gatti joined Boca Juniors in 1976. It was there that he really became a legend and there, naturally enough, that his rivalry with Fillol became more intense. 'Me and Hugo Gatti? It was River Plate v Boca Juniors,' Fillol explained. 'So the media and fans tried to look for a rivalry. That said, he and I are not only very different in the style each of us had but also the way we live our lives. How he lives, the things he says and how I live and the things I say. We each followed our own path, but I have always said that it's good for any player to find a rival. That gives you motivation to improve. It helps you get better.'

At Boca, in the media glare, it became apparent just how good Gatti was at reading the intentions of opponents, anticipating and blocking, often with his feet. He insisted he wasn't really a goalkeeper, but a forward playing in goal and, in keeping with his love of showmanship, coined the term 'hacer vista' – 'to have a view' or 'to watch'. If he stared at the ball hard enough, he claimed, he could make it miss the goal. It was, of course, a nonsensical assertion and yet it hinted at Gatti's ability psychologically to dominate forwards, his brightly coloured shirts and long hair, his capacity to anticipate and his deliberately provocative public statements giving him a shamanistic air.

Those first three years at Boca were Gatti's most successful. He won a Metropolitano title in 1976 and, the following season, Boca conceded just two goals in ten Copa Libertadores ties in reaching the final against the defending champions, Cruzeiro of Brazil. They won the home leg 1–0 but lost the away leg by the same scoreline, leading to a play-off at the Centenario in Montevideo. Neither side could score there in normal time or extra-time, so the game went to a penalty shoot-out. The first nine kicks were scored, but Gatti saved from Vanderley – one of twenty-six penalty saves he would make in his career – and Boca had their first continental title. The next season they won it again, Gatti's Boca beating Fillol's River 2–0 in the Monumental after a goalless draw in the Bombonera to secure progress from the three-team second group phase. Gatti missed the first leg of the final in Colombia as Boca drew 0–0 with Deportivo Cali, but he was back for the home leg as Boca romped to a 4–0 win.

Yet 1978 was also the source of perhaps Gatti's greatest disappointment. Come the build-up to the World Cup on home soil, it became apparent that one of César Luis Menotti's main decisions was over which goalkeeper to select. A knee injury ended up ruling Gatti out but the indications are that Menotti would have chosen Fillol anyway. His decision was fully vindicated as Fillol was named goalkeeper of the tournament, making a stunning save in the final victory over the Netherlands. 'It was the goal [at the Monumental] that has the Río de la Plata behind it,' Fillol recalled. 'Américo Gallego and Daniel Passarella got in each other's way and the ball fell to Rep. He controlled it and from very near the penalty spot took a great shot that somehow I managed to save.' Diving up and to his right, Fillol was just able to deflect the ball over the bar. 'I see that save these days,' he went on, 'and I think it's incredible how I was able to stop that ball from going in. Falling 1–0 down to a team like Holland would have been devastating for us. We had played against Italy in that World Cup and when they scored, we couldn't find a way back into the game. We ended up losing. So that save is still very special for me. It was the best save of my life.'

The sweeper-keeper is one thing, but there is another type that goes beyond that: those – mainly Latin American, usually nicknamed 'El Loco' – goalkeepers who seem genuinely to consider themselves outfield players. The trait really began with Jorge Campos, who played for Mexico at the 1994 and 1998 World Cups. Although official records list him as being 5'8", which would have been small for a goalkeeper anyway, he was probably a couple of inches shorter than that. Born in Acapulco, he turned professional when he was twenty-one, joining the Mexico City side Pumas. They already had a fine goalkeeper, though, in Adolfo Ríos, who would himself go on to be a Mexico international and so, desperate for first-team football, Campos asked to be considered as an outfielder. Playing as a centre-forward, he scored fourteen goals in his first season, yet within a couple of years he had established himself as the first-choice goalkeeper.

He became noted for his brightly coloured kits, which he designed himself – 'My experiences in Acapulco with surfing influenced my choice of bright colours,' he said – and for his willingness to change position if his team needed it. Perhaps the most famous of them came for Atlante against Cruz Azul in 1997 when, having started out in goal, he was moved to centre-forward and scored a spectacular bicycle kick. Given his lack of height and the way his shirts shamelessly drew attention to himself, it would be easy to dismiss Campos as having novelty value only, but he won 129 caps for Mexico and came third in the voting for the IFFHS Goalkeeper of the Year award in 1994.

Still, it would be hard to claim that Campos was a better keeper than José Luis Chilavert, the Paraguayan who was named goalkeeper of the year on three occasions in the nineties by the IFFHS. Campos scored thirty-five goals in his career – although none at international level – but the majority of them came when he was playing as an outfielder. Chilavert got sixty-two, eight of them for Paraguay, and he always played as a goalkeeper.

He was seventeen when he made his debut for his home-town side, Sportivo Luqueño, and after a brief stint at Guaraní, he joined the Argentinian side San Lorenzo when he was nineteen. He had scored five goals in Paraguay – either with free-kicks or penalties – but he was more restrained in Argentinian football and failed to score again until after his move to Zaragoza. It was after he had left Spain in 1991, though, that Chilavert really began to make his mark. At international level, he was one of the over-age players in the Sergio Markarián-coached team that qualified for the Barcelona Olympic Games. He went 267 minutes without conceding a goal in that tournament as Paraguay reached the quarter-final with a group of players – Carlos Gamarra, Celso Ayala, Francisco Arce and José Cardozo as well as Chilavert – who would go on to form the core of the Paraguay side that qualified for the 1998 and 2002 World Cups, establishing Paraguay as one of the leading South American nations. They qualified again in 2006 and 2010, a remarkable achievement for a country with a population of only 6.5 million.

Chilavert joined Vélez Sársfield from Zaragoza. They had always been the sixth team in Buenos Aires, the best of the rest after the five *grandes* and, when he arrived, the only silverware they'd won was the Nacional championship in 1968. By the time he left, ten years later, they'd won four league titles as well as lifting the Copa Libertadores under Carlos Bianchi. Chilavert's dead-balls became legendary. He scored a hat-trick of penalties against Ferro Carril Oeste in 1999. 'I put the first to the goal-keeper's left, the second to his right and then I doubted,' he explained. 'So I decided to put it down the middle and it flew into the roof of the net.' His quick-thinking, barging dithering team-mates out of the way, allowed him to score with a free-kick from within his own half against River Plate. He also con-ceded to a River Plate goalkeeper, Roberto Bonano converting a penalty against him in the Copa Mercosur in 2000. Typically, Chilavert wasn't impressed. 'He hit it really badly,' he said, 'like a wet newspaper.'

He can be a difficult, awkward personality, despite his claims that his on-pitch aggression was merely an act. 'I created an image,' he said. 'For me, with this face, it was much easier to play the bad guy.' During the 2006 and 2010 World Cups, he worked as a co-commentator for the US channel Univision; in press-rooms before matches in South Africa he became a famil-iar sight, huddled in a drab olive-green coat, a baseball cap pulled low over his eyes, gloweringly daring anybody to recog-nise him. He often seemed to hate journalists and he was quite happy publicly to criticise those he didn't respect. 'Not everyone can be a goalkeeper, you know,' he said. 'People think we're only there to stop goals, but that's an entirely mistaken and nega-tive view. To my mind you can't have a good team without a good keeper. Brazil had a fantastic side in 1982 but they also had Valdir Peres in goal. Every time the opposition went forward they scored, which rather proves my point.' He wasn't alone in arguing Valdir Peres as the weak point of that Brazil side but few other professionals have done so quite so bluntly: no notion of the goalkeepers' union for him.

At times, Chilavert was motivated by principle, as when he insisted on the Paraguay squad donating a share of their bonuses from the 1998 World Cup to the back-room staff, or when he refused to take part in the 1999 Copa América, saying the money Paraguay had spent hosting it would have been better spent on education. At other times, it seemed he just had a short fuse, as when he was banned for three games during qualifying for the 2002 World Cup for spitting at the Brazil full-back Roberto Carlos – whom he claimed had racially insulted him by calling him 'Indio' – or when he quit international football in 2003 after falling out with the team hierarchy.

And at other times, his actions were simply criminal as when, in 2005, he was given a six-month suspended prison sentence in France after being convicted of using forged documents in a dispute over the compensation he was due after his two seasons at Strasbourg, whom he had joined from Vélez. He recovered soon enough, though, moving on to Peñarol and scoring four goals in fourteen games as they won the Uruguayan title.

His one regret in his career, he claimed, was that he never had the chance to play in England. 'The football there would have suited my style of play,' he insisted. 'With all the crosses they put over, I would have had lots of opportunities to punch clear. My huge goal kicks would also have gone down well.' As, of course, would his goals. Chilavert's record as the world's top-scoring goalkeeper has been taken by the Brazilian Rogério Ceni but he will always be remembered as the pioneer, the man who made goalscoring goalkeepers more than a mere novelty.

Chilavert may have been the best of los locos, but the most notorious was the Colombian René Higuita. He grew up in Castilla, a barrio of Medellín, playing football and dreaming of being a centre-forward. Many of the games in which he played took place on pitches and under floodlights paid for by Pablo Escobar, the head of the local drugs cartel, who was philanthropic with his profits, building housing for the poor and offering a measure of social security. At seventeen, Higuita, by then a goalkeeper, moved to Bogotà to join Millonarios. He played sixteen games for them and, remarkably, scored five goals.

A year later, he returned to Medellín with Atlético Nacional, a club funded by Escobar and his long-time associate Carlos Molina. He continued to wander from his box, being used by his team-mates as a passing option – often far further forward than even Cruyff would consider wise. 'I think goalkeepers should get more freedom of expression,' he said in an early newspaper interview. 'If we are attacking, I like to move into the centre-circle and exchange a few passes.' It seemed to work: he won two league titles with Nacional and, in 1989, was part of the first Colombian side to win the Copa Libertadores.

With his long hair and flamboyant style, Higuita became an icon of his country. Yes, there were mistakes, most notoriously in the second round of the 1990 World Cup against Cameroon. Having come forty yards from goal to deal with a long clearance, Higuita passed the ball square to Luis Perea. The defender's return pass was poor, but Higuita dallied, tried to jink by Roger Milla and was dispossessed, allowing Milla to run through and score into an empty net. Colombia's coach, Francisco Maturana, took a position of Cruyffian perspective, excusing the error on the grounds the risk was worth it because of the benefits his style of play brought. Higuita, he said, was 'without doubt the saviour of Colombia and not the crazy goalkeeper that some believe him to be. He brings the ball out with competence and great security.'

But there were also moments of brilliance, or at least moments of audacity so striking that they are still referred to years after the event. Had he seen the linesman's flag go up when, in a friendly between England and Colombia in 1995, he opted to deal with Jamie Redknapp's overhit cross by plunging forward onto his hands and kicking the ball away with his heels? If he did, it was evidence of astonishing awareness; if not, then what was the Scorpion Kick? Brilliant, yes, but ludicrously self-indulgent. And yet, without it, would anybody ever have reason to think back to a drab goalless draw? Whatever else he did, Higuita made football memorable.

The 1995 Copa América seemed to sum up his blend of haplessness and anarchic brilliance. Against Brazil in Colombia's final group game, he punched a cross into his own net. But then, in the third-place play-off against USA, he raced forward to take a free-kick, curling his shot against the bar, the rebound falling for Faustino Asprilla to knock in (with a volley mishit so badly the ball bounced about two feet behind the line and spun out of the goal again – but that's not to detract from Higuita's initial strike).

As Higuita's fame grew, Escobar began to take an interest. He summoned the goalkeeper to a meeting in 1987 at which they talked football – Escobar was a genuine fan – and Higuita, at least by his own account, tried to persuade Escobar to give himself up. Four years later, by which time Escobar was in prison (in the loosest sense of the term: it was essentially a luxury resort built to his own specifications), they met again. Higuita couldn't really refuse the summons, but photographs taken at the time, showing the two laughing together, created an uncomfortable impression.

In July 1992, Escobar escaped. He evaded capture for several months, calling in old favours, but as the net closed around him and his access to banks was cut off, he became increasingly desperate and ordered the kidnapping for ransom of Claudia Molina, the fifteen-year-old daughter of his former ally Carlos Molina, with whom he had fallen out. Molina, having seen the photographs of Escobar and Higuita together, and having once effectively been Higuita's employer, turned to the goalkeeper for help. Molina may not have been as powerful as Escobar but he was still a narco chief; there was little Higuita could do but get in the car when it called for him.

He was taken to Molina's house, where he was given a briefcase containing $300,000 to be handed over as ransom. It took time for the kidnappers to make contact, but when they did, Higuita took the money to a location in central Bogotá. Everything went smoothly. Claudia was released, and a delighted Molina gave Higuita $64,000 to thank him.

That should have been the end of it, but naively Higuita boasted of what he'd done in the newspapers and on television. Realistically, all he was guilty of was liaising between two extremely powerful men when it would have been dangerous to refuse but under emergency regulations it was illegal at the time in Colombia to profit from a kidnapping, no matter how incidentally. Higuita was jailed without trial in July 1993, and only released seven months later, having gone on hunger strike. He was never formally charged. That cost him his place at the 1994 World Cup but by the following year, Higuita was back to his best, reclaiming his place in the national side and starring as Nacional reached the Copa Libertadores final for the second time. In the semi-final, he even scored a superb free-kick, the ball glancing in off the underside of the bar as Nacional beat River Plate on penalties.

Despite testing positive for cocaine in 2004, he kept playing, on and off, until he was forty-four. Even in those final days, at Deportivo Pereira, a second-division side in the heart of Colombia's coffee country, he insisted on playing in the same style, and scored five goals in twelve games over two seasons. Finally, in 2010 he retired, and immediately began making noises about becoming a politician. 'When I have finished my career,' he said, 'my name will stay on people's lips and in their minds as a player who brought a bit of magic into the lives of ordinary people.'

5: THEY ALSO SERVE

Most countries in the world are proud of their goalkeepers, seem to think that their tradition is unique, even if that is often undercut by the assertion that there is something a little odd about wanting to be a goalkeeper. Not Brazil and not Scotland, two nations whose goalkeepers have historically – if not always entirely fairly – been held up for ridicule.

'To be a goalkeeper,' the Brazilian saying goes, 'you must be either mad or queer.' Attitudes have changed over the past twenty years or so, but Brazil is probably the only nation with a worse reputation for goalkeeping than Scotland – if only because their travails contrasted so obviously with the abilities of the rest of the side. And while other countries questioned the sanity of goalkeepers, most at least acknowledged the courage – physical and mental – the role demanded. In Brazil, though, the goalkeeper was somehow unmanly (to follow the macho logic of the age that produced the phrase): he was Other – subversive, unorthodox, perhaps even (again, following the rationale of an earlier age) unnatural or ungodly.

That was confusing, because the stereotype of Brazilian football is of subversion, something first set out by the anthropologist Gilberto Freyre, who developed the figure of the *malandro*, the conman or trickster, idealised as the slave getting one over on his master by cunning. 'Our style of playing football,' Freyre wrote in 1938, 'contrasts with the Europeans because of a combination of the qualities of surprise, malice, astuteness and agility, and at the same time brilliance and individual spontaneity … Our passes … our dummies, our flourishes with the ball, the touch of dance and subversiveness that marks the Brazilian style ... seem to show psychologists and sociologists in a very interesting way the roguery and flamboyance of the mulatto that today is every true affirmation of what is Brazilian.'

The *malandro* spirit found its personification in two of the greatest Brazilian players of the thirties, the centre-forward Leônidas and the defender Domingos da Guia, both of whom were black and thus happily fitted the slave-narrative. Uncomfortable as the suggestion that black players were somehow naturally more skilful than whites may be, there was an unfortunate practical explanation, rooted in self-preservation. 'When I was still a kid I was scared to play football,' Domingos said, 'because I often saw black players ... get whacked on the pitch, just because they made a foul or sometimes for less than that ... My elder brother used to tell me: the cat always falls on his feet ... Aren't you good at dancing? I was and this helped my football ... I swung my hips a lot ... That short dribble I invented imitating the *miudinho*, that type of samba.'

Another anthropologist, Robert da Matta, refined Freyre's work and posited that because the laws and codes of behaviour in Brazil, even after the abolition of slavery in 1888, were designed to protect the rich and powerful, individuals lower down the social scale had to find imaginative ways of getting round them – a characteristic he termed '*jeitinho*'. The parallel with football is easily drawn: what was prized was an imaginative response to a problem, a cleverness that could outwit those bigger, stronger or wealthier.

That prevailing ideology raised two awkward oppositions. First of all, how can a goalkeeper express the seductiveness, cunning and imagination that the game is supposed to be about? His job is to be safe and secure, to stifle the creative impulses of others. He is thus cast as he had been in the very origins of the game, as the killjoy, the man who interrupted the fertility rite. And secondly, if the *malandro* spirit that underpins the Brazilian game is the preserve of blacks and mulattos, those who can trace their heritage back to slaves, it follows that those who try to crack down on the creativity, the goalkeepers, should be white. It may even follow – to those who would select their teams by crude racial stereotyping – that the goalkeeper shouldn't be black, despite the fact that Jaguaré, the first great Brazilian goalkeeper, certainly the first to make a name for himself outside of Brazil, had been.

Moacyr Barbosa was black. He was also the goalkeeper widely blamed for the most traumatic event in Brazil's football history, perhaps in the history of the nation, and as such he shaped the Brazilian perception of goalkeeping for half a century.

In 1946, for the first time in over a decade, Brazil elected a democratic government. There was a mood of optimism and growing economic strength about the country, galvanised by the hosting of the World Cup in 1950 and the construction of the Maracanã, the largest football stadium that had ever existed.

A year earlier Brazil had won the Copa América by beating Paraguay 7–0 in a play-off (emphatic as that was, there was a warning in the fact the play-off had only been necessary because Brazil had lost to Paraguay in Rio in their final game of a seven-team group when a draw would have been enough to give them the title). In the World Cup itself, they'd been comfortably the most impressive team. Although they'd drawn their one match in São Paulo, when they'd attempted to appease the local crowd by selecting *paulista* players, at the Maracanã Brazil had won four out of four, racking up nineteen goals. That they could fail to get the draw they needed to be world champions against Uruguay was so inconceivable that, on the morning of that final game, the newspaper *O Mundo* printed a team photograph with a headline declaring Brazil the world champions.

When, two minutes after half-time, a reverse ball from Ademir laid in Friaça, who held off Andrade and, with a slightly scuffed cross-shot, gave Brazil the lead, everything seemed to be going to plan. But, twenty-four minutes from time, Uruguay levelled. The captain Obdulio Varela advanced, and spread the ball to the frail, hunched right-winger Alcides Ghiggia. He had space to accelerate, checked as Bigode moved to close him down, then surged by him, crossing low for Juan Schiaffino to sweep the ball in at the near post. The Maracanã fell silent. Doubt, for the first time, gripped the hosts, and the momentum was with Uruguay. With eleven minutes remaining, Ghiggia again picked up the ball on the Uruguayan right. This time Bigode was closer to him, but isolated, so Ghiggia laid it back to Julio Pérez. The right-half held off Jair and slipped a return ball in behind Bigode. Ghiggia ran on, and with Barbosa anticipating a cross, struck a bobbling shot in at the near post.

Roberto Muylaert, Barbosa's biographer, described the clip of the goal as being like the Zapruder footage of the Kennedy assassination: 'the same drama … the same rhythm … the same precision of an inexorable trajectory'. Even the puff of dust that kicked up as Ghiggia struck the ball seemed to evoke a gunshot. That was the moment of Barbosa's assassination: from then on, his life as a normal citizen was over. The video of the game shows him down on one knee after the goal, slowly, sadly, raising his powerful body as though he knew already the burden he would carry for the rest of his life.

That defeat wasn't just a defeat; it was something that struck at the heart of the Brazilian nation and its burgeoning self-confidence. The playwright Nélson Rodrigues spoke of the defeat as 'our Hiroshima'; it might not have been a particularly tactful image, but what he meant was that it was the greatest single catastrophe to have befallen Brazil, which was only founded as a nation in 1889 and has never fought a war. Paulo Perdigão expresses the same point less outrageously in *Anatomy of a Defeat*, his remarkable meditation on the final, in which he reprints the entire radio commentary, using it as the basis for his analysis of the game almost as though he were delivering exegesis upon a biblical text. 'Of all the historical examples of national crises,' he wrote, 'the World Cup of 1950 is the most beautiful and most glorified. It is a Waterloo of the tropics and its history our *Götterdämmerung*. The defeat transformed a normal fact into an exceptional narrative: it is a fabulous myth that has been preserved and even grown in the public imagination.'

Scapegoats were needed, and they were found in the three black players – Bigode, Juvenal and, particularly, Barbosa. According to the midfielder Zizinho, the press 'killed' Barbosa, even though Ghiggia admitted his goal had been lucky and that

Barbosa had done the logical thing in straying from his near post. Even if it is accepted that he made an error, Barbosa had otherwise had an excellent World Cup, being named goalkeeper of the tournament; such is the goalkeeper's lot.

'Barbosa was excellent in the South American Championship [the forerunner of the Copa América] in 1949,' said the journalist Luís Augusto Simon, who included Barbosa in his book on the eleven best Brazilian post-war goalkeepers. 'The accounts of journalists at the time said he was a great goalkeeper.' Although Barbosa was dropped immediately after the 1950 World Cup, he returned in 1953 for one cap and looked set to be selected for the 1954 World Cup. That might have given him the chance to rehabilitate his reputation but he broke his leg in a match between Vasco da Gama and Botafogo and missed the tournament. 'The biggest impact of his mistake was to make it harder for black goalkeepers with the national team and even in the clubs,' said the journalist and historian Paulo Guilherne, whose book *Goleiros* is the definitive history of the goalkeepers to have played for the Brazil national team. 'It created a paranoia that you could not have black goalkeepers.'

Barbosa himself never escaped that final. In 1970 came what he described as his worst moment as he overheard a woman in a shop saying to her young son, 'Look! There's the man who made all of Brazil cry.' Seven years earlier, if Muylaert is to be believed, Barbosa attempted an act of symbolic expiation, inviting friends to a barbecue at his home in the north of Rio at which he burned the Maracanã goalposts in what Muylaert described as 'a liturgy of purification'. Whether the sacrifice happened or not is debatable, but the way the tale was accepted suggests how eagerly Barbosa's victimhood was lapped up.

In 1993 the BBC tried to take Barbosa to visit the Brazil camp at the USA Cup. Mario Zagallo, who had won the World Cup as a player in 1962 and as manager in 1970, was working with the squad as assistant to the coach Carlos Alberto Parreira. He had been by the pitch at the Maracanã on that fateful day in 1950, operating as security as part of his national service. Recognising Barbosa, he refused him entry to the camp, insisting he would bring bad luck. 'In Brazil,' Barbosa said, 'the maximum sentence is thirty years, but my imprisonment has been for fifty.' He died in poverty in April 2000; a year earlier, Dida had become the first black goalkeeper to play for Brazil since Barbosa's final appearance forty-nine years earlier.

Brazil isn't the only nation to have had a racial issue with goalkeepers; it's just that, having had talented black goalkeepers so early, their subsequent exclusion is more obvious. In Britain, it was common in the seventies to hear managers and pundits explain that black players were all very well as forwards but that they lacked the discipline and concentration necessary to be a defender (a wrong and racist assertion that was all the more weird given that the first black player to win an England cap was a defender, Viv Anderson of Nottingham Forest). It was, presumably, doubly true for goalkeepers.

Whether because of that prejudice or not – and of course it is part of the insidiousness of racism that it is self-perpetuating: if a talented young black footballer sees there are no black goalkeepers, then why invest the time in training to be a goalkeeper? – black goalkeepers took far longer to make the breakthrough in English football than black outfield players. Alex Williams, who succeeded Joe Corrigan at Manchester City, was a pioneer and with the likes of Clayton Ince at Crewe and Walsall, David James at Watford and Shaka Hislop at Reading, the theory was disproved by the mid-nineties.

Yet the first black player to play in the Football League was a goalkeeper. Arthur Wharton was born in what is now Accra in Ghana, but was then Jamestown in the Gold Coast. His father was a Wesleyan minister from Grenada, himself the son of a Scottish merchant, while his mother was the daughter of a Scottish trader called John Gaunt and Ama Egyiriba, a Fante royal. He studied in London, Cannock and Darlington, where he became noted as a remarkable sprinter. He won the Amateur Athletics Association sprint at Stamford Bridge in 1886, retained his title in 1887 and then won the unofficial professional title a year later. 'Sprinting of many kinds has been seen: some sprint bent forward, some with head and shoulders thrown back, but here is a man running away from his field with his body bent forward and running almost on the flat of his foot,' noted a report of that 1886 meeting.

Quick as he was, Wharton preferred to play in goal. He turned out for Darlington and Preston North End before making his league debut for Rotherham United in 1893–94. He was a player who was determined to have fun on the field, hanging from the crossbar, catching the ball between his legs and lying down during quiet passages of play, leaving it as late as possible to spring up and foil an advancing attacker. Newspapers of the time were mildly disapproving of his occasional clowning and eccentricity but it's difficult at this remove to know how much of that was born of exuberance and how much of a genuine pioneering spirit. James Catton, the great *Athletic News* journalist, was a big fan. 'Wharton is indeed a born goalkeeper,' he wrote. 'He never loses his head, and his hands are always in readiness.' Stable he may have been as a goalkeeper but after his retirement from football he became a publican and succumbed to bouts of heavy drinking.

Alex Williams, who made his City debut in 1980, only became aware of Wharton when he was well into his career – 'We signed John Burridge and he told me about Arthur. It was quite strange, I thought I was totally unique. Whatever it was for me, it must have been worse for him,' he said – and his inspirations were, understandably, drawn from the First Division as he was growing up. 'It was very much people like Pat Jennings, Peter Shilton and Ray Clemence,' he said. 'It was a great era for British goalkeepers. Then there was Joe Corrigan, whom I got to know at City. Pat Jennings was my favourite. With Pat, he was such a cool, calm person. He had a way of catching the ball with one hand. He was a quiet, unassuming man, a real gentle giant. I went to see him once at Maine Road and came away impressed.'

At City, Williams found a mentor in Steve Fleet, the youth-team coach. 'He had been understudy to Bert Trautmann and he saw something in me,' he said. 'First and foremost I thought of myself as a goalkeeper, not as a black goalkeeper, but I was quite a unique one.'

In an era in which racism was a major problem in English football and black players were commonly targeted, Williams inevitably suffered abuse; his position exposing him to the crowd behind the goal meant that he could never seek respite in the middle of the pitch. 'There were a number of bad incidents,' he said. 'One of the worst occurred at Everton [in 1982]. It was one of my first games for the club. I ran out for the second half and in those days there were barriers between the crowd and the pitch. A lad had climbed up the barrier and turned his programme into a cross and set it on fire, à la the Ku Klux Klan. I remember playing quite well that day, but I think we lost 2–1. I just focused on going out and playing for Manchester City and being a goalkeeper. You know there are some clubs … West Ham was one of them, it was my fourth or fifth game for the club, we lost 4–1 and I got a lot of stick, but I got clapped off at the end. It helped that I saved a Ray Stewart penalty in the first few minutes.'

His own club's fans, of course, having recognised Williams's quality, responded to the abuse of one of their own with additional levels of support. 'City fans were fantastic,' he said. 'I was born in Moss Side, 200 yards from the stadium and I was a local boy. I was heavily involved with the club and the supporters so I built up quite a rapport with the fans. I was doing work in the community at the time.'

Barbosa's woes may have prepared the ground but before the widespread dismissal of Brazilian goalkeeping there was a further great: Gilmar. Born in Santos in 1930 and taking his name from his parents, Gilberto and Maria, he was part of the great Santos side that won five São Paulo state championships, five national championships, two Copas Libertadores and two Intercontinental Cups, and played for Brazil in three World Cups, winning in 1958 and 1962. A debonair man, he had height, natural authority, a calmness on and off the pitch and a charisma that won him great popularity.

That wasn't always the case though; he knew ignominy as well. His great crisis came in November 1951 in a game for Corinthians against Portuguesa. With a couple of months of the season remaining, both sides were battling for the title. It was expected to be a tight, tense game, but Portuguesa won 7–3. 'It all went wrong,' said Gilmar. 'It was the most disastrous moment of my life.' The rumour got about that Gilmar had thrown the game, something for which there seemed to be no evidence other than the belief he couldn't have let in seven in any other way. He wasn't just dropped, but ostracised, forbidden even to come into the club to train. It was only around six months later, as other goalkeepers proved less effective, that he was allowed to return and, although he went on to establish himself as Brazil's number one, there was always a tension in his relationship with Corinthians – something that contributed to his decision to move to Santos in 1961.

By then, Gilmar was a celebrity. In *Goleiros*, Paulo Guilherne argues that Gilmar was almost as big a figure as Pelé, largely because of the 1958 World Cup, the first won by Brazil. For one thing, he was excellent, not conceding a goal until the semi-final, a run that meant he matched the world all-time goalkeeping record of seventeen clean sheets in internationals. And for another, he was clearly a leader of the team. In the famous photograph of the seventeen-year-old Pelé overwhelmed with emotion shortly after the final, it is Gilmar's shoulder on which he is weeping. He was also a voice of reason amid the superstition that dominated the dressing room. He had worn the number thirteen shirt throughout the tournament but when he turned up for the final he found his blue kit clashed with the shirts the Brazilian federation had hastily bought in a Stockholm sports shop to avoid a clash with Sweden's yellow. The only contrasting shirt he could find had a number three on the back. He would happily have worn it but his team-mates insisted he had to wear thirteen. For a short while there was panic, but then Gilmar calmly sat down, cut out a one from some spare material and had it stitched in front of the three.

It would be an exaggeration to say Gilmar took a scientific

approach to goalkeeping, but he was obsessed with details and, in Sweden, made sure he learned from other nations. Before that tournament goalkeepers in Brazil had traditionally worn long shorts and elbow pads but, seeing his rivals in much shorter shorts, Gilmar switched, arguing that the long shorts, far from offering protection, actually grazed his knees when he dived while restricting his movement. The team doctor, Hilton Gosling, discussed the issue with other medical personnel and came to the conclusion that long shorts were useful for the first twenty minutes of games, keeping a goalkeeper's muscles warm, but thereafter they would restrict circulation and elasticity. Gilmar never went back to the long shorts and other goalkeepers in Brazil followed his style.

That World Cup was also the first to be broadcast live on Brazilian radio, which led to those players involved in the most dramatic action becoming household names: that is, those who had the shots on goal for Brazil and those who saved the opponent's shots. 'All of my street loved listening to the saves of Gilmar on the radio,' said Valdir Peres, who was Brazil's first-choice keeper at the 1982 World Cup. 'When I was a kid, I got used to hearing commentators screaming his name. I thought that he was the best. That made up my mind that one day I was going to be like him.' Valdir wasn't the only one inspired. Six months after the World Cup final a boy was born to the Rinaldi family in Erexim in Rio Grande do Sul. They called him Gilmar and he went on to play in goal for Internacional, São Paulo and Flamengo, earning a call-up to the national squad for the 1994 World Cup. 'My mother was pregnant when Brazil won the World Cup for the first time,' he said. 'My dad decided to give me the name Gilmar. When I started to play football I didn't get too far: with this name I could only be a goalkeeper.'

Gilmar – the original version – was well aware of his image. He loved cinema and, according to Guilherne, was the first goalkeeper in Brazil to think about how he looked on the pitch, making sure there was an aesthetic quality to his movement and dives so that it looked good on film. Gilmar clearly relished his fame and there were regular complaints from club directors that he attended so many parties and events – although he made sure he never drank in public. Whatever his private excesses, they did him little harm and, in 2000, Gilmar was voted the greatest goalkeeper in world football history by *Paris Match*.

Gilmar, though, was an exception; the general perception was that goalkeeping in Brazil didn't attain the standards set elsewhere on the pitch. In the great 1970 side, for instance, Felix was seen as the clear weak link. He seemed to have an infallible capacity for haplessness, something that continued in his life after football when he named his motor repair business after the initials of his daughter, Ligia, her husband, Angelo, and their son Rafael: LAR.

When he was a child, his mother thought he spent too much time on football and tried to stop him playing, but he would leave home at 5.30 each day and collect his boots from the Mussolini stocking factory where his father worked. 'It was our secret,' he said. He started out as a centre-forward, but his courage in flinging himself about on the street meant he ended up in goal. 'In Brazil if a player is no good playing in front, he'll be a goalkeeper,' Felix told Gary Jenkins in *The Beautiful Team*. 'But not in my case. I started playing in goal because generally nobody wanted to play there and I was very courageous. We played on the streets and I would dive on the pavements. I started to like it.'

Even after he started playing for a junior side at CA Juventus, Felix kept lying to his mother, working as an office boy and telling her he was going to become an accountant. Santos took an interest and Felix began to leave work early to go to their ground. Gilmar, another Juventus product, was already there. The director from whom Felix had to seek permission to leave early was a Portuguesa fan and suggested Felix should play for them instead. When Santos were on tour in Argentina, Portuguesa signed him.

Even by the standards of the time, Felix was less than physically imposing, nicknamed '*Papel*' – paper – because he was so thin. He refused to do weight-training to bulk up, saying that would have turned him into 'a robot' and diminished the reflexes that were the basis of his talent.

Having narrowly missed out on the squad for the 1966 World Cup, Felix rapidly became number one when Gilmar and Manga, who had both gone to England, returned tainted by the disgrace of a first-round exit. Felix was João Saldanha's first choice through the qualifiers for the 1970 finals, but after the coach had been to Europe, he came back believing his side was certain to face an aerial barrage. He needed, he said, a more physically imposing keeper, such as Emerson Leão of Palmeiras, then just twenty.

That perhaps made a certain sense and was in the long-standing Brazilian tradition of concern about the physicality of European sides. By the build-up to the finals, though, Saldanha had entered a state bordering on paranoia, pursuing one critic with a loaded gun and making a string of bizarre criticisms of players in his squad. Most notoriously, he claimed that Pelé was shortsighted, but he also insisted that Gérson had mental problems, that Leão's arms were too short and that Felix didn't know how to play in gloves, something of particular concern given that the tournament was scheduled for the rainy season in Mexico.

Saldanha was sacked after a defeat in a friendly against Argentina in the March before the World Cup and replaced by Mario Zagallo. The new coach promptly brought Felix back, at which Leão broke down and left the camp in tears, insisting Felix must be Zagallo's puppet, although he later returned to the squad. At thirty-three, Felix was the oldest player there and it may be that what he did off the pitch turned out to be more significant than what he did on it. He roomed with the youngest player, Marco Antônio, his team-mate at Fluminense whom he had joined in 1968. He was part of the five-man committee with Gérson, Wilson Piazza, Brito and Carlos Alberto that represented the players in their meetings with Zagallo and the Brazilian federation. But perhaps most importantly, he was a joker: he gave everybody a nickname and his general clowning around helped ease the pressure of being under the scrutiny of the world's most fickle media.

On the pitch, Felix was far less impressive. His problems began in the eleventh minute of Brazil's opening game, against Czechoslovakia, when Ladislav Petráš surged through to beat him at his near post. He might, perhaps, have been quicker off his line, but it was far from a glaring error; nonetheless, Saldanha used it to begin a campaign of criticism, even though Brazil came back to win 4–1.

Brazil's second game, against England, was probably Felix's best of the tournament, as he kept his only clean sheet in a 1–0 win. He made a fine save from a Francis Lee header and was then kicked in the face as Lee tried to get to the rebound, leaving him unable to remember the rest of the first half. Two cigarettes in the tunnel at half-time revived him. He rode his luck to an extent in the second half, although he claimed credit for Jeff Astle's notorious miss, insisting it was his speed off his line to close the forward down that forced him to drag his shot wide.

From there, Felix's tournament went rapidly downhill. He let in two soft goals in the 3–2 win over Romania, and had his hands bent back by Alberto Gallardo in conceding Peru's first in Brazil's 4–2 victory over them in the quarter-final. Against Uruguay in the semi-final, he was left looking very silly, sitting hopelessly on his line with the ball in his net behind him, knowing that he'd been yards out of position beyond his near post as Luis Cubilla's far from ferocious shot dribbled past him. The pitch, he explained, had been remarked and he had been confused by the appearance of two goal lines, his feet then tangling as he tried to readjust. Later on, with the score at 2–1 to Brazil, he made a superb reflex save to keep out a Cubilla header. 'I don't know how I could fly the way I flew,' he said, but it was the gaffe for the opener that was remembered. In the final against Italy, he made one tip-over from a long-range Luigi Riva effort, but then, after Clodoaldo's mistake, contributed to the Italians' goal, hurtling from his line and colliding with Brito to leave Roberto Boninsegna and Gianni Rivera with all the time in the world to decide who was going to roll the ball into an open net.

Felix had already won one Rio state championship with Fluminense and he would go on to win four more. He clearly wasn't a bad goalkeeper, but he had had a bad tournament and that confirmed – as much to Brazilians as to outsiders – that Brazilian goalkeepers weren't to be trusted. 'One of the problems,' Guilherne said, 'was that when Brazilian teams played against foreign sides they would usually dominate the game and the goalkeeper from the other team would make lots of saves while the Brazilian would stand back and have little to do. So everybody thought the Argentinians, Uruguayans, Paraguayans, Colombians … were the best. So the clubs took these goalkeepers to Brazil.'

And that, of course, exacerbated the issue because it made it harder for Brazilian goalkeepers to break through and gain top-level experience. And the fewer high-class goalkeepers there were, the fewer role models there were to inspire young potential goalkeepers, reinforcing the message that goalkeeper was no position for a Brazilian.

There may have been for a long time a general disdain for goal-keepers in England, but in Scotland, the situation was a thousand times worse. Bill Forsyth's 1981 film *Gregory's Girl* made clear the contempt in which the goalkeeper was held, exposing the cultural acceptance of the haplessness that spawned the almost universal mockery of 'Scottish goalkeeping'. Gregory, as played by John Gordon Sinclair, is a gangling misfit, hopelessly besotted with Dorothy, the new girl at school played by Dee Hepburn. She turns out to be a skilful centre-forward, and so to accommodate her in the school team Gregory is shifted – demoted – to play in goal. Although he does get a girl in the end – the quirky Susan, played by Clare Grogan – the footballing message is clear: playing in goal is for the oddballs who can't get into the team as an outfielder.

By the eighties, Scottish goalkeeping was so universally recognised as laughable that large swathes of ITV's Saturday lunchtime show *Saint and Greavsie* were devoted to weak jokes at its expense. Any mistake by a Scottish goalkeeper was seized upon and portrayed not as a one-off aberration but as part of an inevitable trend. When foreign goalkeepers were seen making errors, it was immediately asked if he had Scottish blood. The Scottish goalkeeper sat below only mothers-in-law in the list of subjects guaranteed to raise an easy laugh. So low had he sunk in the general estimation that, indignity of indignities, the Scottish goalkeeper was ranked even lower than the foreign goalkeeper (who, of course, didn't like it up 'im and couldn't/wouldn't catch).

It wasn't always so. James McAulay, Harry Rennie, Ned Doig, John Thomson and Jimmy Cowan were all fine goalkeepers, respected north and south of the border. Everything changed, though, on the afternoon of 15 April 1961 when poor Frank Haffey was widely blamed for Scotland's 9–3 defeat to England at Wembley. Jimmy Greaves, who became Scottish goalkeeping's principal critic, was in the England team that day, scoring a hat-trick. The *Sunday Express* was particularly cruel, printing photographs of all nine goals with Haffey in various poses of distress under the headline 'The man who let through 9 goals'.

His nightmare began in the eighth minute as he dived several seconds too late for a Bobby Robson volley from just outside the box. It was 3–0 at half-time, but Denis Law had had a goal ruled out for offside and, within eight minutes of the restart, goals from Dave Mackay and Davie Wilson had pulled Scotland back into it. A minute later, though, Bryan Douglas, the Blackburn winger, struck a free-kick goalwards – Scotland claimed from the wrong place. However far he took it from where the offence occurred, there was no excuse for Haffey's fumble, allowing the ball to slither through his hands and trickle over the line. From then on, England were remorseless, Scotland hopeless, and the scoreline grew and grew.

Was it Haffey's fault? It was his second – and last – cap, the first having come a year earlier, also against England, when he conceded only a Bobby Charlton penalty in a 1–1 draw, and he was a regular for Celtic, so he had some pedigree even if, at twenty-two, he was young for the role. He wasn't Scotland's first choice, or even their second. Bill Brown of Spurs was injured while Airdrie's Lawrie Leslie was ruled out after requiring eleven stitches in an eye wound sustained against Ayr United the previous week. There were those who would have preferred Ronnie Simpson, by then at Hibernian after a hugely successful spell at Newcastle (and later, of course, the goalkeeper who won the European Cup with Celtic), but Haffey, while he could be erratic, was reasonably well regarded.

He was, though, undoubtedly eccentric. He had a habit of singing to keep himself alert while his side was on the attack – and later emigrated to Australia where he made a living as a cabaret singer – while Stuart Cosgrove notes in *Hampden Babylon* that 'in more than one crunch game when the pressure was off and the ball was in the opposition's half, Frank would climb on to the bar and endear himself to the faithful by pretending to sleep on the woodwork.'

A goalkeeper does not concede nine without some help from the rest of his team or without good play from the opposition. 'Always the English will believe the genius of [Johnny] Haynes won glorious victory,' wrote Donald Saunders, a Welshman, in the *Daily Telegraph*. 'Scotsmen will forever blame Haffey for ignominious defeat.' The *Daily Record* was relatively kind, highlighting Haffey's misery rather than cursing his errors.

'It was a terrible game for me to watch,' said Lawrie Leslie, who had been at Wembley despite his injury. 'I travelled with the team and had to sit through it in the stand. It was a poor game all round, nobody on our side played well and I still feel the result was a travesty. Then, as now, the goalkeepers tended to stick together, so that night I found myself wandering around central London with Frank, trying to cheer him up. But, in truth, we were both suffering and couldn't get back up the road quickly enough.'

The most trenchant criticism came from Hugh McIlvanney in the *Scotsman*. 'It was a night [in West End pubs later] when most preferred to identify themselves with Rangers or Celtic rather than Scotland, although the representatives of Parkhead were not rushing to defend the performance of Haffey. The young goalkeeper's was the biggest personal tragedy on a day when there was no shortage of them. He might have saved at least four of the goals, including the vital first in the eighth minute. After that, he erred with the clumsiness and regularity of a substitute in a second-class works team. Admittedly, the actions of some of the players in front of him were liable to convince him he was, in fact, in such a side.'

The *Herald* picked up that last theme. 'Not for the first time [Dave] Mackay and [Denis] Law must be charged with putting their own whims and fancies before the good of the team,' it said. The scapegoat had some defenders, although he did his reputation little good by seeming unfazed by what had happened. He sang to himself in the bath after the game and, when angry fans hurled bottles, cans and stones at the Scotland team bus, he smiled benignly. Given his gloom with Leslie that night, that might suggest shock, but the following day he posed in front of the clock tower at the Houses of Parliament in illustration of the very popular if not particularly good joke, 'What time is it? Nearly ten past Haffey.' Few in Scotland found it funny and when a man was arrested for throwing a lump of concrete through Salvador Dali's painting *Christ of St John of the Cross* in Kelvingrove art gallery, he supposedly claimed that in his drunken state he'd believed it to be a picture of Haffey hanging from his crossbar.

But it takes more than one poor performance, and more than one provocateur in the style of Greaves, to tarnish the goalkeeping of a whole nation. It doesn't help Scotland's cause, of course, that the goalkeeper who let in the most goals in a single game was a Scot, Andrew Lornie shipping thirty-six as Bon Accord lost to Arbroath in the Scottish Cup in September 1885. Given that he was a right-half who volunteered to cover for an absent colleague, though, and that his side, who played in work trousers with mismatching shirts, had entered the competition by mistake, it's probably harsh to blame him too much. Then again, Aberdeen Rovers conceded thirty-five to Dundee Harps the same day.

That thought perhaps, as Nick Hazlewood suggests in *In the Way!*, lay deep down in football's subconscious a feeling that

Scottish goalkeepers weren't to be trusted. From an English point of view, it was a message that kept on being reinforced. Although the Scots had the better of their early encounters against England and held their own until long after Haffey's nightmare, England racked up big scores against Scotland just often enough to keep that flame of doubt alive.

Joe Crozier, the Brentford goalkeeper, for instance, played just twice for Scotland, both times against England in unofficial war-time internationals. He let in eight at Maine Road in 1943 and a further six at Wembley four months later. Freddie Martin was at fault for at least the first and third goals when England beat Scotland 7–2 at Wembley in April 1955, having conceded seven to Uruguay in the World Cup eight months earlier. After Haffey, the evidence kept mounting for those who wished to cherry-pick examples. Stewart Kennedy had a nightmare against England at Wembley in 1975, not only conceding five but doing so in a manner of blundering frenzy. And in 1984 came a reminder of the dark days of Bon Accord as Stirling Albion beat Selkirk 20–0 in an early round of the Scottish Cup. The match programme described Selkirk's keeper Richard Taylor as 'very brave' but in an interview with the *Stirling Observer* after the match 'he did admit ... that he perhaps had not found his right position yet.'

Understandably, Scottish keepers reacted angrily to the stereotype. Alan Rough, for instance, wrote in his autobiography of meeting Bob Wilson on a trip to Wembley for a Rous Cup game against England in 1986. Wilson was born in Chesterfield, but played twice for Scotland having qualified through his father. He claims always to have felt Scottish, but irritated Rough by bringing up the tribulations of previous Scottish goalkeepers at Wembley and asking him if he was nervous he would suffer something similar. Rough 'let him know that past events were no concern ... It was out of character for me, with ten caps to my name, to ask him how often he had played international football. The truth is I was fed up with hearing about this so-called jinx on goalkeepers. From the time the team arrived in the south, I seemed to hear nothing else and I have to confess that I did not sleep as well as usual on the eve of the game.' That may explain why so many footballing clichés are self-perpetuating, although Rough was blameless in a 2–1 defeat.

A decade later, Jim Leighton was still railing at the cliché – and he had no doubt who was to blame. 'I feel a lot of this rubbish started when Frank Haffey let in nine goals at Wembley,' he said in an interview in *Goal* magazine quoted in *In The Way!* 'We have only really had four regular goalkeepers for the good part of twenty-five years: me, David Harvey, Alan Rough and Andy Goram. Nobody is going to tell me that we are all terrible. Then, of course, we had all that stuff that Saint and Greavsie did. Really horrible sarcasm, that's what their programme was all about. It wasn't funny, especially if it was about you personally. Remember, as well, that at the time England were lucky enough to be able to field two exceptional goalkeepers in Shilton and Clemence. So maybe we suffered by comparison.'

Yet Leighton himself was part of the problem. For almost a decade in Scotland he was an excellent goalkeeper, helping Aberdeen to three league titles, four Scottish Cups and the Cup-Winners' Cup. Even English pundits were impressed. Peter Shilton commented that he had 'solved Scotland's goalkeeping problem', while Brian Clough noted, 'Jim Leighton is a rare bird – a Scottish goalkeeper that can be relied on.'

There was always, though, an air of misfortune about him. He had a gawky spindliness and a confused expression that recalled John Gordon Sinclair and, like Gregory, he ended up in goal by mistake. Leighton was a centre-half who had never played in goal when he turned up at a Paisley and District trial. A coach told him to get between the posts and, too nervous to say no, he dutifully took up the role and found he was good at it. Quite why the coach, whom Leighton never met again, ordered him in goal never became clear; he suggested in his autobiography it was because he was 'big and daft'.

In May 1985 Scotland travelled to Iceland for a World Cup qualifier, knowing a win would leave them needing a point away to Wales in their final match to take, at worst, second in the group, setting up a play-off against an Oceanian team for a place at Mexico 86. Leighton was in fine form but the day before the game he collided with David Speedie in training, landing heavily on his neck. He was plagued with headaches for the rest of the day and could barely put his head on the pillow that night. The next day he decided he was fit enough to play, even though he effectively couldn't turn to his right and was still in a lot of pain. With the game goalless, Iceland won a penalty. He dived left and made a dramatic save; 'I could never have flung myself in the other direction anyway,' he said. Jim Bett scored the only goal of the game with four minutes remaining.

That was a misfortune that led to a positive outcome but Leighton's bad luck struck again in the vital game in Cardiff. Mark Hughes put Wales ahead after thirteen minutes, giving them a lead that, if maintained, would have eliminated Scotland (assuming Spain went on, as they did, to beat Iceland at home in their final game). Ten minutes later, Leighton jumped for a cross with Robbie James, whose hand brushed accidentally across his face, his little finger knocking the contact lens out of the goal-keeper's left eye. Leighton searched frantically in his goalmouth but couldn't find it and spent the rest of the half in a panic. It was bad enough that he found himself no longer able to judge distance but nobody in football, not even his club manager Alex Ferguson, knew he wore lenses.

Ferguson, who was Jock Stein's assistant with the national side, laid into Leighton at half-time, bewildered by his dithering. Realising he'd left his spare pair of lenses in Aberdeen, Leighton was forced to admit what had happened and was substituted by Alan Rough. Stein, Leighton wrote, 'turned ashen-faced before turning away without saying a word'. Leighton never saw him again; Stein collapsed in the dug-out during the second half and never regained consciousness. Leighton himself spent the second half sitting on a hamper in the toilet, unable to watch a game he knew he might be responsible for losing. Only the noise of the crowd told him Davie Cooper had equalised with a late penalty.

Ferguson moved to Manchester United in 1986 and Leighton followed his manager south for £500,000 two years later. And that was when things began to go wrong. His first season at Old Trafford went relatively well, at least from a personal point of view. Although United finished only eleventh, Leighton kept fourteen clean sheets and conceded only thirty-five goals in his thirty-eight games. He was outstanding in a 1–0 defeat at Liverpool on his debut, making one-handed reflex saves to deny John Barnes twice and Jan Mølby, while one parry he made later that season from Aston Villa's Alan McInally, diving up and to his left to deflect away a ferocious volley with an outstretched left hand, was breathtaking.

But the next season he became increasingly erratic. He bafflingly fumbled a Graham Baker cross over his line while under no pressure in a 2–2 draw against Southampton at Old Trafford and endured a miserable game in a 5–1 defeat to Manchester City that brought, he said, 'a sharp escalation' in the abuse he received from the Stretford End. His Scottishness didn't help, predisposing the crowd to distrust him, as Richard Kurt makes clear in *United We Stood*, his fan's account of United between 1975 and 1995. 'One day,' he wrote, 'they'll discover that there's a goalkeeping chromosome and that it's always been hideously deformed north of the border.'

As Leighton became increasingly nervous he suffered stomach ulcers and 'bouts of migraine', his anxiety intensified by the fact that he never got the 'public show of support' from Ferguson he felt would have helped. Ferguson, under intense pressure himself, was having doubts about Leighton. 'In the run-up to the Cup final, he showed incredible nervousness,' Ferguson wrote in *Six Years at United*. 'There was a constant debate between Archie Knox [Ferguson's assistant] and myself about what we should do. We rested him a couple of times and gave Les Sealey a chance.' They considered dropping Leighton after a shaky performance in the FA Cup semi-final against Oldham but stuck by him for the replay in which he played well. Ferguson took Leighton aside and told him he was the best goalkeeper Scotland had had in thirty years, although he later admitted that he was 'very sensitive' and that 'at Aberdeen he had been protected by the success of the team, two tremendous centre-backs in front of him and his own resulting confidence.'

The manager's patience was eventually exhausted after the 3–3 draw against Crystal Palace in the FA Cup final. Leighton was badly at fault for Palace's first, caught in no-man's land as Gary O'Reilly's header from a right-wing Phil Barber free-kick looped in off Gary Pallister. He then misjudged the John Salako cross from which Ian Wright rammed in Palace's third. 'As we were trooping off the field,' Ferguson said, 'I looked at Jim Leighton and I knew he was a beaten man. In the dressing room, he sat with his head between his knees and it was then that I knew he had to be left out of the replay.' Sealey seemed far less cowed by Palace's aggression and aerial approach and United won 1–0.

Leighton was devastated. He removed any evidence of the United part of his career from his house and, in his autobiography, written ten years later, he said he'd never speak to Ferguson again: 'Ferguson's decision shattered me. I knew that, just as surely as he must have done, from the moment he broke the bad news to me, and I cannot find it in my heart to forgive him.' From the Cup final on, he spoke to Ferguson only when called to his office. Ferguson acknowledged that 'people recognised that [decision] as a distasteful illustration of sheer callousness' but remained adamant he had made the correct call: 'I can't apologise for doing something that needed to be done.'

The following season, Leighton played just once, in a League Cup tie against Halifax, and after loan spells with Arsenal and Reading he returned to Scotland with Dundee in 1992 with his reputation in desperate need of rehabilitation. Instead he found further frustration, in the form of what he calls their 'cocky, arrogant' manager Simon Stainrod, who dropped him after a 6–3 defeat to Partick Thistle, saying he couldn't cope with the backpass rule. Leighton's autobiography adopts a basic tone of self-justificatory bluster – as many do – undercut by the frequent admission of blunders. During his dark spell at United, the errors crept in to his performances for the national team. There was a dropped cross in a 3–2 win over Cyprus in a World Cup qualifier in February 1989. That September 'I was at fault with the first goal, failing to beat Srecko Katanec to a cross' as Yugoslavia came from behind to beat Scotland 3–1 and end their long unbeaten run. And then, in the World Cup itself, just a month after the trauma of the FA Cup final, there came the inevitable mistake. Scotland needed a draw against Brazil in their final group game to reach the second round and, with eight minutes remaining, the score was 0–0. But then an Alemão shot bounced just in front of Leighton, he fumbled and Muller tucked in the goal that knocked Scotland out. 'He got up after the ball had gone in and was clearly angry with himself,' Ferguson said. 'Most keepers would have been out of goal like a flash, blaming their defence. He certainly had every right because it was a hard shot after the Brazilians had been allowed to walk through the Scottish defence without a tackle. Jim was too honest.'

Leighton's form returned in lengthy spells with Hibernian and then Aberdeen, but the haplessness on the key occasion never deserted him. In the 1998 World Cup, when the decision to select him led Andy Goram to announce his retirement from international football a fortnight before the tournament, Scotland were again drawing with Brazil when a Leighton parry cannoned off Tom Boyd and back into the net. It wasn't an error, but it was typical of his bad luck. Morocco's second goal in the final group game, though, when Leighton got only a weak hand to Abdeljalil Hadid's shot so it looped up and dropped just under the bar, was a clear mistake. Yet, error-prone as he was, Leighton racked up ninety-one caps – more than any other Scot apart from Kenny Dalglish. All goalkeepers make mistakes of course; Leighton's misfortune is that he made so many in key games and in one season-long spell that came to dominate perceptions of his career.

Even his farewell was tainted by ill luck. In 1999–2000, by which time Leighton was forty-one, Aberdeen reached the Scottish Cup final, in which they faced Rangers. It could have been the perfect end for Leighton, a fifth Scottish Cup and redemption after the trauma of his previous Cup final ten years earlier. But three minutes in, Rod Wallace challenged Leighton for an Andriy Kanchelskis cross and caught him in the face with his knee. After lengthy treatment it became clear Leighton couldn't carry on and, without a goalkeeper on the bench, the forward Robbie Winters had to take over in goal. Aberdeen lost 4–0 and Leighton's career ended with him being stretchered off having broken his jaw.

Had he not been quite so blighted, Leighton might have changed the perception of Scottish goalkeeping; it was Andy Goram, though, who did so. His binge-drinking, unfortunate habit of being spotted with loyalist extremists and generally shambolic lifestyle made him an erratic figure but his abilities were such that Rangers endured his recklessness for seven years; indeed, in 2001 Alex Ferguson, needing goalkeeping cover, took him to Manchester United for a brief loan spell. 'Andy's positional sense was uncanny, and on the rare occasions he came for crosses, he dealt with them well and punched superbly ...' said Walter Smith, his manager at Rangers. 'His timing and reactions were second to none.'

Yet when he moved to Ibrox from Hibs in 1991, Goram was well aware he was being brought in because Chris Woods, the incumbent, was English at a time when Uefa restricted teams to three foreigners in European competition. He was noted as a fine shot-stopper, but at 5'11", he was extremely short for a goalkeeper. 'When you're a goalkeeper under six feet tall, your relationship with your centre-halves is pivotal,' he said.

Goram's positional sense had come from working with the former England keeper Alan Hodgkinson at Oldham. For a fortnight he found the exercises boring and pointless, on one occasion belting the ball away down the plastic pitch at Boundary Park in frustration. 'Quite honestly, I didn't know what he was talking about to begin with,' he said, 'nor did I understand what he was attempting to do through his specialised training, possibly because I thought I could amble along and teach myself rather than bother with the technical side of keeping goal.'

Until then, Goram had basically been stopping shots and working on crosses. He told his manager, Joe Royle, that he didn't want to work with Hodgkinson any more. Royle insisted on a trial period, during which Oldham played Fulham. 'In training Hodgy had been asking me to look at a couple of situations and had advised me on how I should deal with them whenever they came up in an actual game,' Goram said. 'They came up this time. Not once but twice. Two incidents which we had looked at and worked on in training happened in the same ninety minutes and I took Alan's advice and made saves which I might not have made without his guidance.' He found himself taking up positions automatically then querying why he was there before realising Hodgkinson's methods had worked on him subconsciously. 'Basically his credo is simple: he tells you to look at where you were positioned when you lost a goal and then ask yourself if you could have been better placed.'

Goram and Hodgkinson worked together again with Rangers and the Scotland national side. Hodgkinson had also been short for a keeper. 'The movement of your feet and how important that can be to carry you up to that top corner of the goal,' Goram said. 'I can't do that from a standing jump, so it's a question of getting your feet right as you move across the goal and then making your jump.'

At Hibs, Goram's coach was the 6'4" Peter McCloy, once of Motherwell and Rangers. His style of coaching was completely different to Hodgkinson's. He 'wanted most of the work to be done low, around your feet,' Goram said. 'I think it was probably because ... while he could make the high balls from a standing jump quite easily he was worried about the low ones.'

Hodgkinson also worked with Leighton at Manchester United, where the goalkeeper said he was one of the few supportive presences as his form disintegrated, but it was after a disagreement with Hodgkinson, whom he felt was favouring Goram, that Leighton retired from the Scotland national team in 1998.

Goram's unreliability reached its peak in 1994 and very nearly led to his being forced out of Rangers. Struggling with a back injury, he went to Mallorca for a week with his family to recuperate. On his final day there, he met his former Oldham teammates, who were drowning their sorrows after being relegated from the Premier League. He joined them, kept drinking and woke up after lunch the following day, having missed his flight home. His family, he discovered, had flown home without him, leaving him with no bags, no passport and only £40. So he kept drinking. When a Dundee United fan baited him the following night, he lashed out and broke his cheekbone. The Oldham party then went home, leaving Goram alone. Eventually, police tracked him down and handed over his passport, which his wife had left for him at the airport. In disgrace and with his back still troubling him, Goram missed the Scottish Cup final. Ally Maxwell took his place; coming out for a short backpass, he smashed his clearance into Christian Dailly, allowing Craig Brewster to roll in the winner.

It was Maxwell's mistake but Goram seemed more at fault. His ability, though, earned him a reprieve and, for all his binges, he worked extraordinarily hard in training, always looking for an extra edge. He even adopted an all-white kit at the suggestion of Ally McCoist. 'When I'm through one-on-one,' the forward said to him, 'I just look at the goals and nothing else and I just slip it in. But if I see this great fat thing in white coming towards me, I'm going to think twice. It might cost me a split second and I might miss.'

He may have been a tabloid staple and a regular in magazine lists of football's bad boys, but he was also a key presence as Rangers completed their run of nine league title wins in a row. In an Old Firm game at Celtic Park he made one stunning save from a close-range Pierre van Hooijdonk volley, diving to his left and pushing the ball away with his outstretched right hand. 'I saw Van Hooijdonk's body shape, and I knew he had to go to the far post, so I took a chance and hurled myself,' Goram said. 'When I watch it now, the Celtic fans are up in the air when he hits it. They *know* it's a goal and they're up in the air. When they come back down, though, their hands are on their heads before they've even landed.' Walter Smith described it as the greatest save he'd ever seen. It was moments like that that persuaded him to put up with all the problems Goram brought, that led Ferguson to describe Goram as the greatest Scottish goalkeeper there's ever been, that began to make the jokes about Scottish goalkeeping seem very dated.

By the time Sunderland paid £9 million to Hearts in 2007 to make the Scotland international Craig Gordon the most expensive goalkeeper in British history and the second most expensive in the world, it seemed almost natural. *Almost:* 'everyone said the same thing about the old joke about Scottish keepers,' Gordon said. Although persistent injury problems cost him his place in Sunderland's first team, a string of excellent performances after his initial return from a broken arm were largely responsible for the turnaround of form that kept Sunderland in the top flight in 2009–10, while his reflex block to keep out a Zat Knight header against Bolton in December 2010 is probably the greatest save by a Sunderland keeper since Jim Montgomery's fabled double save in the 1973 FA Cup final. But after a second broken arm and the emergence of the young Belgian Simon Mignolet, he was released on a free transfer in 2012, an example of the fragility of a goalkeeper's role.

In fact, with the dependable Allan McGregor replacing Gordon in the Scotland national side, it's probably fair to say that by the time Craig Levein became national manager in 2009, Scotland were stronger in the goalkeeping department than in any other position.

Behind the thick green hedges the shouts mingle with laughter. Nobody answers the door, but it doesn't really matter because if you walk down the side of the car park you can get in through the back gate anyway. The academy run by the former Brazil goalkeeper Zetti in São Paulo is a relaxed place. He sits under a canopy, drinking coffee with Carlos, once his rival to be the national team's keeper. In front of them, on an Astroturf pitch not much bigger than a tennis court, a coach tests the ability of four boys to flop down to their right and stop low shots. They range in age between about seven and ten and the smallest of them, in all honesty, isn't very good, but Zetti doesn't care about that. This is an academy for anybody who wants to make themselves a better goalkeeper, whatever age they are, whatever ability.

'There was a need for this sort of academy,' Zetti said. 'I had the idea of opening a place for kids. Professional clubs don't have the space so I wanted to reach wider. Clubs just want to sign players at fourteen who are already tall and strong and have the basic skills. Here it doesn't matter if a kid is short or fat; I just want to show them how to train without the structures of a professional club. Before this we never had an academy specifically directed to training goalkeepers. We have 250 students. Over the first four years [he opened the academy in 2008] we've had 500 graduates. People asked what I was doing setting up an academy for goalkeepers. But São Paulo is so big that if you have a good idea somebody will want to take you up on it.'

Zetti was born in Porto Feliz in the state of São Paulo in 1965. He started out playing volleyball and basketball 'so I had good coordination with my hands. When I was fifteen I was already playing indoor football at school and I was already standing out. I was really bad as an outfielder, but I was really good in goal. I was already tall. I didn't have a sophisticated technique. I didn't know how to dive, but I was learning.' After playing for a string of local sides he joined Guarani in 1986, before signing for Palmeiras. He moved to São Paulo in 1990 and won back-to-back Libertadores titles with them, amassing seventeen caps before he retired, after stints at Santos and Fluminense, in 2001. He coached a string of clubs in the years that followed – twelve in six years – before setting up his academy.

'I was responding to demand,' he said. 'A lot of parents came to me because I was a famous goalkeeper and asked where their kids could train. Even my boy when he was fourteen decided he wanted to be a goalkeeper. Maybe he wasn't good enough to be a professional but he needed a place to see if he could be a professional.'

Four or five decades ago, you suspect, when Felix was giving hope to opponents called on to face the best side in the world, such an academy would have seemed almost a perversion: goalkeepers were a necessary evil but who, seriously, would want to train to become one? Brazil mocked its own goalkeepers and the rest of the world, delighted to spy a weakness, joined them. Emerson Leão, the goalkeeper in the 1974 and 1978 World Cups, was rather more competent and attracted little scrutiny from the world's media but in 1982, as the old romance returned to Brazil after those more pragmatic tournaments, so too did the questionable goalkeeping. Valdir Peres suffered nothing like the torments Felix had in 1970, but when Andriy Bal's long-range effort bobbled through his arms to give the USSR the lead in their first group game, the world looked on knowingly.

The failings of Brazilian goalkeepers were familiar, and this fitted the pattern: as Brian Glanville put it, Valdir was 'the latest in the line of inept Brazilian keepers'. Perhaps that was unfair, a case of a player's poor form being assumed to fit a general principle. Certainly Paulo Guilherne is inclined to be sympathetic. 'Valdir Peres played some great games and made some very good saves,' he insisted. 'In 1981 he saved two penalties from Paul Breitner in a friendly [against West Germany]. He was very good before the World Cup. Maybe a loss of confidence made him make that mistake in the first match against the USSR.'

Carlos had a good World Cup in 1986, conceding only one goal in his five games and that certainly not attributable to an error. He was remembered, though, for a cynical but unpunished foul on France's Bruno Bellone in extra-time in the quarter-final and then being the hapless stooge of instant karma in the shoot-out as Bellone's penalty hit the post, bounced back, hit him on the back of the head and trickled over the line.

It was at the next World Cup that opinions began to change. The breakthrough came with Taffarel, although if Nielsen, who coached him with the national team between 1989 and 1994, is to be believed, the groundwork for Taffarel's emergence began much earlier. Nielsen had been a gifted goalkeeper himself, playing for Fluminense, Flamengo, Botafogo and Vasco da Gama as well as Brazil's Olympic side in 1972. 'Many, many kids come to be a goalkeeper now,' he said. 'It's changed a lot. Before, no. Before, to be a goalkeeper was very, very difficult because nobody like to play as a goalkeeper. Everybody wanted to play like Pelé or Garrincha. I remember our goalkeeper Gilmar but he was a long time ago and kids didn't care for him. All kids wanted to play at the front, not at the back. I was very bad with my feet. My brothers played very well, so my father was very smart and told me to go in goal. Goalkeeping was for people who couldn't play with their feet.'

When Nielsen emerged, goalkeeping coaching was in its infancy and at most clubs the keeper trained with the rest of the squad, doing little other than having shots pinged at him. 'The mentality has changed,' Nielsen said. 'More Brazilians want to be goalkeepers than thirty or forty years ago. In Brazil thirty years ago, our goalkeepers were very, very bad. All the foreign press spoke badly about our goalkeepers. It began in 1970 with the World Cup in Mexico. Everybody spoke badly about Felix that he was a very bad goalkeeper. At that time we had a lot of foreign goalkeepers in the league – from Uruguay, Argentina, Paraguay, Colombia – Andrade, Fillol, Mazurkiewicz … Our goalkeepers were not in good shape so we had to change.'

Brazilian football generally had to change. Tim Vickery has argued convincingly that while British football aped the factory production line or the pit, Brazilian football, in its earliest days, became a mechanism for subverting social hierarchies. In Britain, Vickery wrote in Issue Six of The Blizzard, 'physical strength and reliability' were valued while 'the gifted individual has often been mistrusted, seen as a wayward figure, worryingly undependable.'

There was no industrial revolution in Brazil and the attempts of Getúlio Vargas, the president from 1930 to 1945 and again from 1951 to 1954, to develop the country while preserving the existing social structure left a semi-feudal limbo in which rich and poor were treated almost as different species. In football, though, by performing a trick that dumps an opponent on the floor, the pawn could become a king. Brazilian crowds still roar when they see a defender humiliated.

That prioritising of cunning – the delight in an individual outwitting somebody higher up the social scale – lies at the heart not only of Brazilian football, but perhaps Brazilian culture in general, as Da Matta lays out in his theory of jeitinho. Vickery sees that need to get one over an individual opponent springing from a general problem in Brazilian society with self-esteem. Eric Hobsbawm once described Brazil as 'the world champion of economic inequality'; when life appears so stratified the appeal of football as a means of challenging the social order is obvious. The corollary, though, is that in such circumstances, the importance of victory is inflated. 'Of course, winning is important everywhere,' Vickery wrote. 'But here it reaches new heights. I have heard the same line time and time again from many in the Brazilian game. Deep down, they say, Brazilians don't really like football. They like victories.'

That is borne out by attendance figures for the Brazilian league, which can fluctuate dramatically according to how well a club is doing, or by the extraordinary outpouring of grief and recrimination after the defeat to Uruguay that cost Brazil the 1950 World Cup. The negative reaction to that defeat was the scapegoating of Barbosa; more positively, it contributed to the development of the back four, which helped Brazil to the 1958, 1962 and 1970 World Cups, providing enough defensive cover for the individuals to play. If the systematised approach with which England won the World Cup in 1966 provoked disquiet, the glories of 1970 quelled the doubts. But the 1970 World Cup was played in the heat and altitude of Mexico, where sustained pressing was all but impossible. Come 1974 in a wet West Germany, systematised pressing returned to crush Brazil.

Brazil needed to beat the Dutch in their final second-phase group game to reach the final. They lost 2–0, had Luis Perreira sent off and found their basic principles shattered. Brazil had always relied on a deep-lying midfielder to control the game – Dida in 1958 and 1962, Gérson in 1970. In 1974 Roberto Rivellino occupied the role. He was supposed to stroll around in front of the defence initiating attacks but every time he got the ball he found a phalanx of white shirts closing him down. Most observers were taken by the attacking possibilities of Total Football, the way that players interchanged; this was the other side of it, the hard pressing that stifled opponents.

Northern European football, generally, was on the rise. The game in the Netherlands and West Germany had gone professional in the previous decade. A year after England's World Cup win, Celtic had won the European Cup, beginning a northern European domination of the competition that lasted until 1985 and the ban on English clubs that followed the tragedy at Heysel. As early as April 1963, Brazil had had warning of what was to come, losing 5–1 to Belgium and 1–0 to the Netherlands as part of a European tour. Those results were shrugged off; a few days before leaving they'd hammered Argentina 4–1 in the Maracanã. Even before beating Brazil at the 1974 World Cup, though, the Dutch had put four past both Uruguay and Argentina earlier in the tournament. The lesson could not be ignored: this was the future and the traditional South American game was outmoded.

Argentinian and Brazilian football met the challenge in very different ways and, as Vickery says, the way they responded was conditioned by the relationship between the game and the military dictatorships that ruled each country in the mid-seventies. Juan Perón, having returned to power in Argentina in 1973, died a year later, and was succeeded by his wife, Isabel, who bore her husband's name but shared little of his political acumen. Even he had struggled to control the extreme elements of his own support, as was seen in the Ezeiza massacre in June 1973. Then, as a crowd of around two million waited at the airport to welcome Perón on his return from exile, far-right extremists hidden on the speaking platform shot and killed at least thirteen members of the leftist Peronist Youth. With inflation rocketing as the economy contracted, the country was so divided as to be all but ungovernable, which led to the military coup of 1976. Dissent was ruthlessly suppressed, but as the junta pursued its dirty war, torturing and murdering opponents, football turned away from the pragmatism of the sixties to the bohemian romanticism of César Luis Menotti.

Menotti didn't just define a way of playing; he defined a way of thinking about the game. For Argentinians, football is what Vickery terms 'a cultural and philosophical manifestation'. The game there breeds coaches who view football as a way of living out their ideals; football is more driven by theory and principle in Argentina than anywhere else in the world. Brazil, by contrast, reacted to the dictatorship by lurching into pragmatism. Perhaps it was winning for the government, perhaps it was winning for people oppressed by the government, but it wasn't defining itself against the government; it was defining itself by victory and, broadly speaking, developed in harmony with the government.

The regime, which had been so desperate for the propaganda coup of a third World Cup win that it had arranged for the players to go on a NASA training course before the finals in Mexico in 1970, became increasingly involved in football. Cláudio Coutinho, a captain of artillery, was the fitness coach at that tournament and he went on to be technical director in 1974 and then head coach in 1978. Even the establishment of a national championship in 1971 was explicitly part of the government's attempts to create a sense of unity across the whole nation.

Military rule came to an end in 1985 – although the first truly civilian election wasn't held until four years later – and the twenty-one years of army control are now generally remembered as having been an appalling period in which the government tortured and murdered to cling to power in the face of widespread opposition. It's true there were student uprisings in the late sixties, including the March of the 100,000 in Rio de Janeiro in 1968, but there were far bigger demonstrations across the country in support of the regime, which was perceived by many as the quickest way to implement neoliberal economic reforms. The historian David Aarão Reis even dismisses the term 'military dictatorship', suggesting that as the coup against João Goulart was supported by 'business, political and religious leaders, entities of civil society such as the lawyers' organisation and the council of bishops, the right-wing in general', a more accurate term is 'civil-military dictatorship'. As the art historian Claudia Calirman argues, they were 'seeking security and wary of the spread of Communism, social reforms, and the increasing popular movements'. Although human rights abuses eventually led the Church to withdraw support and to increasing opposition to the junta, as the historian Glenda Mezarobba wrote, 'claims surrounding the obligations of the democratic State or the rights of the victims of the military regime, [were] issues that did not mobilise – or, it would seem, even interest – the majority of Brazilians.' For many, the military government was a distasteful but necessary solution to a crisis.

Most intriguing in terms of the dictatorship's impact on football is the view of the economist Celso Furtado. He was a committed opponent of the regime and described it as 'military-technocratic', the result of an alliance between the armed forces and middle-class technical specialists. The term 'technocrat' was used almost immediately after the coup, initially to describe the financial officials the military placed in charge of the economy. It had a justificatory sense: never mind democracy, these people were the experts and so should be trusted. To a large degree (certainly from the right-wing perspective of the regime) the economic technocrats did succeed: inflation came down in the seventies and there were huge benefits for skilled workers, although there was mass unemployment among the unskilled. A credit squeeze led by the USA in 1981 brought an end to the boom but infant mortality dropped, literacy rates rose, as did the number of homes with indoor plumbing and with access to radio and TV, while life expectancy went up from fifty-five to sixty-six between 1960 and 1988.

The technocrats, the number-crunchers with their clipboards, also had their impact on football. The stereotype of Brazilian football as a happy-go-lucky game made up on the spot by playboys who had just wandered off the beach has always been misleading. It may have had a swagger and a love of the individual but even as early as 1958 the national side was backed up by an array of sports staff including a dentist and a sports psychologist. In the seventies, as systematised football became accepted as the only way to play and the coaching instincts of the former player became less respected, the technocrats took over.

'Today football is made by technocrats, but also by commerce and marketing,' said Leão. 'It's not about romance. What is a technocrat? Somebody who learned from a teacher in college or from a computer and not from the field. Now I'm going to tell

you the Brazilian disaster: in the junior section of many professional teams the coaches are one hundred per cent technocrats.
The president of the team believes in those people, because they
come and present a wonderful training plan.'

Coutinho's appointment for the 1978 World Cup was part
of that process. He explicitly tried to ape the Dutch with his
theory of 'polyvalency' – essentially a variant of Total Football.
The failure of that model – Brazil finished third and the success
of Argentina with something that resembled the old-style football – led to a reversion under Telê Santana at the 1982 and 1986
World Cups but, by 1990, under Sebastião Lazaroni the model
was a German-style sweeper system. The technocrats lived by
their statistics. Murici Sant'anna, one of the country's leading
physical preparation specialists, found that the distance covered by players in games doubled between the mid-seventies
and the mid-nineties and so concluded that if midfield elaboration had been overrun by the Dutch in 1974, two decades later
there was no hope of returning to the freedom and creativity
of 1958–70. He decided that not only did Brazilian players have
to match European players physically but that with time on the
ball diminished and physical contact increased, there was no
point trying to elaborate as the great Brazilian sides had; the
fewer passes there were, the numbers appeared to show, the
more chance there was on an attack yielding a goal. Creative
central midfielders such as Didi, Gérson and Toninho Cerezo
were replaced by tacklers and battlers such as Dunga, Edmilson
and Felipe Melo.

It worked – up to a point. Brazil reached three successive
World Cup finals between 1994 and 2002, but they never captured the imagination of the world – or indeed their own fans
– as the earlier incarnations had. Brazilian football, Zizinho
wrote in his autobiography in 1985, 'has given the central midfielder, the man who has seventy per cent of his team's possession in his hands, the specific function of destroying, when it
should be to set up the play'. Pragmatists may regard that as
an unavoidable evil but surely even they would accept that
with the rise of the technocrats a certain magic has been lost

from Brazilian football over the past four decades. Where it has gained immeasurably from the involvement of more rigorous coaching, though, is the goalkeeping.

'In 1970 we started goalkeeper coaching with Raul Carlesso,' said Nielsen. Carlesso was a teacher of physical education in the army. With the Palmeiras goalkeeper Valdir de Moraes, he sourced from Yugoslavia a series of videos about training goalkeepers and began using them at the 1970 World Cup in Mexico. He later wrote a book outlining the twenty-five attributes he believed were necessary to be a good goalkeeper. 'If you'd had all of them you'd have been superman,' said Guilherne.

'I think Carlesso was very important in our history,' said Nielsen. 'He was my coach with the national team, but his methods of training were very slow. He wasn't the first goalkeeping coach, but he was the best. He was from the army. He hadn't been a goalkeeper himself, but he had good observations about goalkeeping. Before it had just been shooting in training. He started to change things. He worked on the fundamentals.'

Valdir Peres was also starting out in the early seventies. He was born in Garça in the state of São Paulo in 1951 and started playing for his local side from the age of sixteen. 'The coach took goalkeeping training,' he recalled. 'It was just shooting, shooting, shooting. Other players practised passing and crossing and heading but we goalkeepers got nothing on handling or anything like that.' He didn't even wear gloves until he moved to Ponte Preta in 1970.

'My coach there wasn't a goalkeeping coach,' he said, 'but he would send us to the military school in Rio to get all the exercises they had stipulated for goalkeepers. That's how I found out what the national team was doing.' He moved on to São Paulo in 1973 and within six months had been called up to the full national squad, although he was a reserve at the 1974 World Cup and didn't actually make his debut until the following year. 'They sent us to the military school for training,' he said. 'Everything was run by the military at that time.'

The head goalkeeping coach there was Valdir de Moraes. He was born in Porto Alegre in 1931 and joined Renner, a small provincial team, in 1947, starting to play with the first team when he was eighteen. In 1954 Renner upset the usual favourites, Gremio and Internacional, passing undefeated through the whole season to win the state championship. That raised the players' profiles, but it wasn't till 1957 that Valdir left Porto Alegre for São Paulo. A year later, he started playing for the first team of Palmeiras, where he was a regular for ten years. 'For the whole of my career,' he said, 'the only training was shooting, players kicking at the goal but no more than that. As I was approaching the end of my career, I started to think about the possibility of doing a specific kind of training. I felt the need not just to play but to watch other goalkeepers. So, in that last year of my career I played but I also trained together with the other goalkeepers. I started doing what I intended to do afterwards.'

He retired in 1968 and began work in a hunting and fishing store he owned in São Paulo. Every day, the Palmeiras coach Osvaldo Brandão, the man who had persuaded Valdir to leave Porto Alegre, came for a chat. Eventually, he asked him to start work as his assistant. Valdir agreed, on condition he could work with the goalkeepers. 'I saw the mistakes of Brazilian goalkeepers and of others because I travelled the world,' he said. 'I heard criticisms about our goalkeepers that elsewhere were expressed in a different way. Elsewhere they accepted goalkeepers made mistakes and mistakes were part of the game. And I also felt there was a need for a more specific and focused kind of training.'

It was in 1970 that Valdir began working as a coach.

I was heavily criticised at the time. "Why is it necessary to have specific training for goalkeepers?" people asked. But I believed and fought for it, and Senhor Brandão kept supporting me until it took off and worked. Then it was easier. Once everything fell into place, the goalkeepers themselves started to spread the word about the work we were doing because they felt it was helping them.

'Today, goalkeepers start from the junior categories with this kind of training, so they take it for granted. But back then you could see the interest of goalkeepers in working at something other than shots on goal – at technical training, the repeated training of movements, for example. It was helping them. And I always told the goalkeepers with whom I worked, I don't care about today, the day of the game, if he made a mistake or something like that. I am worried about tomorrow – I don't know how you are going to come to the next training session after a game in which you had an unhappy moment or were the best player on the pitch. If the former, you're going to come unhappy and beaten. I will work on the psychological aspect. The session after a game, I would work more on the psychological aspect than the technical or physical. To know what happened, to study that also, because it's not only about kicking the ball.

Leão saw the attitude change over the course of his career. 'When I began as a goalkeeper you didn't have specific coaching,' he said. 'But then goalkeeping coaching began, maybe not in a sophisticated way, but something. Before that, goalkeepers were self-taught.'

That didn't mean they were necessarily bad and the perception that even the best Brazilian goalkeepers were inferior clearly irritates him. 'They said that the Brazilian goalkeeper couldn't come out of his goal to take crosses, that he was always stuck on his line because Brazilian forwards went straight for the goal so would take a shot rather than crossing,' Leão said. The theory actually makes some sense, but just because few Brazilian goalkeepers were called upon to leave their line didn't mean that none of them were any good at it.

'When we went to West Germany in 1974 somebody bought a film of the great goalkeepers to learn their techniques, the techniques of European goalkeepers, and specifically the technique of dealing with crosses,' Leão said. That in itself was indicative of the changing mindset. When Osvaldo Zubeldía set about revolutionising the Argentinian side Estudiantes in the sixties, he used videos from the USSR in his coaching. In preparation for both the 1970 and 1974 World Cups, Brazil similarly, in looking for instruction, were forced to turn to a European resource.

What they found on the tape, though, surprised them. 'After dinner one night,' Leão said, 'we put on the video to watch. We got a big shock: seventy per cent of the film was me. In 1973 we'd played a friendly game against Germany which we won 1–0. Gerd Müller was the centre-forward. The German team always tried to play the ball in to him, so I would come out to try to stop it getting to Müller. He wasn't very big but he was a great finisher, so I tried to get there first. So the movie was full of me playing against Müller. That proved the Brazilian concept was wrong. We thought the Brazilian goalkeeper wasn't so good.'

Leão himself did much to change the perception of the keeper. It wasn't just that he was clearly a far better player than Felix, the man he succeeded in the Brazil goal, it was that he understood how to promote himself and had the hardness of personality and the ambition to overcome the doubters. 'In my day,' he remembered, 'they always said goalkeepers should pass unnoticed. Other players cost more money. But I put my name on my shirt. I would even wear hoops to be noticed more. They said a goalkeeper should be discreet, that if the forward couldn't see you it was easier to make saves from them. I was more aggressive, really went to the ball.'

It wasn't just on the pitch. He sold shirts with 'Leão' printed across the chest and advertised chicken and underwear. 'I was the first goalkeeper to market myself as a brand,' he said and, in doing so, he added to the sense that goalkeepers were somehow acceptable, not just joke figures. 'Leão was very important,' said Guilherne. 'He tried to get good salaries for goalkeepers, to make it a good job that was well-paid. He became president of the players union. He promoted his image. He was intelligent.'

Nielsen took the principles laid down by Carlesso and applied them in his own coaching career. 'I used a lot of the fundamentals: repetition, repetition, repetition,' he said. 'If you have good fundamentals you have confidence. You have to make it automatic. It's like driving a car or typing. At first it's difficult but after a year you don't even think about it.' Although he speaks of the 'physical, technical and tactical' aspects of goal-keeping, perhaps his greatest contribution was on the psychological side.

He began working with Taffarel in 1989 when the goalkeeper was twenty-three. Born in Santa Rosa in Rio Grande do Sul in 1966, Taffarel became the most celebrated Brazilian goalkeeper since Gilmar. 'For me it's a huge honour to know I kept goal for Brazil for ten years playing in a position in which only one can play,' he said. 'Being a goalkeeper is like that: you either play or you don't. You have to be the man to be the goalkeeper and I can say without any false modesty that I was a man born for it. I was born to play in goal.'

They're stirring words, the insistence on the 'manliness' of goalkeeping presumably a riposte to those who saw it as a position for the 'mad or queer'. But actually, the man who was born to play in goal was Claudio, which was how Taffarel was known until he had a shocker in a Gaucho youth championship final against Brasil de Pelotas in March 1984. He decided from then on that he would rather be known as Taffarel. He made his debut for Internacional's senior side in October 1985 and within a couple of years had established himself as first choice, winning the Bola de Ouro as the best player in the championship in 1988. He made his international debut the same year, playing all four matches as Brazil saw off Australia, Saudi Arabia and Argentina to win the Australian Bicentenary Cup.

Taffarel was also a regular in the Brazil Olympic side that took silver in Seoul that year, establishing his reputation as a penalty specialist. In the semi-final victory over West Germany, he saved one in regulation play and then a further two in the shoot-out. 'That was the best feeling I ever felt in football,' he said. 'I never felt myself shake like that. The entire stadium was behind me. I could feel the vibrations of all the spectators. A football player needs to learn how to play with happy moments and sad moments. I only started to learn it at that moment.' Brazil, though, lost 2–1 to the USSR in the final.

'He was only 1.80m [5'11"] tall which is short for a goalkeeper,' Nielsen said.

Taffarel started playing volleyball and so he was good at jumping, had good reactions. He was a very good goalkeeper but he was in very bad physical condition. He didn't have the patience or the stamina to keep training. He would come up panting and ask to stop saying he couldn't do more. So slowly, step by step we did drills so he became stronger and quicker. He was very technical.

'In '89 he was the first-choice goalkeeper for the national team and everybody said they had confidence in him. But after a season, when we got to Italy and were preparing for the World Cup, Taffarel's level went down. He was especially emotional. I called him. "Come here. Sit here please." I said, "You are now very bad. You don't need more strength. You just need to sort out your emotions." He was worried. He was very young; it was normal. When the competition came near, he was nervous because all the press came about his head. I said, "You're coming to play but only with your body. Your spirit has stayed away. Why? Are you afraid about the tournament?" He said he was. I told him all the people were [afraid], that it was normal to feel nervous inside, not to sleep well. I said, "If you need to stay in the rest room, no problem. We don't need you training today."

'I took the responsibility. I talked to [the coach Sebastian] Lazaroni. I said to Taffarel that we didn't need him training unless he brought everything, brought his spirit. He said, "Okay." I said, "Okay." He went to the rest-room.

'The next day he comes ... phewww ... smart, smart, quick. "Come here." He comes. "Are you all complete?" "Sure, sure."

'Before the first game, against Sweden we went to look at the pitch one day before. I said to Taffarel, "Tomorrow you start the competition here." I said, "You are a good goalkeeper and you are playing very well. I'm sure you'll play very well tomorrow because now you are prepared for the start of the competition. After the game tomorrow, I'll give you a hug."

'And he played so well in the tournament he was signed by Parma. He was the first goalkeeper from Brazil to play abroad. He was only the fifth foreign goalkeeper to play in Italy.

Psychologically, that was a huge moment. 'Brazil started giving importance to the goalkeeper with Taffarel – the fact he went abroad and played in two World Cups and was a fantastic guy,' Zetti said. For Guilherne, it was Taffarel who 'opened the market for other Brazilian goalkeepers'; suddenly European clubs began to treat Brazilian goalkeepers with respect, began to sign them. 'After Taffarel,' he said, 'it was possible for a goal-keeper to be a hero, as an idol. Kids started wanting to be a goal-keeper. I think Taffarel was the turning point.'

'Before Taffarel, there was no credibility for Brazilian goal-keepers,' said Valdir de Moraes. 'Now we have goalkeepers all around the world, hundreds of them. I myself went to train goalkeepers in Saudi Arabia. The biggest thing for us now, the thing that shows the advance, is that you have a lot of goalkeep-ers going abroad to play.'

Even Leão, who is sceptical about Taffarel's abilities having coached him at Atletico Mineiro, acknowledges his influence. 'Please don't take Taffarel as the great example of a Brazilian goalkeeper,' he said. 'Why did he play so much for the national team? He was a good – not an excellent but a good – goalkeeper. He was fortunate in the World Cup with penalties and then he was undroppable. And he played at a time when Brazil was look-ing for a goalkeeper.'

The trade route was opened and Taffarel was followed to Italy by the likes of Dida, Doni and Júlio César. 'Brazilian goalkeep-ers were always there,' Júlio César said. 'It's just that people in Europe didn't notice and maybe in part it was down to Taffarel. He certainly was my hero.'

Arguably the best Brazilian goalkeeper after Taffarel, though, never played in Europe. Marcos was eighteen when he joined Palmeiras in 1992. He retired twenty years later never having played for another club. He didn't even become the regular number one until 1999, when an injury to Velloso gave him his chance. He starred in a penalty shoot-out in the quarter-final of the Copa Libertadores as Palmeiras beat their São Paulo rivals Corinthians, earning the nickname São Marcos. Palmeiras went on to overcome River Plate in the semi-final and Deportivo Cali, also on penalties, in the final, while Marcos was named player of the tournament, goalkeeper of the tournament and man of the match in the final. They won another penalty shoot-out against Corinthians in the semi-final the following year before being beaten on penalties by Boca Juniors in the final.

He then had a spectacular World Cup, keeping four clean sheets as Brazil won the tournament in Japan and South Korea. That prompted interest from Arsenal but, having reached London, he decided he couldn't leave Palmeiras. He eventually retired aged thirty-eight, having played 532 games for them in the Brasileirão.

By then the idea that Brazil might produce good goalkeepers sought after by European clubs no longer seemed outlandish. If anything, the problem was that Brazilian goalkeepers had become too popular. 'This had a positive side but also a negative side for Brazil,' said Zetti. 'Goalkeepers started to go abroad – usually foreign clubs signed only forwards and attacking mid-fielders. This showed we also had great goalkeepers. But on the negative side we went ten years in Brazil without a great goal-keeper. Over time we lost reference. So you had nobody chal-lenging Júlio César for the national team.' Both Zetti and Leão were seriously concerned about the future with Internazionale's Júlio César, who for a time was probably the best goalkeeper in the world – his performance in a World Cup qualifier away to Ecuador in 2007, when he just about single-handedly earned Brazil a 1–1 draw, for instance, was outstanding – clearly past his peak.

For two decades or more, Brazilian goalkeeping has been at least the equal of that of other major nations, but it remains a particu-lar style of goalkeeping, the reasons for which lie in the path the Brazilian game took half a century ago. There was a time when Brazil led the world in tactical terms. Other nations had been experimenting with a back four through the fifties, but it was Brazil who got it right, and the 4-2-4 formation with which they won the World Cup in 1958 led to a period of frantic experimen-tation elsewhere as the old certainties were shown to be flawed and radical possibilities were opened up. Over the next decade, the old-school W-M was all but phased out as teams all over the world – at the highest level at least – adopted a back four. There were two basic ways of structuring that: a team could play with a *libero*, one player sweeping behind three or occasionally four defenders, at least two of whom had man-marking duties; or it could employ a flat back four that pushed high up the pitch, using an offside trap to prevent players getting behind it. In the latter approach, which dominated the thinking in northern Europe, it was essential to have a goalkeeper who was prepared to leave his box and operate as a sweeper-keeper.

In Brazil, though, the tendency was for defences to sit deep. When the defender Marinho Peres, who had captained Brazil at the 1974 World Cup, joined Barcelona from Santos, he was bewildered by how high a line he was asked to play by the coach Rinus Michels, the great pioneer of Total Football and the Netherlands coach at that World Cup. 'Michels wanted the centre-backs to push out to make the offside line,' he explained. 'In Brazil this was known as the donkey line: people thought it was stupid. The theory was that if you passed one defender, you passed all the others.' This had been a constant in Brazilian football since the 1919 Copa América, when they'd split their full-back pairing so one went to the ball and the other covered behind, and was maintained in the 4-2-4 in which one of the central defenders, the *quarto zagueiro* (fourth defender) played almost as a holding midfielder, coming out to meet the attack as the other centre-back mopped up behind him.

'What [the Netherlands and Barcelona captain Johan] Cruyff said to me was that Holland could not play Brazilians or Argentinians, who were very skilful, on a huge pitch,' Marinho went on. 'The Dutch players wanted to reduce the space and put everybody in a thin band. The whole logic of the offside trap comes from squeezing the game. This was a brand new thing for me. In Brazil, people thought you could chip the ball over and somebody could run through and beat the offside trap, but it's not like that because you don't have time.'

Brazil, though, remained distrustful of pressing and looking for offsides and that had a knock-on effect for their goalkeepers. With the game stretched and defences generally sitting deep, there was rarely any need for goalkeepers to act as sweepers. 'Goalkeepers in Brazil are not used to playing outside their box,' said Nielsen. 'It's difficult for them. Elsewhere they play more outside the box.' This was something that went beyond the supposed technical deficiencies with crosses of which Leão spoke. When Brazilian goalkeepers have gone overseas, the one country in which they have been consistently successful is Italy – where the tendency has been to play with a *libero* and a deep-lying defence. The problems Júlio César had at Internazionale at the start of 2011–12 were surely in part down to the high line imposed by their new coach Gian Piero Gasperini (not that he was the only Inter player to struggle).

Not even Italian defences are as deep-lying as those in Brazil, though. Nielsen remembers Taffarel playing for Brazil in a friendly against England at Wembley and against Italy in Milan in 1992 after two years at Parma. 'He kept coming off his line for crosses,' he said, standing up from the table and showing exactly what he meant by designating two trees as goalposts and advancing five or six yards in front of them. 'Standing leaving a big space. I asked why and he said that in Europe players don't shoot at goal if you leave space at the near post.' Taffarel was a keeper who did his homework. In that game against England he saved a penalty, calmly standing still and catching the ball with ridiculous ease as Gary Lineker, looking for a forty-ninth international goal that would have equalled Bobby Charlton's England record, dinked the ball down the middle. 'It was a great moment for me, to save a penalty at Wembley,' Taffarel said. 'I'd seen him do that in some game before so I decided not to dive.'

Nielsen cited a goal Jorginho scored past Germany's Bodo Illgner in a friendly in Porto Alegre in 1993 and Maicon's against North Korea at the 2010 World Cup as examples of Brazilian players being quick to exploit that sort of gap. He even suggested the goal Ronaldinho scored past David Seaman at the 2002 World Cup, curving a free-kick over his head as he ventured off his line in anticipation of a cross, as another example, repeating the well-known anecdote of Cafu, the Brazil right-back, who had been in the Real Zaragoza side when Nayim beat Seaman with a preposterous lob from the halfway line to win the 1995 Cup-Winners' Cup, telling Ronaldinho to look out for Seaman's advance. It may be true, but Seaman came no more than four yards off his line; while there's no doubt he could be slightly flat-footed, it's hard to blame him in this instance; hard too to believe Ronaldinho could be so confident of hitting such a small gap – if he was that accurate, why not just aim for the much larger space at the near post? The probability remains, whatever Ronaldinho may say, that it was actually a mishit cross.

Still, the very fact that story has some credibility in Brazil suggests just how predisposed their goalkeepers are to staying on their line. Even Ubaldo Fillol, noted in Argentina as a goalkeeper who stayed on his line, a counterpart to Hugo Gatti, was considered crazily adventurous in Brazil in his one season at Flamengo. 'Fillol was a good goalkeeper in Argentina,' Nielsen said, 'but not in Brazil. He was very bad because he was caught off his line all the time. There was a very big expectation because he was a World Cup-winning goalkeeper, but he was awful.'

The willingness to criticise such an august name, albeit one who was thirty-four by the time he arrived in Brazil in 1984, was itself perhaps indicative of growing Brazilian self-confidence. Over the two decades or so that followed, no nation had such a clearly defined style of goalkeeping as Brazil; the problem now is to sustain it. That is their worry. Scotland's goalkeepers have no such obvious stylistic quirk; their misfortune is that the respect they have earned of late has arrived just as the Scottish game as a whole is in a desperate slump.

6: THE PATIENT ENGLISH

Peter Shilton, stretching up and to his left, reached out with his right hand. Peter Nogly's powerfully struck shot had swerved violently in mid-air, but Shilton, somehow, had read it and reacted. As his right hand arced across, it intercepted the ball at a point at which his body, stretching slightly backwards, was approaching the horizontal, four or five feet off the ground, and turned it away. Nottingham Forest survived again. 'Goalkeepers are normally expected to save shots from that distance,' Shilton said in his 1982 book *The Magnificent Obsession*, 'but this was an out-of-this-world shot.' He had, he explained, reacted slightly late, unsighted by the players in front of him. 'The other problem,' he went on, 'was that the shot started going to my right and then went to my left. I couldn't get into position quickly enough to save it with my left hand, so I had to bring my other arm across, while in mid-air, to give myself extra momentum and push the ball away with my right.'

It seems astonishing to hear something that happened so rapidly analysed in such a way, but this, surely, is an example of time slowing down for somebody who was absolutely focused and at the top of his game – an example of the former Ajax general manager David Endt's view that 'the seconds of the greats last longer than those of normal people.' (That said, recent theories developing and refining the pioneering work of Benjamin Libet, a researcher into neural activity, suggests the sensation of time slowing down is the brain's attempt to explain what the body is doing by instinct while offering the ego the comforting thought that it remains in control.)

That save from Nogly was the finest save of many as

Nottingham Forest beat Hamburg 1–0 in Madrid to win the European Cup in 1980. If it wasn't Shilton's finest game – and he had many fine games – it was certainly his best performance in such a high-profile match. It had been a complete display of goalkeeping. He'd made reaction stops and well-judged dives. He'd shouted and gesticulated constantly, organising a defence that remained magnificently resolute in the face of sustained pressure. He'd come off his line to cut out through-balls and dominated his area. And when technically orthodox goalkeeping wasn't possible, he'd improvised superbly, as when he'd thrown himself forwards into a crowded box, fists stretched out with his body parallel to the ground four feet below, to punch a Horst Hrubesch flick away from Jürgen Milewski.

Whether he was actually, as many claimed, the best in the world, it's impossible to say, but Forest wouldn't have swapped him for anybody; he was absolutely the right goalkeeper for that team. Given that he had succeeded Gordon Banks, and was still only sharing the England shirt with Ray Clemence – with the likes of Joe Corrigan and Jimmy Rimmer providing solid back-up – there was every reason for England to be proud of its goalkeeping heritage. 'Some countries,' Shilton later wrote in his autobiography, 'are known for producing quality things, Switzerland its watches, Italy its cars. British football was always renowned for the general quality of its goalkeepers.' Actually, most major football nations seem to think they have a unique tradition of goalkeeping and it would perhaps be truer to say that England consistently produced good goalkeepers of the sort it admired. Which is to say, goalkeepers who were safe and reliable and, as though by right of birth, escaped that terrible foreign habit of flapping at crosses.

There was something paradoxical in the English attitude. On the one hand, the goalkeeper was regarded less as an enigmatic loner than as a freak, somebody both untrustworthy and slightly pitiable. Yet at the same time, a certain kind of goalkeeper seemed to represent the very best of Englishness: courageous, unfussy and unflappable – and if he was perhaps a little weird, well, where was the harm in that?

Leigh Richmond Roose and William Foulke may have been extroverts, but they were exceptions and British football soon settled to a more cautious, understated style. In *The Goalkeeper's History of Britain*, his eccentric but engaging attempt to trace the changing culture of the country through its goalkeepers, Peter Chapman recalls watching football on television for the first time in 1956, a friendly between England and Germany. Reg Matthews, then Coventry's keeper, dived to his left, caught the ball, sprang up and bounced it to the edge of his box. 'He looked concerned to rid himself of the ball as quickly as possible and, with it, all evidence of his save,' Chapman wrote. 'He seemed embarrassed by the whole affair, guilty for having attracted attention to himself.'

Coventry at the time were in the Third Division. Of the four home international keepers at the time only Jack Kelsey of Wales and Arsenal played in the top flight. Northern Ireland's Harry Gregg played for Doncaster Rovers and Scotland's Tommy Younger was with Liverpool, both then Division Two clubs. The goalkeeper, Chapman concluded, neither needed nor sought recognition: in the spirit of those ordinary men who had left mundane jobs to fight in the previous decade, goalkeepers simply did their duty when they were called upon to do so. Even the England goalkeeping top, a yellow woollen jersey, spoke of a deliberately downbeat outlook. It seems laughably bizarre a little later in the book when Chapman's father criticises Lev Yashin for, as he saw it, flashily wearing a white number one on the back of his black (or very dark blue) shirt, yet – World Cups aside, when Fifa insisted upon it – it wasn't until Gordon Banks in the late sixties that the number one began to appear on the back on England goalkeeping tops. Goodness only knows what Chapman's father would have made of the yellow-and-black zig-zag effort foisted on Shilton at Euro 88, or the red splurge David Seaman modelled at Euro 96, or the interlocking turquoise crosses Joe Hart wore at Euro 2012.

The assumption was that English goalkeepers were the best in the world. Perhaps, by the mid-fifties, after Hungary had come to Wembley and obliterated any thought that England's outfielders were the best in the world, the superiority of the English keeper was all there was left to cling to. The only question at the time was whether the pinnacle had been Sam Hardy or Harry Hibbs.

'Safe and Steady Sam', like so many before him, started out as a centre-forward at Newbold White Star, but went in goal in a friendly and excelled. He joined Chesterfield in 1902, signing his contract by the light of a lamppost after haggling his initial fee up from five to eighteen shillings, before moving to Liverpool in 1905. He won a league title there, then moved to Aston Villa, where he twice lifted the FA Cup. Slim and only 5'9½" in height, his great strength was his positional sense. He was, according to a 1959 *Encyclopaedia of Sport* published by Sampson Low, noted for his 'calm judgement' and was 'invariably in position when the shot was made'. He was 'hardly noticed on the field', 'as unspectacular in goal as he was quiet and modest off it'. The pen portrait in the programme for the 1913 Cup final described him as 'confident and reliable ... Exceptionally cool in action, and clever in anticipation, and with sound judgement. Particularly quick in getting down to ground shots.'

That sense of anticipation could at times seem almost preternatural, as the Villa and England forward Billy Walker recalled. 'The first time I played for the juniors against the seniors with Sam Hardy in goal, I got a loose ball, beat a couple of men and raced towards Sam,' he said. 'He was leaning against the left-hand post as I looked up. I hit the ball hard to the right-hand side and when I looked up again, there was Sam taking the ball easily into his chest as if he had been there all the time. Only he and I knew that a second before he had been leaning against the left-hand post. In the dressing-room afterwards, Sam said to me, "Young Bill, why did you fire at the right-hand post?" I replied, "Because when I looked up you were standing at the left-hand one." He smiled at me and said, "I saw you looking up. Did you expect me to stay there?" As I got to know the greatest of all goalkeepers I got to know better.'

As the early football writer Bruce Campbell put it, 'Hardy ... is not a statuesque goalkeeper, neither is he given to making any fuss, but he is safe as anyone can be, and his anticipation is simply wonderful. Many times I have heard people declare that Hardy is a lucky keeper, because so many shots go straight at him. That, of course, is the criticism of people who cannot read between the lines, and the fact is that Hardy gets into positions for shots before they are made. He has no mannerisms worth talking about, and his telegraph address might well be, "Consistency, Birmingham."'

Hardy won twenty-one caps for England, but more than that, he defined what English goalkeeping was. He laid down the standard against which others would be measured. When Liverpool had to replace him, they looked for somebody as similar as possible, and came up with the Belfast-born nineteen-year-old Elisha Scott, who had been playing for Linfield and Broadway United, and had been rejected by Everton for being 'too young'. The 1959 *Encyclopaedia* noted that Scott was 'strangely like' Hardy and 'positioned well'. He was 'modest and quiet' with 'nothing of the showman about him'.

Off the pitch, Scott was an eccentric, obsessed with goalkeeping. On one occasion, the story is told, he was walking through Belfast when he passed the Everton striker Dixie Dean, a player with whom he'd had a series of duels in Merseyside derbies. Dean touched his hat in acknowledgement at which Scott, so closely had he studied Dean to try to understand his prodigious heading ability, sprang instinctively forward as if to save an attempt on goal. That may be an urban myth but it gives some indication of the intensity of Scott's personality. He was incorrigibly superstitious but on the pitch, Scott was the model of imperturbability.

Harry Hibbs was from the same mould. Half an inch shorter than Hardy, he was, according to the 1959 *Encyclopedia*, 'safe rather than spectacular', his positioning, based on careful study of opponents and a sharp memory, so good that 'he gave the impression that forwards were shooting straight at him'. Other goalkeepers revered him. 'What he taught me, I should like to teach others,' said Sam Bartram, who remains probably the best English goalkeeper never to win an international cap. 'And principally this has to do with positional play. You can make the other fellow, the oncoming forward, put the ball exactly where you want it if you position yourself correctly. Always seek to narrow his shooting angle. Don't stand stiffly, but be ready in every muscle to spring to the ball when it is loose. On the other hand, don't jitter about in the hope of putting him off – a good forward is too intent upon his manoeuvring and the finish to his run to bother about a jack-in-the-box keeper.'

Hibbs too was unfailingly loyal and modest, spending his entire career with Birmingham City: he never finished higher than ninth in the First Division, lost the one Cup final he reached and earned only £8 a week during the season (£6 in summer) at a time when Ricardo Zamora was earning £50. As such, as Chapman put it, Hibbs 'consolidated the British tradition of goalkeeping.'

Hibbs's successor as the best in England was Frank Swift. '[Hibbs],' Swift said, 'was a master of angles and each time we played Birmingham I learned something new from him ... I gave him six inches in height [by which, confusingly, he means he was six inches taller] and have frequently made what seemed amazing saves only because the length of my arms enabled me to reach the ball; yet, short as he was, I have seen him make similar saves without any last-minute excitement, purely through his amazing positional sense.'

Swift joined Manchester City in 1932 as a seventeen-year-old, and the following year, when they reached the Cup final, he squeezed into the sidecar of a friend's motorcycle to make the trip to Wembley. His friend had only one eye and, whether because of that or not, crashed on the way south, turning bike and sidecar over. Seeing no serious damage had been done, the two set off again and arrived in time to see Everton beat City 3–0. Swift was working in a gasworks at the time, but he gave up that job when his wages at City were doubled to £1 a week. He made his debut on Christmas Day the following season, being knocked unconscious early in the game at the Baseball Ground and then being at fault for two of the goals as Derby County beat City 4–2. He sat up with his brother analysing what had gone wrong and, after only a couple of hours' sleep, turned up at Maine Road for the return fixture. He was selected again – on his nineteenth birthday – and kept a clean sheet in a 2–0 win. Swift established himself as a regular as City reached the Cup final for the second successive season, but at nineteen he was still dreadfully prone to nerves.

'As the days passed,' he wrote in his autobiography, 'I still couldn't quite believe that I was going to keep goal in a Cup final. One moment I'd be on top of the world, then I'd get terrible fits of despondency and tell myself I was far too young to think about playing in a Wembley side. I never confided in anyone, but I tell you I was plenty worried.'

He roomed with the team captain, Sam Cowan, who sat up till 3 a.m. bathing a poisoned big toe in a bowl of hot water and talking, Swift later believed, to make him sleep late and so given him less time for nerves. He even fell asleep on the coach on the way to the game, but his anxiety was reawakened when a policeman tried to prevent him joining his team-mates inspecting the pitch, taking him to be a young spectator. When he saw a senior colleague too nervous even to tie his own bootlaces, Swift panicked and admitted he might not even have made it onto the pitch had the coach Alec Bell not slapped him and given him a tot of whisky.

Once the game started, things only got worse. Seeing the Portsmouth keeper Jock Gilfillan had decided against wearing gloves despite the rain, Swift left his in the back of his net, and then blamed himself as a shot from Septimus Rutherford slipped through his hands to give Pompey a half-time lead.

Fred Tilson, City's centre-forward, told Swift at half-time not to be so gloomy, and vowed to score twice in the second half. He did, the second coming with two minutes remaining, but as time ticked by, Swift became increasingly anxious. When the whistle blew, he passed out, and had to be revived with the physio's sponge. It made him a hero – a great goalkeeper with human frailty. That, though, along with a habit for occasionally exaggerating dives for the sake of amusing himself and entertaining the crowd, led the 1959 *Encyclopaedia of Sport* to claim that 'Swift might have been the greatest of all time, but for a tendency to showmanship.' He loved to entertain, on and off the pitch, delighting onlookers – although it's hard to imagine how – with his impressions of a woman getting out of a bath and a man eating fish and chips.

His final joke is all too well known. After his retirement, he worked as a journalist for the *News of the World* and travelled with Manchester United for their European Cup quarter-final against Crvena Zvezda in Belgrade in 1958. After two attempted take-offs in the snow at Munich on their return, the mood was tense, but was lightened as Swift boomed down the aircraft, 'You are now asked to fasten your seat-belts – very tightly.' The third attempt to take off was not aborted but the plane never left the ground, crashing through the perimeter fence, clipping a tree and ploughing into a house. Swift was one of the twenty-one who died in the crash.

As a goalkeeper, even those made sceptical by Swift's supposed flashiness admired his huge hands and great strength. Raich Carter, the great Sunderland and Derby inside-forward and an England team-mate, said that Swift was so big, so dominated the goal, that trying to score past him felt like trying to force the ball into a matchbox. What really marked him out, though, was his ability to initiate attacks, hurling the ball downfield with great accuracy – something almost unknown in English football at the time and something Swift only started doing after watching a water-polo match.

He became England's first-choice keeper after the Second World War, and captained them in the famous 4–0 win over Italy in Turin in 1948. Swift that day gave one of the great performances, standing firm as the England goal came under prolonged siege. At one point early in the second half, he pounced on a header from Guglielmo Gabetto as it cannoned down off the bar. As the Italians protested it had crossed the line, Swift invited a photographer onto the pitch so he could inspect the scuff mark on the ground that proved he had kept it out of the net.

Yet he was dropped for Tottenham's Ted Ditchburn six months

later and played for only a year after that, retiring aged thirty-six to become a sales rep for a confectionery firm. Ditchburn, who had bought his first boots with pennies thrown by spectators at prize fights before which he acted as a warm-up act, was a less flamboyant figure; just right, Chapman argued, for the post-war austerity. He was replaced by Bert Williams of Wolves, a less sober alternative but less showy than Swift. This, for Chapman, was England feeling its way back after the war, rediscovering a measure of self-expression.

Next came the unflappable Gil Merrick, who was 'never unnecessarily spectacular'. Nicknamed 'the Clutch' for his impeccable handling, he made his debut in 1951 three weeks after Churchill's re-election as though to emphasise a returning self-confidence about Britain. The world had moved on, though, and when Ditchburn played his last game in 1956, shortly before the retreat from Suez, Chapman saw 'a line in the sand' for the old keepers and the old way of doing things. The new era was characterised by the transition from a roll-neck to an ordinary round neck on the keeper's jersey – and by a battle to be England number one between the twenty-year-old Alan Hodgkinson of Sheffield United and the year-older Eddie Hopkinson of Bolton.

Frank Swift had been the first great goalkeeping hero of a Cup final and with his humble background, his simple love of the game, his image as a gentle – if occasionally overly flashy – giant and his deference to royalty, he fitted a very British template. The second goalkeeping hero of an FA Cup final also felt woozy at the final whistle, but he could hardly have been a more different figure.

What happened in the 1956 FA Cup final made him famous but in the extraordinary life of Bernhard Trautmann it was barely a footnote. Born in Bremen in 1923, he joined Tura, the local amateur football club, at the age of eight and at school played both football and *Völkerball*, a preferred sport of the Nazis similar to dodgeball. In 1933 he joined the Hitler Youth. At the time, around a third of all German children were members and for Trautmann, with his love of sport, it was a natural step. He was one of only sixty members from the Bremen region to be selected to spend a year in a castle in Silesia to work on the land – the *Landjahr*, portrayed as a great honour and part of the general programme of indoctrination for the brightest and fittest (and most Aryan) of the nation's youth.

On his return, Trautmann began an apprenticeship at a vehicle maintenance plant in Bremen, starting work in January 1939. He still played football on a Sunday morning, usually as a combative centre-forward. When Germany invaded Poland that September, Trautmann was enthusiastic. In his memoir *Trautmann's Journey*, he remembered almost hitting his father for ruminating that the invasion almost certainly meant war with Britain, which he saw as unwinnable.

A week after his seventeenth birthday, in August 1940, Trautmann signed up, years of propaganda having convinced him of the justice of the German cause. He didn't have the academic qualifications to become a pilot, as he wished, so initially he trained as a wireless operator. Failing his test, though, he was sent to an air district communication division, a land-based unit in the Luftwaffe. In June 1941 he headed east, across Poland, to join the invasion of the USSR. At the beginning of July, Trautmann – by then known as Bernd – and his company were ordered to remain behind in the forest near Zhitomir to await maintenance supplies arriving from Krakow. They would be left either to barter for food in nearby villages or to forage in the woods for the two weeks or so it would take for the equipment to arrive. Trautmann decided the process would be much easier if they had a car, so fiddled with the ignition and the distributor on an Opel P4 that was supposed to be travelling on with the rest of the unit towards Kyiv. The ploy failed as the army towed the car and then sent for Trautmann to fix it, something he did with such ease his secret was soon discovered. He was court-martialled and sentenced to nine months in jail.

On his second day, Trautmann suffered a burst appendix. He was transferred to an army hospital where he proved so useful as he recovered that doctors managed to delay his return to the jail by three months. By then, his sentence had been reduced and so, when the hospital finally let him go, he was sent to rejoin the army near Dnipropetrovsk in southern Ukraine. There, after becoming lost on manoeuvres and spending a night in the forest, Trautmann inadvertently witnessed an SS massacre of local civilians. As winter fell, he was transferred to Vitebsk in Belarus and then to Smolensk. It was horrendously cold and seeing the conditions in which Soviet prisoners were kept fostered disillusionment. In January 1942 he applied to join the *Fallschirmjäger*, the Luftwaffe's parachute regiment, at least in part because it meant two months training back in Berlin where it was warm and rations were adequate.

Having qualified, which meant completing just six jumps, Trautmann was returned to Belarus to fight partisans near Bryansk. So ferocious was the fighting that the safest place for the paratroopers to sleep was in the trees, strapped to branches with their parachute webbing. By 1943 the Germans were in retreat on the eastern front. Trautmann was shot in the leg, but returned to combat after the bullet had been removed. Then, in July, with his unit outnumbered fifty to one by an enemy tank regiment, he was taken prisoner by the Soviets. Three days later, a German counter-attack secured his release.

By July 1944, when he was transferred to the western front following the Allied landings in Normandy, he had won two Iron Crosses and was one of only 800 of the 3,000 in his original regiment still alive. He fought the Americans just outside Paris and the British at Arnhem. He was buried under rubble for three days following the bombing of Kleve. Finally, in March 1945, as the Allies crossed the Rhine, Trautmann gave up and made a break for home. He was captured by the Americans who then released him. As he fled he hurdled a hedge and landed among a British signals patrol. After being briefly interrogated by a senior officer Trautmann was told to sit against a tree, whereupon a soldier approached him with a tin mug. 'Fancy a cup of tea, Fritz?' he asked.

Trautmann was transferred to the POW Camp at Marbury Hall in Cheshire and then to Ashton-in-Makerfield where he drove lorries round local farms. Soon Sunday football became part of his regular routine, initially between teams of POWs but, in time, a match was arranged between a POW side and local opposition. Trautmann played at centre-half but suffered a slight injury early in the second half. The referee advised him to go off and have it treated but Trautmann refused, prompting an argument that was resolved only when the POW goalkeeper persuaded Trautmann that they should swap positions. The Germans won with ease and Trautmann's career as a goalkeeper had begun.

Repatriation began in September 1946, starting with those who had been opposed to the Nazi regime. As a member of the Hitler Youth and the *Fallschirmjäger*, Trautmann was considered to be a hard-core Nazi sympathiser – as he had been until the war in the east began the process of disillusionment. As the mood softened, POWs were allowed out on Saturdays to watch football. Trautmann became a fan of Ted Sagar, the Everton goalkeeper, and began studying him to improve his own game.

The order for Trautmann's repatriation came in March 1948 but he opted to stay for a further year. Part of the reason was that a local girl, Marion, was pregnant with his child, but there was also his pride: he didn't want to return home in poverty to a defeated country. He began playing for St Helens Town, where his name underwent another mutation and became Bert. He abandoned Marion and Freda, his daughter, and, in January 1949, finally headed home for a month. The day he left, members of the St Helens club presented him with a travelling trunk full of food and £50 in cash – some indication of how popular he had become. He found Germany an alien, broken country and returned to England with some relief.

In 1949 he signed for Manchester City, prompting a predictable backlash. Over 25,000 turned up at Maine Road to protest against the decision and there was fury in the letters pages of the *Manchester Evening News*. 'When I think of all those millions of Jews who were tortured and murdered, I can only marvel at Man City's crass stupidity,' wrote 'a disgusted season-ticket holder'. But then the communal rabbi of Manchester, Dr Altmann, wrote an open letter to the newspaper. 'Despite the terrible cruelties we suffered at the Germans [*sic*],' he said, 'we would not try to punish an individual German, who is unconnected with these crimes, out of hatred. If this footballer is a decent fellow, I would say there is no harm in it.' There were taunts and shouts of '*Sieg Heil!*' at his first game, a defeat to Bolton, but by the end of the season Trautmann had been accepted. He was clearly an exceptional goalkeeper, noted for his courage in leaving his line to engage in physical confrontations with forwards and for his rapid distribution.

It was the FA Cup final in 1956 that secured Trautmann his enduring place in English football history. He'd played in the final the previous year, when City had lost 3–1 to Newcastle and had been cheered to the rafters as the first German to play in a Cup final. The following year was different as Trautmann received a number of poison pen letters from Tottenham fans, angered by a cynical foul he'd made on George Robb in the closing minutes of the semi-final.

By then, Trautmann had become such a popular figure to City fans that they rallied to his defence. 'It was a darn bad show and left a nasty taste in one's mouth,' Globetrotters from Ardwick wrote in a letter to the *Manchester Evening News*. 'Both Manchester City and Manchester United fans are proud of Bert's record, both on and off the field. And if ever he walks into our pub – or any other pub for that matter – he would find that all the lads are with him and think a lot of him.'

Joe Hayes put City ahead after three minutes of the final, but Birmingham City levelled on the quarter-hour through Noel Kinsey. Trautmann was forced into a number of saves but two goals in quick succession just after the hour turned the match decisively City's way. Jack Dyson got the first before Bobby Johnstone finished off a smart counter initiated by Trautmann. City seemed comfortable, but with sixteen minutes remaining, Trautmann charged out to dive at the feet of Peter Murphy, Birmingham's inside-left. The forward's knee caught the side of his head and knocked him unconscious. When he came round, he insisted on playing on, despite the fact he was staggering around in clear distress. He later admitted he couldn't remember any of those final minutes but he played superbly, making a brave save to take the ball off the toes of Eddie Brown and clearing a high ball from Murphy. Somehow, City held out. It was only days later it was discovered his neck was broken.

Trautmann had been named Footballer of the Year that season, but 1956 rapidly became the worst year of his life. First he was told he would never play football again and then, just a month after the Cup final, his six-year-old son John was knocked over and killed. Although Trautmann made his comeback on Christmas Day that year, he was never quite the same again. He remaining staggeringly popular, though, and his testimonial, in 1964, drew an official crowd of 47,000, although it's thought as many as 60,000 may have squeezed in.

The injury to Trautmann began to change the perception: previously, danger had just been part of the goalkeeper's lot; now there was a sense that he needed to be protected. At an inquiry into the death of Celtic's John Thomson in 1931, the Celtic manager Willie Maley said, 'I *hope* it was an accident.' His sceptical tone cast doubt and Sam English, the Rangers forward who had caught Thomson with his knee, was haunted by the death, but no other account seems to suggest the incident was anything other than terrible bad luck following the sort of collision in which goalkeepers were inevitably involved. The day Thomson died, George Blyth of Hibernian broke his leg in a game against St Bernards, while William Paterson of Airdrie was stretchered off at Falkirk.

Goalkeeping was dangerous, but it was part of the goalkeeper's unemotional, unflappable ethos – in Britain at least – that they didn't complain about it. 'I don't know if you have ever been thrown into a fight which you did not seek,' John Ashcroft had written in 1906. 'At the onset you are in a kind of sliver of nervousness, but once you have had a smack on the jaw, your diffidence has disappeared, and you scarcely notice the hard knocks you receive in the fray. So it is in goalkeeping. The best incentive to good work is to rough-and-tumble early in the game ...'

Ten years before Thomson's death, the Dumbarton goalkeeper Joshua Wilkinson, having survived three years in the navy during the First World War, died following a match against Rangers. The cause of death was recorded as peritonitis, and the Glasgow press were united in insisting there had been no particular rough play during the game. Wilkinson's father, though, was sure football was to blame. 'He certainly met his death,' he wrote in a letter to the *Glasgow Evening News*, 'by a rupture of the small bowel caused by some blow received during the match.'

Then, in 1936, the Sunderland goalkeeper Jim Thorpe died following a game at Roker Park in which Chelsea had come back from 3–1 down to draw. Most initially blamed the keeper for the dropped point: he had misjudged a clearance for Chelsea's second and then, seeming distracted by the onrushing Joe Bambrick, had missed a backpass to gift the Chelsea forward the leveller. 'Thorpe,' Argus reported in the *Sunderland Echo* the following Monday, 'has shown some excellent goalkeeping this season, but he seldom satisfies me when the ball is crossed. On Saturday, his failures had an entirely different origin, and I can come to no other conclusion that the third goal to Chelsea was due to "wind up" when he saw Bambrick running up.' Two days later, Thorpe died in Monkwearmouth and Southwick Hospital, a series of blows sustained in what had been a physical game having prompted a recurrence of a diabetic condition.

Argus was horrified. 'I know many,' he wrote, 'who would give anything now to feel that they had not uttered the harsh words they spoke in the heat of the moment regarding Jimmy Thorpe's failure to prevent the two Chelsea goals in the second half last week. They did not know that the man whose failures were cursed was actually a hero to carry on at all. Neither did I know, and I confess now that I myself would give anything to have been in the position to have known and never to have given pen to what I wrote.'

Startled by Thorpe's death into an acknowledgement there was a serious problem, the *Echo* demanded a change in the laws of the game. 'It has frequently been advocated that a goalkeeper should be given protection from an opponent while in possession of the ball,' Argus wrote. In other words, he should neither be charged nor kicked at in an endeavour to dispossess him.

This rule has been in operation on the continent and there is no valid reason why it should not be made to apply in this country …' It would take high-profile incidents in three successive FA Cup finals in the late fifties, though, before any action was taken.

At least what had happened to Trautmann had been an accident, pure and simple, and had made no impact on the result. The next year, though, the game was effectively decided by a challenge by the Aston Villa outside-left Peter McParland on the Manchester United goalkeeper Ray Wood that, if not malicious, was at least culpably reckless. Wood broke a cheekbone and was knocked unconscious and ended up trotting around on the left wing as Jackie Blanchflower took over in goal. McParland scored twice as Villa won 2–1.

The following year, United, riding a wave of public sympathy after the Munich air crash, were beaten 2–0 by Bolton Wanderers, Nat Lofthouse bundling both the ball and the goalkeeper, Harry Gregg, over the line to score the second. What Lofthouse had done was – just about – within the laws of the game and fully within its traditions. Gregg's handling, in truth, had been poor all game and, when he could only parry a Dennis Stevens shot into the air, even a modern forward would have every right to go for the dropping ball as it looped towards the goal line. Gregg got there first, but was off-balance, and Lofthouse's challenge – while it would certainly be considered a foul today – didn't have to be especially forceful to knock him into the net.

Nonetheless, given what had happened to Ray Wood the year before, the goal provoked an outcry. 'It was an early sign,' Chapman wrote, 'that the goalkeeper was drifting to be just another member of the team.'

Gregg, anyway, was part of a new breed of goalkeeper who felt less constrained by their penalty areas. He had been criticised for leaving his line too frequently, often having to remove his cap to head the ball clear, but on 5 February 1958, after a 3–3 draw away to Crvena Zvezda that secured United's passage to the semi-final of the European Cup, Frank Swift sat down with Gregg and urged him not to be a keeper who stayed on his line.

Gregg's style wasn't the only change in the English game. Chapman's attempts to link England's goalkeepers to the national outlook at times become more parlour game than serious history, but he is surely right to link De Gaulle's veto on UK entry into the Common Market to France's 5–2 victory over England in Alf Ramsey's first game as manager: seventeen years after the war had ended, any illusion of British superiority or lingering sense that the French might be grateful had vanished. Ron Springett, Chapman noted, had been particularly poor in that game – English goalkeeping could no longer be relied upon.

With the likes of Fulham's Tony Macedo – born in Gibraltar of a Spanish father – and Chelsea's Peter Bonetti – born in Putney to Swiss parents – starting to establish themselves in the First Division, goalkeeping in the early sixties began to take on a continental sparkle. Others, with no such genetic excuse, also began to challenge the notion of the goalkeeper as the diffident loner who kept out of trouble. Liverpool's Tommy Lawrence was a case in point. 'He comes so far off his line he plays like a defender,' said the Manchester City manager Joe Mercer after the 1966 Charity Shield in which Liverpool beat Everton 1–0.

Even Gordon Banks, who rapidly became Ramsey's preferred choice for the national side, wasn't as stolid as many of his predecessors. Chapman remembered seeing him cost Leicester a goal against Arsenal at Highbury with a moment of unnecessary flamboyance. 'I saw him dive high to his left to a free-kick from outside the penalty area, when he should have moved his feet to the ball more before take-off,' he wrote. 'There was no need for him to have made quite such a flourish of his heels in mid-air.'

Where Banks did fit the tradition, though, was in being almost an accidental goalkeeper. He was not somebody who grew up with a burning ambition to be England's number one and directed his whole life to achieving that aim; it was just something that came along. He was born and raised in Sheffield, the youngest of four brothers. He played football at school, and was gifted enough to make six appearances for Sheffield Boys, but he estimated he went to only around twenty professional matches in his childhood, something he blamed on poverty.

After finishing school, Banks got a job bagging and delivering coal, which left him exhausted. At the weekend, though, he'd drag himself along to his local park to watch the amateur matches that were played there. Before one game, he was recognised by a player from a team called Millspaugh. They were short of a keeper and asked Banks if he could play for them. He dashed back home to get his boots, but didn't have any shorts so played in work trousers stained black with coal dust.

Banks did well enough to be invited back and continued to impress, receiving an invitation to play for the Yorkshire League side Romarsh Welfare. In his first game, Romarsh were beaten 13–2 and when they lost his second 3–1, he was despatched back to Millspaugh. Banks left the coal yard to become an apprentice bricklayer, which not only left him far fresher at weekends, but also gave him time to train twice a week. The improvement in his form was dramatic and, at the end of his first full season with Millspaugh, he was signed by Chesterfield. His excellence there helped Chesterfield reach the final of the FA Youth Cup and, having broken into the first team, he had played just twenty-three matches when Leicester City bought him. So vague was Banks about professional football at the time that he didn't even know which division they were in.

Twice he played in losing FA Cup final sides before lifting the League Cup in 1964, but it was his performances for England that made his name. He won his first cap in 1963 and was the clear first choice by 1965. He was excellent in England's first four matches at the 1966 World Cup, keeping clean sheets in all of them, but in the semi-final he was at least partly responsible for Portugal's goal, which brought the score back to 2–1 with eight minutes remaining: he flapped at a cross allowing José Torres a header that was punched off the line by Jack Charlton; Eusébio converted the penalty. 'Such errors could no longer be interpreted as in character,' Chapman noted. 'He had become a solid, efficient and almost old-fashioned type of British goalkeeper, appearing to have restrained his "spectacular" side, to the benefit of his "safe".'

England, of course, went on to win the World Cup, but the moment for which Banks will always be remembered came four years later, in a group match against Brazil at the World Cup in Mexico as he made a save that, in England at least, is widely regarded as the greatest ever. Banks described it in his autobiography:

> Tostão, a smooth, sophisticated player, came to the near post and I went with him as I sensed that Jairzinho would try to find him with a diagonal pass. What I didn't see was Pelé running beyond his marker Alan Mullery at the back post. Jairzinho lofted a dipping centre high in the direction of Pelé and I suddenly had to scamper back across my goal. Pelé got above the ball and powered it low and hard towards the corner of the net. It was a perfect header. I was now into a dive to my right and as the ball hit the ground just in front of the goal line I flicked it with my outstretched right hand as it came up and managed to divert it over the bar. Alan Mullery told me later that Pelé had been shouting 'Goal!' as I reached the ball, and Pelé himself was generous enough to tell me he considered it the greatest save he had ever seen.

The real genius, as Francis Hodgson pointed out in *Only the Keeper to Beat*, was that Banks dived slightly backwards, giving himself an extra fraction to get to the ball, which by then had enough bounce on it that he could flick it over the bar. Had he dived straight for the ball, the chances are that it would simply have bounced over his arm, even had he got there in time.

Yet the odd thing is that by the time Banks was making the save that confirmed him – in the eyes of England at least, and quite possibly Brazil – as the best in the world, he had left Leicester. Not because a bigger club came calling or because he had grown frustrated with life at a team of Leicester's stature, but because Leicester were so confident in the ability of a teenager already at the club that they felt it was worth cashing in on Banks. That teenager was Peter Shilton.

Shilton was single-minded about goalkeeping from a frighteningly early age. Although he was a gifted outfield player as a schoolboy, goalkeeping was always his first love. In *The Magnificent Obsession*, in fact, it's described how Shilton would play outfield until his school side had the lead, and then go in goal to try to protect it. Even then he took goalkeeping so seriously that he'd come home and draw diagrams to try to understand why he'd made mistakes or let goals in.

Although he grew rapidly up to the age of nine, he then seemed to get bulkier rather than taller, and when he started training at Leicester aged eleven (technically, as he couldn't be signed on schoolboy terms until he was thirteen, Shilton was merely 'using their facilities'), there were concerns over his lack of height. Shilton responded by drawing chalk marks on his garage floor and stretching himself out to try to touch the lines with fingers and toes. He would swing from the balcony between his parents' grocery shop and the flat upstairs, attaching weights to his feet or having his mother or father pull at his legs. The exercises may not have made him any taller – he ended up a touch over six feet tall – but his arms are two inches longer than would be normal for somebody of his height.

Shilton's first coach at Leicester, George Dewis, tackled the problem of Shilton's height in a more orthodox way, making him practise catching the ball at the highest possible point. In practice, that meant it often appeared that Shilton was taking the ball behind his head. Dewis admitted there were times when the habit made him so anxious he could hardly bear to watch, but Shilton always maintained that it was merely momentum carrying him back and making it look as though he were taking the ball a fraction too late.

Banks first saw Shilton when he was thirteen. 'He'll be having you out the team soon,' Dewis said as they watched him make a string of saves from first-team players. Banks laughed, but four years later it was true. Shilton, he acknowledged, wasn't just gifted, but had that 'vital mixture of determination and dedication'.

Obsession really was the word. As a schoolboy, Shilton spent six months fretting about punching the ball, unable to understand why sometimes he flapped at punches and sometimes made solid contact. After studying boxers, he realised he was trying to punch too far from his body, so added a punchbag to his training regime.

He set up poles at various points in the box so he could practise the positioning and the different types of save necessary from varying positions. 'When we're talking about the difference between shots from eighteen yards and twelve yards, we're talking about maybe a fraction of a second,' Shilton said. 'And it's this very fine point of goalkeeping that the majority of keepers never go into. After the work I did, I felt I was unbeatable … as confident of stopping shots from, say, ten or twelve yards as from eighteen or twenty.'

That level of focus and attention to detail remained with him throughout his career. He worked on building his strength and physical power, strapping a bag of shale to his back and jumping on and off a low wall surrounding the pitch. He would insist on staying on the training pitch until his touch had returned or he'd ironed out a minor technical flaw. Shilton admitted he was the same in everyday life, insisting his house was immaculately tidy. 'If something doesn't interest me, I'm useless, but if it does, then I've got to get really involved in it and everything else goes by the board,' he explained. 'I don't like to see things out of place.' When Shilton decided against doing O-Levels, his mother asked him what he would do if he didn't make it. 'I've never even thought about it,' he replied. 'I'm just going to do it.'

So confident was Shilton, so determined to make his impression early, that aged seventeen he gave Leicester an ultimatum. Given that Banks had won the World Cup the previous year, that took tremendous chutzpah and Shilton must surely have thought he would be sold. As it was, it was Banks who went. The then-Leicester manager Matt Gillies claimed in *The Magnificent Obsession* that Banks had fancied a change, but that is certainly not the impression Banks gave.

That book, written in collaboration with Jason Tomas, also hinted at a tension between Shilton and Banks. (Shilton, it should be said, doesn't come out of either that book or his auto-biography, published in 2004, as a particularly likeable figure, complaining about the most minor faults or misunderstandings with almost everybody he'd worked with or come across; the curse, perhaps, if we're being charitable, of the perfectionist.) Shilton suggested in *The Magnificent Obsession* that he initially adopted some of Banks's mannerisms, which led people to say they looked similar, but he insisted Banks never took him aside or offered any special coaching and admitted that he resented the fact that Banks never came out and said that what Shilton had achieved he'd achieved alone. They seemed friendly enough when Shilton appeared on *This Is Your Life* in 1986, and by the time of his autobiography, Shilton was complaining about the rumours that they hadn't got on. Whatever their relationship, there were clear differences in style between the two keepers. Shilton, perhaps because of his superior physique, was more aggressive than Banks, and made a point of organising his defence, of commanding his whole area.

Banks moved to Stoke for £56,000, a sizeable fee, but even so that seemed a bargain alongside the new goalkeeper's record West Ham United set by paying £67,000 to land Bobby Ferguson from Kilmarnock. Tony Waddington's emerging and stylish side won the League Cup in 1972 – still the only trophy Stoke have ever won – with Banks the hero of the semi-final victory over West Ham, in which he pushed a Geoff Hurst penalty over the bar. A few weeks later he was named the Football Writers' Footballer of the Year and when he kept a clean sheet for England against Scotland at Hampden Park at the end of the season, he seemed at the peak of his powers.

The next season, though, began badly for Stoke and in the October, a day after a defeat at Liverpool, Banks's career was brought abruptly to an end. Driving home for Sunday lunch, he was still fuming about a refereeing decision the day before when his Ford Granada was held up by a crawling lorry and a car that was stuck behind it. He pulled out to overtake, but didn't see the Austin A60 van that was coming towards him. The crash cost him the sight in his right eye.

Banks set about trying to make a comeback. 'Goalkeeping is all about geometry and geography and with one eye I set out to re-educate myself about angles and positioning,' he said. He spent weeks working alone, refamiliarising himself with the dimensions of his box. But when he started facing shots, he realised he couldn't get the timing of the pace of the ball right. At the end of the season, he accepted he was never going to get back to his former level and gave up his playing career to become a youth coach at Stoke. He did make a return four years later, joining Fort Lauderdale Strikers in the NASL, on one occasion riding a white horse onto the pitch as part of a cowboy-themed game. He reckoned he was only seventy-five per cent of the player he had been, but he was still named goalkeeper of the year.

Seeking a replacement for Banks, Stoke turned to the most obvious candidate: Shilton. The £335,000 they paid to sign him at the start of the 1974–75 season was three times the previous British record for a goalkeeper and outstripped even the £300,000 Juventus had paid for Dino Zoff. His first two seasons there were good and Stoke finished fifth then twelfth, despite losing no fewer than five players to broken legs. Shilton, though, was frustrated by an attacking style that often left him exposed; he accused his team-mates of being unprofessional and showing a lack of character, and was dismayed by the appointment of the inconsistent Alan Hudson as captain.

However frustrated he might have been, Shilton never let up his own quest for self-improvement, and turned to Len Hepple, a dance teacher from Hexham in Northumberland for help. Hepple showed him how to 'turn from the hips when upright' which, Shilton explained in his autobiography, 'enabled me to save a valuable second when turning', adding:

> Len also taught me to have my weight slightly forward, shoulders also forward and knees slightly bent when addressing a shot … He taught me to throw my head forward first when

taking off on a sprint. I found this helped my initial propulsion and subsequent momentum. To this day I see goalkeepers dancing up and down on their toes, especially when a free kick or corner is about to be taken. Len told me not to do this because you lose a vital second when taking off. He taught me to keep my feet light and close to the ground, moving them as if skating on ice. Many goalkeepers keep their feet too far apart, which puts them at a disadvantage when saving shots from close range. Len Hepple taught me to keep my feet closer together and collapse my legs down when saving shots from close range.

The aim was to lose the stiffness from his body, to become 'like an object which can be seen shimmering through a heat haze'; the practice perhaps explains the slightly mannered, apparently over-dramatic, nature of many of Shilton's saves.

Shilton, though, no matter how much he was improving, couldn't do it all alone. Behind the scenes, the Stoke experiment was beginning to fall apart. At the end of the 1974–75 season, the club had announced record losses of £450,000, and the pressure to bring the overdraft under control increased in January 1976 when the roof of the Butler Street stand was blown off. Jimmy Greenhoff and Hudson were both sold, Mike Pejic followed and the coach Tony Waddington resigned, furious at the way he'd been made to break up his squad. With George Eastham in temporary control, Stoke drifted to relegation.

Shilton's departure was inevitable, the only question being where he'd end up. It was Brian Clough and Nottingham Forest who swooped, paying £270,000. Contract negotiations proved rather trickier than the initial deal. Shilton had always been financially aware. At nineteen he had designed a goalkeeping top with a zip so it could be worn as a V-neck in warm conditions and as a roll-neck in the winter, only for the FA to rule it illegal. Later, he pioneered the move away from the traditional (in England at least) green goalkeeper's top, playing in all white. He was also one of the first players to use an agent, and as a result had a contract that stipulated an annual pay rise in line with inflation (given the financial problems he would later have, his acuity early in his career now seems desperately sad). Clough, not surprisingly, held little truck with agents and, at the initial meeting, hid behind the door of his office, tripping up Shilton's two representatives with a squash racquet. The deal was eventually concluded a couple of weeks later in a pub.

Shilton by then had developed into one of the best two goalkeepers in the country but Ray Clemence was keeping him out of the national side. Shilton suggested Don Revie, England manager from 1974 to 1977, had never been keen on him, which may be true, but he was also paying the price for an error in the crucial World Cup qualifier against Poland in 1973.

England, needing a win to qualify for the 1974 World Cup ahead of their opponents, attacked for almost the whole ninety minutes. The Polish goal was peppered with shots, but England found Jan Tomaszewski, the goalkeeper famously dismissed as 'a clown' by Clough, in outstanding if unorthodox form. 'I've never played in a more one-sided game in my life,' said Norman Hunter, but England couldn't score. Then, twelve minutes into the second half, Tony Currie lost possession on the Polish left to Henryk Kasperczak. His pass forward was intercepted by Hunter but, for once, he was a little tentative, and Gzregorz Lato nicked the ball from him. He cut inside and, as Robert Gadocha created space with a forward run across his line, slipped the ball right for Jan Domarski. Emlyn Hughes lunged, but was too late to block the shot. It shouldn't have mattered; the ball, struck well but not ferociously, was only a yard or so to Shilton's left. As he went down, though, the ball squeezed under his body and in.

'It wasn't an easy shot for me to deal with,' Shilton said, 'because, apart from the fact that Domarski struck the ball exceptionally well, the Wembley pitch that night was very greasy and I was a bit unsighted by Emlyn. Unfortunately I made the mistake of trying to make the perfect save. In that sort of situation, I should have concentrated just on getting to the ball, knocking it behind for a corner or something like that. But I attempted to hold it by scooping it in to my body, and the pace beat me.'

At the other end, Tomaszewski kept making his imperfect saves. Allan Clarke converted a penalty, but a draw was enough for Poland. Tomaszewski, the clown, was the hero. As he recalls, though, he nearly wasn't.

It was obvious England would attack from the opening minutes, and because of that and because I was so bewildered by the atmosphere, I made a crucial mistake that could have ended everything before it had begun. I was about to kick the ball, and I put it down to run it out to the edge of the box, and I didn't notice Allan Clarke. I just saw some shadow of a white shirt, so I grabbed at the ball. I got a hand on it, and I was kicked by Clarke. It wasn't a foul, but the referee whistled and gave us a free-kick. That's how we survived and that was what woke me up. I started to play a normal game after that.

I remember hardly anything from the game. During the game, it was so noisy we were going crazy. With 100,000 people screaming for England we couldn't hear our own thoughts, so I only realised something special had happened when I was in the shower after the game. I was in the shower naked when the vice-president of the Polish Football Federation, Mykłoska, came running in fully dressed, came under the shower and hugged me. There are only two situations I really remember from the game. The first was the penalty by Clarke. I tried to look at Clarke to try to work out where he would put his shot – right or left or whatever. There's always something the player shows – he will glance one way or the other, but not Clarke. He was really confident, standing there knowing he was going to score, and he did score. I was a bit embarrassed by him. Then there was a situation where Clarke hit a shot from 6m [19ft], and I fell to the right and I felt something hit me, and realised I'd saved it. It was a corner kick, so I started organising my defenders, and then I saw Clarke standing, confused, as if he couldn't understand what had happened.

Clough later apologised to Tomaszewski for the clown comment, saying he had been deliberately denigrating Poland to try to strengthen his bid to take over from Alf Ramsey as England manager (he had resigned from Derby County thirty-six hours earlier), but the jibe accurately reflected what many in England felt about that style of goalkeeping at the time. Tomaszewski wasn't conservative or secure, he didn't look comfortable or safe; he just got in the way. Even early in the second half, when Tomaszewski had already made a series of fine saves, the commentator Barry Davies was left incredulous as he opted not to attempt to catch a swerving shot from Currie: 'Why did he punch?'

Particularly in goalkeeping, in which styles are so individual and the craft itself so misunderstood, it's dangerous to highlight one key moment after which nothing was ever the same again, but Tomaszewski's performance at Wembley perhaps was the keystone of a general change of attitude. Shilton, certainly, began thereafter to look less for the technically perfect save than the simply effective one. English crowds, meanwhile, had a British example of pragmatic unorthodoxy to learn from: Pat Jennings.

Bob Wilson called Jennings 'the most naturally gifted goalkeeper I ever set eyes on' and described him as a 'one-off', admitting that even though he was Arsenal goalkeeping coach during Jennings's stint at the club, there was no sense in which he could be coached. Nor, he eventually acknowledged, should he be imitated. As a young goalkeeper, Wilson had idolised Jennings (despite being four years older than him) and had tried to model his game on the Northern Irishman's before eventually accepting he was unique. 'He was an amazing shot-stopper,' Wilson wrote, 'brilliant at picking high crosses out of the air, sometimes one handed, [had] an amazing ability to save with his feet, cool enough to dribble his way out of trouble and all performed with what seemed to be a totally unflappable temperament.'

The fact that Wilson first revered Jennings and later became his coach says much for Jennings's longevity. He became the first British player to play over 1,000 games in a career that lasted from his debut for Newry Town in August 1961 to Northern

Ireland's game against Brazil in Guadalajara during the 1986 World Cup. In that time, he won two FA Cups, two League Cups and the Uefa Cup, was four times Tottenham's player of the year, Footballer of the Year in 1973 and Players' Player of the Year in 1976. He even scored in the Charity Shield of 1967, beating Manchester United's Alec Stepney with a mighty clearance. 'I hardly knew a thing about it,' Stepney said. 'Play was at the other end of the field and as Pat made his long clearance, kicking out of his hands, the ball seemed to be dropping in the area where [the defender] Bill Foulkes would be expected to clear.' Foulkes, though, let the ball drop, leaving Stepney, who had moved to the edge of his box, stranded. 'The ball bounced in front of me,' he went on, 'and soared in a long, slow, agonising arc over my head and into the goal.'

(It's only fair to note that, embarrassed as Stepney was, he became a goalscorer himself and, six seasons later, he was Manchester United's top scorer at Christmas – admittedly with just two goals. He'd taken a penalty in a sudden-death shoot-out against a Spanish side in a pre-season friendly and had converted it so impressively that Tommy Docherty nominated him as United's penalty-taker in the absence of Willie Morgan, who usually took them. It was at Leicester, who had Peter Shilton in goal, that Stepney was given his first chance of a league goal. 'When he saw me pick up the ball and place it on the spot he never said a word,' Stepney wrote. 'He's too professional for that, but the look on his face said everything. I drove the ball well wide of him to score the first goal of my career.')

When he was eleven, Jennings played in the local Under 19s league, excelling at saving low shots and having little chance with anything that went above head height, although as there were no posts on Newry meadow referees often gave him the benefit of the doubt. His team – known as Shamrock Rovers although they had no affiliation to the Dublin club – reached the cup final in his first season but he was left out for a bigger boy. Jennings was given a medal, but insisted it meant nothing to him. It looked for a time as though that disappointment would be the end of his football career as the local league was disbanded and, for the next five years, Jennings turned to Gaelic football. 'It taught me to accept hard knocks,' Jennings said. 'The physical contact was tremendous and the result is a few cuts and bruises don't worry me.'

After school, Jennings worked felling trees for a timber firm, building up his body further. This time, when his brother Brian, who played for Newry Town, asked him to fill a gap at the club, he was big enough and tough enough. They won the Irish Junior Cup in his first season. His form earned him a call-up to the Northern Ireland side for the World Youth Championships, at which they beat Belgium and Czechoslovakia, drew with Sweden and Bulgaria and survived the toss of a coin to reach the final. England beat them 4–0 but Bill McCracken, the great former Northern Ireland defender who had helped pioneer the offside trap at Newcastle United in the early 1920s, was watching the game in his capacity as a scout for Watford. Jennings had one more day working for the timber firm before the Fourth Division club offered him a contract.

Despite suffering badly from homesickness he was an ever-present in 1963–64 and developed the self-assurance to insist on playing his way. 'You'll never be a keeper, son, until you get your head kicked in a couple of times,' the manager Bill McGarry said to him. 'I happen to think that the good goalkeepers are those who don't get their head kicked in,' Jennings replied. It wasn't that he lacked courage, far from it, but – unlike Wilson – he was never a goalkeeper who would hurl himself at the feet of opponents. The next summer he moved to Tottenham. He would spend thirteen years there before joining Arsenal for a further eight.

Throughout, he remained placid, seemingly imperturbable, something that perhaps disguised his astonishing speed. Against Wolves in the 1972 Uefa Cup final, for instance, he made a stunning save, charging back and tipping a Danny Hegan volley over the bar after his miscued clearance had presented the midfielder with a chance. Jimmy Greaves said he was the fastest player at Spurs and that he was a decent outfield player in practice. Greaves also recalled a moment in Arsenal and Liverpool's FA Cup marathon in 1980 when Jennings and Willie Young exchanged a one-two rather than Jennings doing what most keepers of the time would have done and just belting it out of play.

He wasn't a true sweeper-keeper, but Jennings was a potent attacking weapon with his fine distribution, both with his long kicks and hard, flat throws that could initiate breaks rapidly. He had two clear unorthodoxies: he would catch balls one-handed, taking advantage of his vast, bucket-like hands, and he made a lot of saves with his feet. Unlike Shilton against Poland in 1973, he was rarely caught trying to make too orthodox a save. 'I have never found coaching manuals much use,' Jennings said. 'On the contrary, the "advice" they contain is often misleading and some of the pet theories about goalkeeping are wide of the mark.'

He preferred to find his own solutions. Some came from his background in Gaelic football, but he also learned from experience, which seems to have taught him, beyond anything else, that there is more luck and chance in football than most are prepared to admit. 'A proportion of goals,' he said, 'result from deflections by defenders or shots hitting divots and changing direction. But most of all you have to safeguard against an opponent miskicking. A mishit shot is the one most likely to finish in the bottom corner of the net after you have prepared to deal with a power drive. And, believe me, First Division stars miskick like schoolboys, even if they don't always admit it. More than once I have seen the scorer of a vital goal go on television after a game and explain, tongue in cheek, how he "bent" the ball past me when we both know he intended his shot to go in the opposite corner.'

That willingness to improvise was perhaps best demonstrated in the 1982 World Cup, in Northern Ireland's famous 1–0 victory over Spain. The hosts had benefited from some generous refereeing in their previous two games, being awarded a penalty in each, and the baffling sending off of Mal Donaghy after sixty-one minutes suggested the Paraguayan referee Hector Ortiz was no less minded to give Spain the benefit of the doubt than his predecessors. As the game headed into injury-time, a pass was played into the box for Juanito to chase. As the forward closed in, the ball bounced about a yard in front of Jennings. 'I could see that the ball was too high for Juanito to reach,' he wrote in his autobiography, 'and I sensed that if I made contact with him I might be penalised and the game could slip from our grasp. So I knew exactly what I was doing when I tipped the ball over his head and dived to retrieve it. Later I was told that millions of viewers, watching on television all over Britain, had their hearts in their mouths at that instant. I can only repeat that, however it looked, I had the situation under control.'

When Clough paid £270,000 for Shilton, there were doubters. Clough, always happy to conjure up directors saying idiotic things he could then prove wrong, insisted one board member had asked him what the point was in paying so much for a player who wouldn't be involved for eighty-five minutes of a game. Whether or not that was literally true, it was representative of a general attitude: if a goalkeeper had to make a save, the logic seemed to run, something must have gone wrong somewhere else on the field. Why not, then, invest heavily in outfielders who could make sure the goalkeeper was as underemployed as possible?

Yet the impact Shilton made was undeniable. He arrived five games into the 1977–78 season, at which point Forest had conceded six goals. The next six would take a further fourteen matches. By the end of the season, Forest had conceded just twenty-four goals, a league record; as Clough walked down a line of players to collect the Championship trophy, he extended his hand towards Shilton, acknowledging his extraordinary contribution. 'If I'd been a centre-forward,' Clough said, 'and I'd got past Burnsy and Lloydy [Kenny Burns and Larry Lloyd, Forest's two centre-backs], you've then got to get past Shilton, and Shilton came out and he used to cover the goal. When I played five-a-side with them I'd never pack it in till my side was winning, but to get past him with his huge shoulders – a magnificent body – was a killer.'

Clough respected other players, but with Shilton it went further. If he hadn't already had Barbara, Jim Montgomery joked when he was signed as Forest's reserve keeper, Clough would probably have married Shilton: he saw clearly not just how important Shilton was in himself, but the effect he had on other players. 'With Shilton in goal,' Clough said, 'it gave everyone more confidence. It spread through the side ... The defenders felt safer, and the forwards thought if we could nick a goal, there was more than an evens chance that the opposition wouldn't score at the other end.'

Shilton himself was very conscious of the importance of making himself so dominant that opponents were psychologically cowed by him, feeling compelled to attempt the perfect finish. In *The Magnificent Obsession*, he reproduces diagrams to show how a goalkeeper, by advancing, can force the forwards to play through-balls into wider areas or, by pushing out the defensive line, could encourage forwards to shoot from longer range. So confident was he in claiming crosses that apart from a man on each post, Shilton would refuse to allow any other defenders in his six-yard box while defending corners.

So intense was the psychological impression he made that opponents began to believe Shilton would sell them dummies – much in the way Sam Hardy had at Aston Villa before the First World War. 'I had a great chance with a header and I knew I just had to thump it square into the net,' the QPR defender Terry Mancini said of a game against Leicester that Shilton rated as one of his best. 'But he shaped to cover that side, so I glanced it for the other corner ... and he was standing there laughing at me as he caught it. He's a magician.'

He was also a great organiser of a defence, the unseen job for which he believed goalkeepers never got sufficient credit. 'People see the shots I save, the crosses I take and what have you, but they don't see the confidence, determination and discipline I can instil into a team by shouting the right things at the right time,' he said. 'It's *got* to be done. This sort of responsibility should be shared, but the man at the back – the last line of defence – should still be the dominant one. All the play is in

front of him and he can see so much more than the other players.' The best games, he said, were the ones in which he didn't
need to make a save; he offered the second leg of the European
Cup semi-final against Ajax in 1980 as an example. Forest, leading 2–0 from the first leg, lost 1–0, but were relatively comfortable in holding Ajax at arm's length.

There were, of course, dangers in being so proactive, seen
perhaps most clearly in the 1980 League Cup final when Forest
were beaten 1–0 by Wolves. It was a poor game, something for
which a new design of ball was widely blamed. 'Players found it
difficult to weight passes correctly,' Shilton said, 'and the ball's
tendency to bounce higher than the standard type made control difficult.' The goal came midway through the second half.
Wolves had been noticeably direct, trying to bypass Forest's
midfield and when Peter Daniel played in another long angled
ball from the right there seemed little danger. 'I gauged it was
going to carry through to me but it seemed to dip then suddenly drop short,' Shilton said. 'David Needham and I were both
thrown by this. Having expected to head the ball clear David
had to rapidly adjust. I too had to adjust, and we clashed. As
we staggered apart, we saw Andy Gray tapping the ball into the
empty net. I had to blame myself. I never left my line unless I
was sure of winning the ball.'

In that regard, there was a clear stylistic difference between
Shilton and his rival for the England goalkeeper's position, Ray
Clemence. Clemence had been a left-half as a schoolboy, but
went in goal for his youth team in a cup final, was spotted by
Scunthorpe United and signed by them in 1965. Even then he
nearly quit, so down was he after a string of defeats. At nineteen,
though, he was signed by Liverpool for £20,000 and after three
years as understudy to Tommy Lawrence, established himself
as a first-teamer. Gordon Banks noted that, 'Liverpool pushed
back onto Ray Clemence when opposing teams were putting
them under pressure and gave him comparatively little space to
come out for crosses. But Peter Shilton always wanted that area
immediately in front of him free. He's great on crosses and if
the opposition have the ball in a wide position, and he can see

they're going to hit it into the middle, he'll immediately push the defenders out to give himself room to take it.'

So when the ball was in the box, Clemence was reactive and Shilton proactive; when it was outside the box, Clemence effectively acted as a sweeper at times as Liverpool pushed out. Shilton was less inclined to do that, preferring to hang back to try to psych his opponent out and draw an error from him. Bafflingly, Ron Greenwood, the England manager, went through a spell of alternating between Clemence and Shilton rather than selecting one over the other; given the differences between them, it's hard to see how that could have achieved anything other than confusing the England back four.

Eventually, in the build-up to the 1982 World Cup, Shilton became the undisputed number one, and he went on to win a record 125 caps. In the eighties, despite leaving Forest for Southampton and then Derby, he *was* English goalkeeping, his unflappability and consistency such a paradigm that John Burridge, an eccentric who played 771 league games in England and Scotland for a total of twenty-nine clubs, went to a hairdresser's with a photograph of Shilton and demanded a similar perm.

So committed was Burridge to the path of self-improvement that he would have his wife throw fruit at him when he wasn't expecting it to try to improve his reflexes. He may not have had Shilton's talent, but Burridge followed him in his recognition of goalkeeping as something approaching a vocation, a skill to be practised and developed obsessively. He then took that obsession to Oman, where he was struck by a penalty save made by a part-time foreman at Muscat airport in a training match. 'I saw how you saved that penalty and I can see in you that you can go very far,' he said to him. 'Concentrate, train hard and I will promise you I'll get you to England.' The goalkeeper, then playing in the Omani third division, was Ali Al-Habsi. Within four years, he'd joined Bolton Wanderers, and four years after that he became a Premier League regular and crowd favourite at Wigan.

Through no fault of his own, Al-Habsi has come to seem symptomatic of the most recent trend in English goalkeeping:

decline. Even in the days when foreign goalkeepers were widely mocked for their supposed discomfort under high balls and their preference for punching over catching, there has been a willingness on the part of English clubs to turn to them. After Trautmann came the Yugoslav Petar Borota.

He joined Chelsea from Partizan in 1979 and made over 100 appearances for them. He even broke Peter Bonetti's record of sixteen clean sheets in a season in 1980–81 but was never able to shake off his reputation for eccentricity. Twice in his final year at Partizan he had conceded goals by putting the ball down in a crowded penalty area as though to take a free-kick when the referee hadn't blown for one, while at Stamford Bridge he would backheel the ball to team-mates in his own box to enliven dull games. He was one of four early Yugoslav goalkeepers in England: Ivan Katalinić, having won four league titles with Hajduk Split, moved to Southampton in 1980; Yakka Banović, who was born in Australia, played thirty-five games for Derby after joining them in 1980; and Raddy Avramović joined Notts County in 1981, helping them to promotion back to the top flight, before moving to Coventry.

And then there was Bruce Grobbelaar. Born in South Africa in 1957, the son of a British Fusilier, he moved north to Zimbabwe with his family when he was two months old. During the civil war in the 1970s, he fought as a tracker on the side of the government against rebels led by Robert Mugabe and Joshua Nkomo. Simon Kuper, getting a lift with Grobbelaar in Cape Town in 1999, noted how sharp his eyesight remained as he showed off his ability to read street signs at 100 yards. He was stationed in the bush and then on the border with Mozambique. One of his closest friends was shot dead five yards from where Grobbelaar was standing. 'If war teaches you anything it is the appreciation of being alive,' he said. 'Losing a game is not a tragedy after experiencing border raids and having to eat beetles because you are out of rations. I will never apologise for laughing at life and enjoying football.'

The war over, and lost, Grobbelaar turned to sport, signing for Durban City. He had been a prodigy not merely at football but also at baseball, rugby and cricket, claiming he was a better wicketkeeper as a teenager than Dave Houghton, who went on to a Test career for Zimbabwe. He was offered a trial by West Brom, but problems with his work permit meant he ended up playing in Canada for a year with Vancouver Whitecaps before returning to England with Crewe. In twenty-four games for them, he scored a penalty, earned a booking (apparently for wearing a face-mask of an old man during the kick-in) and impressed sufficiently to catch the eye of Liverpool. The Liverpool manager Bob Paisley spoke of seeing Grobbelaar warming up by having one of his team-mates blast a ball at him from the edge of the six-yard box. 'He not only stopped everything, but caught it,' Paisley said. 'I could have left even before kick-off.'

At Anfield, Grobbelaar immediately made himself unpopular by insisting he was out for Ray Clemence's first-team place. The defender Alan Hansen recalled most of the established players thinking 'he needed to be taken down a peg or two'. But within weeks Clemence was sold to Tottenham and Grobbelaar, who in the interim went on honeymoon with his best man as his wife, an air stewardess, had been called upon to work on a flight to Barbados, was first choice.

He made mistakes – a dropped cross against Peterborough, a misguided dribble out of goal in Moscow, a miscue against Sheffield Wednesday – and there was always the possibility that he'd misjudge a high ball, come careering out of his box or start wandering upfield with the ball at his feet, but that was balanced by his brilliance. 'Until Bruce burst on the scene,' said Bob Wilson, 'it was a rarity for a keeper to go for a high ball beyond twelve or thirteen yards from his goal or to sweep up behind his defence more than twenty-five-to-thirty yards from his goal line. His philosophy knows no limits. If a ball is in the air long enough to allow him to catch it seventeen yards from goal, then attempt to catch it he will.' In a sense, it was part of his genius; like Gatti, he always argued the forays prevented more goals than they cost and only an extrovert, the sort of person who borrowed a spectator's umbrella during a rainy game and threw oranges back at a Spanish crowd that had been pelting him, would have dared make them. Paisley's faith in him never wavered, and he insisted Grobbelaar would have been an England regular had he not been committed to Zimbabwe. The match-fixing allegations that blighted the end of his career cast a shadow over his reputation, of course, but for a decade at least Grobbelaar extended the Liverpool model of goalkeeping as laid down by Lawrence and Clemence.

As Shilton's career went on, the number of foreign keepers swelled. By the advent of the Premier League in 1992, there had been Hans van Breukelen and then Hans Segers, both Dutch, at Nottingham Forest, the Canadian Craig Forrest at Ipswich Town, the Australian Mark Bosnich and the Dane Peter Schmeichel at Manchester United and the Czechs Pavel Srníček, Jan Stejskal and Ludek Miklosko at Newcastle, QPR and West Ham respectively. They were the start of a wave. By the end of the 2011–12 season, of the twenty Premier League clubs, only four had an English goalkeeper as first choice. As ever in discussions of the impact of foreigners in a league, cause and effect are hard to disentangle, while the correct balancing of quality against quantity is extremely difficult to judge – which, after all, is better for an England manager picking three keepers for a twenty-three man World Cup squad: four goalkeepers playing at the very highest level, or twenty playing at a much lower level?

Shilton retired after the 1990 World Cup at the age of forty. He'd made vital saves in that tournament against Belgium and Cameroon, proving himself still a master of one-on-one situations. Against West Germany in the semi-final, he'd made one stunning reflex block from a Jürgen Klinsmann header, but questions had been raised both over his technique in the penalty shoot-out and the way he was beaten by Andreas Brehme's deflected free-kick. Shilton insisted he paid for almost recovering as the shot looped off Paul Parker; as he back-pedalled desperately he couldn't get sufficient height in his leap and he ended up shoving the ball into the roof of the net. 'Many match reports asked serious questions of me, saying it was a soft goal and suggesting if I had jumped another inch or so I would have tipped the ball over the bar,' he said. 'The journalists who wrote such things revealed just how little they understood about goal-keeping. In similar circumstances, I have seen the majority of goalkeepers rooted to the spot in no man's land. They are never criticised for it because TV commentators and a good many supporters think, "He had no chance of getting that" ... if I had remained rooted to the spot and looked on helplessly as the ball sailed over my head, I'm sure not a word would have been said.'

Chris Woods had been waiting a long time for his chance to succeed him. After impressing as an eighteen-year-old in the 1978 League Cup final for Nottingham Forest – when he had deputised for the Cup-tied Shilton – he had been forced to leave the club in search of regular first-team football, going first to QPR and Norwich and then to Rangers before returning to England with Sheffield Wednesday. He proved himself an excellent goalkeeper, but desperately unlucky to find Clemence and Shilton ahead of him for the national team. After making his debut against the USA in 1985, he played a further fifteen times (although only four of them were in competitive matches, one of which was in the final group game in Euro 88 after England had already been eliminated) before Shilton's retirement and then another twenty-seven afterwards. By 1990 – still only thirty, relatively young by goalkeeping standards – he was probably already just past his best and the overriding memory of him in an England shirt is of his knees buckling slightly as Norway's Lars Bohinen fizzed a shot over his left shoulder in a World Cup qualifier in Oslo in 1993. England lost that game 2–0 and Woods played only one further game for his country, finishing as he had begun with a friendly against the USA.

Still, there seemed little reason for England to panic about the goalkeeping situation. David Seaman took over and, although he had a habit of being caught flat-footed, he became as consistent for England as Shilton had been, winning seventy-five caps despite the presence around the squad of goalkeepers as good as Tim Flowers and Nigel Martyn.

His moustache and pony-tail jarring with his Yorkshire gruffness, there was always a sense that Seaman wasn't taken entirely seriously. Certainly his habit of signing his autograph

'Safe Hands' occupied an uneasy middle ground between posturing and an almost self-mocking self-confidence. Arsenal fans may recall the long years of reliable stolidity but others remember Seaman as much for his mistakes as his brilliance. There was his desperate leaden-footed scramble across his goal line as Ronald Koeman dinked a free-kick past him in a vital World Cup qualifier against the Netherlands in 1993. There was the outrageous Nayim shot from the halfway line that looped over Seaman's backpedal as Real Zaragoza beat Arsenal in the Cup-Winners' Cup final in 1995. There was the slowness of his reaction as Dietmar Hamann thumped a low free-kick past him as Germany beat England in a World Cup qualifier in 2000, in the final game at the old Wembley. And there was his helplessness as Ronaldinho, whether by design or by fluke, curled a free-kick over his head in Brazil's victory over England in the quarter-final of the 2002 World Cup.

The German journalist Uli Hesse remembers meeting Seaman in a fish-and-chip shop in Kings Langley in the 2000–01 season. 'When he left, the Turkish owner said to me, "Did you talk to him?" I said, "No. The only thing I could think of was, 'You should have saved that Hamann strike at Wembley.' He laughed and said, "Same with me. I always want to thank him for not saving a penalty against Galatasaray [in the Uefa Cup final in 2000] and then I decide not to." The funny thing is that, a few months later, in the build-up to the [Germany v England] game in Munich in September 2001, people over here made fun of Seaman and said it was strange that England, the home of the game, had this clown and we had Oliver Kahn, the best keeper in the world. Well, and then Seaman makes the best save of the game and England win 5–1.'

That save, getting down quickly to push a Jörg Böhme shot round the post, was typical of Seaman. Essentially, apart from the moments when his feet became rooted – if only he'd been introduced to Len Hepple, Shilton's dance teacher from Hexham – Seaman's greatest quality was his reliability, but he was also capable of startling reflex saves, none better, perhaps, than the one he produced in the 2003 FA Cup semi-final against Sheffield

United, his 1,000th senior appearance, as he dived backwards and to his right to claw a Paul Peschisolido header away from goal. A month later, he captained Arsenal to victory over Southampton in the FA Cup final, his farewell appearance for the club.

After impressing at QPR, Seaman joined Arsenal in 1990 and conceded just eighteen goals in thirty-eight games in his first season as Arsenal won the title. In the third-last game, away at Sunderland, he made a fine diving save up and to his left to push wide a late Gary Owers curler to protect a goalless draw and earn Arsenal a point that kept them four points clear of Liverpool. He went on to win a League Cup and FA Cup double in 1993 and the Cup-Winners' Cup a year later, although it was his performance against Sampdoria in the same competition the following season, capped by a save from an Attilio Lombardo penalty in the shoot-out, that stands out. Although he played a significant part in the double-winning seasons of 1997–98 and 2001–02, Seaman's finest spell of form probably came in Euro 96, when he saved a Gary McAllister penalty against Scotland, was magnificently imposing in the 4–1 win over the Netherlands, making a superb block from Dennis Bergkamp just before half-time when the score was 1–0, and then turned away Miguel Ángel Nadal's kick in the quarter-final shoot-out victory over Spain.

It was after Seaman that the problems set in for England. His last match came at the age of thirty-seven in a European Championship qualifier against Macedonia FYR in 2002 after he had been beaten direct from a corner by Artim Šakiri. He was succeeded by David James, who never inspired the same confidence Seaman had at his peak, his frequent but unpredictable sallies from his box seemingly making his back four wary about pushing high up the pitch, which in turn meant spaces opened up between the defensive and midfield lines. That was horribly apparent in England's World Cup qualifier away to Austria in 2004 when James-induced panic turned a 2–0 lead into a 2–2 draw, the equaliser coming as an Andreas Ivanschitz drive deflected off Steven Gerrard and squirmed under James's dive.

James was dropped for Paul Robinson after that, but his vulnerability to long shots allied to his misfortune in a European Championship defeat in Zagreb when a Gary Neville backpass hit a bobble and hopped over his attempted clearance to give Croatia the lead meant he was never secure in the role. Scott Carson then made an awful error against the same opposition at Wembley, allowing a long-range Niko Kranjčar drive to slither through his hands as England failed to qualify for the 2008 European Championship. Was he a bad goalkeeper or just one who, promoted perhaps too soon, made a hideous career-defining gaffe on his competitive international debut? Perhaps the truth is that it's quite easy for a country with one outstanding goalkeeper to appear as though it has a fine stock. So long as Shilton was playing, England could look at the likes of Clemence, Corrigan, Woods, Gary Bailey and Dave Beasant and feel secure. They played only occasionally, little was expected of them, and a performance of competence was enough to reinforce the perception of strength in depth. Shilton could make a mistake and, with his history of excellence, be quickly forgiven; a mistake by a less-established goalkeeper, though, would lead to suspicion – something even Shilton experienced after his gaffe against Poland in 1973. What England found after Seaman was that no keeper ever managed to become established before making an error that brought calls for them to be dropped. Of course, a player of the quality of Shilton made fewer errors than lesser keepers but to an extent England's goalkeeping crisis of the first decade of the twenty-first century was the result of bad luck, errors at the wrong time generating panic, which in turn made the environment for each new keeper increasingly anxious.

With Chris Kirkland and Ben Foster regularly injured, it was West Ham's Rob Green who ended up as England's first-choice at the 2010 World Cup. He had already proved himself a goalkeeper to whom unfortunate things happen, rupturing a groin muscle while taking a goal-kick in a B-international against Belarus in 2006, allowing Vitaliy Kutuzov to roll in a simple finish. What happened in Rustenburg against USA, though, was far worse as he allowed a soft shot from Clint Dempsey to dribble under his body. England had looked comfortable at 1–0; the goal sucked the confidence out of them and they ended up drawing, costing them top spot in the group and setting up the humiliating 4–1 defeat to Germany in the second round.

The catastrophe of English goalkeeping seemed clear, generating much handwringing but few solutions. At one point things seemed so bleak there was talk of trying to persuade the Italian Carlo Cudicini or the Spaniard Manuel Almunia to naturalise. And then Joe Hart, born in 1987, blessed with bulk, agility, sharp reflexes and an aura of confidence, came along and everybody could breathe easily again. The performances of Birmingham City's Jack Butland, born in 1993, in the Under-20 World Cup in Colombia in 2011, commanding his box, saving a penalty, dominating one-on-ones and letting in only one goal in four matches despite England being under pressure in all of them, suggests Hart may soon have competition.

If a Clemence–Shilton style rivalry does develop, England would be extremely blessed. History suggests that the period between 2002 and 2010, while rocky by England standards, was not a crisis, but that the period from 1963 to 2002, when, the three-year Woods interlude aside, four keepers – Banks, Clemence, Shilton and Seaman – dominated the position, was a highly unusual period of consistency and stability.

7: TOMMY AND JO-JO

Éclair Douala don't exist any more, and even when they did they weren't a major force in Cameroonian football. They never won the league – never so much as reached the Cup final. For most of their existence, they were a nondescript second-division side. And yet, not only was Éclair the club where Roger Milla first played league football, but in the early seventies it boasted the two goalkeepers who would go on to be the greatest in African history: Thomas Nkono and Joseph-Antoine Bell. The rivalry between Tommy and Jo-Jo, as they came to be known, would dominate Cameroonian football for almost two decades. 'When you had these two goalkeepers it was something great for the country because the whole country talked for twenty years about Thomas Nkono and Joseph-Antoine Bell,' said Bell. 'I can imagine that young players wanted to be goalkeepers, because we were real goalkeepers and became role models.'

They could hardly have been more different either in personality or style. Bell is ebullient and self-confident, these days an engaging and outspoken television pundit and a consistent critic of the Cameroonian football authorities; Nkono is far more reserved, although certainly not without self-confidence, a quiet man who largely stays out of the limelight. There is a social difference as well: Bell was educated at boarding school, while Nkono was a boy from the countryside who lived with his sister and then the club president after making the move to Douala.

I met Bell on the top floor of his house in a comfortable suburb of Douala, a study rendered trapezoid by the slant of the roof. He had a laptop propped on a pile of books in front of him, while a guitar rested alongside him on the sofa. The shelves behind him were crammed with books in French on the history of art and with thrillers in English. It's possible that they belonged to his wife but Bell has clearly embraced the fact that his life is now more about words than balls. To an extent, that was always the case.

'I've always known that I was a goalkeeper,' Bell told me. 'I was playing up front but knowing that I was a goalkeeper. I started playing in goal when I was really young, maybe five or six. When I got to boarding school, I organised my housemates to play, but I didn't play goalkeeper. I was playing up front and nobody knew I was a goalkeeper.'

At the time, going in goal simply wasn't the done thing in Cameroon, which may explain why Bell hid his vocation at least until his early teens. 'They used to force someone to be the keeper,' he said. 'But nobody needed to force me. I felt goalkeeper was a position of responsibility, which it is. I enjoyed it because of that, because I knew if there was a goal it was my responsibility. And because it was my responsibility I had to make them play the way I wanted and so that's why I behaved as I did. I had leadership ability and this gave me the opportunity to use it.' And because he'd spent so much time playing outfield, Bell was unusually comfortable with the ball at his feet, which of course helped when it came to leaving his box.

In Bell was embodied the urge for integration that had gripped various goalkeepers over the preceding century. For him, that process of bringing the goalkeeper back into the body of the team was completed with the change in the backpass law in 1992 and he was mystified that that wasn't how Fifa presented it. 'I was good enough with my feet that it didn't matter when they changed the rule on backpasses,' he said. 'I went to [Sepp] Blatter and I told him he was wrong to say they were taking some privilege away from goalkeepers. I told him if he said that he would have problems because nobody likes to have privileges taken away from them. You need to say you have integrated the goalkeeper in a real football game. Now they are allowed to play like the rest of the team but they have something extra. If you say you have taken a privilege then they will not play, but if you say they've been integrated then they have to improve with their feet.'

Nkono also began as an outfielder. I met him at a tennis club in the hills overlooking Barcelona, where he works as a goalkeeping coach for Espanyol, the club he represented for almost a decade. The academy he runs in the city has produced players such as Carlos Kameni, who has followed Nkono at Espanyol and was Cameroon's keeper when they won gold at the 2000 Olympic Games; Didier Ovono, whose career took him to Allianza of El Salvador and Dinamo Tbilisi of Georgia before he settled at Le Mans and who was a central presence in the Gabon side that lost unluckily in the quarter-final of the African Cup of Nations in 2012; and Gorka Iraizoz, goalkeeper for Athletic Club of Bilbao as they reached the Europa League final in 2012. 'I try to give them a methodology of the work,' he explained. 'To give them vision. To make them play well with the hand and the foot. To make them handle the ball well. To do analytical work. In the past it was just about stopping goals, but now it's completely different. You must be able to continue the play in modern football.'

Nkono was born in 1956 in Edea, a small town to the southeast of Douala, but soon moved to the village of Dizangue, about ten miles west on the other side of Lake Ossa. 'I was just playing with friends and family,' Nkono said, but there were days when he would run back to Edea after school just for a game. 'When I had holidays I went to Edea to play some games because my mother's family was there,' he went on. 'I played as a midfielder or a forward when I was young but then my big brother told me I had to go in goal. He played in a team in Edea. When I went there I played maybe one or two friendly matches with this team and some scout saw me and asked if I wanted to go to play for Éclair of Douala. I said okay. It was a big opportunity for me. My big sister lived in Douala so it made sense for me to go there and to play. I had some chance because she lived only fifty metres away from the club. In my first season we were promoted.'

Even in such basic details comes the first disagreement in the accounts of Bell and Nkono. 'He came to Éclair the year I moved,' Bell said. 'The boy who was my sub was supposed to play that year but he was not good enough and the chairman didn't really trust him. We had a stadium somewhere not far from here and one day the other goalkeeper was not there. The chairman said to Nkono – because he came from a village and he was doing him a favour getting him there – he told him that the worst one will go in goal. So he said, "Villager, you will go to the goal." And because he came from the village, didn't have many friends and didn't talk very much, he went there and did his best to show his will to help. And this is the way he started his career.' Nkono, for his part, insists he was signed as a goalkeeper but played as a forward sometimes in training.

In 1973, soon after Nkono had started playing for Éclair, they reached the semi-final of the Cup. They were drawn against Canon of Yaoundé, then five or six years from their peak, when they were one of the greatest club sides Africa has ever known. It should have been a two-legged tie, but the first leg in Douala was abandoned when Éclair's president-manager was denied entry to the stadium over a dispute long since forgotten. The Cameroonian federation ruled that only the second leg, the game in Yaoundé, should be played, making it effectively a one-off match. That was Nkono's great stroke of luck. 'I couldn't play in the first game because I had some injury in my shoulder,' he said. 'I would only have been able to play as a forward.'

Nkono was fit enough to go in goal in the game in Yaoundé and excelled in a 1–0 defeat. 'I played my way to a transfer,' Nkono said. 'From the first minute people were asking, "Who is this? Who is this guy?" It wasn't like now when you have mass media. People didn't know me.'

'After that game the decision to sign him was unanimous among the first-team players,' said the Canon defender Jean-Paul Akono. 'I remember that game vividly. I took a penalty against him and he saved it – and held it – like it was the easiest thing in the world. He made you doubt your own ability to play football. One of the managers of the Canon club, Mr Clement Obou Fegue, who was director general of the water corporation, was the one who realised that Thomas Nkono should be signed.'

The decision was one thing; actually getting the deal done something else. Fegue went to the area of Douala where Nkono was living with Éclair's president. 'All the people wanted to kill him because he wanted to take me away,' Nkono said. 'It was not a very good neighbourhood and so he was threatened and I had to come out: "No, no. This team is going to sign me, please ..." That was the first contact. Then Éclair were relegated to the second division and I moved to Canon.'

When he did join, though, he wasn't an automatic first choice. 'The coach at the time was the former international Eboa Laurent, Canon's first-team goalkeeper was called Matuke and he was a good goalkeeper, so when Nkono joined the team, the coach decided to rotate them,' Akono recalled. 'One would play two games and then the other would play two games. Then we had a crucial Cup match in Douala against Dinamos in 1973. We beat them 3–1 in the quarter-final in Yaoundé. In the second leg it was Matuke's turn and he conceded four goals and they were virtually eliminated because his performance was a disaster. The coach decided to bring on Nkono for the last few minutes. He made some brilliant saves, and Canon managed to equalise, to score four goals, and finally qualified.'

Bell is almost two years older than Nkono and there is a clear sense that he helped to pave the way for his rival. Nkono is almost universally described as 'a natural' but it wasn't that Bell enjoyed hour upon hour of expert tuition. On the contrary, he was self-taught and if his was a talent that achieved great-ness through hard work, it was he who managed and guided that work. 'Goalkeepers were always a bit mysterious,' Bell said of the environment in which he grew up as a footballer. 'He was different from the others. He could be a bad goalkeeper but because he did different things from the rest of the team he would be looked at as somebody special.'

What changed was the arrival in Cameroon in 1974 of the great Yugoslav goalkeeper Vladimir Beara. 'He was the first goalkeeper trainer I had,' Bell said. 'He brought a lot to me especially. I worked with him in the national team. At club level I had to do it myself. I really helped myself a lot because I did it with my own mathematics at school – at that time there was no television so I couldn't learn from the image of anybody – so I tried to work out the best way to avoid contact, the best way to take the ball easier ... But Beara was the first coach who could tell me I had to work hard, that was the first thing: never to complain about the amount of work you had to do at training. With Beara you finished with the rest of the team and he would take twenty or thirty minutes more for goalkeepers.'

Beara was one of the best European goalkeepers there has ever been, almost certainly the greatest Yugoslav goalkeeper ever. When Lev Yashin collected his European Player of the Year award in 1963, he insisted that the best goalkeeper in the world wasn't him, but Beara. He was born in Sinj, in what is now Croatia, in 1928 but even in the early eighties he would turn up at Hajduk's training and hold his own against younger keepers in penalty shoot-outs.

The Yugoslav's reputation was never as great as that of Yashin, but even in England he garnered something of a cult status following an international at Highbury in 1950 in which he pulled off a string of improbable saves as Yugoslavia held England to a 2–2 draw. But it wasn't just his athleticism and reflexes that impressed; there was also a grace and a majesty to his goalkeeping. As Bob Wilson said, 'There was an entertaining, aesthetic air about him,' which was perhaps appropriate for a player who once studied ballet. That, Wilson went on, was 'why his jumps and dives with feet curled and body perfectly poised appealed. He kept goal on his toes, like a coiled spring, always ready to pounce.'

Although he attracted the nickname of 'the ballet dancer with the hands of steel', Beara always felt his development owed more to the training techniques of one of his first coaches, Luka Kaliterna. 'My confidence in goal, the way I seemed to be able to catch a ball easily, and my technique for taming shots I put down to Barba Luka,' he said. ('Barba' is a familiar term in Split for an old man – loosely it translates as 'uncle'.) 'It was a simple drill we did in practice. He made me catch a small ball about the size of a baseball and after that it was very easy for me to catch a football.'

Beara played sixty times for his country, winning silver at the 1952 Olympics when Yugoslavia, having overcome the USSR 3–1 in a replay after a 5–5 draw, had the misfortune to run into the great Hungary side of Puskás, Hidegkuti and Bozsik in the final. His greatest disappointment, though, came in the 1954 World Cup, the second of the three in which he played, as Yugoslavia lost to West Germany in the quarter-final. 'We scored an own goal after eight minutes, and then had ten great chances, but ended up losing 2–0,' Beara said. 'If the game against the USSR was our most dramatic, this was our un-luckiest.' According to Wilson, Beara was so restricted by injury that he could barely move to try to stop Helmut Rahn's decisive late second.

It wasn't just bad luck that undermined Yugoslavia that day, though. 'At the time, the president of the FA was Rato Dugonjić [a senior politician who headed the department of youth],' Beara said. 'We were promised that if we got through the group we'd each get a Vespa, which at the time cost $100 in Italy. But then on the day of the Germany game, Dugonjić came and said there were no scooters, and that it wasn't good for us to play like the bourgeoisie when other people had to work just to buy food. Suddenly we were public enemy No.1, and we hadn't even asked for anything. So after that, we were depressed.'

Politics also intervened in Beara's club career. He won three league titles with Hajduk, before making the highly controversial move to one of the great rivals, Crvena Zvezda, who, it is rumoured, sold their team bus to finance the deal. Quite why he went has never been fully established. Some suggest the move was directed by the authorities; others point out that Beara's wife was Serbian. Either way, it proved a success for both player and club, as Zvezda won four out of the next five league titles.

Beara clearly wasn't fazed by the move, but then he gives the impression of being a man who isn't fazed by much. He always cut a relaxed figure on his goal line, preferring to trust in his ability rather than in any mechanical learned technique. He even eschewed walls while facing free-kicks. 'Somehow it always seemed easier when I could look at a player eye to eye,' he said. 'My time was the time of romantic football. There were still lots of good moves, dribbles and attractive goals. Tactics still hadn't eaten football. It was the playing style of the 1962 World Cup and then in England in 1966 that started the new era of football when the ball was no longer the most important thing in the game.' Some things, though, he believes will never change. 'A good goalkeeper,' he said, 'still has to be a lot like he was in my time. He has to have courage and self-confidence.' Those were the qualities he tried to pass on to the Cameroonians, having been despatched to West Africa as part of Tito's programme to extend the reach of the Non-Aligned Movement, which sought to steer a middle course between US and Soviet influence.

It wasn't just Yugoslavia that sent coaches to Africa in the sixties and seventies. Many Europeans and South Americans went for political reasons, but many more went out of curiosity, with a pioneering spirit or simply because it was possible to make a decent living there; African football, by the seventies, had a credibility it had never had before. This was the great age of African self-assertiveness as colonialism was cast off and swathes of the continent gained independence. In football that was reflected with the establishment, in February 1957, of the Confederation of African Football and the staging, later that year, of the first African Cup of Nations. As the competition grew and African football became increasingly self-confident, Africa boycotted the World Cup after being allotted only half a place for the 1966 tournament (the best African team playing off against the best Asian team for one of the sixteen available slots).

The action was successful and Africa was guaranteed a slot at the 1970 tournament. Morocco won the qualifying competition and so became the first African side to play at a World Cup finals since Egypt in 1934. They took a single point but African improvement was rapid. Tunisia became the first African side to win a match at a final tournament when they beat Mexico in 1978; Algeria and Cameroon were both eliminated only on goal difference in 1982 before, in 1986, Morocco became the first African side to make it through the first round. It's much harder to judge the strength of the club game in Africa, given the lack of matches against teams from other continents but, given how rare it was for an African player to move abroad then, it's safe to assume it was, in comparative terms, significantly stronger than now and that its quality would have risen along with the quality of African national sides. Certainly the atmosphere in which Bell and Nkono grew up was one of optimism for football and new opportunities.

'When Beara came there had been nothing before,' Bell said. 'He was here for one and a half years, holding camps but not every month. So when you went there you had to keep something from what he was saying, what he was telling you and bring it back to your club and put it into effect yourself. He was the first to say that handling was something important. I've seen many goalkeepers dropping balls and I don't enjoy it because I learned how to handle the ball and I know that handling is important. Keeping the ball is your main job, not just pushing it away. So, if you have to push it away it must be to a safer situation. But with him, I learned how to do it, why to do it.'

Nkono also benefited from Beara's teaching – undermining the claim that his talent was purely instinct; he may have had great natural ability but he also benefited from instruction. 'I thought it would be easy to play with my talent but what I didn't realise was the intensity you needed,' he said. 'From the point we started training with Vladimir Beara everything changed. I started working on technical aspects. They created a special role for Beara in order to improve the technical aspects – blocking the ball, crosses, diving … he created a machine for me to practise punching the ball. He taught me to coordinate jumping with punching the ball.

'I was called to the national team. I'd work for instance on Mondays and he'd say, "Okay – we'll see you on Wednesday for

(top left, *PA Images*) Taffarel celebrates after saving Phillip Cocu's penalty as Brazil beat the Netherlands in a shoot-out in the 1998 World Cup semi-final. (top right, *PA Images*) Gilmar punches clear during Brazil's victory over Sweden in the 1958 World Cup final. (left, *Getty Images*) Arthur Wharton, goalkeeper for Preston and Rotherham, and the first black player to appear in the Football League. (above, *PA Images*) The hapless Frank Haffey claims a cross in Scotland's 9–3 defeat to England in 1961.

Peter Shilton makes a save on his England debut against East Germany in 1970 (*PA Images*).

Two of the early English greats: Harry Hibbs of Birmingham (left) and Sam Hardy of Aston Villa (right, *both pics PA Images*).

(left) Frank Swift catches a cross in a Home International match against Scotland (*PA Images*).

(centre) Gordon Banks saves a penalty from Geoff Hurst as Stoke City beat West Ham in the League Cup semi-final in 1972 (*PA Images*).

(bottom) Manchester City's Bert Trautmann struggles on with a broken neck in the 1956 FA Cup final (*Getty Images*).

The ballet-trained Yugoslav keeper Vladimir Beara in practice. (*Getty Images*)

The great Cameroonian rivals, Joseph-Antoine Bell, (left) and Thomas Nkono (below, *both pics Getty Images*).

Peter Schmeichel wasn't just a great shot-stopper; his long throws often started counter-attacks (*PA Images*).

Oliver Kahn, prime example of the muscular school of German goalkeeping (*PA Images*).

Sepp Maier and his famous big gloves make a save against Italy in the 1978 World Cup (*PA Images*).

The two greatest Italian keepers: Dino Zoff (left) and Gianluigi Buffon (right, *both pics PA Images*).

Milutin Šoškić, who influenced the development of US goalkeeping, hurls himself into a challenge playing for the rest of the World against England in 1963 (*PA Images*).

(left) Iker Casillas flies over his team-mate Carles Puyol as Spain beat the Netherlands in the 2010 World Cup final (*PA Images*).

(below) Barcelona's Victor Valdes punches clear of Manchester United's Wayne Rooney in the 2011 Champions League final (*PA Images*).

Four literary number ones (clockwise from top left): Albert Camus, Yevgeny Yevtushenko, Vladimir Nabokov (*three pics Getty Images*) and Osvaldo Soriano (*PA Images*).

the second session of the training. The stadium was four kilometres away. I had pain in all my body. So I was thinking, I'm going, I'm not going ... We had a training session at four o'clock and finally at three-thirty I decided I wasn't going. The next training session, the coach told me he didn't want me in the national team because I'd missed the training sessions. That changed my mentality and I understood I needed to go to training sessions if I wanted to be a professional goalkeeper. I was better than other players, but they didn't call me up. I missed three or four training sessions and get-togethers. And when he called me again, I was on the bench.'

At club level, though, it wasn't long before Nkono established himself in a side that would go on to win four domestic titles in six years, the African Champions Cup in 1978 and 1980 and the Cup-Winners' Cup in 1979. 'At that time we had probably the best team in the world,' insisted the midfielder Théophile Abega, who would go on to captain Cameroon at the 1982 World Cup. 'The best midfield, the best defence. Football was different then: it was the football of talent, natural football. Now it's about who runs fastest, who jumps highest, who kicks it hardest. At that time it was technical football.'

It was the Champions Cup ties in which Nkono really excelled. There were epic games against Enugu Rangers of Nigeria, Green Buffaloes of Zambia and Hafia of Guinea in 1978 and Bendel Insurance of Nigeria and the Zairean side AS Bilima in 1980. At home, where tens of thousands of fans packed into the vast open bowl of the Ahmadou Ahidjo, Canon were confident; facing a similar intensity of support away was very different. 'There were matches in which we were completely rattled,' said Abega. 'It was like Tommy was playing alone against the opposing side.'

It wasn't just that he was calm, radiating confidence, he also had a psychological effect on opponents. 'Nkono discouraged the attackers from the opposition side,' Akono said. 'Some of his saves were provocative. If you shot from long-range, he would hold the ball. We went to games thinking nobody could ever beat us. There were games when the opposition was much better than us but he would rise to their level. There were many occasions when it seemed he was beaten but would do something like a miracle.

'He was a phenomenon. He was very strong when everybody was fragile. It's hard to describe the influence he had on the team. He was a genius but he was also the hardest worker in the team. It wasn't just in matches; he didn't like conceding goals in training sessions. He was an extremely hard worker. It was very reassuring having him behind you so you knew if you made an error, there was someone who could correct it.'

For a country to have one great goalkeeper was unusual in Africa; two was unprecedented. Even if Nkono and Bell had had videos to draw on, they would have found little local inspiration. Goalkeepers are often the forgotten men but that seems doubly true in Africa. The written history of the African game is limited anyway and what does exist is heavily focused on the exploits of skilful midfielders and goalscoring forwards. 'It was simply far harder for them to train,' said Claude Le Roy, the highly respected French former coach of Cameroon, Senegal, DR Congo and Ghana. 'With all the stones, or the bottle-tops lying around on the pitches they use, of course people found it unbelievable that Africa could create goalkeepers. There weren't the conditions for it.'

There was probably only one truly exceptional African goalkeeper before Bell and Nkono: Robert Mensah. Born in Cape Coast, where football was introduced to West Africa by an Anglo-Jamaican schoolteacher called Mr Britton, he made his name with Mysterious Dwarfs, whose stadium today is named after him. He moved west to Sekondi Independence Football Club in 1963, but after the coup in 1966, he returned home to the Dwarfs. Noted for the black shirt and the checked cap he wore in honour of Lev Yashin, he won his first national call-up in 1968 and joined the Ghanaian giants Asante Kotoko the same year.

They had played the great Zairean side Tout-Puissant Englebert in the 1967 African Champions Cup final, the tie being awarded against them when they refused to take part in a play-off after two draws, and with Mensah in goal they went on to be one of the major sides of the turn of the decade. Kotoko lost to Ismaili of Egypt in the semi-final in 1969, and then beat them at the same stage the following year before again facing Englebert in the final. Kotoko drew the first leg 1–1 in Kumasi but Mensah was exceptional in Lubumbashi, inspiring his side to a 2–1 win.

By 1971, when he moved on to Tema Textiles Printing, Mensah was recognised as the best goalkeeper in Africa, almost certainly the best goalkeeper the continent had known. That April, he was stoned by the home crowd as Ghana won 3–1 in Liberia. In June he was sacked by his club for a no-show while away on international duty. Three days later, he made three good saves but could not prevent Ghana losing 1–0 to Togo and so failing, for the first time, to qualify for the African Cup of Nations. It was, the headline insisted, 'THE DAY GHANA STOOD STILL'. It would stand even stiller in Mensah's honour before the year was out.

He returned to Kotoko and it was for them, on 28 October, that he played his last game – not, of course, that the newspapers reported it as such at the time – keeping a clean sheet as Kotoko beat Sekondi Hasacas 1–0. Knowing what was to come, there is a plangent banality to the formalities of the match report. Hasacas, the *Daily Graphic* noted, were denied not by Mensah but by 'too much elaboration in front of goal'. Yaw Sam got the winner, heading in a cross from 'young Albert Essumang'. His last major game, at least by the *Graphic*'s estimation, had been – appropriately enough – against Ismaili in the quarter-final of the African Clubs Cup, a game Kotoko won 3–0. Mensah was chaired from the field at the final whistle.

The day after the Hasacas match, Mensah returned to Tema, by then a concrete new town, the old fishing village having been turned into a thriving port by Nkrumah's reforms. That night, a brief piece in the *Graphic* of 1 November reported, he was stabbed with a broken bottle outside a bar in Tema.

More details emerged in the *Graphic* the following day. Inspector C. J. Acquaye of the local police said that a quarrel had arisen between Agya Awere and Joseph Ackersou, two local men who were drinking in the bar. A third man, a thirty-one-year-old electrician called Isaac Melfah, was remanded in custody, accused of having followed Mensah from the bar after the fight and attacked him. As for Mensah, he had been operated on and the prognosis seemed positive. By the time the public read that, though, it was already out of date: aged thirty-two, Mensah died in hospital, at 0230 on Tuesday, 2 November 1971.

'He was,' the columnist Addo Twum asserted (and the capitals are his), 'a Big man with Big hands and Big heart and no doubt, Ghana's foremost goalkeeper. Robert stood more than six feet tall and he handled a football with the same contemptuous ease that Joe Louis treated the gloves … There will be many good goalkeepers but there will never be another "Yashin" Mensah who will be remembered in his black jersey and magic cap. He had a superb sense of anticipation, great physical fitness and the courage and confidence to go down to the feet of dangerous attackers. And of course, those magic hands that could pick a ball out from the air as simply and effortlessly as the feet of legend Pelé scores goals, will be seen no more.'

His funeral became a procession of tragedy, as the body was taken from Tema to Kumasi, home of Kotoko. It was for them he had played his greatest games, most notably in their epic victory over Tout-Puissant Englebert in the African Clubs Cup final of 1968. There were, the *Graphic* reported, 'thousands of mourners, young and old … Schoolchildren refused to attend classes and rushed to the airport and the sports stadium to pay their last respects … there was wailing and weeping at the nooks and corners of the city. Traffic stood still as taxi-cabs, private cars and commercial vehicles wrapped in the red traditional colour of Kumasi lined up in the streets tooting their horn signifying their last post to Robert Mensah …'

Direct evidence as to his ability, in the form of video clips or photographs, is limited, but the regard in which he was evidently held speaks as eloquently as any highlights reel. An accompanying news story reported that, 'A tro-tro driver today died at the Okomfe Anokye Hospital after drinking his head off following the death of Robert Mensah.'

Ohene Djan, Ghana's first sports minister, recalled Mensah's performances for the national team at the African Cup of Nations in Sudan in 1968, when he was named goalkeeper of the tournament. 'For his brilliant performance in the national team the nation, nay, the entire continent of Africa, will mourn him with fitting tributes and eulogy,' he said. 'Robert is no more, but his sparkling performance will endure for ever.' The Sports Council of Côte d'Ivoire, proving respect for Mensah was not limited by nationality, made a donation to Mensah's widow.

Kwesi Prempeh, the director of Kotoko, was keen to make sure nobody thought Mensah had been murdered because of his club affiliation. 'If such a wrongful notion was not discarded, there is bound to be reprisals and retributions and Ghana football will be the worse for it …' he said. 'Allow justice to take its course.'

Mensah's cortege went on to Cape Coast, where he had begun his career with the Dwarfs. His coffin was presented at the town hall and then taken, via Victoria Park where a bust of the queen still glowers over the dusty parade ground where football was first played in West Africa, to St Francis's Cathedral, where he was buried. That day, the *Graphic* printed on its back page a photograph of a concrete slab near a kiosk selling cigarettes and soft drinks 150 yards from the Credo Bar in Tema. It was spattered with Mensah's blood.

That is a poignant image, but perhaps the best tribute is a song released in Mensah's memory by the Ghanaian guitar band the Negro Kings, imagining a conversation between Mensah's Kotoko team-mates, Ibrahim Sunday and Osei Kofi:

Sunday: What is the matter Kofi?
Kofi: What is it?
Sunday: Someone has robbed us.
Kofi: Ah! Truly it is the known who dies prematurely.
    Robert, if it is destined that you should die so untimely, then rest in peace.
    If it is just that your life is cut short, descend into someone so your name is immortalised.

The whole Ghana bids you farewell.

May God be with you for the good work you did for Mother Ghana.

The greatest tribute, of course, would have been if Kotoko could have gone on to win the African Champions Cup. Refused permission by CAF and the Ghanaian federation to postpone their semi-final against another Ghanaian side, Great Olympics, they played the first leg in Accra on 13 November. Wearing black armbands and with Essel Mensah in goal, Kotoko drew 1–1. A week later, Sunday Ibrahim converted Kwame Nti's cross in the final minute to give Kotoko a 1–0 win.

That set up a final against Canon Yaoundé of Cameroon. Kotoko won the first leg 3–0, Aburakri Gariba scoring twice before Albert Essuman, the 'Baby Pelé', added a third. Aggregate scores weren't the deciding factor, though, so when Canon won the second leg 2–0, the game went to a play-off. Essuman had a goal disallowed after forty minutes and Emmanuel Etémé gave Canon a seventy-second-minute lead. When the Ethiopian referee Ayele Tessema disallowed what the *Graphic* called 'a perfect equaliser' as Essuman headed in a corner, Kotoko stormed off the pitch and refused to return. The game was awarded to Canon, and football, once again, had denied a sentimental favour to one of its greats.

So why then? What was it about Cameroon in the mid-seventies that suddenly yielded two of the world's greatest ever goalkeepers? Le Roy went into the forests and mountains where the Bassa people live. He was particularly struck by the ability of players of that ethnicity to jump and seemingly hang in the air. 'I had a curiosity about this,' he told Ian Hawkey in *The Feet of the Chameleon*, 'and one day I went to the village of François Omam-Biyik, who was one of my best centre-forwards, near a place called Pouma. I had noticed the balance and coordination of many of the players from that region and I thought, "Hey, it wasn't coaching that gave them that." When I went to the village I found people were playing a special game. It uses a small ball, and it is a bit like head tennis and the court was the space between two houses. If I head the ball and it hits your house, I win. If I save the ball that you have headed, I win. And so on. And I was told they start doing this from very, very young. That's why you get so many players with such great co-ordination especially from the Bassa regions, and you get this fantastic jumping quality ... It's not just Omam-Biyik. There's also all the goalkeepers from there.'

It's a tempting theory. Edea is only around twenty-five miles west of Pouma on the road from Yaoundé to Douala. Nkono, though, has no knowledge of such a game and neither does Bell who, anyway, is from further west. So if the tribal pastime isn't the reason, then what? 'Coincidence,' said Nkono, and he's probably right. Beara's influence and the growing prestige of Cameroonian football created the environment in which a talented goalkeeper could thrive – and secure a profile-boosting move to Europe – but the fact that two players of such gifts should come along at once to take advantage was just chance. And once Bell and Nkono had shown what was possible, the tradition was established: children saw them as role models and European clubs had a sense that Cameroon was a country you could look to for goalkeepers.

It was at the 1982 World Cup when Nkono first emerged as a global star, conceding just once in three drawn matches against Peru, Poland and then Italy. 'When you compare the goalkeepers who played at the 1982 World Cup, Nkono was arguably the best,' said Abega. 'His judgement was great. He was very relaxed. He had a great sense of timing, of anticipation. He had a habit of surprising the attacker. He was not a nervous goalkeeper who betrayed tension. With a cool head, he would let the player get to the end of his action and then pounce on him. He was alert, like a cat. He looked like someone who was sleeping when the attacker came, which gave him an edge, because he would then pounce on the ball.'

The tournament earned Nkono, by then twenty-six, a move to Espanyol, where he would spend the next nine years, playing 241 league games. Club commitments, though, jeopardised his place in the national team, opening the door for Bell. He was, for instance, recalled to Spain after two matches at the 1984 Cup of Nations in Côte d'Ivoire to play a league game for Espanyol. 'I wanted to go back to Côte d'Ivoire,' he said. 'There were no regulations then to force teams to release players. There was nothing official – when you went to the national team the federation and the team decided between them. The federation said it wasn't necessary to go back so I didn't go.'

That – clearly – was a great opportunity for Bell. Did Nkono think he might have helped persuade the federation not to bother recalling him? He said nothing, but smiled in a way that left little doubt what he thought. Bell took his chance. He kept clean sheets against the hosts in the final group game and against Algeria in the semi-final as Cameroon went through on penalties and sealed his nomination as goalkeeper of the tournament as the Lions beat Nigeria 3–1 in the final to lift the Cup of Nations for the first time. Bell was named in the team of the tournament again in Morocco four years later as Cameroon won the title for the second time.

Both men agree the competition spurred them to greater heights. 'I always say that although we had a great rivalry, I was lucky to have somebody like that because I knew he was doing well so I had to do better than that,' Bell explained. 'When he was in Yaoundé and I was in Douala I wasn't thinking about my reserve; I was thinking about him. He helped me a lot.'

They appear at least at first to have been able to keep their rivalry not merely civil but cordial. In part that was because Nkono was so placid but – as Bell sees it – his own generosity should not be discounted. 'The main difference between us is the way we started,' Bell explained. 'He just started playing. When he was leaving his home that day he didn't know he was going to play goalkeeper. He played from one minute to the next. He never really had to think about what he was doing. The main difference comes from that, that I planned ahead of time what I was going to do. I knew what I needed to improve and how it had to be improved. I remember him telling me he was having some difficulty diving on his right side. Because I had thought about this before, I told him it was normal. Everybody had a good foot, so of course when you take a step from your good foot it's going to be better than off your wrong foot. So you have to practise on your bad side. We worked on it together with the national team because at that time we didn't have a goalkeeping coach, so I was directing our training. We were good friends because we had to help ourselves.'

The differences in style, though, did cause problems and, if Bell is to be believed, led to him being undervalued at home. Former internationals queue up to pronounce Nkono the greater of two great keepers. 'In terms of how they commanded their goal line, Nkono had a lot more authority, even if Bell had more charisma in terms of presenting himself to the outside world,' said the great Cameroon forward Roger Milla. 'I had more difficulty playing against Nkono, because the way he put himself in a position as a goalkeeper put him in a better position to anticipate the moves you were about to make. I didn't play that many matches against Bell, but I had fewer difficulties against him.'

Akono, Abega and Jean Manga-Onguene, another Canon teammate and the African footballer of the year in 1980, all emphasised that Nkono was a natural talent whereas Bell's skills were learned – although, of course, all three played with Nkono at club level, which may explain their preference. 'If you asked all the players in the national team which goalkeeper they trusted the most, they'd say that they felt a lot more reassurance when they knew it was Tommy,' said Jules Nyonga, who worked with the national side as either coach or assistant coach between 1984 and 1996. 'He was a strong goalkeeper with rapid reactions and great reflexes when he came out for balls inside his box. Bell was less reassuring. Tommy was a strict person when it came to basic points. We allowed them the freedom to organise the defence for set-plays. Tommy always wanted to have a man on each post; Bell preferred to leave the near post free but have one person behind him. Tommy insisted on naming the players in each position: number one is you, number two is you, number three is you ...'

Nkono was rather blunter when asked to compare himself to Bell. 'One of us was a very good goalkeeper,' he said. 'The other was a genius.' Although you suspect that is what Nkono thinks, the line was offered with no great arrogance and was followed immediately by a fit of giggles. 'I had more talent,' he went on. 'Bell wasn't very tall; he played more by his perception and anticipation. And for the lack of height he compensated with anticipation. I was a player who didn't move from the goal, but I could adapt to other systems.'

Bell insisted he didn't get the credit he deserved because his method of goalkeeping, like Peter Shilton's, was at its most effective when he didn't have to make saves. 'Every coach will say he needs his lines to be closer, but they always forget one line, which is the goalkeeper,' he explained. 'This is why I always pushed behind my defenders, then they can play higher and you move the offside line higher up the pitch. Then every through-ball is going to be mine. If I stayed back, every through-ball would be a very good pass. But I was there, stopping the attacks with my feet. That was completely unusual. When I did that people were shouting at me to go back.'

He saw organising his defence, preventing the creation of chances, as a more valuable skill than saving shots – and, reading between the lines, it seems his volubility in doing so may have ruffled feathers. 'The problem for me was being a leader,' he said.

A leader means you know where you are going and what you are doing, so you are not afraid of criticism or of what people think. You know that you know. If you do not have this leadership ability you cannot afford to attack people: you do what people want you to do. You stay behind and if there is a goal, you say, 'Oh, it's my fault.'

I was controlling my box every Sunday, talking, talking, talking, talking, and only when they saw what I was doing in Europe did they admit it was right. There was a journalist from the Netherlands who told me he was a good friend of Johan Cruyff and he said he knew who I was because at Ajax they used videos of me to show how they wanted the goal-keeper to play.

A goalkeeper is just like insurance. When you buy insurance it's not to use it. You have somebody very good, but it's just in case the worst should happen. The best way to stop them scoring is not to let the opposition have a shot on goal. This is why I started going out for crosses. A good cross is when the ball meets the head [of the forward] but if somebody comes and intercepts the cross you will never know if it would have been a good cross.

In other words, to place the rivalry in the context of its parallel in Argentina, Bell was the Gatti and Nkono the Fillol. What really seems to have riled Bell is that others couldn't see the impact alternating between the two keepers had on the rest of the team. Cruyff liked Bell because he swept up behind his defence, allowing them to play a higher line; with Nkono the back four had to drop deeper. 'They had to adjust but it wasn't something they were talking about,' Bell said. 'It was something that happened on the field and I would say I was quite alone in knowing there was something like that. When I was not there, nobody would tell them to play deeper.'

He even blames Cameroon's exit in the quarter-final of the 1990 World Cup on that deficiency. 'They played deep and nobody told them to move forward and even you could say we lost against England because of that,' he said. 'If I'm not there and they move up then the through-ball is really dangerous. You could see the way we were playing was not always quite the same. Players would go up if they knew they had somebody who could cover behind. But you have to have a coach who understands. It was not something we were always able to plan because sometimes you didn't have a coach who could make a difference.' England's equaliser and winner in that game both came from penalties awarded after Gary Lineker had been fouled running on to through-balls – the sort of passes Bell's style of proactive goalkeeping was designed to cut out.

That suggestion of weakness on the part of coaches hints at

the darker aspect to the Bell–Nkono rivalry. It's clear Bell still feels resentful about what happened in 1990. Nkono had been the first choice at the 1986 Cup of Nations, at which Cameroon had lost on penalties to the hosts Egypt in the final, but Bell was back in favour two years later when Cameroon regained the title in Morocco. Having qualified for the World Cup in impressive fashion, Cameroon were among the favourites at the 1990 Cup of Nations in Algeria.

They were a shambles, losing to Zambia and Senegal before a meaningless win over Kenya in their final group game. Nkono had been first choice for the tournament, but amid the disappointment, he was replaced by Bell, who was widely expected to be first choice for the opening game of the World Cup against Argentina. 'We had a very bad Cup of Nations,' Nkono said. 'There were big problems in the national team.' He got to Yugoslavia for pre-tournament training to be told he was going to be second choice. 'I asked why,' he said. 'The coach [the Russian Valeri Nepomniachi] said he wanted to change the system and play with a keeper like a *libero*. In the Senegal match in the Cup of Nations I was playing like a *libero* so there was no argument to justify the decision. I said to the coach I wanted to go back to Barcelona but Nyonga, Manga and Nepomniachi eventually convinced me to stay in Yugoslavia.'

Preparations went badly. Cameroon lost a string of warm-up games in Yugoslavia but Milla, who had been imposed on the squad by the national president, Paul Biya, offered some hope when he came off the bench against Hajduk Split and scored twice, turning a 3–0 deficit into a more respectable 3–2 defeat. 'We had a meeting with Milla, Bell, [Emmanuel] Kundé, [Eugène] Ekéké ... the senior players,' Nkono said. 'And we said we couldn't go to the World Cup playing that sort of attacking football. We had to change the system and change to 4-4-1-1. We decided which players had to be sacrificed. And the player to go was Milla. All the squad said to the coach this was what we needed to do. We changed the system for the last match – against Yugoslavia – I played and we won 1–0. The next day we went to Italy.

'We did the last training session and it was spectacular. People began to say they couldn't understand why I was on the bench.' Bell, though, was still the number one. Even worse for Nkono, in those days a team had to name seven substitutes – rather than being able to bring on anybody else from the squad as has been the case since the 1994 World Cup – and Bell didn't want Nkono on the bench. Why, I asked Nkono. '*Falta respeta*,' he replied. 'He has no respect.'

But then Bell gave an interview to a French newspaper in which he – with some justification, even if the timing were questionable – criticised Cameroon's preparations. Hours before kick-off, the order came to drop him – nobody quite knows from whom, but Bell's protest that the decision was 'political' is almost certainly true. 'I was going to the stadium just to watch the match,' Nkono said.

> I got my wife tickets for the match. I thought it was a very bad team and we were going to lose. And suddenly the coach said I was going to play. Five hours before the game.
>
> I asked, 'Five hours before the first game of the World Cup? How can I play?' We had a meeting with all the coaches and I asked why they were changing their mind. They said I'd played the last match and not to forget that. So I was trying to reach my wife to tell her things had changed. She'd gone out shopping with the wives of the other players and this was before mobile phones.
>
> Then I had to take a decision. I was talking to [the third-choice keeper] Jacques Songo'o. I said no way. I had no confidence in the coach. I was looking for my wife. The federation, the minster of sports, seven or eight people were telling me I had to play and I was saying I didn't feel ready. They said if I wasn't going to play they would play Songo'o, and if he didn't want to play they would put an outfielder in goal. I had experience. Songo'o was very young [actually, he was twenty-six, but he was very inexperienced compared to Bell and Nkono]. So I agreed to play. I went to talk with the president of Cameroon, Paul Biya. And eventually I agreed to play this match.

At half-time, as the players left the pitch, Diego Maradona, who knew Nkono slightly from their time playing for different clubs in Barcelona, came up to him and asked, 'What are you doing here? I thought Bell was the man?' Despite the chaos, Nkono kept a clean sheet and retained his place in the side through the tournament as Cameroon became the first African nation to reach the quarter-final.

Bell was back in favour by the 1992 Cup of Nations, letting in just one goal in four games. He even saved Eugène Yago's kick in the semi-final shoot-out against Côte d'Ivoire, but Cyril Makanaky and François Omam-Biyik had already missed when Bell himself stepped up to take Cameroon's fourth penalty. Alain Gouaméné saved and the Ivorians went through to the final in which they beat Ghana 11–10 on penalties after another goalless draw.

Gouaméné, uniquely for a goalkeeper in Cups of Nations, was the hero, not letting in a single goal in five games, although it said much for the general West African disdain for goalkeepers that rather than being hailed for his abilities, it was widely reported that he had been aided by *muti*, supposedly stuffing an elephant's tooth down his sock to make him appear as large as an elephant in the eyes of opposing forwards. Thankfully he retained his own agility. It may sound absurd, but the story was taken seriously enough that, twelve years later, after a series of disappointments, the Ivorian federation finally paid the three witchdoctors who claimed they were responsible: $2,000 cash and two bottles of whisky. Côte d'Ivoire promptly qualified for their first World Cup.

The rivalry between Bell and Nkono reached its bitterest point in the USA in 1994. Cameroon had failed even to qualify for the 1994 Cup of Nations, but it's arguable that no country arrived in the USA with such a depth of goalkeeping talent. There was Nkono, there was Bell and there was also Songo'o. He is very much the third part of the trinity, but in the IFFHS poll of the best goalkeepers of the twentieth century, Nkono was the highest-placed African with Bell second and Songo'o sixth. He won forty-six caps in total and had lengthy and successful spells at Metz and Deportivo la Coruña, where he was part of the side that, in 1999-2000, won the club's first league title. He was named African Goalkeeper of the Year in 1996 and won the Ricardo Zamora award for the best goalkeeper in Spain in 1996–97. He was, by any measure, a great goalkeeper, but he wasn't as good as Nkono or Bell. The problem with having three great goalkeepers is that you can only play one of them and it was Songo'o's misfortune that he spent much of the best years of his career in the shadow of Bell and Nkono.

Songo'o, then thirty, was playing for Metz at the time; Bell at thirty-nine was calling time on his career with Bordeaux; while Nkono, at thirty-seven, had just moved to Club Bolívar in La Paz after spending the three seasons following his departure from Espanyol with smaller sides in Catalonia. 'I went to Bolivia to use my little English to help a friend of mine who was a Fifa agent,' he explained. 'I went with him to look at a player who was playing there. When I got there I was watching a training match and I decided I wanted to play. The president saw me and said, "Who is this goalkeeper?" They said, "It's Thomas Nkono." "Can we sign him?" They were putting together a very good squad for the Copa Libertadores.' He went on to win three league titles there, but Bolívar never made it beyond the quarter-final of the Libertadores, losing to Olimpo of Paraguay at that stage in 1994 and Sporting Cristal of Peru three years later.

Nkono was a late call-up to the World Cup squad and Bell was the clear number-one choice. He was selected for the opening game, a 2–2 draw against Sweden, but the plan – at least according to Jules Nyonga, then the assistant coach – had always been for Nkono to come in for the second game, against Brazil. 'He was playing in Bolivia at the time, so had a better understanding of the South American game,' Nyonga explained. 'Psychologically Tommy was there, so we decided it was Tommy round whom we would build the match strategy. The day before the match we confirmed that Tommy would start and we told him at breakfast.'

By chance, Nkono remembers, all three goalkeepers were sitting at the same table when the decision was revealed to them.

'I was playing better,' he said. 'They didn't have confidence in Bell. They had a meeting with the coaches and decided finally that I would play this match. They thought I had more skill in one-v-one situations and they thought that would be valuable against Brazil.'

But in the few hours between breakfast and the technical meeting at 11 a.m., something changed. 'I'm not sure so don't want to be categorical, but I think Bell held a meeting with [the Cameroon coach] Henri Michel to complain that politicians were sidelining him from the team,' Nyonga said. 'Bell went and held this meeting with the players and told them that the coaches had picked him as the goalkeeper of the match but that the politicians didn't want him to play.'

Nyonga is a quiet, bespectacled man, but there was clear anger in his voice as he recalled the events of that day.

Jean Manga-Onguene and I didn't know about these manoeu-vres or even the possibility there might be a change from the team we had confirmed for the match. The players told Bell that if he had been picked he had to play. During the 11 a.m. technical meeting, Henri Michel asked the question very bluntly to the players, 'What have you decided?' Manga and I were stunned after all that we had prepared. Milla stood up and said they had decided they wanted Bell. Michel said he agreed with the players. Then I told Henri Michel that if he agreed with the players then I had nothing to do with the decision. Then I stormed out of the meeting. Manga stood up, for a moment hesitated, but then stayed and took a back seat.

We were beaten 3–0. Bell summoned a meeting after the match saying he had something to tell the players. We got into the room for a meeting. Bell said he knew he would be lynched when he got back to Cameroon because he had con-ceded three goals and already before that match politicians didn't want him to play. And he said that he knew there was one person in that room who didn't want him to play. I said, 'I suppose you're talking about me? Then I'm going to tell you what exactly transpired.' I told the players how we had prepared throughout the training sessions prior to that game for Nkono to be the goalkeeper. This was confirmed the day before the technical meeting. I said I would like to understand what happened after breakfast and before the technical meeting. I said this wasn't how things are done, that it's not the players who decide who should be in the team especially after the coaches had ruled on it. I pointed out Henri Michel was there to contradict me if what I said was wrong. And I tried to explain the build-up and how we reached our decision.

The first person who stood up after I made that speech, almost in rebellion, was Jacques Songo'o. He insulted Henri Michel, calling him names, saying he was useless and didn't have a personality. Another person who stood up was [André] Kana-Biyik. He said, 'We are fed up with all the meetings. We are fed up with all the intrigue.' We knew something serious had gone wrong with the national team.

Bell remains unrepentant. 'In 1990 Nepomniachi came and told me openly, "Your country doesn't want you to play because of politics,"' he explained. 'In 1994 Henri Michel got the players and told them he wanted me to play but the politicians didn't and they said, "No way." We were not courageous enough in 1990. We didn't understand what happened but in 1994 we didn't want it to be like that and they don't have to say who is going to play. Whoever the coach wants to play is going to play. They really had some problems with me, but I can understand their problems. We have been used through politics to understand that if somebody stands up and says this is not right, then he is a dangerous man. I was not dangerous to the country, but the people in charge of the federation didn't like those who stood up and said what they thought. It means they were afraid of leaders.'

The only person who didn't seem overly bothered was Nkono. 'Tommy was calm,' Nyonga said. 'He never got annoyed. Michel decided it should be Songo'o who should play in the third game, almost as a way of paying him back for the hard remarks he'd directed at him. And Kana, who'd also reacted angrily, was asked to play, despite having a knee injury, instead of Emile Mbouh, who was really the first-choice. At 2 a.m. before the game I called Roger Milla and a sports commentator of the time, then I went to see the Minister of Information, who was the government's envoy with the team, the head of the delegation to the World Cup, and I told him he should go and see Henri Michel because I knew it was going to be terrible. But Henri Michel said he wasn't going to change. And we were beaten 6–1. After the match he came back to the hotel and spent the whole night drinking whisky and he had to be carried to his room.'

'We lost those games not on the field but in the hotel,' said Nkono.

Neither he nor Bell ever played for the national team again.

8: LAND OF THE GIANTS

No career surely, has ever had such a finale as Peter Schmeichel's at Manchester United. At the beginning of the 1998–99 season, he'd announced he would be leaving the club the following May. He'd won five Premier League titles and three FA Cups but with three minutes of injury time remaining in the Champions League final and United trailing to Bayern Munich, it seemed he would leave Old Trafford without European success. United won a corner on the left. Schmeichel, knowing 'something pretty extraordinary had to happen', charged forward from his goal to 'make a nuisance of myself'. He did just that, outjumping three Bayern defenders to get a touch on the cross. The ball fell for Dwight Yorke at the back post, but was hoofed half-clear to the edge of the box. Ryan Giggs mishit a low shot but Teddy Sheringham, on the six-yard line, hooked it just inside the left-hand post. 'I have no doubt whatsoever,' Schmeichel said, 'that my sudden rush up the pitch was a contributory factor in that goal.'

Two minutes later, of course, Sheringham flicked on another corner, Ole Gunnar Solskjær stabbed it in at the back post and United were European champions. It was then that Schmeichel, captaining the side with Roy Keane suspended, went forward to lift the trophy, a fitting conclusion to eight years of consistent excellence. He kept a clean sheet in a record 42 per cent of the 292 league matches he played for United in that time.

Schmeichel wasn't just a fine goalkeeper, though, he also seemed to define a new style of goalkeeping. Gordon Banks had bulked himself up carrying bags of coal and Peter Shilton had worked hard to build up his shoulders, but Schmeichel was at another level. It wasn't just that he was muscular, gym work enhancing already broad shoulders; he practised looking big, spreading himself as far as possible in a star jump. 'I played handball up until I joined United, both as a goalkeeper and an outfield player,' Schmeichel said. 'That [star jump] is a big part of being a handball goalkeeper and I brought that move into football. It is a very effective way of saving a chance. If you're on the line and someone has a header, the chances of you reacting to where it goes are slim, so this technique helps you to cover as much of the goal as possible.' In 1906, writing in *The Times*, Leigh Richmond Roose had spoken of the importance of giving an 'impression of strength'. That was precisely what Schmeichel did.

He also stood out for his distribution. He certainly wasn't the first goalkeeper to initiate attacks with long throws from the back – Frank Swift, for instance, was a pioneer in English football – but Schmeichel was notably adept at it, helped of course by the fact that he was hurling the ball out to the wings to make the most of the pace and talent of Ryan Giggs, Andriy Kanchelskis and David Beckham. 'When I get hold of the ball, I try to create counter-attacking possibilities,' he said. 'It's not always successful, but the tactic unfailingly forced the opponents to turn around and head for their own goal. This can be both strenuous and demoralising.'

Although born in Copenhagen, Schmeichel was a Polish citizen until he was seven through his father, whom his mother had met through her work as a ship's nurse in the Polish port of Gdynia. He started playing for his local club, Høje-Gladsaxe, from the age of nine, and went in goal straight away. He said he doesn't remember exactly why, but wonders whether the coach thought sticking him in goal was the best way to keep the wild kid out of trouble. He was only partly successful; Schmeichel was one of the great bawlers, always screaming at his back four – or, as he put it, 'directing, yelling, warning, moving players from one position to another ... trying to plug any holes before they appear.' In that as well as his physique, he was Shilton's heir.

He soon moved on to Hero, a bigger club with a well-respected youth set-up, graduated to Hvidovre and then, in 1987, at the age of twenty-four, to Brøndby. He won four titles in his five seasons there before moving to United. A season later, he was one of the major reasons Denmark won Euro 92, turning in a superb performance in the final, one early save from Jürgen Klinsmann, diving full-length down to his left to deflect a shot around the post, setting the tone.

When he arrived at United, Schmeichel found 'the goalkeepers were usually left on one side and allowed to stand there kicking half-volleys to each other' while other players performed technical drills. He insisted on changing that, getting the goalkeepers involved so they became more part of the team, better equipped to initiate counter-attacks.

Perhaps only Eric Cantona had a bigger influence on United's transition from underachievement to dominance. In 1992–93, as United won the league for the first time in twenty-six years, Schmeichel kept twenty-two clean sheets. Four years later, it was his performance at Newcastle as much as Cantona's winning goal that shifted the momentum of the title race. His plunge to his left to push out a John Barnes header was particularly memorable. And in 1998–99, after a wobble in the autumn that led to his announcing earlier than intended that he would be leaving the club at the end of the season, he returned to superlative form for the treble run, making a stunning save to his left to keep out Dennis Bergkamp's last-minute penalty in the FA Cup semi-final replay against Arsenal. Probably his greatest save, though, was the one he made in a Champions League group game away to Rapid Vienna in December 1996 as he got down to René Wagner's close-range header and, in a manner that recalled Gordon Banks's famous save from Pelé, managed to flick the ball up and over from the bar from almost on the goal line.

The saves, though, were only a small part of it. He made brilliant reaction stops, but he was always adamant that it was 'better to keep things simple and safe than to be spectacular ... If a striker sees his goalbound shot saved with a minimum of fuss it can be very unsettling for them and the goalkeeper has gained the upper hand.' His real strength was his presence, the way he was able to project an aura of invincibility. 'You cannot underestimate [he presumably meant overestimate] the power of psychological strength in the midst of a football match,' Schmeichel wrote in his autobiography. 'It's of huge importance to me that my opponents are intimidated by my presence between the posts. It doesn't matter whether it's a striker who has broken through alone to face me in a one-on-one situation, or a midfield player lining up a long-range shot. No matter who it is, they have to know that I'm prepared for them one hundred per cent, that I'm ready to do anything with my power to stop them from scoring.'

In 2000 Schmeichel finished seventh in an IFFHS study to determine the greatest European goalkeeper of the twentieth century. In 2011, when the same body polled its members to determine the best goalkeeper of the preceding twenty-five years, Schmeichel was fourth, beaten by Edwin Van der Sar, Iker Casillas and Gianluigi Buffon. Casillas, standing a touch under six foot, is an exception and Van der Sar's greatest strength, for all his height, was his ability to sweep, but Buffon, at 6'3", follows the Schmeichel model almost exactly. He too is muscular and athletic, his skills honed through another sport that requires blocking, although in his case not handball but volleyball, which his sisters Guendalina and Veronica play professionally.

It's easy to say with hindsight but there was something inevitable about Buffon becoming a sportsman. His mother, Maria Stella, was three times Italian champion at shot-put and a national record-holder in the discus, his father Adriano competed in the shot-put while his uncle, Dante, played international basketball. Buffon has always said that his favourite place in the world is I Bagni Unione 1920, a beach he used to go to with his sisters and cousins. 'Their favourite pastime,' he wrote in his autobiography, 'was as follows: they tied my hands behind my back and I had to clear obstacles doing somersaults. How many knocks on the head I took! But I like to think it was that way that I overcame the fear of throwing myself about, diving on the ground even when there isn't snow to soften the landing.'

After Buffon's remarkable debut, as a seventeen-year-old, in a 0–0 draw between Parma and AC Milan in November 1995, much was made of the fact that he was a *figlio d'arte*, the next in line in a family noted for producing members of a particular profession. That had nothing to do with his parents, though, but was a reference to Lorenzo Buffon, who won six *scudetti* in the late fifties and early sixties, five with Milan and one with Internazionale, and was a second cousin of Buffon's grandfather. Sport and goalkeeping were in the blood.

Schmeichel emerged almost from nowhere in Denmark: Troels Rasmussen and Ole Qvist were decent enough keepers, but it says much for the more general standing of Danish goalkeeping that most non-Danes asked to name a Danish keeper before Schmeichel, if they could come up with anybody, would name Niels Bohr, the Nobel Prize-winning physicist who played for the Copenhagen side AB in 1905 (his brother Harald was part of the Denmark national team that took Olympic silver at the 1908 Olympics, but any chance that Niels might go on to similar honours vanished when he let in a soft goal against the German side Mittweida and admitted he'd been distracted by a mathematical problem he'd been mulling over). Buffon, though, quite apart from his family tradition, was part of a proud goalkeeping heritage that stretched back to the days of De Prà, Combi and Olivieri.

One morning in the autumn of 1965, a desperate man presented himself at the offices of *Il Corriere dello Sport* in Rome. He asked to see the editor, Antonio Ghirelli, who reluctantly left his desk and walked down the stairs. Waiting for him, he found Giuseppe Moro.

Moro had been arguably the most naturally talented goalkeeper of his generation in Italy. 'When they ask me who I consider to be the greatest Italian goalkeeper, I say, "Moro" without any hesitation,' said his contemporary, Giorgio 'Kamikaze'

Ghezzi, who won the European Cup with AC Milan. 'Watching him was fantastic. He was magical.' The poet, film director and intellectual, Pier Paolo Pasolini, who watched him play for Roma at the Stadio Olimpico in the mid-fifties, compared him to Ricardo Zamora.

Moro's record in facing penalties was extraordinary, saving a barely credible forty-six in his career. He played nine times for Italy, his finest performance coming at White Hart Lane against England in 1949 when he made a series of outstanding saves to keep the score at 0–0 until two goals in the final quarter-hour turned the game England's way. He was never consistent, though. 'He alternates the wonderful with such huge blunders that it seems as though he wants to make them,' wrote the great Italian journalist Gianni Brera. 'Despite leaving this unpleasant suspicion, many admire him.'

By the time Moro arrived at the offices of *Il Corriere dello Sport*, though, such admiration was a distant memory. Shunned by the football community in Italy and unable to make a living, he'd been forced into unofficial exile and was living in Tunisia. Struggling there, he decided he needed catharsis: he wanted to tell his story.

Ghirelli called down a reporter called Mario Penacchia and over the four days that followed, he listened to Moro's story. *Il Corriere* published their account under the headline 'A Desperate Life' in ten parts running between 16 November and 1 December 1965. It became a sensation, one of the best pieces of football journalism ever produced in Italy, provoking such a torrent of reaction that *Il Corriere* devoted two further pages to readers' comments.

Moro, it's fair to say, had his dark side. He stole his grandmother's bread money to buy a football. He pinched fruit from farmers. On another occasion, having riled his father, he jumped out of the window of his family's second-floor apartment to escape. When his father tried to follow him, he broke his leg. Moro's talent for goalkeeping emerged early and he joined Treviso as a sixteen-year-old in 1937. It was, he said, only during the Second World War, though, when he was sent to the Sicilian front, that he really learned how to dive as he flung himself to the ground during aerial bombardments. He deserted and spent the next few months on the run, narrowly evading capture.

After the war, Moro resumed his career, rarely staying at any club more than a year. He passed through Fiorentina, Bari, Torino, Lucchese, Sampdoria, Roma and Verona. He habitually fell out with directors and with other players so that when his career came to an end in 1956, few were interested in helping him find a future in the game.

He was awkward and spiky but he was also unlucky. For instance, in 1947 Treviso had planned to sell him to Lucchese, whom they played in a crucial game towards the end of the season. Treviso had been unbeaten at home until then but they lost that afternoon and many accused Moro of throwing the game. Once the allegation had been made, it proved very hard to shake off. He didn't help himself in that regard: there were occasions at Fiorentina and Roma when he deliberately let in goals after, as he saw it, being insulted by coaches, team-mates or directors. His prickliness harmed his chances with the national team. At one point the great forward Valentino Mazzola told the national coach, Vittorio Pozzo, that if he didn't pick Torino's goalkeeper Valerio Bacigalupo, none of the other Torino players would play, so great was their distaste for Moro.

At the end of his career, Moro begged all his former employers for help. He was ignored. When he died, in 1974, the only footballer to pay his respects was Dino Zoff, who gave the Moro family one of his Italy shirts. 'In my memory, like that of all passionate football fans, Moro remains a great artist of goalkeeping, a true legend,' Zoff wrote.

It was Zoff, of course, who dominated Italian goalkeeping after Moro, being voted second to Yashin in that IFFHS poll to determine the best goalkeeper of all time. He was the first baby born in the village of Mariano del Friuli in 1942 and so he appears in the local register for that year as 'No. 1'. It became common to say of Zoff that he was 'born flying', that goalkeeping was his destiny. And yet for a long time there were serious doubts about him, not least about his height. His coach at his local club Marianese had great belief in him, but trials at Juventus and Inter overseen by Renato Cesarini and Giuseppe Meazza ended in rejection.

A growth spurt in his late teens took him up to 6'1", after which things became much easier for him. Zoff joined Udinese's academy and was quickly promoted through the age-group teams, making his debut for the first XI in September 1961 at the age of nineteen. It went appallingly as Udinese lost 5–2 to Fiorentina. 'It was a tragic thing for me,' he told *Il Corriere dello Sport*. Over the days that followed, Zoff went frequently to the cinema and would shrink into his seat as a news programme showing highlights of the game appeared on the big screen.

Udinese were relegated that year but after a season in Serie B, Zoff was given another chance in the top flight with a transfer to Mantova. It was there that he first began to show glimpses of the goalkeeper that he'd become. 'I wasn't in a hurry,' he said. 'I knew what I wanted and that's what I did. Mine was a vocation.'

By 1967, AC Milan were ready to sign Zoff, only for Napoli to steal in and take him. For the deal to be validated, though, a postal worker had to be persuaded to backdate the correspondence to make it look as though it had been done before the midnight deadline. His debut was almost as complicated. The club wanted him to make his debut in a friendly against Independiente, but he was doing his military service in Bologna and couldn't leave until mid-afternoon. Fortunately Zoff is a motor-racing enthusiast – he writes a Formula One column for *La Repubblica* – so he hopped into his Alfa Romeo Giulia Sprint and sped down the *autostrada*. He got to the San Paolo barely an hour before the game but nevertheless played well, earning himself the nickname the Nembo Kid (the Italian version of Superman).

At Napoli, Zoff won his first call-up to the Azzurri. Italy had lost the first leg of a European Championship quarter-final 3–2 away to Bulgaria and, with the second leg scheduled for Naples, the national coach, Ferruccio Valcareggi, gave Zoff a surprise debut. Italy won 2–0 to qualify for the final stages – then comprising just four teams – which they ended up hosting. Zoff retained his place for the semi-final, in which Italy beat the USSR on the toss of a coin after a goalless draw. They drew the final 1–1 against Yugoslavia before beating them 2–0 in the replay. Zoff was second choice to Enrico Albertosi at the 1970 World Cup but thereafter he took over as the regular first choice. Between October 1972 and June 1974, Zoff went a record 1,143 minutes without conceding a goal in international football.

During that spell he moved from Napoli, where he had spent some time sidelined by a fractured fibula, to Juventus for the colossal sum of 300 million lire. It was the beginning of an extraordinary run. Over the eleven seasons that followed, Zoff played every single league game – a total of 330. A play called *Perseverare humanum est* was written about his understudy, Massimo Piloni, who spent virtually his whole career on the bench. Zoff won the *scudetto* in his first season at Juve, going 903 minutes unbeaten, a record that would stand until AC Milan's Sebastiano Rossi took it in 1993–94. That same season, Juventus reached the European Cup final, where they were beaten by Ajax; had Juve won, Zoff might have pipped Johan Cruyff to the Ballon d'Or. As it was, he finished second.

In 1976 Gianni Agnelli, Juve's owner, appointed Giovanni Trapattoni, then just thirty-seven, as coach. He was only three years older than Zoff and the two found an almost instant understanding. At the first training session, Zoff asked Trapattoni whether he should use the informal 'tu' form of the second-person pronoun or the formal 'lei'. Trapattoni said he was happy with 'tu' because by asking the question, Zoff had shown the respect their positions merited. Not that they didn't have fallings-out. On the opening day of the 1979–80 season, Juventus faced Bologna at home. Earlier in the week, Trapattoni had told Zoff that if Giuseppe Savoldi took a penalty against him, he should dive to his left. Bologna did win a penalty and Savoldi did take it. Zoff did dive left, but Savoldi went the other way and scored. Zoff launched a torrent of abuse at the bench.

A year after Trapattoni's arrival, Juve won the Uefa Cup with an all-Italian team, a unique success in Italian history. Even by then, though, there were suggestions that Zoff was coming to an age at which he should be contemplating retirement. Enzo Bearzot named him captain of a Juventus-dominated Italy for the 1978 World Cup, at which he was blamed for a defeat to the Netherlands, both Dutch goals coming from long-range strikes. Brera suggested Zoff's eyes might be going.

But Bearzot retained his faith and Zoff was captain again at the 1982 World Cup, his crowning glory. He will forever be remembered for '*la Parata*', the save he made, swooping down and to his left not merely to block but also hold Oscar's header on the line, in the second-phase victory over Brazil. At the final whistle, Zoff ran to Bearzot, who was being interviewed on television, and gave him a kiss. Taken aback, Bearzot called it 'a gesture beyond our Friulian modesty'.

Italy went on to beat Poland in the semi-final and West Germany in the final, leaving Zoff to hold the trophy aloft, a moment immortalised in a stamp designed by the painter Renato Guttuso. The most iconic image, though, was a photograph taken of Zoff, Bearzot, the winger Franco Causio and the president of Italy Sandro Pertini playing *scopone*, an Italian card game, as they flew back from Madrid. Placed on their table was the World Cup.

Zoff and Pertini developed a close bond, so much so that when Zoff retired in 1983, Pertini wrote him a very affectionate letter – discovered in the former president's archive in 2010 – recalling that flight and how it pained him to learn Zoff was calling an end to his career. Zoff wrote back to say he was very moved and that it 'sweetened a bitter moment'. That 'bitter moment' was defeat in the 1983 European Cup final in Athens to Hamburg, who won thanks to a speculative long-range shot from Felix Magath. Zoff's last game came in a friendly for Italy against Sweden on 29 May 1983. He was named man of the match, but said, 'I can't save myself from age.'

Zoff was succeeded by Giovanni Galli and even before Buffon there came four more greats: Walter Zenga, nicknamed

Spiderman for his agility and cursed forever by his misjudgement of a cross in the 1990 World Cup semi-final; Angelo Perruzzi, under six feet tall but compact and muscular, three times named Italian goalkeeper of the year; the pugnacious Gianluca Pagliuca, who broke Zoff's record for the most Serie A appearances; and the tall and reliable Francesco Toldo.

Even more than Toldo, Buffon was a physical monster, muscular enough to attract the nickname Superman, something he appreciated enough to wear a Superman T-shirt under his goalkeeping top at times. He makes little of the athletic environment in which he grew up other than to note how his parents indulged his passion for sport.

He started as a midfielder for a local youth side, Canaletto, and was good enough to play for the age group one year above him. One day they didn't have a goalkeeper, so he went in goal, returning to his usual berth in midfield for the next match. He made such an impression, though, that twelve months later, the age group two years above him called him up to play in goal for them in a local tournament which they won. He moved from Canaletto to Perticata, a club with links to Inter, and went back into midfield.

Then came Italia 90. Buffon was twelve, and the tournament, and in particular the performances of Thomas Nkono, overwhelmed him. For all the rich tradition of Italian keepers, it was the Cameroonian who was Buffon's model. 'Football entered my life in a thousand ways,' he said. 'A lot of it was through the TV. I discovered Cameroon at the 1990 World Cup, but I'd got to know their great goalkeeper Thomas Nkono, who is still my idol, already before when he played in goal for the Espanyol team that knocked Arrigo Sacchi's Milan out of the Uefa Cup in 1987.' Such was his respect for Nkono, that Buffon named his first son Thomas.

It was Buffon's father who persuaded him finally make the switch to goalkeeping. 'One day,' Buffon recalled, 'he said to me, "Gigi, why don't you be a goalkeeper for a year?" ... I believe that my father had caught a glimpse of something, watching me in that brief spell as a goalkeeper some time before. I was thirteen. In that moment I decided that I would be a goalkeeper. But Perticata were only interested in me as a central midfielder. So I changed clubs again. My real career began at Bonascola. . . It was the late spring of 1991. I was tall, slim and I was a goal-keeper. Nine months were enough to become one. I was a goal-keeper and not just any old one. Personal conviction aside, the others were saying it. I realised that some important clubs were interested in me. Three were looking at me: Bologna, Milan and Parma.' He opted for Parma, where he came under the influence of Ermes Fulgoni, a coach he said became like a second father to him, drilling him constantly with cross after cross and shot after shot.

There are some stylistic similarities between Buffon and Nkono, most notably in the fact that Buffon, as is the Italian way, is essentially a reactive goalkeeper. He commands his box, intimidates forwards with his size and makes fine reaction saves, but rarely leaves his box to sweep up behind the defensive line although he showed in 2011–12, as Juve won the league under Atonio Conte, that he is capable with the ball at his feet, that his skills as a midfielder haven't entirely left him. Understandably, though, the goalkeeper to whom Buffon is most frequently com-pared is Zoff. They are the two outstanding keepers in Italian history. They have both had outstanding careers at Juventus. They both won the World Cup and, before the final of Euro 2012, much was made in Italy of the possibility of Buffon emulating Zoff by winning the European Championship as well. In terms of ability, it's hard to split them. Zoff believes that the young Buffon was the greatest goalkeeper there has ever been, better even than Yashin, but thinks that in his thirties he was better than Buffon is in his thirties.

In terms of personality, though, they could hardly be more different. Zoff was known as a *Musone* – somebody with a long face and a stoical disposition (the term deriving from the Italian version of Gloomy, a pipe-smoking aeroplane mechanic who appeared in a handful of Mickey Mouse cartoons in the 1930s). He was a leader who spoke little and so when he did speak his words carried additional weight and significance. Buffon is also a leader but far more outspoken and demonstrative than Zoff, even if he doesn't reach the levels of fury Schmeichel used to when berating his defence. He has at times, for instance, celebrated penalty saves by clambering on the fence separating fans from the pitch.

Buffon has always had a close relationship with fans. He has often professed to be a supporter of Genoa, from the days when he would visit his mother's parents in Liguria, but he made a habit of following Carrarese when he was in the youth set-up at Parma. He would travel to away games with the ultras, sitting in the *curva* with them, and later bought the club, appointing his wife Alena as president in summer 2012. On one occasion during his time at Parma, Buffon went to the Artermio Franchi to watch a Coppa Italia tie against Fiorentina in which he wasn't playing. Parma and Fiorentina ultras clashed outside the ground and, as Buffon drove away in his Porsche, he saw the head of Parma's ultras staggering around, bloodied and bruised. Buffon stopped, opened the passenger door and urged him to get in. The *capo*, known as '*il Volpo*' – the Fox – was initially reluctant to leave his fellow ultras but eventually agreed. As they drove away, though, Buffon's car was stopped by police at which the *capo* scarpered. Having been recognised, Buffon was allowed to continue. Just as he reached the junction outside the stadium, the *capo* flagged him down. Buffon again let him in and they drove back to Parma, where they went clubbing until the early hours.

In a sense that was typical of Buffon. He is strong-willed and not afraid of controversy – and prone to errors of judgement. In 2000, for instance, he caused outrage by asking to wear the number eighty-eight shirt, later claiming to be unaware that, as H is the eighth letter of the alphabet, it is seen by neo-Nazis as representing the phrase, 'Heil Hitler'. He only asked for it, he said, because he'd been refused permission to wear 00. 'I chose eighty-eight because it reminds me of four balls and in Italy we all know what it means to have balls: strength and determination,' he said.

As a teenager at Parma, he was well aware of how good he was and so approached his debut with no apparent fear, even though he was seventeen and the opposition was the Milan of Fabio Capello. When it became apparent that he was still considered back up to Luca Bucchi, he became frustrated and demanded a move. Similarly at a training session during the 1998 World Cup, for which the twenty-year-old Buffon was selected largely to gain experience, he asked what he was doing there when he was third choice behind Pagliuca and Toldo and refused to dive for shots. Cesare Maldini, the coach, sent him to the dressing-room in disgrace.

In his autobiography *Numero Uno*, published in 2008, Buffon admitted to have tried 'a joint' as a teenager, although he recounted how he'd turned down 'a pill' (presumably ecstasy) when a friend offered, aware of the risks and the consequences it could have for his career. The revelations confirmed Buffon as an instinctive rebel, as candid and as willing to break taboos and expose hypocrisy as he had been on the *curva* at Carrarese.

He also, to general shock given his aura of invincibility, admitted he had suffered from depression between December 2003 and June 2004. 'I fell into depression,' he said. 'I was in the care of a psychologist. I never understood why then, why not before, why not after. Perhaps that was the moment of my passage from youth to adulthood, even if I was no longer very young, even if it had been thirteen years since I had abandoned my family to go and live alone, even if my career wasn't at a standstill. Far from home, with my team Juventus who weren't doing well at the time. What do you call it? A year of transition. But this couldn't be the explanation. What was happening to me? It was simple really. I wasn't satisfied with my life and football, my job. They were complicated months, difficult to manage ...'

The trigger perhaps came in 2003. Buffon had probably the best season of his career in 2002–03 and Juventus won the *scudetto*, but the Champions League brought intense disappointment. The final, against AC Milan at Old Trafford, finished goalless and went to penalties. It was 1–1 as Alessandro Nesta stepped up to take Milan's fourth kick, Paolo Montero having just missed Juve's fourth. Nesta scored and Buffon was left demoralised: 'I was convinced that I'd saved it and instead it went in. I was certain he'd shoot to the left and I dived there. But too early with respect to the ball, which instead had a strange trajectory and surprised me. When Shevchenko arrived at the spot for the last penalty, I was already in the dressing room, the adrenaline that had accompanied me until that moment had abandoned me.'

After the game, Buffon stood in a corridor outside the dressing-room, winding down with a cigarette and, hardly aware he was speaking aloud, asked, 'When the fuck will I get another chance like this?' The Juve director Roberto Bettega, a goalscoring legend of the club, happened to be walking past. 'At Juventus,' said, 'they tend to come along rather a lot.'

But Buffon became consumed by self-doubt, a staggering revelation for somebody who had always seemed so confident: 'It was as if my head weren't my own, but someone else's: as if it were continually elsewhere.' His legs would tremble involuntarily and he found himself acting out of character: after Italy's draw against Denmark at Euro 2004, for instance – 'a horrendous game', as he notes – 'I was the only one who smiled.' He began to think that everything in football and around his life was superficial and cited a line supposedly from Marilyn Monroe with which he vehemently disagreed: 'Better to cry in a Rolls Royce than on a full tram.' He wanted for nothing from a material point of view, he said, but slipped into despair because he lacked certain human values. The danger all goalkeepers face is thinking too much, that the nature of their position gives them time to dwell on doubts.

When Schmeichel left United in 1999, Buffon's only real rival as the best in the world was the man who'd been at the other end in that Champions League final in Barcelona, Oliver Kahn. So closely did Kahn fit the template of the hulking modern keeper that at one point he had to stop going to the gym because his muscle mass was so great it was restricting his movement. Not for nothing was he nicknamed *Der Titan*.

Kahn was born in Karlsruhe in 1967. His father, Rolf, who

had been born in Latvia, was a midfielder for Karlsruhe, and he joined the club at the age of six. He was called into the Karslruhe first-team squad in 1987, initially as back-up to Alexander Famulla, whom he finally succeeded in 1990. He was not just a fine goalkeeper but a great motivator in the best Karlsruhe side of the professional era. In the second round of the 1993–94 Uefa Cup, they lost 3–1 away to Valencia but then thrashed them 7–0 in the return in what became known as the Miracle at the Wildparkstadion. They went on to beat Bordeaux and Boavista before losing to Casino Salzburg in the semi-final.

Kahn's performances in that run caught the eye of Bayern Munich and, after he had been named German goalkeeper of the year in 1994, he moved there for £2 million. He went on to win eight league titles, six DFB Pokals, six DFB Ligapokals, the Uefa Cup and then, finally, after he had excelled in a penalty shoot-out against Valencia, the Champions League in 2001. He was noted both for his reflexes and his aggression and for his ability to seemingly out-psych opposing forwards, something that stemmed, as it did for Schmeichel, in part from his size and in part from his volubility.

He was the best goalkeeper at the 2002 World Cup but, as is so often the way for goalkeepers, he faltered at the last, fumbling a Rivaldo shot to gift Ronaldo the opener in the final against Brazil. He was playing with two damaged fingers but refused to use them as an excuse. 'That had nothing to do with it,' he said. 'There is no consolation. I have to live with this mistake myself. Because of it, everything is lost. It was my only mistake in seven games, and I was punished. That's ten times as bitter.'

For all his brashness, though, Kahn didn't seem to cope with the mistake well. He was involved in a number of on-field mis-demeanours the following season, the worst of them coming in a game against Bayer Leverkusen as he grabbed Thomas Brdarić round the neck. Although only booked for the incident, Kahn offered to resign the captaincy of Bayern, but refused to apolo-gise. 'That's Kahn,' he said. 'Those are my emotions. I will not let the moralists take anything from me.'

While supposedly injured he was caught playing golf all day, then partying until 5 a.m. Bayern fined him but Kahn was regularly photographed after that drinking champagne and smoking with a twenty-one-year-old blonde woman called Verena Kerth. His wife, Simone, the mother of his four-year-old daughter, meanwhile, was heavily pregnant. An attempt at a reconciliatory holiday failed because Kahn spent so much time on the phone to Kerth. As Kahn's form slumped and his belligerence increased, it was widely assumed that Kahn, then thirty-four, after years of devotion to goalkeeping was going through some sort of midlife crisis. He never fully recovered. Although he went on to win a further four Bundesliga titles, all four of his European Goalkeeper of the Year awards and all seven of his Bundesliga Goalkeeper of the Year awards came before his divorce. Like Buffon, Kahn was a physical monster, an aggressive and imposing presence; like Buffon, it turned out the aura was not quite as invincible as it had seemed.

Kahn, of course, like Buffon, was coming from a fine tradition. Heinrich Stuhlfauth had dominated the landscape before the Second World War but the so-called *Wunder von Bern*, when West Germany beat Hungary in the 1954 World Cup final, a match widely seen as having restored a measure of German self-esteem after the war, created a new goalkeeping hero. Toni Turek had what *Kicker* described as 'the game of his life' in the final as West Germany came from two goals down to win 3–2. One save from Nandor Hidegkuti had the Germany commentator Herbert Zimmermann screaming, '*Turek, du bist ein Teufelskerl! Turek, du bist ein Fußballgott!*' – 'Turek, you are a devil of a man! Turek, you are a football god!' Zimmermann was later forced to apologise by the German church which considered the comment blasphemous.

Turek was born in Duisburg in 1919 and had impressed enough in his youth career that his name appeared in one of the fabled notebooks compiled by Sepp Herberger, Germany's coach between 1936 and 1964, who had spotted him as a seventeen-year-old (Herberger's notebooks are the sacred texts of early German football history; he kept a daily diary throughout his career and managed to avoid mentioning the Second World

War once). Turek worked as a baker until being sent to the eastern front. There he narrowly escaped death when a shell fragment struck his helmet – there was still a splinter in his skull when he won the World Cup – before being taken prisoner by the Americans. 'I lost my best years to the war,' he would often note and his international career came to an end just four months after that World Cup final. He died aged sixty-five, having spent the last eleven years of his life in a wheelchair, the result of a mysterious disease that left him paralysed from the waist down. As a goalkeeper, his main quality seems to have been his judgement; numerous team-mates spoke of seeing him leaving shots they thought were flying in only for the ball to flash wide. He may not have laid down a stylistic template but Turek did create the notion of the goalkeeper as fighter, a battling last line of defence in the way his compatriot and fellow former prisoner of war Bert Trautmann did in England at roughly the same time.

Hans Tilkowski, who played in the 1962 and 1966 World Cups, kept the flame alive, but the next great German keeper was Sepp Maier. He won four Bundesliga titles and three European Cups with Bayern Munich, with whom he spent his whole career, and was West Germany's goalkeeper as they won the European Championship in 1972 and the World Cup in 1974. From 1966 to 1979 he played in a record 442 consecutive Bundesliga matches. He struggled at times with crosses – a couple of high-profile errors meant that when West Germany came to Wembley for the European Championship quarter-final in 1972, a cabal of Bayern players wanted him dropped – but eventually he became noted for the understated sense of authority he radiated. 'A goalkeeper needs to exude a sense of calm,' he said, 'and make sure he doesn't fall asleep. There's no need to make a daring leap if you're standing in the right place to begin with.' Although that sounds very like what Schmeichel would later say, Maier's style, he claimed, was typically German. 'It's got to do with being responsible and giving serious thought to everything.'

Yet he was far from blandly serious: on the contrary, he was famed as a joker. Having once helped out on a busy flight when there were only two flight attendants on duty, Maier would regularly serve drinks on planes, eventually being named as an honorary steward by Condor airlines. During a game between Bayern and Bochum in May 1976, meanwhile, he gave chase to a duck that had landed in his penalty box at the Olympiastadion.

Maier was also innovative in his use of gloves. It had been common for several years for goalkeepers to wear gloves, particularly in wet conditions, but Maier wore enormous ones; in that sense he was the first to look like a keeper of the modern era. 'Tight gloves just didn't feel right,' he explained. 'Large gloves are like a soft cushion for the ball so it won't rebound very far. Throw a tennis ball against a wall and watch how far it rebounds. But throw a tennis ball against a curtain and it drops to the ground almost vertically. Big gloves swallow velocity. Today the materials are thicker anyway, and players generally wear larger sizes. If your hand calls for a size nine glove, it's normal in today's game to wear size eleven or twelve. Back then I was one of the few keepers who did that.'

Maier was an inspiration for the man who replaced him in the West Germany goal, Harald 'Toni' Schumacher. His horrific foul in the 1982 World Cup semi-final, when he charged from his goal and smashed into Patrick Battiston so hard that he knocked the French defender out, damaged his vertebrae and dislodged three teeth, tends, understandably, to overshadow any consideration of his career, but he was also a genuinely talented keeper. Schumacher himself insisted he had not meant to foul Battiston. That is perhaps disingenuous but it's also true that the foul tends to be judged by its consequences rather than by Schumacher's intentions. That he was reckless, dangerously so, is hard to deny but essentially all he did was jump across the line of the opponent, something common enough among goalkeepers. Certainly nobody trying to hurt an opponent would go in with their hip.

By then Schumacher had already won a Bundesliga title with Köln and the 1980 European Championship with West Germany. He played on the losing side in two World Cup finals – and was voted second-best player at the 1986 World Cup – before his international career came to an end in 1987 after the release of his autobiography in which he made allegations of substance abuse against various team-mates.

Maier put the consistency of German goalkeeping down to thinking; Schumacher insists it was all about planning. 'Even in 1972, I had a dedicated goalkeeping coach at my club,' he said. 'At the time, I worked on my throwing with an Olympic javelin thrower and improved my leaping ability with the help of high jumpers. It was revolutionary, but today's keepers are benefiting from what we found out back then. We're the example the others follow and definitely the number one in terms of goalkeeping coaching. For years now, Germany has been ahead of the other European heavyweights. Today's pros are genuine elite athletes. With the help of extensive computer analysis, the training programmes are personally tailored, and much more detail is applied to the craft. Youth development and continuous training after that are the fundamentals. If you don't understand that, you'll never make it into the world-class goalkeeping elite. The way you appear in public and a healthy dose of self-confidence are also essential for a modern goalkeeper, and your body language is another important factor.'

It was Schumacher's long-time deputy with the national side, Gerry Ehrmann, who went on to become the most influential German goalkeeping coach of the nineties noted for the power and direct approach of his charges. Six players who came through his 'Flugschule' at Kaiserslautern went on to play in the Bundesliga: Roman Weidenfeller, Tim Wiese, Florian Fromlowitz, Tobias Sippel, Luis Robles and Kevin Trapp. As David Gohla noted in a piece in Kicker, they were all 'Porsche-driving, toned, solarium-tanned, coiffed and wearing gold chains – and all great goalkeepers, especially their reactions to close-range shots – not surprising, considering Ehrmann's training methods.'

Born in 1959, Ehrmann had played just two Bundesliga games when he left Köln, where he had been Schumacher's understudy, for Kaiserslautern in 1984. There he replaced Ronnie Hellström and with his aggressive style soon became a favourite of the Westkurve, his muscularity earning him the nickname the 'Chuck Norris of the Palatinate'. He was never entirely secure under high crosses but his reflexes and ability in one-on-one situations meant he was never dropped for long and he was part of the team that won the Bundesliga in 1991. It was after retiring in 1996 (although he briefly returned in 1997–98 in response to an injury crisis) that he had his greatest impact.

His coaching was intense, designed to build up a goalkeeper both in terms of physique and confidence, although he insists that he rarely encouraged his students to follow him into the weights room. He had them train in a weighted vest for ninety minutes once a week and worked occasionally on abdominal strength or the back muscles but talk of regular gym work, he says, is 'bullshit'. 'Jumping power and strength are the basic requirements,' he said. 'The courage to stand tall and not turn away when a ball is struck from three or four metres away is very hard to arrive at. We train on the basis of situations that occur during the game. I shoot hard thirty or forty times from five metres at a narrow angle to the goal. The boys have to stay standing and react. We repeat things over and over until they become automatic. You don't have time to think during a game but if you repeatedly respond to certain things, you are programmed and it becomes automatic.'

The focus is on an aggressive self-confidence, something Ehrmann looks to establish with unrestrained training sessions. 'Self-confidence is essential for a goalkeeper,' he said. 'A principle of mine is, "Winners do not doubt and doubters do not win". Whether it's 50,000 or ten spectators doesn't matter. In the end it comes down to keeping the ball out of the net. We practise game situations. No ifs or buts. I want absolute focus and determination in training. I have no problem if they wipe me out going for a rebound. It's the only way to do it. You have to make decisions and then go through with them. You should not go easy on either yourself or your opponent – without just blindly knocking people over.'

A goalkeeper's attitude, he insists, has a knock-on effect on his team-mates. 'The way the goalkeeper is influences the rest of the team,' Ehrmann said. 'For a striker it makes a difference whether he knows that the goalkeeper will go right in there in a certain situation or whether he has the feeling that this is a coward who never comes out.' What is vital is size but also the projection of size, the psychological appearance of size, which both gives confidence to a goalkeeper's own team and discourages the opposition. This, perhaps, is the logical outcome of a position that has tended to be associated with victimhood: what Fatty Foulkes and Leigh Richmond Roose did in carrying the game to opponents who sought to charge them has become institutionalised.

Milutin Šoškić doesn't look much like a goalkeeper. A slight stoop makes him seem shorter than he really is and with his white hair and sunken cheeks he is physically unimposing. Yet there is a sprightliness to him and, when he holds up his hands, the bumps and scars of his profession are obvious. And then there is his jumper. Whether consciously or not, when we met in a Belgrade hotel early in 2011 he was wearing the same powder blue he had worn throughout his career at Partizan and then at Köln.

Like so many goalkeepers, Šoškić began as an outfielder and fell into goalkeeping almost by mistake. 'I do not want to sound immodest, but I had good qualities to become a player – a midfielder,' he said. 'Until I was fourteen, I played volleyball, basketball, handball also. And one day all of a sudden there was no goalkeeper for the Partizan youth team. The team went to play some games in the provinces and the coach asked if there was any guy who thought he could be a goalkeeper. So I said, "Yes, I can be a goalkeeper." They asked how I could do that when I'd always played outfield, but I was a handball goalkeeper. I was good in goal that day and I started to like it.' And so was set in motion a series of events that not merely made him one of the finest goalkeepers of his era but also facilitated the rise of the USA as a major goalkeeping power.

Šoškić always believed his greatest game came at Old Trafford in the second leg of the 1966 European Cup semi-final, but he'd never been able to find a video of the game. I spoke to Nick Coppack of *Inside United* magazine and he confirmed there was nothing in the archives at Old Trafford. But then, a few days before I left for Serbia, there came a remarkable stroke of luck. Somebody at the Old Trafford museum had been sorting through a load of unmarked old tapes, intending to hand them over to the North-West Film Archive, when he came across highlights of the second half of that game. A quick transfer to DVD and Šoškić was reunited with at least some of his memories.

Partizan had won the first leg 2–0 thanks to goals in the first quarter-hour of the second half from Mustafa Hasanagić and Radoslav Bečejac, but they were almost entirely on the back foot in the second leg at Old Trafford. The game in Manchester could hardly have been more different. 'It was practically a game of one goal, and for ninety minutes Manchester United were attacking it, crossing, crossing, shooting,' Šoškić said. 'My perception is that Manchester was one hundred per cent the better team, but for such a good team they played quite foolishly. All the time they persisted with high balls. [Velibor] Vasović, [Branko] Rašović and me, we quite easily picked up those balls.'

Frankly, the video does little to support Šoškić's claim that it was his greatest game, although it is a slightly oddly edited selection. He did palm away one cross in spectacular style, but his main involvement was the concession of a goal with seventeen minutes remaining. Nobby Stiles cut in to the box following a short corner and drove the ball across goal. 'I was saving everything, but Nobby Stiles was close to the goal,' said Šoškić. 'The ball came to [Fahrudin] Jusufi and he intentionally missed it and then I was deceived. But Stiles at the end of the game came to congratulate me.' That's a generous interpretation; Jusufi, in fact, was nowhere near the ball and the ball cannoned in tamely off Šoškić's knee.

'There is one moment that has stayed in my memory,' he went on.

The goal was quite near to the fans – they were so close I could have shaken hands with them – and they kept trying to distract me. At one point around the end of the first half they threw a sandwich at me. The sandwich hit me on my shoulder and landed two or three metres in front of me and in a split second I made a decision. I took the sandwich, I unwrapped it and took a bite, and the other part of the sandwich I kissed and put it near to the goal. I think this gesture was a shock for the fans. They were passionate fans, but after that they left me alone. Maybe they saw some meaning to what I did, and after that I was allowed to play normally. Before that they'd been throwing coins – I even collected the coins and put them in the goal. But I didn't react. I didn't let myself be provoked. Maybe in other situations I would have allowed myself to react, but with the whole English football tradition – the whole English tradition but especially the football tradition – I felt that I was playing at a shrine of the gods.

It was wonderful, a full stadium of 60,000 people or so. There was one Yugoslav flag. I was happy that we went through, but I couldn't understand how one team could keep playing in such a way. They had the players available to play in a different way. They were a very strong team, a very good team and if they'd played another way I think I would have conceded five or six goals. Even in Belgrade, United could have won. They missed some incredible chances here. It was unbelievable to me. But we scored two goals and in that European campaign that season we didn't concede a single goal at home.

It was that run to the final that defined Šoškić's career. Partizan beat Nantes without too much bother in the first round, then drew Werder Bremen in the second round. 'What we experienced in Bremen I didn't experience again in my sixty years of being in football,' said Šoškić. 'Only God could decide who would advance. It was the toughest game I ever played in and it will never be repeated any time in the world. We won 3–0 at home, with three late goals.

'But when we got there, the pitch was frozen and the fans were in the ground one-and-a-half hours before kick-off. It was a hostile atmosphere, very hostile towards us, so we were sort of frightened. Around the pitch there were policemen with walkie-talkies. In the game you felt like they could kill us, that they would destroy us. Maybe that was my best game. Our players were frightened and on top of everything, the Germans went 1–0 up with an early goal.' Yet dreadful as he makes it sound, there is a sparkle in Šoškić's eyes as he tells the tale. This is what he lived for, and so the perversity that lies at the heart of the goalkeeper's soul is displayed again: essentially, the harder it was the more he liked it.

'The person who gave us strength in that game was the referee [Thomas Wharton, an engineer from Glasgow who was nicknamed 'Tiny' because of his height],' Šoškić said. 'He was from Scotland, almost two metres tall. He was the only guy who protected us. He was not biased for us, but he was honest. He saw what was going on but he tried to protect us. I don't remember his name, but he is a referee I can never forget. He came there without fear; he was a really big guy, so strong he could probably have beaten up any of the players.

'I don't know how I kept them out, but I know I was more in the air than on the ground. If Bremen had kept calmer they would have scored five or six goals against us, but they were also anxious and I always say there is a god in this life. This game was not football; it was a war. The Germans after the game apologised for their brutality in a telegram, apologised that they were too hard. One German I spoke to said, "I knew Yugoslavs, but I didn't know they were so brave."'

Partizan faced Sparta Prague in the quarter-final. They lost 4–1 in the first leg in Czechoslovakia. 'In Prague, I didn't play,' said Šoškić. 'I was sick, I was ill, and I stayed in Belgrade. I watched the game on television and when it was 4–1, my father came to the room where I was lying in bed and started shouting. "You are out," he said. "You are out!" And I said, "No – we will beat them in Belgrade." That was a strange game. Sparta came like millionaires. They were a hundred per cent sure they were going through. The whole atmosphere was odd; none of our fans thought it was possible we would not go through – they were confident in our football, and we scored goal after goal. We won easily.' On the same night Manchester United won 5–1 away to Benfica in one of their defining European displays, Partizan won 5–0 at home to Sparta.

Old Trafford proved the high point for Partizan. It wasn't just that they lost 2–1 to Real Madrid in the final in Brussels, despite having led through Vasović's goal; it was the manner of the defeat. 'It was in a way the tragedy of my life,' said Šoškić. 'First we lost a great generation and second we lost a final which we should have won. The directors sold a lot of our players and Partizan for a long time after that didn't have a good team. We went 1–0 up and I didn't have a lot to do – maybe only fifty per cent of the job I'd had in the previous game. Real had experience. We were sort of lost – we didn't even try to make some dives to win a penalty.'

Many of the players who were sold off were told they were leaving on the day of the game. 'Only two hours before kick-off they told me I was going to Köln,' Šoškić said. 'The whole organisation was terrible: some players went by plane, some went by train, some went in private cars. A few hours before kick-off Uwe Seeler, who was a representative of adidas, came into our dressing room and gave us new boots, offered us a hundred dollars to play in them. I was the only one who didn't take them. Out of solidarity I allowed them to paint three stripes on my boots, but I didn't take the money. I wouldn't have taken a thousand dollars or a hundred thousand. We had a private shoemaker who made our boots in Belgrade; they were better than the adidas boots. There were many things it's better to forget.'

Šoškić went on to the Bundesliga where he had to deal not merely with a new club and a new way of life, but also with the memory of Werder Bremen fans. 'I played with Köln against Bremen exactly one year after the Partizan game, the same kick-off time even,' he said. 'And when we went out onto the pitch, the emotions were coming back to me, the same as I'd felt when I was running out with Partizan one year before.

'And now I came out with a new team, with a German team. I had my team-mates, but I'd known them only a few months. I was very insecure in that game; the atmosphere was very hostile and practically every ball I missed. Very often I had to grab the rebound because I lost the first shot. My team-mates knew I was having problems with the hostile atmosphere. In the second half, the score was 1–1 and I intentionally went out earlier, alone, and I said to myself, "Why are you frightened? Calm down." The second half was practically a repeat of the Bremen–Partizan game. I saved so well I broke their morale and we won 3–1. I took my Partizan shirt with me and wore the same shirt I wore in the final in Brussels. The Partizan shirt was plain, so I stitched on a Köln badge. That game was the last time I could wear that shirt because it was torn apart. They kept saying to me, "Why don't you wear that shirt?" But I couldn't because it was torn apart.'

That pale blue shirt had been a totem for him. 'The wife of the Köln president bought me a lot of goalkeeper shirts from England, bought from the most exclusive shops, but I persisted with my Partizan shirt,' he said. 'When it was torn apart, even after that I didn't take those new shirts – I thought they were too good to play in so I took the normal goalkeeper's shirts. Her shirts were too good for a football pitch.'

Šoškić had a brief stint as manager of OFK Belgrade before returning to Partizan to serve as goalkeeping coach for eleven years. In 1993, though, he received an invitation that would change his life and the course of football in the USA. Bora Milutinović, whose brother, Milorad, had been a team-mate of Šoškić at Partizan, had been appointed national coach in 1991 and needed somebody to look after the goalkeepers. 'There were good goalkeepers there before I got there,' Šoškić said. 'I don't want to exaggerate my role, but I think they didn't have enough good continuity work. They were self-taught and they didn't have good coaches who were former goalkeepers. After that time the number of kids who were playing football became bigger and bigger, and from such a big reservoir it's not a problem to find some good players.'

Šoškić found talent almost immediately. 'When I got there, in the club where I was working there was a kid who played basketball, and I saw from his name he had German ancestry, and I said, almost as a joke, that I would make a goalkeeper out of him.' That player was Brad Friedel. In the twelve years Šoškić spent working for the US Soccer Federation, he also had significant impacts over the careers of Juergen Sommer, Marcus Hahnemann, Kasey Keller and Tim Howard. 'I put the emphasis on the things I'd learned to become a good goalkeeper,' Šoškić said. 'They accepted it. There were some little problems in terms of the way of training, but there was no big resentment. In some cases there were asking, "What do I need to do this for? What do I need to do that for?" but most of the time they accepted it.'

Occasionally that meant eccentric drills. A film released by Partizan in 1962 shows Šoškić training, performing handstand push-ups on a rickety bench, doing pull-ups from the branch of a tree and hurling himself around a bare, dusty goalmouth. Conditions in the US were rather more sophisticated, but Šoškić's training sessions required little in the way of complicated equipment. He would teach his goalkeepers positioning by making them lie down with their back to the ball to show which position best covered the goal. On one occasion he had a load of sand delivered to the training ground and made his goalkeepers train on that so that when they returned to the grass their spring was much greater. 'They felt like they were flying,' he said.

Šoškić's priority, though, was positioning. 'I think the goalkeepers from the United States, but also from England and Germany,' he said, 'put more emphasis on physique, on stature, but for me it was not too difficult to change the method of work. I persuaded them that a goalkeeper must not only be a goalkeeper – he can even act outside the penalty area. The most difficult thing for me was to teach them how to behave in the goal, to come out off their line and make the goal smaller. It was not difficult for me to teach such things to children of eight, ten or fifteen years old, but for an older goalkeeper, if he got used to falling back, then it's not so easy to change him and persuade him it's better to go forward, that you have to go towards the ball and cut off the angle. It was difficult for me to persuade them that by doing that you can make a goal that is eight yards across seem only five yards across. I had to teach them to get the positioning right.

'I made them learn to play like a sweeper, so that they could intercept sometimes the ball, to watch, to make the position already when the attacking player has the ball, to watch the positions of all the players and at times to try to get into the position of the opponent before he receives the pass. In eighty per cent of the cases, he will guess right, and then there is no shot to save.'

There are two critical points here. The first is that issue of size: the rise of the US keeper coincides with the rise of the gym-toned keeper. Of course, US football in general rose through the nineties thanks to the spark provided by hosting the 1994 World Cup and the subsequent establishment of MLS, but it seems fair to suggest that the emphasis on physique suited the mindset of US sport. As John Murphy, a former goalkeeping coach of New England Revolution, put it in a piece in *Soccer Journal* (the official magazine of the National Soccer Coaches Association of America) in 1997 when asked why the US was producing so many top-class goalkeepers, 'The oversimplified answer is that the American keeper is brave, competitive and athletic. They have the classic American trait of being good with their hands too.' That latter argument seems fundamental. Tony Waiters, the former Blackpool keeper who won five caps for England and served for a time as director of NSCAA's Goalkeeper Institute, cited 'the carryover of throwing, catching and fundamental handling of a ball from traditional American sports such as [gridiron] football, basketball, and baseball.'

The other is the reluctance of the American keeper to leave his line. It's not a universal trait by any means but there is a very puzzling section in an article in *Soccer Journal* in which Tony Di Cicco, who had made one appearance in goal for the USA but was by then the highly successful coach of the US women's team, is adamant that with an offside line set thirty-five yards out, goalkeepers should be no more than two or three yards off their line. Perhaps in the women's game, with shorter goal-keepers, an extra element of caution is necessary, but he cites as an example of the dangers of advancing too far the goal Ray Houghton scored for Ireland against Italy in the 1994 World Cup, when his mishit shot floated over Gianluca Pagliuca. It seems a strange goal to choose, for a number of reasons. For one thing, the Italian defensive line is not thirty-five yards out, but has retreated to just inside its own box to deal with a long ball and Houghton recovers possession only because of a weak clearing header from Franco Baresi. There is nothing about Houghton's body shape to suggest he is about to attempt a chip; Pagliuca is rather set for a drive, and therefore pretty much in the right position. What undid him is that Houghton then cut across and under the ball, floating it over the keeper in a way that was both unintentional and unpredictable. This, surely, was an example of one of those freakish goals Johan Cruyff was prepared to accept in exchange for the benefits offered by an advancing keeper.

Whatever the rights and wrongs of that particular goal, though, the more general point is that Šoškić found himself standing counter to a culture in which keepers were reluctant to advance. In that regard, Šoškić is part of the mainstream of European tradition (outside of Italy) and the fact that his ideas seemed so fresh and were so effective probably says much about the general standard of US coaching at the time. 'What fasci-nates me the most is that despite an acknowledged lack of true goalkeeper coaches in this country, we see some of the most proficient skills coming from our players in goal,' wrote the NSCAA coach Giovanni Pacini in that piece in *Soccer Journal*. The poor quality of coaching in the USA, especially for the under-fourteens, was a major issue for him, and he even sug-gested that American goalkeepers succeeded where outfielders didn't because a goalkeeper's career tends to be longer than that of an outfielder and they thus have time to recover from poor early coaching. That may seem overly pessimistic but it does hint at something more fundamental: the USA probably isn't producing high numbers of high-class goalkeepers *per se* but it is producing vast quantities in comparison with what went before and relative to other positions. Athleticism and hand-eye co-ordination would seem to underlie that phenomenon but Šoškić must also take credit for having helped forge so many high-class goalkeepers from that raw material.

Yet in some ways, Šoškić remained defiantly eccentric. 'Always in the end I would say that the ball is of feminine gender,' he insisted. 'The ball is a she not a he, and so you have to stand tall and grab it. If you don't do that, but you run after her, you will never catch her. I was the biggest opponent of gloves – even today I am. The palms are much better than gloves. It's like wearing gloves when you are with a woman. When I went to Germany, I was punching the ball and I only wore gloves if it was raining, but I was not a big fan. I don't know why they wear gloves – are they protecting their fingers? Are they afraid of broken fingers? Or is it the fear of the power of the ball? I cannot understand it.'

In total, Šoškić spent twelve years in the USA. His English remains uncertain, but he clearly loved his time there. 'In the USA it's wonderful to be a coach,' he said. 'They are eager to learn and to work. They are eager to tap into your knowledge and your passion. It's possible that one day there will be more exports from there than from Brazil or Argentina. First of all they are mentally strong, physically they are good, they're eager to work, they're keen to learn. They have everything you need.'

He found that desire for self-improvement in abundance.

'A friend of mine had a football camp, and he asked me to join this camp so it got a better name – for advertising,' he remembered. 'I told them not to tell their parents anything, just to work. A kid turned up at training, nine years old. The family was very rich, multi-millionaires. I worked with this boy, and all the family was really good looking, like they belonged in Hollywood. At the first training session I always tried to get to know my students to see how they walk, how they run. Most of them were okay, something to work with, but this one kid, he was a disaster. He was short, he was ... funny. But I tried. He was very keen. He remembered everything I told him, but his mother showed up after training. First I was shocked by her beauty, and then she asked, "How's my boy?"

'I said, "This is your boy? Do you love him?"

'She got mad with me and said of course she did; he was the only son she had.

'And I said, "Lady, you are the best teacher for him, the best coach for him, the best friend for him. You are his mother. You are the person who can help him the most. I cannot judge your boy yet. My problem is just to see him walking."

'So she got mad with me again. And my friend was unhappy because of what I'd said to her. The family had a lot of money and for ten days the kid came but the parents didn't. And I was working really hard to try to teach him. Probably every day he was going home and his mother was asking how things were going and he was telling her everything was going well. When the training camp ended, she came to pick up her son. And she came to me, and she told me she had come to apologise. So I asked why. And she said it was about the other day when we'd had a falling out. And I said, "It was not a falling out. You asked me a question and I answered you."

'"I didn't come because of that," she said. "I came to offer a solution. Would you like to become the personal coach of my son?"

'They offered me double the salary I was on. I said, "Lady, you don't have the money to pay me."

'"We?" she said. "*We* don't have the money?"

'And very calmly I said, "You don't have the money to pay me."

'And again she was angry, and I said, "My dear lady, I will explain to you why. I've known your son for ten days. I've taught him only the first letter, and I'm supposed to teach him the rest of the alphabet. But it's like learning to be a marine, and when I start to torture him, you will come to me and we will again have a problem and you can't pay to soothe my nerves. But I will always be here to train your son out of love for him and because he's so eager to learn."

'I had several such situations. I worked a lot with children and I always worked very seriously. The only complaint parents ever had about me was that I was too serious. I always said to the parents, "Here, at training, I am the parent."'

What Šoškić really admired was mental toughness. 'A goalkeeper must be hard with feelings, for the simple reason that the whole team, all ten outfielders, can work for a result and the goalkeeper can spoil it all,' he said. 'There are goalkeeping coaches who are selfish. When I started to work, my intention was that the guy I was training became better than me, and I'm happy when I today watch Tim Howard and Brad Friedel and I see they are doing so well. And I often tell my friends, these are my goalkeepers, these are my guys.'

Tony Meola, it's pretty clear, wasn't and Šoškić seems baffled by Milutinović's decision to make him first choice for the 1994 World Cup; Friedel suggests that Milutinović wasn't a huge fan of Meola either but had inherited him as captain. 'He was already old and was always standing on his heels,' Šoškić said. 'He was a film star. When there was a shot he was always on the back foot, but it's much better to go forward. If you've been taught one way when you're young it's very difficult to change.' Meola perhaps embodies the muscular ideal of US goalkeeping: he was an all-round sportsman who captained his high-school basketball team and was good enough at baseball to be drafted out of college by the New York Yankees.

Meola was the first of the new wave of US keepers to move to England, although he managed just eleven games, only two of them in the league, for Brighton before returning home. Juergen Sommer was next, also starting at Brighton, for whom he played one league game before going to Torquay United, Luton Town and Queens Park Rangers. Then came Kasey Keller, who totalled almost 300 games in England for Millwall, Leicester, Tottenham and Fulham and had a lengthy stint in Germany with Borussia Mönchengladbach. He was another who worked with Šoškić. 'He listens to you,' Keller said. 'He's not someone who says, "This is the way you have to do it because this is how I did it." He's here to work for us and he realises that. He doesn't push you into things.' Ian Feuer was a regular back-up for a number of English clubs between 1994 and 2002 and Marcus Hahnemann totalled 276 league games for Reading and a further 40 for Wolves. The two American keepers of the past decade to have really stood out, though, are those that had the closest relationship with Šoškić: Friedel and Howard.

Friedel was a natural, blessed with such hand-eye coordination that he was happily catching a basketball from the age of two-and-a-half. He had success in college soccer with UCLA and played for Galatasaray before, after a frustrating wait for a work permit, joining Liverpool in 1997. It was at Blackburn where he really made his name, though, playing 287 league games for them before moving on to Aston Villa and then Tottenham. He also won eighty-two international caps earning a reputation for reliability interspersed with moments of athletic brilliance.

Šoškić's favourite, though, seems to have been Howard. 'Manchester United asked me to write for them my opinion of Tim Howard,' he said. 'When he joined Manchester United, he went from the US national team directly to London and he was fifteen minutes crying on my shoulder, because he all of a sudden became not only a very good goalkeeper but also a very rich man. Every time I see him he hugs me and asks if I need anything. But my biggest reward is the pride I have in my goalkeepers. I don't need anything else; that satisfaction is enough for me. The financial situation was not so good; for sure I'd have made more money if I'd stayed in Serbia, but I worked at what I liked.'

Howard was also a talented basketball player, but he became a professional football player a month before graduating from high school, spending a season with the North Jersey Imperials before moving to the MetroStars. It was from them that, in 2003 he moved to United. Although Howard spent four years at Old Trafford, an error towards the end of his first season overshadowed his time there. United led Porto on away goals heading into the last minute of their last-sixteen Champions League tie when Howard tamely parried a Benny McCarthy shot, allowing Costinha to prod the ball over the line from close range. That was the goal that prompted José Mourinho's charge down the touchline, and as such Howard's error had a huge impact in establishing Mourinho as one of Europe's brightest young managers as his Porto went on to win the Champions League that year.

'When Tim Howard went to Manchester United,' said Šoškić, 'I knew that US goalkeepers liked all the time to catch the ball. Friedel today likes to punch the ball away. I told Tim Howard the number one thing is to only try to catch balls you are one hundred per cent sure you can hold. Everything else, just punch it into the corner. And what happens? He made some phenomenal saves in the first half of the season, he was brilliant, then they played Porto and he made a mistake. He knocked the ball down and Costinha scored. A good goalkeeper is a goalkeeper who saves what can be saved. If he saves what it is impossible to save, then he is even higher than a good goalkeeper.'

No matter how powerful or agile a goalkeeper, there is always a mental aspect. Howard went on to become the first American to play in a winning FA Cup final side and was named in the PFA team of the season for 2003–04, but he never seemed quite as confident again at Old Trafford and was never able to re-establish himself as a regular first choice. It took a move to Everton in 2007 for him to rediscover his form.

Among the greats of the modern age, Iker Casillas stands out in not being a physical giant. He is a little under six feet tall and lacks the bulk of the likes of Schmeichel, Kahn or Buffon but for over a decade he has been at the forefront of a great generation of Spanish goalkeepers, from Santiago Cañizares and José Molina to Pepe Reina and Victor Valdés. As with all goalkeeping generations, you wonder whether there is an element of coincidence about so many coming along at once, but a Uefa seminar in 2010 suggested Spanish keepers develop quickly because playing on hard pitches encourages them to learn their angles so they don't have to dive. And, like the USA, Spain has an admirable recent record in sports that involve the hands. They took silver behind the USA in the basketball at the 2008 and 2012 Olympics and bronze in handball in the 2000 and 2008 games, while the traditional Basque sport of pelota requires both tremendous reflexes and hand-eye co-ordination. Unlike the USA, Spain also has a fine tradition of goalkeeping.

The founder, of course, was Ricardo Zamora, feted across continental Europe as the greatest of his era. After Zamora came Antoni Ramallets. He was born in Barcelona in 1924 and spent most of the Civil War helping to dig earth to create bomb shelters. He played for Mallorca, San Fernando and Valladolid before joining Barcelona in 1947. He soon became a regular but when he was called up to the national squad for the 1950 World Cup, he was widely perceived as being third-choice behind Juan Acuña of Deportivo la Coruña and Ignazio Eizaguirre of Valencia. Sure enough, Eizaguirre played in the first game, a 3–1 win over USA, but then, for reasons that remain opaque, Ramallets was selected for the second, against Chile. He made an outstanding save from Atilio Cremaschi as Spain won 2–0 and was inspired again as England were defeated 1–0, earning the nickname 'the Cat of the Maracanã' for his agility. Spain didn't win a single game in the final pool but few doubted that Ramallets had been one of the stars of the tournament.

Ramallets was hailed as the successor to Zamora, winning the Zamora trophy as the best goalkeeper in Spain on five occasions as Barcelona lifted six league titles and five cups. 'Zamora is a legend from whom all others follow,' he told Jimmy Burns in an interview quoted in *La Roja*. 'He was a man who personified, like no other, the solitary figure of the goalkeeper in all its potential for greatness: a strong personality, who saw the imperative of limiting failure. The goalkeeper depends on his team-mates. But only he can win or lose a match and that's what makes him such a key figure.'

As well as winning thirty-five caps for Spain, Ramallets played seven times for the unofficial Catalan national side. Zamora, of course, whatever his political beliefs, was also a Catalan;

after Ramallets, the baton of Spanish goalkeeping was carried by Basques. The sample size is small and the line of Zamora-Ramallets-Iribar-Arconada-Zubizaretta could easily be coincidence, but it is tempting to believe that those who felt – or grew up in areas that felt – somehow alienated from the Spanish state were more naturally inclined to take up the self-imposed solitariness of which Ramallets spoke.

Ramallets was succeeded by José Ángel Iribar. He was born in Zarautz in 1943 and, although he played forty-nine times for Spain, was always proudly Basque, managing the unofficial Basque national team in 1988 and then again between 1992 and 2010. He began his career at Baskonia but after a superb performance in a shock victory over Atlético Madrid in the Copa del Generalísimo, he moved to Athletic of Bilbao for 1 million pesetas in 1962. Initially a back-up to Carmelo Cedrún, another Basque Spain international, Iribar got his chance through injury in October 1964. He was a regular for the next sixteen years, helping the club to two cups and to the final of the Uefa Cup in 1977. In 1970–71 he kept clean sheets in a record ten successive home games.

He was also outspoken in support of Basque rights, campaigning for the release of political prisoners. In December 1975, a month after the death of Franco, Iribar and the Real Sociedad captain Inaxia Kortabarria led their sides out at Atocha for the Basque derby carrying between them the Ikurriña, the Basque flag that was banned at the time. 'I think it marked an important step which helped a great deal the process towards the legalisation of the Ikurriña …' Iribar said. 'The fact is that it was that derby between our two teams that had endured as my best football memory – and that is despite the fact that we lost 5–0.'

Two years later, Iribar was the Athletic captain in the famous game against Barcelona at Camp Nou at which the stands were bedecked with hundreds of Catalan and Basque flags in a celebration of regional pride. 'The dictatorship had ended and we were in a transition towards democracy and there was a general expression of joy in the stadium that day,' Iribar told Burns, 'a real hunger for liberty on both sides so that the game became a reflection of all that was happening. You could feel a real sense of happiness of being part of a democratic process and of winning freedom – you could feel it in the stadium, the streets ...'

Iribar insists he would have coped with the modern game but for him the reintegration of the goalkeeper into the body of the team is a matter for regret. 'I fear the worst,' he said in an interview with *El País* in 2006, 'that they will eliminate the goalkeeper or make the goals bigger. The figure of the goalkeeper is the hardest hit in the evolution of football and, at the moment, that which has changed the most over the past twenty years. Now you have to be more of a footballer, in quotation marks, than in my time. You have to use your feet, you have to be transformed into something more complete. But the point remains making saves to provide security. Making saves allows you to set the pace of play of your team, to boost the attack immediately or slow the game down, letting time tick away. On the pitch, the goalkeeper thinks the most.'

Television, he believes, has harmed the perception of goalkeepers. 'Previously our goals were sung about, not visualised,' he said. 'Now the feeling you get of seeing a goalkeeper on television is quite different. I don't know how you can tell a goalkeeper to watch a video to correct his mistakes. That's torture and will leave his self-esteem in tatters. Before children would imagine football. Value has been lost. I imagined football because I heard it on the radio. There were commentators who were so good that we were transported to the scene of the action and we would see a goalkeeper's style, how each one was ... people like me didn't go to the stadium or went only a couple of times a season. I went to Atocha very few times. I imagined everything reading newspapers or listening to the radio and, of course, I did not see the failures. They spoke of the good play. I remember a picture of Sanduce, the Alavés goalkeeper ... he was like a superhero! How he flew!'

Modern football Iribar sees as overly showy – 'I was practical in life as on the pitch,' he said – but his concern about mistakes, his desire, if not to cover them up, then at least to allow them quietly to be forgotten, lies at the heart of a very Spanish insecurity. All goalkeepers have that fear to an extent, of course, that desire to deflect blame, but in Spain it seems particularly pronounced.

Iribar was replaced in the Athletic goal by Andoni Zubizaretta, who was born in Vitoria but grew up in Aretxabaleta. He played in the Athletic side that won back-to-back league titles and the cup under Javier Clemente before moving to Barcelona in 1986. He played over 300 games for them, winning four successive league titles and the European Cup as part of Johan Cruyff's Dream Team before moving on to Valencia where he racked up another 150 league games. He made his Spain debut in 1985 and accumulated 125 caps over the thirteen years that followed, making him at the time Spain's most capped player.

Between Iribar and Zubizaretta in the Spain goal came another Basque, Luis Arconada. Born in San Sebastian, he spent fifteen years at Real Sociedad, winning two league titles and amassing sixty-eight caps. His fine reflexes and powerful wrists earned him the nickname '*El Pulpo*', 'the Octopus', but his career was defined by an incident in the Euro 84 final against France. He had had an excellent tournament, producing a series of brilliant saves in the victory over West Germany in the group stage and then against Denmark in the semi-final. Twelve minutes after half-time, Michel Platini bent a free-kick over the wall. There was little power on the shot and as Arconada flopped on the ball at his left-hand post, there seemed no significant danger. The ball, though, somehow squirmed between his arms and his chest and slithered over the line. The report in *El País* called it 'the most child-like error in the history of the European Championship'.

Nothing else he did seemed to matter, none of the brilliance or the bravery, the double-save against Denmark, the penalties he kept out in the Copa del Rey final against Atlético Madrid in 1987; one mistake blighted the lot. When Spain won the European Championship in 2008, the Sevilla goalkeeper Andrés Palop, Spain's third choice, wore the shirt Arconada had worn in the 1984 final to collect his medal from Platini, who was by then the Uefa president. 'He deserved an important tribute,' said Palop. 'I had the chance to get this shirt and I was clear that if we lifted the trophy I was going to wear it ... because historically he's remembered for a terrible error, but it's fair that we remember he was a great goalkeeper who made great saves both for Real Sociedad and in the shirt I was wearing.'

Although Zubizaretta is generally revered, his career in the national team also ended with an error. Spain led their 1998 World Cup group match against Nigeria 2–1 when, under no pressure, he inexplicably diverted a low Garba Lawal cross into his own net. Sunday Oliseh thrashed in the winner five minutes later and, despite drawing against Paraguay and thrashing Bulgaria 6–1, Spain failed to make it through the group stage.

The terror of failure, of the defining error, thus seems a constant thread in the Spanish tradition and, if Iribar is to be believed, it is getting worse as television replaces imagination and football's collective memory focuses on often replayed mistakes rather than the saves of legend such as the one Zamora made from Martin Ventorlá in the dust of the 1936 Copa del Rey final. Even Ramallets had his defining error at a key moment – arguably two of them. Barcelona had beaten Real Madrid, who had won the first five European Cups, to reach the final of the sixth, in 1961, and were firm favourites against Benfica. They even took the lead from a fine Sándor Kocsis header before Ramallets, charging off his line rashly, made it easy for Domiciano Cavém to square for José Aguas to tap in. Worse was to follow. José Neto chipped in a cross and the ball looped backwards off the head of the Barça defender Enric Gensana. It should have been a simple enough matter for Ramallets, with no player within ten yards of him, to pluck the ball from the air, but he seemed mesmerised by its flight and shovelled it weakly against the inside of post from where it spun back behind the line and out again. The referee Gottfried Dienst, superbly placed, gave the goal, and Barcelona were behind and on their way to a 3–2 defeat.

Riffing on Peter Chapman's idea that the goalkeeper is the sporting embodiment of the island English nation, and admitting the idea is 'whimsical', Jimmy Burns suggests that Spanish goalkeepers, or at least those who have played for the national side, have taken their lead from Don Quixote. 'He ... personifies those high ideas which were supposed to make Spain great, a bastion against the enemy as well as an excuse for failure.' Quixote, of course, was an arch-outsider, living outside the usual customs of society to follow his own eccentric code of honour.

And then, defying the fear, came Iker Casillas, not an outsider, not a Catalan, not a Basque, but a unifying figure from Móstoles on the edge of Madrid. Yet he does have a Basque forename, as does his brother Unai, the result of his parents having lived in Bilbao. His father, who served in the civil guard, had been posted there and it was there that his mother fell pregnant. One day a shoemaker who begged on the street near their apartment told her that he had foreseen that her son would be a great goalkeeper and that he would play for an all-conquering Athletic side, taking his place in the great pantheon of Basque keepers. A few days before the baby was due, though, the Casillas family returned to Madrid and so it was the local team there who benefited from the goalkeeping ability the shoemaker had prophesied. It would be absurd, of course, to suggest that Casillas had somehow picked up the Basque talent for goalkeeping while in the womb but his links with Bilbao are significant, if only because – symbolically at least – they make him seem like a player of all Spain and not just Madrid. As Spain followed up their World Cup win by retaining the European Championship in 2012, their coach Vicente del Bosque praised his understated leadership; Casillas was captain for all three successes. Casillas's friendship with Xavi, which dates back to their time playing together in Spanish youth teams, has been a major factor in overcoming the Real Madrid–Barcelona rift that has undermined spirit in previous squads and, given the rancorous nature of their rivalry under José Mourinho and Pep Guardiola, could easily have done so again.

Perhaps Casillas was fortunate that his parents' return to the capital meant he became a Real Madrid player immediately, without any intermediate club. Certainly he was lucky to get his chance as early as he did. Casillas was sixteen and sitting in a classroom at the Instituto Cañaveral de Móstoles when the call came, a concierge arriving at the door and summoning him to the director's office. He was nervous, wondering whether he was about to be punished for something but the director greeted him with a proud smile. Real Madrid had just been on the phone to ask whether, with Bodo Illgner injured and Santiago Cañizares doubtful having suffered a blow to the chest, Casillas could be released to join the club for their Champions League trip to play Rosenborg in Trondheim. At the time, he was playing in the third division with Real Madrid's C team and, although he didn't play, sitting on the bench in Norway elevated him in the pecking order.

His childhood seems to have been made up of unfortunate escapades. When his parents gave him a chick as a pet, he decided he would prefer it to be more eye-catching, so coloured it in with a felt-tip. Not liking the result, he sought to wash off the ink so put the bird in a toilet and pulled the chain. It drowned. When he was seven, he was given his father's pools coupon to post. He forgot, costing the family a little under a million pounds as all fourteen predictions proved correct.

Casillas's abilities as a goalkeeper first emerged when his father took him to the park to play football, smacking shots at him. Every year Real Madrid organised a series of trials for hopeful youngsters to try to impress. When he was ten, Casillas got through the first round and was placed in goal for the second. On a bitter day, in which he shivered in just a thin shirt, he conceded five goals in a 7–1 defeat for his team and assumed his chance had gone. He was wrong; Antonio Mezquito, head of the youth section at Real, decided to take him on.

Another injury to Illgner gave an eighteen-year-old Casillas his debut in September 1999. At the end of that season, he became the youngest keeper to win the Champions League. He came off the bench to replace César Sánchez in the final two years later as Real won the Champions League again. When Real claimed La Liga in 2012, it was Casillas's fifth championship. He was named IFFHS goalkeeper of the year every year from 2008 to 2011, becoming the first goalkeeper to win the award four years running. 'The great thing about Iker is the natural way he has always confronted things,' said the former Spain goalkeeper Paco Buyo, who worked with him at youth level. 'His maturity, coolness and calmness give him the serenity with which he plays. This serenity is eventually rewarded.'

Would Casillas look as strong in weaker sides? In games for both Real Madrid and Spain, he is almost invariably the less involved goalkeeper and that perhaps contributes to his reputation; after all, a goalkeeper's errors will always count against his reputation more than saves count for it. Then again, there have been matches when Casillas has almost single-handedly kept Real in contention. After one league game under Manuel Pellegrini, the sports daily *AS*, which usually marks players out of three, rated his performance as a four. Playing for good teams helps, and he was extremely fortunate to get his chance so early, but Casillas has been too consistent for too long to be regarded as anything other than a truly exceptional keeper.

Victor Valdés too started young, given his chance at Barcelona when Roberto Bonano suffered a spell of poor form in 2002–03 and made first choice in 2003–04, as he turned twenty-one, when Rüştü Reçber began the season badly. Since then he has won the Zamora trophy five times while embodying the ideal of the sweeper-keeper. Liverpool's Pepe Reina, meanwhile, although his role with the Spain national team often seems to be that of a cheerleader, was named the best goalkeeper in the Premier League three seasons in a row between 2006 and 2008.

Yet for all the success of Valdés and Reina, it may be that their reputation is enhanced by the reflected glow of Casillas. Valdés has always been prone to mistakes and Reina made an unusual number of errors in 2011–12. As England found in the seventies and eighties, the perception of strength in depth is easy to maintain when there is a true great in the front line, whose brilliance ensures mistakes will be forgiven as he protects the reputations of understudies who are never exposed.

Casillas is not merely a great but perhaps represents the

beginning of a new phase of goalkeeping. He is far from the spindly outcast of old-fashioned myth, but neither is he anything like as bulky as Schmeichel or Buffon. Flexibility, agility and reading of the game, perhaps, have begun to take over from the muscular aggression of Ehrmann's *Flugschule*. In Germany too, there seems to have been a turn away from the likes of Kahn to the tall but relatively slender Manuel Neuer. Ron-Robert Zieler and Marc-Andre ter Stegen are similarly built. Hugo Lloris of France and Buffon's back-up Salvatore Sirigu, even Joe Hart and Jack Butland, while athletically built, are agile rather than hulking. The era of the real giants, perhaps, has passed.

9: THE FEAR OF PENALTIES AND OTHER EXISTENTIAL QUANDARIES

The forward steps up, watching the goalkeeper. The goalkeeper stares back. Two men in the sparse crowd look on, mumbling to one another. It's a familiar scene, a classic Mexican stand-off transferred to a small football stadium in Austria, the final scene of *The Goalkeeper's Fear of the Penalty* [*Die Angst des Tormanns beim Elfmeter*], directed by Wim Wenders and released in 1972. Having little credible competition, it usually comes near the top of lists of the greatest football films but it actually has very little to do with football.

The protagonist, Josef Bloch, played by Arthur Brauss (who nine years later would play Lutz, one of the German team in *Escape to Victory*), is sent off for committing a foul, leaves the stadium, meets a cinema cashier, spends the night with her and then murders her. The book on which the film is based, Peter Handke's 1970 novel, features even less football; in that version, Bloch has long since retired and is working on a construction site when he commits his murder.

At times, the vagueness about details – 'a championship game', 'a tour to South America' – or painstaking descriptions of the mechanics of a corner can make it seem as though Handke has no great knowledge of football, but in fact he was a keen fan and in 1969 wrote a poem called '*Die Aufstellung des 1. FC Nürnberg vom 27.1.1968*' ['The Line-up of 1. FC Nürnberg on 27.1.1968']. It lists in formation the eleven players who played in Nürnberg's Cup victory over Bayer Leverkusen, with the kick-off time detailed beneath, a neat way of indicating how, to fans, there is a poetry in the cadences of a list of names, each of which, packed with memories of past glories and the potential of future ones, carry a meaning far greater than the simple signifier may suggest (even if he lists a player in the starting line-up, Leupold, who was actually used as a substitute). The dissonance between the apparent simplicity of the signifier and the complexity and layered meaning of the signified is a consistent theme of Handke's work.

In both film and novel of *The Goalkeeper's Fear of the Penalty*, the title is explained by a climactic scene in which Bloch, having had some sort of breakdown that leads him to question the connection between words and the objects they describe, wanders into a football stadium during a match. A penalty is awarded, at which – in the novel – Bloch turns to the man next to him, 'a salesman', and explains that, 'The goalkeeper is trying to figure out which corner the kicker will send the ball into … If he knows the kicker, he knows which corner he usually goes for. But maybe the kicker is also counting on the goalie's figuring this out. So the goalie goes on figuring that just today the ball might go into the other corner. But what if the kicker follows the goalkeeper's thinking and plans to shoot in the usual corner after all? And so on, and so on.'

In the film, which, while far from conventional, sticks far more closely to the template of the detective story than the overtly existentialist novel, the man Bloch speaks to in the stadium is a policeman and he is in his home town rather than an unnamed Austrian border town. There the metaphor is explicit: Bloch has chosen not to go on the run, instead returning home and living the life of an innocent man. The policeman is a friend of his but Bloch has no idea whether he suspects him of the murder; if he doesn't act like a suspect, he thinks, there is no reason for anybody to suspect he is one as there were no eyewitnesses to the killing.

In the novel, there is nothing to link the goalkeeper's thought processes at the taking of the penalty with Bloch's attempts – such as they are – to evade capture. 'When the kicker starts his run,' Bloch says in the book's penultimate paragraph, 'the goalkeeper unconsciously shows with his body which way he'll throw himself even before the ball is kicked and the kicker can simply kick in the other direction … The goalie might just as well try to prise open a door with a piece of straw.'

The theme is picked up by the Argentinian writer Osvaldo Soriano in his short story '*El penalti más largo en el mundo*' ['The Longest Penalty in the World'], published in 1995. It tells of Estrella Polar, a team of lumbering no-hopers who, thanks to a series of 1–0 wins – 'a long litany of laborious, horrible triumphs' – end up facing the eternal champions, Deportivo Belgrano, away on the final day of the 1958 season, trailing them by just a point. With three minutes to go, Estrella Polar take a 2–1 lead; the title, suddenly, is in their hands. It is then that the referee, Herminio Silva, intervenes: 'He stretched out the game until Padín entered the box, and when Padín had barely approached a defender, the referee blew.' Penalty.

'In those days the penalty spot wasn't marked with a white dot,' the story goes on, 'and you had to count out twelve yards. Herminio Silva didn't have the chance to pick up the ball because Polar Star's right-back, Colo Rivero, had knocked him out with a bloody nose.' A mass brawl erupted and carried on until nightfall, at which the game was suspended. The league decided that the final seconds – just the penalty, in other words – should be played out behind closed doors the following week.

The next day, Gato Díaz, Estrella Polar's goalkeeper, practised by facing penalties from a long line of townspeople. That night, playing cards back at the club, Díaz approached the club president.

> 'Constante [Guana, Belgrano's penalty-taker] always kicks to the right,' he said [beginning to outline a dilemma similar to Bloch's].
> 'Always,' said the president of the club.
> 'But he knows that I know.'
> 'Then we're fucked.'
> 'Yeah, but I know that he knows,' said el Gato.
> 'Then dive to the left and be ready,' said someone at the table.

'No. He knows that I know that he knows,' said Gato Díaz, and he got up to go to bed.

Gato stopped training, asking what the point was. Instead he began pursuing a 'blonde from Ferreira', sending her flowers and taking her to the cinema. She refused to kiss him, though, saying she might do so at the dance on Sunday, but only if he had saved the penalty earlier that afternoon.

'And how do I know?' he asked.

'How do you know what?'

'Which way I need to dive?'

The traffic in the valley was stopped. People gathered outside the ground, craning for a vantage point. A line of fans stretched two miles long to relay the outcome from the stadium. At quarter to four, Silva blew his whistle and Guana placed the ball on the spot, walked back and began his run up.

Díaz took a step forward and lunged to the right. The ball flew spinning in circles toward the middle of the goal and Constante Guana knew immediately that Gato Díaz's legs would carry him right to where he could deflect it to the side. El Gato thought about the dance that night, in his belated glory, and how someone should run to block the ball in the corner because it was still in play.

Even as the news passed down the chain, though, the linesman began flagging. Silva, the referee, who was an epileptic, had had a fit and had collapsed. He hadn't seen the penalty, and so it needed to be retaken. Guana, having lost his nerve, passed the ball to Padín. 'The ball went left and Gato Díaz dived left with an elegance and a confidence he would never have again.' He saved it and Estrella Polar were champions.

The story had its basis in fact. The Argentinian journalist Ugo Splendore travelled to Valle de Rio Negro, where Soriano had grown up, and discovered that the writer had been involved in a similar incident in 1953 or perhaps 1954. Born in Mar del

Plata, Soriano had moved to Cipolletti, near Neuquén, when he was three. Until a knee injury forced him to give up the game, he was a keen centre-forward and played for a local side called Confluencia, the inspiration for Estrella Polar. 'He didn't play football well: he had crooked legs and a powerful kick, nothing more than that,' Pepe Santos, a childhood friend of Soriano told Splendore. 'But he had a superior mind; he was a thinker.'

When Soriano was fourteen (or perhaps fifteen), Confluencia played a decisive match at home against Union Allen Progresista, from the much larger town of Allen. With twenty minutes remaining and the score goalless, the referee awarded Confluencia a penalty. He was attacked by players and officials from the away team and abandoned the game as a mass brawl ensued. The league ruled that the penalty and the remaining twenty minutes should be played behind closed doors a week later. The Union keeper saved the penalty, Confluencia failed to find a winner in the final minutes and the title went to the bigger side. Union's keeper, the precursor to Gato, was called Benjamin, was tall and thin and wasn't in love with a blonde from Ferreira. The version Soriano wrote, then, becomes a form of wish-fulfilment, an enhanced version of reality.

Yet there is no happy ending to the story. The narrator met Gato two years later. He was married by then, not to the blonde from Ferreira but to Colo Rivero's sister. His heroism had faded and he was 'a ruin'. The narrator took a penalty against him and scored. 'Some day, when you're older,' the goalkeeper said, 'you're going to go around talking about how you scored a goal against Gato Díaz, only by then nobody will remember me.'

Soriano's tale thus becomes less about the existential dilemma of the goalkeeper than about the fleeting nature of glory: there'll always be another penalty; you might save the one that wins the championship but there's always 'an insolent teenager' waiting to beat you.

Handke's novel, though, breaks off as soon as the kick has been taken. Perhaps the goalkeeper whom Bloch sees saving the penalty himself faced a kick from somebody like Soriano's narrator. That we never find out, though, leaves the impact of

Handke's penalty hanging, imbuing it with a universality. After all Bloch's talk about guessing left or right, 'The kicker suddenly started his run. The goalkeeper, who was wearing a bright yellow jersey, stood absolutely still, and the penalty kicker shot the ball into his hands.'

The choice, the process of having to make decisions, becomes too much for Bloch; he sees that deciding whether to dive left or right is essentially futile – and then paradoxically it's shown that that paralysis could actually still be effective as the goalkeeper Bloch is watching saves the kick; although whether he is gripped by the same indecision is impossible to say. Perhaps, like Taffarel facing Gary Lineker in that friendly at Wembley, he simply knew the taker had a habit of dinking the ball down the middle. In that, Bloch's fear of the decision echoes precisely that of the existentialists: after the 'death of God' as heralded by Nietzsche, man must be accountable to a moral code of his own devising. Nietzsche saw the death of God as a profound, if terrifying, liberation; others, most notably Kurtz in Conrad's *Heart of Darkness*, saw merely 'the horror' of a world without transcendent meaning. Little wonder that Bloch, in the midst of his breakdown, as signifier and signified separate, unhinging words from their meanings, as his whole epistemology falls apart, cannot face making any decision. 'What number should one start counting at?' he asks.

It is the fact of making a decision that does for Bloch but what he and El Gato Díaz describe perfectly is the nature of the decision: the game of bluff and counter-bluff gone through by forward and keeper. Both experience versions of game theory, which was developed in the 1940s to consider situations in which what one party should do depends on what the other party should do and vice versa. The theory was commonly used to determine policy during the Cold War and led to nuclear proliferation. (Country A and Country B squabble. Country A doesn't know if Country B has the bomb, but reasons that if it doesn't there are two outcomes: A doesn't get the bomb so the squabbles continue; A does get the bomb and B has to toe the line. If B does have the bomb, there are equally two outcomes: A doesn't get the bomb and so it has to toe the line; A does get the bomb so both have it and there is détente. Country A thus reasons that, in all situations, it's better to have the bomb than not.) The penalty, as a self-contained event, offers an almost ideal example of a situation to which game theory can be applied and so a number of economists have studied it.

Both goalkeepers and penalty-takers develop habits which are revealed by study over time: some forwards will always shoot left, for instance, or some goalkeepers will always dive right. Steven Levitt, the co-author of *Freakonomics,* co-wrote a paper with Pierre-André Chiappori and Timothy Groseclose called 'Testing Mixed-Strategy Equilibria when Players are Heterogeneous: The Case of Penalty Kicks in Soccer' based on a study of 459 penalties from the Italian and French leagues. One goalkeeper in their study dived left for all eight of the penalties he faced, although only two of the kicks went that way.

In the 1970s Jan Reker, a Dutch manager who went on to become the chief executive of PSV Eindhoven, began to compile a vast card index on thousands of players, recording, among other things, where he liked to place his penalties. The goalkeeper Hans van Breukelen worked with Reker at PSV and stayed in touch even after Reker left the club. He would often ring him before Netherlands international matches to ask about opponents. It was in 1988 that his work paid off. In the May, PSV faced Benfica in the European Cup final. Van Breukelen called Reker before the game to ask about penalty-takers. The match finished goalless and went to a shoot-out. Both teams scored their first five kicks, but Van Breukelen saved the sixth from António Veloso and PSV won the title. A month later, in the final of the European Championship, the Netherlands were two goals up against the USSR when Van Breukelen conceded a penalty. Following Reker's advice again, he went the right way and saved from Igor Belanov. Reker's research had led directly to both PSV and the Netherlands becoming European champions.

Now such research into penalty-takers is considered almost mandatory. Before each penalty in the shoot-out in the World

Cup quarter-final between Germany and Argentina in 2006, for instance, Jens Lehmann pulled a sheet of crumpled hotel note-paper from his sock before replacing it. On it, in pencil that Lehmann complained was hard to read as the paper became soaked in sweat, Germany's goalkeeping coach Andreas Köpke had jotted advice about likely Argentinian penalty-takers (including the numbers for certain players, presumably fearing Lehmann might not recognise them):

Riquelme left
Crespo long run-up/right short run-up/left
Heinze left low
Ayala 2 waits long time, long run-up, right
Messi left
Aimar 16, waits long time, left
Rodríguez 18, left

Germany's back-room staff had, it was reported, analysed 13,000 kicks. The scrap of paper became almost a holy relic both for Germany and for those who advocate increased use of statistics in football. Yet its effect may be overstated; only two of the seven actually took penalties. Both of them, though, behaved as pre-dicted. Ayala went to Lehmann's right and he got down to save; Rodríguez did go left, but hit his penalty well enough to defeat Lehmann even as he dived the right way.

But the crib-sheet might also have had a psychological impact. Germany, who had gone first, scored each of their first four pen-alties. Ayala's miss meant that by the time Esteban Cambiasso stepped up to take Argentina's fourth kick, he needed to score to keep the game alive. Lehmann consulted the piece of paper. There was nothing on it about Cambiasso, but Cambiasso didn't know that. Germany had never lost a shoot-out since their very first, against Czechoslovakia in the European Championship final in 1976; Germans are famously meticulous; Lehmann had gone the right way for all three kicks up till then, even though Julio Cruz was also missing from Köpke's list; *of course* Cambiasso would think they would have data on him. This was precisely the dilemma outlined by El Gato Díaz, but transplanted onto the penalty-taker: Lehmann didn't know, but Cambiasso thought that he knew and he thought he knew that Lehmann knew that he knew. So, take the kick as he normally would, or go the other way? He went right, but not near the corner, about midway between ground and bar. Lehmann, diving to his left, saved comfortably.

Nobody, perhaps, has studied penalties as thoroughly as the economist Ignacio Palacios Huerta. He started recording how penalties were taken in 1995 when he was still a graduate student at the University of Chicago, and in 2003 published a paper on the theme entitled 'Professionals play Minimax'. A friend of Huerta's also knew Avram Grant and so, as Simon Kuper and Stefan Szymanski revealed in *Why England Lose*, when Chelsea reached the Champions League final against Manchester United in 2008, he put the two men in touch. Huerta sent Grant a report making four key points about United and penalties.

It's no great secret that all players have a 'natural side' – almost everybody gets more power by striking with the instep which means it is easier for right-footers to strike the ball to their left and for left-footers to strike the ball to their right. So much is obvious – although of course some players feel they are more accurate sidefooting shots and so put their penalties the other way. Huerta told Grant that the United goalkeeper Edwin van der Sar had a marked tendency to dive to the striker's natural side. He pointed out that 'the vast majority of the penalties that Van der Sar stops are those kicked to a mid-height (say, between 1 and 1.5m) and hence penalties against him should be kicked just on the ground or high up.' Secondly, he noted that Cristiano Ronaldo was adept at waiting for the keeper to move and then placing his shot the other way; it was essential, then, that Petr Cech stood up as long as possible. If Ronaldo checked his run, meanwhile, eighty-five per cent of the time he put his kick to the right. Huerta's final piece of advice was to go first if possible; sixty per cent of penalty shoot-outs are won by the side taking the first penalty, presumably because the pressure of knowing you have to score to save the game gets to sides.

The extent to which Huerta's advice was adhered to is impossible to say, but what is clear is that he was right. Rio Ferdinand, the Manchester United captain, won the toss and turned to his bench to ask whether United should go first or second. John Terry, Chelsea's captain, presumably trying to influence him, offered to go first – but Ferdinand ignored him. Michael Ballack and Juliano Belletti both scored going to their 'unnatural' sides – that is, to Van der Sar's left.

Carlos Tévez and Michael Carrick had both scored for United, so it was 2–2 when Ronaldo stepped up. Cech stood motionless, Ronaldo checked his run and then, as Huerta had predicted, shot to the right. Cech saved.

Lampard, right-footed, went to his right and scored. Ashley Cole, left-footed, went to his right – that is, his natural side – and Van der Sar went the right way, getting to the shot but being unable to keep it out. Terry went right – the unnatural side – as Van der Sar dived the other way. Had Terry not slipped, he would have scored and won the final; as it was, he fractionally misdirected his shot and it hit the outside of the post. Salomon Kalou, also right-footed, went to his right. In other words, all bar Cole went to their unnatural side. Van der Sar went to the natural side four times out of six, following precisely the pattern his track record suggested he would.

Because five right-footers had gone to their unnatural side and the one left-footer had gone to his natural side, the first six Chelsea penalties all went to Van der Sar's left. As Nicolas Anelka came forward to take Chelsea's seventh kick, needing to score to keep the game alive, Van der Sar pointed to his left side as if to say he had worked out Chelsea's strategy and he knew where they were directing their kicks. All six previous kicks, after all, had gone that way. Anelka is right-footed. If Chelsea were following Huerta's advice, the plan was to aim at precisely that part of the goal Van der Sar was indicating. Anelka suddenly was caught in Bloch's dilemma: the keeper knew, but he knew that the keeper knew (or rather, he thought he knew that the keeper knew). He went left, to his natural side and, even worse, at precisely that mid-height Huerta had warned against. Van der Sar saved and United were European champions.

Duffy, the detective created by Dan Kavanagh (a pseudonym of Julian Barnes) who plays in goal for his Sunday side, follows Bloch in his hatred of penalties, albeit in a more prosaic way – 'He didn't like the penalty spot. For a start, it was much too near the goal.' In practice, the reverse appears to be true. Goalkeepers seem to relish penalties because nobody expects them to save them and the usual polarities are reversed. Concede a penalty and it's one of those things; save one and you become a hero – an inversion of the goalkeeper's usual role as scapegoat. 'The scorer's fear of the penalty – *that* would be worth writing a novel about,' as Sepp Maier said of the Handke book. There may be those who wonder whether, to take the 1990 World Cup semi-final as an example, Peter Shilton might not have been better served trying to guess which way penalty-takers were going rather than diving after the ball had been struck, but the criticism and sympathy he received was all but indiscernible beside that dished out to Stuart Pearce and Chris Waddle, both of whom missed as England lost to West Germany. The shoot-out also offers the goalkeeper a rare chance of immediate glory. In open play, even a brilliant save in the final minute never feels as decisive as a last-gasp winner; there is always another phase to be defended. In shoot-outs, though, the final save is definitive. Parry the last kick, turn it round the post or over the bar, and that's it, the game is over and it's the goalkeeper who's won it.

Fear them or not, the notion of a penalty was devised by a goalkeeper, William McCrum, who played for Milford Everton in Armagh. Initially fouls near the goal had been punished by a free-kick taken from where the offence had occurred but as defenders even in amateur games took increasingly extreme measures to prevent the opposition from scoring, McCrum suggested an unopposed shot at goal, rather than allowing defenders to pack the goalmouth as they had previously. His proposal was adopted in local games and then taken up by the Irish Football Association, which submitted the idea to the

International Football Board. Despite opposition – Corinthians, believing none of their players would ever deliberately employ foul means, refused to contest penalties – the IFB accepted the proposal and it passed into law on 2 June 1891.

The first penalty awarded was for Royal Albert in a game against Airdrieonians, a player now known only as McLuggage scoring past James Connor. Then, as now, penalties were taken from a spot twelve yards from goal, but goalkeepers could advance up to a line marked six yards from the goal line. In 1905, they were forced to stay on their line and, in 1929, they were forbidden to move until the ball had been struck, a rule later amended so they can move so long as they don't come forward off the goal line.

McCrum, meanwhile, was frozen out of the family linen-milling business because of his supposed lack of commercial nous. They provided him with a stipend, but he lost most of that gambling in Monte Carlo and, when the mill went bankrupt in 1931, was forced to sell his possessions. He died in an Armagh boarding house a year later.

Penalties at times seem almost discrete from the game, self-contained moments of drama with their own rules in which football is stripped down to its barest essentials: ball, goal, attacker, keeper. As such, penalties, and particularly penalty shoot-outs, shift the emphasis away from the technical towards the psychological. Shoot-outs are not just about striking the ball cleanly or getting a good spring, they're also a game of bluff and double bluff. Antonin Panenka's famous penalty to beat Maier in 1976 is easily accomplished: most players of any age at any level can dink a ball twelve yards into the middle of the goal; the majority could even do so with a measure of disguise, even if Panenka insists it is harder than it looks. It took him two years of practice before he dared use the technique in a game. 'It's always been a fight between shooter and keeper – who can keep his nerve longest?' he explained. 'No keeper will stay in the centre – that's what I based my strategy on. The keeper is waiting and when I bring my foot to the ball, he is choosing one side or the other. When I kick the ball lightly, the opponent is already on the move and can't recover. However, if I kicked it too strongly, he could make some reflex save. And that's why I used slow lobs. It takes a while but the keeper can't get back.'

What really set Panenka's effort apart was circumstance: he dared to do it for Czechoslovakia at the end of a shoot-out against West Germany in the European Championship final. Get it wrong, and he'd have become a figure of fun, the showboating gambler who not merely cost his country their only major title, but did so while looking ridiculous. As it was, he got it right, correctly guessing that Maier would dive. The nerve he showed led to that sort of penalty being named after him and earned him such respect that a cult Spanish football magazine took his name.

No goalkeeper has ever had a more decisive impact on a more important shoot-out than Helmut Ducadam. True to type, he is an outsider, a loner with a shadow across his soul. 'If I hadn't become a footballer, I definitely would have become a psychiatrist,' he said. 'I always liked to walk in the street and look at people and think, "What is in his mind?" I like poker. I play poker. I'm good.'

So good that, in 1986, in the greatest game of poker he ever played, he saved each of the four penalties Barcelona took against him in the shoot-out of the European Cup final and so won the title for Steaua Bucharest. It was a wholly implausible victory; no side from the east had ever won the European Cup before, and with the final played in Seville, and Barcelona fans outnumbering Steaua fans by a factor of 250 to 1 in the stadium, few gave them much chance. But they held out for a goalless draw and, by the end of extra-time, the tension had told on Barcelona to the extent that Bernd Schuster had stormed out of the stadium after being substituted.

It's easy to see how Ducadam, simply by his physique, would intimidate anxious opponents. He remains an enormous presence. The moustache is a little sparser now and his waistline has expanded with the passing years, but when he stood up from behind his desk in his office at Steaua's stadium to act out his finest moments, he became again the giant figure who filled the goal in Seville. 'I was a specialist at saving penalties; it came naturally to me,' he said. 'There are some goalkeepers who are better than me in open play but who are not so good at saving penalties, but some goalkeepers have this gift.'

It was common at the end of training for Ducadam to bet other players that they couldn't beat him from the spot. He preferred to try to read players in their run-up; not for him the sort of detailed notes used by Lehmann. 'Barcelona had won their semi-final against IFK Gothenburg in a penalty shoot-out,' Ducadam said, before – as though following Bloch's logic – expressing the benefits of ignorance. 'We watched a lot of Barça games before the final, but we never watched how they executed penalties. Maybe that was an advantage for Steaua, because maybe the Barcelona players thought I knew how they took penalties – and maybe they changed strategy just for that game. If you know a player and know his strategy, you make your own strategy according to how he has performed before. You're at a disadvantage because he can change his side to shoot, knowing this. I never took notes like Lehmann.

'It depended a lot if it was a left-footed or a right-footed player because nearly all players in my day sidefooted penalties. Eighty per cent of left-footed players hit their penalty to their left and eighty per cent of right-footed players to the right. There is more power striking the other way across the ball. Only five per cent of penalties are taken technically. Even if the goalkeeper knows where it is going, the chances of stopping it now are very low because of the power.'

The shoot-out, Ducadam acknowledges, was a unique opportunity. 'I dreamed of playing in a final – not the European Cup final, just any final – and becoming the most important guy on the field,' he said. It was rare enough to get that chance; the shoot-out meant that the possibility was there not merely to be the most important guy, but to be widely acknowledged as such.

Steaua's regular penalty-taker was Mihail Majearu, and he stepped up first. He side-footed his effort firmly to his right but it was nowhere near the corner. Urruti, the Barça keeper, dropped on the ball to save and for the first time since the game had kicked off, the momentum seemed to shift against Steaua.

On the goal line, Ducadam stood tall, staring straight at José Alexanco as he placed the ball on the spot. As Alexanco walked back, Ducadam bent at the waist and stayed poised, hands resting on the tops of his thighs. 'You have to have the serenity in your mind to focus on what you have to do,' he went on. 'In Seville I put myself in the situation of the players who took the penalties.' Alexanco, right-footed, clipped the ball to Ducadam's right. The shot was at a comfortable height, not too near the post and just at the right point of Ducadam's dive for him to beat the ball away. 'The most important was the first one,' he said. 'If you save the first, the next one becomes much easier to save. You have to have luck when you save penalties.'

Laszlo Bölöni's kick was struck at almost exactly the same place and Urruti produced a replica of Ducadam's save. Ducadam, meanwhile, was engaged in his own private game of scissors-paper-stone. 'I think the second shooter from Barcelona thought I would go left because I went right for the first one,' he said. 'The logic of the player was that he should go to the same side because he thought the goalkeeper would go the other.' Sure enough, Angel Pedraza also hit his shot to Ducadam's right. It was low and heading just inside the post when Ducadam's outstretched right hand intervened; it was his best save of the night. As Ducadam walked away, fists clenched in celebration, the ball was thrown back from behind the goal. Instinctively, a man absolutely in the zone, he twisted to his right and punched the ball away again. After two penalties each, it was still 0–0.

Having seen so many others fail, Marius Lăcătuş decided it wasn't the time for subtlety and, dispensing with finesse, belted the ball just to the right of centre. It crashed in off the underside of the bar. Ducadam continued his mind-games as Pichi Alonso stepped up for Barça. 'The third penalty was the easiest,' he said. 'The taker thought I would go to the left because the first two I had gone to the right. I dived a bit early, but it was the easiest for me to save because it was predictable.' It wasn't a good penalty, misdirected enough that it almost crept under Ducadam, but he got his body down quickly enough and saved with his ribs. Anxiety in the crowd became desperation; a debilitating hush fell over the Sánchez Pizjuán.

Gavrila Balint rolled his penalty to his left as Urruti dived the wrong way, meaning Marcos had to score. 'Watching it again on television after many years,' Ducadam said, 'I realise that the fourth taker for Barcelona didn't have a clue what he should do, because I'd saved all the other penalties on the same side. I watched him and had eye contact with him. I played a trick on Marcos. I shaped to go to the left and then to the right, then I went left.' Marcos's penalty was struck without great power, and Ducadam saved easily. Steaua were European champions and Ducadam was the obvious hero.

It was a great moment, but it became a desperately poignant one; that was the last serious game Ducadam ever played. He essentially disappeared. In the paranoid world of Ceaușescu's Romania, this led to a flurry of rumours suggesting he'd somehow offended a member of the Ceaușescu family, perhaps by refusing to hand over a car he'd been given as a bonus, and been punished as a result. Some said his arms had been cut off – that certainly isn't true – and others that his arms had been broken.

The truth, as Ducadam explained it, is rather more prosaic, although hardly less traumatic. 'I'd had pains in my right arm for six months before the final,' he said. 'I got drugs from the doctors to control them, but the medicine wasn't strong enough. One day that summer I was with my friends in my home town and I fell over. I put my hand down to protect myself and the aneurysm went to the artery and blocked the circulation for the whole arm. I had surgery, some kind of bypass. In 1988 I had another operation and [in 2010] I had another operation with modern technology.' In September 2012, he had further surgery after being rushed to hospital amid fears he may have to have the arm amputated.

Ducadam did make a brief comeback after that second operation, playing a handful of games for Vagonul, a small team in his home town of Arad. He even scored with a clearance from his own box, but he knew he was far from the standards he'd previously achieved and so retired, initially taking a job working at a customs post on the Hungarian border before Steaua offered him an ambassadorial role. 'Maybe I was unlucky,' he said, 'but maybe I was lucky as well. If it had happened just a few weeks earlier nobody would want to interview me now.'

Five years later, when the second and so far final eastern European side won the European Cup, it was again a goalkeeper who turned out to be the hero. Stevan Stojanović was also the captain of Crvena Zvezda. Dika, as he is nicknamed, is a man who radiates calm, even as tear gas billows at the window as it did the first time I met him, at a Yugoslav league match in Novi Sad in 2001. Yet he was almost remembered in that 1990–91 campaign for a horrendous error.

Yugoslavia was clearly approaching the end as Zvezda, a highly talented side packed with gifted technical players, approached the semi-final against Bayern Munich. They were underdogs, but played superbly in Munich, scoring two brilliant counter-attacking goals to lead 2–1 after the away leg. Before the return, at the Marakana in Belgrade, the first ordnance of the war was fired as Croat nationalists launched three Ambrust missiles into Borovo Selo, the village near Vukovar where Siniša Mihajlović had been brought up.

The atmosphere in the Marakana crackled with intensity: this wasn't just a major football match but, everybody knew, probably the last major football match to be played in Belgrade for years. When Mihajlović put Zvezda ahead with a deflected free-kick midway through the first half, the game seemed won. But twenty minutes into the second half, Bayern won a free-kick in a similar position. The *libero* Klaus Augenthaler took it, catching the ball sweetly but directing it straight at Stojanović. He was momentarily unsighted, but under no pressure it should have been easy enough for the goalkeeper to gather. As it was, the ball squirmed through his arms and slithered between his legs to dribble over the line.

'Before the semi-final, I hadn't made a single error in the European Cup,' Stojanović insisted.

I'd had good performances before that game. And also that game I was good, but that moment could have turned my career, my life, everything, because of one big mistake.

It was a little bit wet. It was not raining during the game, but the pitch was wet. In my head I knew that Augenthaler had a powerful kick. I knew it would come quickly and I was thinking only about it going through the wall or down the side of the wall. As the ball came to me I thought, 'Great,' and it's difficult to explain. I did everything in the way you would coach someone. I didn't stand with my legs apart, but the ball hit me on the arm and took a deflection and that was the only way it could pass through my legs. If it had happened a second time I would have saved it. But it happens only once in a lifetime. But that is a big law of goalkeepers: you've never saved a shot until you have the ball in your hands. I thought I had it and maybe thinking that cost me a millisecond in a lapse of concentration.

I was lying down on the pitch and everything was quiet – almost 100,000 people. [Robert] Prosinečki passed me to get the ball out of the net and he said, 'Come on, Dika, let's go.' Of course I was immediately aware of what a big mistake it was, but the score was still enough to get us to the final, and that gave me confidence. They could say what they wanted, I thought, but the most important thing was that we went to the final. Now we are talking about that mistake in a positive way, but I can't imagine what it would have been like if we had then not reached the final.

They nearly didn't. Five minutes later, Manfred Bender scored a second and the scores were level on aggregate. What followed was twenty minutes of astonishing football as two fine, attacking sides laid into each other. Both teams had chances, none better than the opportunity Roland Wohlfahrt had seven minutes from time as he ran on to an Olaf Thon through-ball, beating the Zvezda offside trap and clipping the ball over the advancing Stojanović. As Wohlfahrt hit it, he must have thought he'd scored; the trajectory seemed perfect and the ball appeared to be heading just inside the left-hand post. Stojanović, on the ground, turned and watched, a despairing hand already beginning to appeal for offside. This time, though, luck was with Stojanović: in the air, the ball began to fade a fraction to the left, and when it bounced, it drifted further that way, hitting the post and bouncing back towards Stojanović, finding just the right angle to elude Stefan Effenberg as he hurtled into the box.

'I thought the ball was going in, but some force took it and it hit the post,' said Stojanović. 'It was unbelievable. If it had come back normally, Effenberg would have scored. When something like that happens you start to think it's destiny that you will go through.' In the final minute that destiny was fulfilled, Augenthaler's attempt to clear a Mihajlović cross sending the ball spinning up and over a flat-footed Raimond Aumann and into the corner. 'It would have been unjust if we had not gone through,' said Stojanović. 'In Munich we played two halves where we were the better team. In the first half here, instead of being 2–0 up we let them back into it. For three halves we were better.' And yet in the end Zvezda reached the final because one goalkeeper made a terrible error and was saved by a stroke of luck, while the other was undone by an outrageous and unpredictable miskick.

The final, against Marseille, was a dreadful anti-climax as two sides noted for their attacking prowess cancelled each other out. A desperate goalless draw led to a penalty shoot-out. 'I saved enough penalties,' Stojanović said. 'I cannot say that I was a specialist or that I was considered a specialist. I always tried to move as late as possible. There are a lot of players who look at the goalkeeper. He sees the goalkeeper move and then he shoots to the other side. On the other hand as the goalkeeper if you can stay still as long as possible on the line then you can confuse the penalty-taker. It's a game of nerves. The only advantage the goalkeeper has is that that's the only situation in the whole of football in which the goalkeeper has nothing to lose.

'I had a book where I would note down where players put penalties. You couldn't guarantee players would shoot to the same side but it was some indication. For example, when I saved a penalty from Hugo Sánchez [against Real Madrid in the quarter-final in 1986–87], I knew that he shot to the right side. Manuel Amoros [who took Marseille's first kick], though, I didn't know because I'd never watched him. I looked him straight in the eye and I noticed he was not calm. He didn't look me in the eye, but put his head down. If a player is calm, he looks at you. I looked at him and I sort of knew he would shoot to my right side.'

Stojanović went that way and saved. Marseille converted their other three kicks, but Zvezda, who had gone first, scored all five of theirs to win the European Cup. By the following year, Zvezda were forced to play home games in Sofia because of the war and the bulk of the squad had been sold off. Zvezda have never been so good since.

Nobody, perhaps, exemplifies how penalties can be an opportunity for a goalkeeper so well as Zetti, the Brazilian who runs the academy in São Paulo. That he was a fine goalkeeper is not in doubt, but his reputation was made by the 1992 Copa Libertadores final against a Newell's Old Boys side managed by Marcelo Bielsa. São Paulo lost the first leg 1–0 in Argentina, but a sixty-fifth-minute penalty from Rai levelled the aggregate scores at the Morumbi and the game went to a shoot-out.

'You can do specific training for penalties,' Zetti said. 'We knew it could be a draw and might go to penalties. So fifteen days before the final we began penalty training with Valdir de Moraes. We did more training than usual. You live the game: you think about it all the time. Newell's had got through the semi-final [against América de Cali] on penalties. Valdir de Moraes watched every game they'd played and took notes.

'I tried to remember the notes. But I was so nervous with 70,000 people shouting their support that it was difficult. And I didn't recognise all the players so you try to remember their numbers. Four of the players followed the notes; only one didn't. Alec Sandro [one of the São Paulo coaching staff] was standing in the centre-circle pointing to which way the penalties would go.'

Zetti saved from Eduardo Berizzi and, after Ronaldão had missed, from Alfredo Mendoza. After each side had taken four kicks, São Paulo led 3–2. Fernando Gamboa had to score. Zetti denied him and São Paulo had their first Libertadores title. It made Zetti a hero and it led to a clamour for him to be included in the national side, particularly after Taffarel's struggles in the USA Cup the following year. Initially Zetti was left out of the squad for the 1993 Copa América by Carlos Alberto Parreira, who preferred Carlos and Taffarel, but after the right-back Branco was injured he called up Zetti to replace him in the squad. 'There was a lot of pressure from press and supporters to pick me,' Zetti said. 'I thought I'd have nothing to do. I was in an uncomfortable position.'

He was selected, though, for the third group game against Paraguay and then, seemingly because of his reputation as a penalty specialist, for the quarter-final against Argentina. 'We had a great team,' he said. 'I touched the ball once in the whole game then I let in a goal from a corner and there was nothing I could do after that.' The game finished 1–1 and went to penalties. This time, the supposed penalty expert failed to save any of Argentina's six kicks and, when Boiadeiro finally became the first player to miss, Brazil were out. That's not to blame Zetti, but merely to point out that consistency in penalty-saving is rare. And, of course, against Argentina, Zetti hadn't had Valdir de Moraes's notes to guide him.

So if notes, if foreknowledge of previous performance, make such a difference, what should a penalty-taker do? What strategies can the taker and goalkeeper use to get through the infinite regress of knowing that he knows that he knows that he knows ...? Many players involved in shoot-outs are probably irregular takers. In their case they should probably just aim for their favourite corner and hope for the best: they probably won't have left enough data for the goalkeeper to know what their usual strategy is and trying something that doesn't come naturally is only likely to lead to mistakes.

A regular penalty-taker cannot simply aim for the same corner over and over again without variation. If he does, then the goalkeeper knows exactly which way to dive. That seems to be understood, almost intuitively. In the study by Levitt,

Chiappori and Groseclose, no player who took at least four penalties went the same way with every one. (Did they, as in Bloch's
and El Gato Díaz's examples, come up against a keeper who,
they knew, knew which way they usually went? Or did they just
vary instinctively?)

But neither can players simply develop a pattern: alternating,
say, or putting every fourth kick the other way to the previous
three. Eventually the pattern would be uncovered. Equally, a
player should still favour the side to which he feels more comfortable kicking (in the majority of cases, the natural side, that
is, to the left for a right-footer) because that will give him the
greater chance of scoring even if the keeper does go the right
way. Go to the weaker side and the chances of missing the target
or striking the ball badly and so making a save more likely are
increased.

The same is true for goalkeepers: go right more than left
and penalty-takers will work it out. Even pursuing a rational
strategy like Van der Sar's and going to the kicker's natural side
more often than not can, when recognised, become a weakness.
In fact, game theory suggests the process of making the choice
of left or right is far more complex than either Bloch or El Gato
Díaz make out.

Huerta studied 1,417 penalties taken between 1995 and 2000.
If the kicker went to his natural side and the goalkeeper went
the other way, the success rate was 95 per cent (the other 5 per
cent missing the target). If the kicker went to his unnatural side
and the keeper went the wrong way the success rate was 92 per
cent. If the keeper went the right way, the success rate fell to 70
per cent if the kicker went to his natural side, 58 per cent if he
went to the unnatural side. From this Huerta calculated that
the ideal strategy was for a kicker to go to his natural side 61.5
per cent of the time and the unnatural side 38.5 per cent, which
is actually remarkably close to what most regular penalty-takers do. For goalkeepers, the best strategy – if he is diving rather
than standing still – is to dive to the kicker's natural side 58
per cent of the time and his unnatural 42 per cent. Again, the
reality was remarkably close to the theory: in 57.7 per cent of

cases the keeper did go to the taker's natural side. The Levitt, Chiappori and Groseclose study showed 57 per cent of goalkeepers dive to their right, the natural side for the majorty of takers.

What is more significant than the overall percentages, though, is the pattern. Huerta looked at twenty-two penalty-takers and twenty goalkeepers, calculating success rates according to the side each chose and also using game theory to formulate a model of the best approach to take. In around 95 per cent of cases, the takers and keepers followed the ideal – Levitt, Chiappori and Groseclose found the same, although there was that one goalkeeper who always dived left. Regular penalty-takers and goalkeepers, in other words, are capable of achieving a sufficient level of randomness that makes a mockery of lists like Lehmann's or existential crises like those suffered by Bloch and El Gato Díaz.

As the examples of Ducadam, Stojanović and Zetti show in their different ways, life, perhaps especially the life of a goalkeeper, is uncertain. Good goalkeepers have their reputations damaged by one unfortunate mistake; others are thrust into the limelight by one or two saves. There is a randomness about it that is unsettling. Bad things happen to good people and we don't necessarily get what we deserve, an unpleasant truth the Bible seeks to justify in the story of Job. If a good man is undergoing horrors, the scripture says, it must all be part of God's plan; he is being tested, and will have his reward for facing down those trials in the next life. As Christian faith declined following the Age of Enlightenment, this inherent unfairness began to occupy writers and thinkers.

No sportsman, surely, so regularly confronts the arbitrariness of the fates as the goalkeeper. A deflection, a bad bounce, a gust of wind, a momentary misjudgement, a brilliant strike, and everything for which he has striven in the rest of the game can be wiped out. It makes sense, then, that, as John Turnbull points out in his essay 'Alone in the Woods: The Literary Landscape of Soccer's Last Defender', a disproportionate amount of what little serious fiction there is about football concerns goalkeepers.

The goalkeeper, after all, is the one player who has time to think, who can be imagined having an internal life. The goalkeeper is all too aware of danger. He cannot run and chase and play the game to forget, but must wait, always exposed, always with time to dwell. The phenomenon of teams dropping deeper and deeper when defending a lead late in games, of suffering panic as the realisation of vulnerability overwhelms them, is common; that awareness is always there for goalkeepers. In his remarkable 1983 book *The Game*, the ice-hockey goaltender Ken Dryden reflects on his fear of the puck, of how he is always conscious of the ephemeral nature of a save as opposed to a goal which, even in defeat, will stay for ever in the official record.

And then there is the fact that so many intellectuals have been goalkeepers: Albert Camus, Vladimir Nabokov, Yevgeny Yevtushenko, Henry de Montherlant, Evelyn Waugh, Mustafa Badawi, Julian Barnes and Pope John Paul II, for instance, all played in their youth or at amateur level. Arthur Conan Doyle played for Portsmouth. Even Che Guevara, despite suffering from asthma, insisted on taking part in games with his men, keeping an inhaler tucked behind the post in case he found himself short of breath.

The reverse is also true: a disproportionate number of goalkeepers seem articulate. There are intellectuals who kept goal and goalkeepers who were intellectual. In rare cases, they even become poets. Giuliano Terraneo, for instance, was a very good if not great goalkeeper who joined Torino in 1977, initially as back up to the highly regarded Luciano Castellini. Terraneo kept a clean sheet on his Torino debut in a Turin derby and then saved a penalty from Gianni Rivera in his next game against Milan but what really made him stand out was the fact that he wrote poetry. He was vocal politically as well, something highly unusual for footballers at the time. 'I vote for the radicals,' he said. 'I believe in their battles, in them not being a party but people. I have listened to their arguments and their projects in my village, Briosco, in Brianza: and I had no doubt about which side I'm on.'

He would organise plays involving his fellow villagers,

answering Pier Paolo Pasolini's call to create a relationship 'between an audience of flesh and bone and characters of flesh and bone that act on the stage.' Pasolini loved football, calling it 'the last sacred representation of our time. While other sacred representations, even mass, are in decline, football is the only one that remains among us. Football is the spectacle that has replaced the theatre.'

Terraneo seemed almost self-consciously to take it upon himself to live up to that ideal. He wrote poems that he would share with a handful of journalists and occasionally read on Radio Gamma. He wrote one, entitled '*Ragazzo Triste*' – 'Sad Boy' – about the death of his sister at the age of three. Another, '*Tu*' – 'You' – was about Luciano Re Cecconi, the great Lazio midfielder who was shot dead when he pretended to rob a jewellery store for a joke. He wrote '*Tu*' on a trip with Torino for a game in Nicosia. As his team-mates messed around, playing cards and phoning wives and girlfriends, he stayed alone in his room composing poetry. Suffering was his great theme; perhaps not surprisingly, he was a great admirer of the early nineteenth-century enlightenment poet Giacomo Leopardi. 'I like his pessimist-realism,' he said. 'It's close to my way of feeling.'

In the 1980–81 season, Torino published *Noi Granata*, a magazine edited by the journalist Bruno Colombero but supposedly written and produced by the players, that ran for eight issues. 'They'd done similar things in Perugia and Genoa,' the Torino midfielder Renato Zaccarelli said. 'Perugia came out with a paper edited by the players in tabloid form but with a certain irregularity. Let's say that ours was the first serious attempt at an actual publication produced by football players.' It was Terraneo, of course, who was responsible for the promotion and development of *Noi Granata*, writing a column and interviewing a number of public figures including Enrico Enrietti, the president of the Piedmont Region, Diego Novelli, the mayor of Turin, Renzo Righetti, the president of the Lega Calcio and Franco Reviglio, the Minister of Finance. He became noted for his probing questions and his focus on social issues. His column, meanwhile, gave a frank insight into the dressing-room and would correct press reports as, for instance, when Paolo Pulici and Francesco Graziani were said to have had a fight.

Terraneo went on to play for Milan, Lazio and Lecce but he never got the move he apparently really desired, which was to England. He even adopted the green or yellow shirts commonly worn by English goalkeepers, to the annoyance of some Italian journalists. 'A goalkeeper's class starts from the kit,' wrote *Guerin Sportivo*'s Vladimiro Caminiti. 'A goalkeeper is not a goal-keeper if he does not care for his kit.' He was typical, though, of the intellectual strand in goalkeeping.

Of the intellectuals who kept goal, Camus was probably the writer who most engaged with football, and it surely is no coin-cidence that Richard Locke's discussion of *The Goalkeeper's Fear of the Penalty* in the *New York Times Book Review* observes the sim-ilarities between Joseph Bloch and Meursault, the narrator of Camus's *L'Étranger*. Camus also mentions football in the back-ground of *The Fall*, *The First Man* and *The Plague* as one of those unavoidable details of life that need no gloss.

That he saw football, with its precisely delineated area and clear rules, as a useful metaphor for life was obvious from an interview that appeared in *France Football* in 1957. 'I quickly learned that the ball never came to you where you expected it,' he said. 'This helped me in life, above all in the metropolis, where people are not wholly straightforward.' Football was, in other words, a reminder of life's unpredictability.

In Algiers, where Camus joined Racing Universitaire d'Aeger in 1928, it became almost an obsession.

I fretted with impatience from Sunday to Thursday, for train-ing day, and from Thursday to Sunday, match day. So I joined the university men. And there I was, goalkeeper of the junior team. We used to play hard. Students, their fathers' sons, don't spare themselves. Poor us, in every sense, a good half of us mown down like corn ... The hardest team was Olympic Hussein Dey. The stadium is beside the cemetery. They made us realise, without mercy, that there was direct access. As for me, poor goalkeeper, they went for my body. There was

Boufarik … that great big centre-forward (among ourselves we called him Watermelon) who always came down with all his weight, right on my kidneys, without counting the cost: shin massage with football boots, shirt pulled back by hands, knees in the distinguished parts, sandwiches against the post … in brief, a scourge. And every time Watermelon apologised with a 'Sorry, son' and a Franciscan smile.

Camus would make sure he got Watermelon back as and when he could 'but without cheating'. That was vital, for, in the phrase that has become so well known it is almost a cliché, 'after many years in which the world has afforded me many experiences, what I most surely know in the long run about morality and the obligations of men, I owe to sport.'

In Paris, Camus supported Racing, because they, like his university side, played in blue and white. He would go to games and when in 1957 he was spotted by a newsreel crew at the stadium, his irritation at being asked to focus on something other than football was clear. He hurried the discussion on from the Nobel Prize he had won earlier that year to the Racing keeper. 'We shouldn't blame him,' he said. 'It's when you're in the middle of the woods that you realise how difficult it is.' That phrase – '*au milieu des bois*' – is highly telling. To play in goal is like being in the forest: it is to be prey to all manner of hidden predators.

And when mistakes happen, they haunt a goalkeeper. Moacyr Barbosa never shook off Alcide Ghiggia's goal at the Maracanã. The thought of Scott Carson conjures images of his error against Croatia. The Leeds goalkeeper Gary Sprake will always be remembered for throwing the ball into his own net in front of the Kop. Even Stojanović, the captain and hero of Zvezda, knows how close his error in the semi-final came to defining his life as a negative. Goalkeepers may be adamant that they have no fear of penalties and that Handke's novel is based on a misconception, but for all that, the epigraph to the novel encapsulates a deep-rooted fear: '*Der Tormann sah zu, wie der Ball über die Linie rollte …*' ['The goalkeeper watched as the ball rolled across the line …']. Perhaps the goalkeeper referred to here was blameless, but somehow the mind conjures horrors like Luis Arconada's for Spain against France in the 1984 European Championship final, or Rob Green's for England against the USA in the 2010 World Cup, or Massimo Taibi's for Manchester United against Southampton (which effectively ended his career at Old Trafford: he was named man of the match in his first two games, made the error in his third and then gifted Chelsea their first in a 5–0 win over United at Stamford Bridge in his fourth; there wasn't a fifth). Or, indeed, like Stojanović's against Bayern.

Ronnie Blake in Glanville's *Goalkeepers Are Different* has similar nightmares when, after the senior goalkeeper breaks his arm, he realises he is likely to be called up to the first team for the first time for the following week's game at Liverpool: 'in one of them, I was keeping goal at Anfield, in front of the Kop – I knew I was at Liverpool, although there wasn't any noise or anything – and this ball was trickling slowly, slowly past me, over the line. I was on the ground; I kept trying to get up and stop it, it was only a yard or so away, but every time I tried, I couldn't make it, something was holding me back.'

The Brazilian writer Sérgio Sant'Anna's short story '*No Ultimo Minuto*' discusses exactly the same sort of error, featuring a goalkeeper who obsessively watches replays of his critical mistake on television, seeing in a paused slow-motion shot the moment at which his side won the championship, before the ball slipped through his grasp and the championship melted away:

> I feel the ball in my arms and against my chest. I know our fans are going to scream and applaud, relieving their nervousness in that last attack of the game. I have the ball securely and firmly against my chest and, suddenly, I feel that emptiness in my body. I'm holding air. The ball is escaping and penetrating softly into the goal. The ball doesn't even make it to the net; it just lies there slightly over the fatal line. And I grasp desperately to reach it, pulling at the ball there inside. But it's too late; everybody's already seen that it was a goal. The stadium explodes and I feel my own head bursting apart. I see and hear all of that: their team hugging each other, the

buzz of the crowd, the fireworks, and our team running to confront the referee, in a useless attempt to have the goal disallowed. I hear and see all that, but it's like everything is very far away, without any relation to me.

Once again, the goalkeeper is left isolated, remote, psychically as well as physically.

Perhaps no goalkeeper so embodies the anxiety that lies at the heart of goalkeeping as Carlos, who played for Corinthians and Brazil. He is tall and lean, but that aside doesn't look much like a sportsman. With his sparse curls, his long nervous fingers and a face made to look thinner than it really is by the length of his nose, he has a slightly academic air, his polo shirt perhaps suggesting a teacher who helps out with PE or a politician off for a bracing game of squash. What he actually wanted to be is an architect. Like Bloch, like Meursault, Carlos has his great crime – not a murder, admittedly, as he is keen to stress, but a cynical unpunished foul on the France forward Bruno Bellone three minutes from the end of extra-time in the World Cup quarter-final in 1986. And, again like Bloch and Meursault, he seems all but unmoved by the crime while suffering doubts and neuroses about life itself.

For him goalkeeping was always an intellectual pursuit – quite literally, at first, for he had to conjure the image from words. He started playing football in the streets of his home town of Vinhedo in the state of São Paulo with no model to guide him. 'You had social clubs,' he explained. 'You had the radio as well. You didn't have matches on television so you listened to games. When you listened to the radio the most spectacular play would be around the goal: you either had a goal or you had a save from the goalkeeper. So when I played I tried to imitate what I heard and imagined.'

Carlos was a gifted sportsman so started taking football a little more seriously than others he'd kicked about with on the streets. 'I started playing at amateur clubs and I played as a defender,' he explained. 'I had a good sense of position but I was afraid of heading the ball. I didn't have skills – that's why

I played as a defender – but I had a good reading of the game. At the time there was a thought that the goalkeeper was just a player who couldn't play outfield so nobody wanted to do it. But I liked it. I already liked it. At school I did high jump and I played basketball so I knew how to spring. I was twelve or thirteen when I decided goalkeeper was my position.'

He rose quickly. 'I started out playing against keepers my age but because nobody wanted to be a goalkeeper I started playing with older people,' he said; whether he was being modest or simply expressing how underappreciated goalkeepers were in Brazil at the time is unclear. 'When I was fourteen I would play with people twenty years older than me. Sometimes they would get mad at me because I couldn't save everything.'

Then came his big break. 'Ponte Preta [a team from Campinas who were one of the stronger sides in the Paulista region in the seventies] would play training matches against amateur clubs and one day I was playing in the match before that game,' he said. 'A coach from Ponte Preta saw me play and asked if I wanted to join the club. I was thirteen or fourteen.'

But Carlos found he didn't much enjoy the life of a footballer. 'I spent three months training with Ponte Preta,' he explained. 'I'd go to school in the morning, have lunch and then go to train. I didn't want this for my life. I liked football, but to be a professional goalkeeper … I didn't enjoy it because of the pressure. Even though I was playing with people my own age, there was a responsibility to play well. I didn't enjoy that; I wasn't comfortable. I went there one morning and told them I wanted to quit, but the coach who had taken me to Ponte Preta insisted. He spoke to my father. So we agreed that I'd move school to be nearer to the club.'

The way he said it, though, made it clear that he wasn't overly enthusiastic. 'A lot of my friends wanted to be professionals but didn't make it, so even though I wasn't enjoying it I had a responsibility to them,' Carlos said. 'By 1973 I was already with a professional team but really I wanted to be an architect. But I realised that I was already earning money playing football so I decided to dedicate myself to that.'

Ronnie Blake, in Glanville's *Goalkeepers Are Different*, goes through similar agonies when called up to Borough's reserve side: 'I'd got this picture in my mind, me standing in the goal there, and behind the goal Mike and about a dozen other of the lads, leaning over the wall, calling out advice, telling me what I ought to do and ought not to do, and up in the stand, where I could see them, because there'd hardly be anybody else there, the old man, Mum and my sister.' So bad is his fit of nerves that Ronnie considers asking for a transfer to 'Manchester, Liverpool, Birmingham, anywhere … anywhere outside London.'

What made the shackles harder to break was that Carlos turned out to be very good. 'It wasn't easy to enjoy being a goalkeeper, but once I'd been called up to the national team they kept picking me,' he said. 'I played in the South American championship and in the 1976 Olympics in Montreal.' The following year he turned professional and Ponte Preta reached the final of the Paulista championship, losing to Corinthians. It brought Carlos to prominence and earned him a call-up to the national side. He went to the 1978 World Cup as back-up for Emerson Leão.

After Telê Santana became national coach in 1980, Carlos began to get more and more opportunities in the national team, but he still wasn't happy. 'The pleasure,' he said, 'came from the titles and the accomplishments. But I really had to fight against anxiety. I thought too much. I would be frozen with indecision. Something would come in my mind and then I would change. Sometimes I'd be in the national team thinking, "I've got to get better. There's other goalkeepers who could be in my place." And yet there I was in the national team. There was a contradiction. Maybe the way I started influenced my whole career, generated this sense of not belonging.'

In *Simple Goalkeeping Made Spectacular*, Graham Joyce makes the case forcefully that goalkeepers are not existentialist heroes: 'What a load of cock!' as he puts it. He's right, of course, up to a point: just because Camus was a goalkeeper doesn't mean that every goalkeeper is prone to fits of neurotic self-analysis: they're not all 'complex brooding outsiders'. But then he himself acknowledges that 'too much imagination is bad for a goalkeeper' and you wonder about somebody who rails against the suggestion that goalkeepers are 'alienated' and yet seems so uncomfortable about preconceptions of his chosen profession, constantly attacking the supposed pretensions of 'literary' novelists and Oxbridge types. He refers to Nabokov as a 'paedophile hiding behind irony' yet at times he seems prepared to defend any goalkeeper, whatever the evidence, against those who would do them down. 'Paul Robinson and David James,' he wrote, 'have had to endure in front of them a ragged line-up of prima donnas, hopheads, dimwits, basket cases and *Hello!* magazine fashion shows.' Never mind that some might argue that one of them had concrete feet and the other persistently made bad decisions; it must be the outfielders' fault.

In fact what's notable about both Joyce's book and Francis Hodgson's *Only the Goalkeeper to Beat* is how angry they both seem, determined to make the case for goalkeepers while raging against prejudice and misportrayal. 'Goalkeeping,' Hodgson wrote, 'remains an unknown and rather unloved activity. The goalkeeper is there to carry the blame, to be laughed at, and to look decorative as he gets beaten by the kind of over-emphatic goal all players love (but usually fail) to score. It isn't fair, it isn't right. But these are still clearly the attitudes that goalkeepers have to put up with.' Which, in a certain light, might seem like alienation.

Carlos, certainly, by his own admission, had too much imagination, always doubting, always wondering if he were worthy of his place in the side. 'Despite that I was consistent,' he said. 'When I got an idea in my head I'd work really hard to do it well. I was saying, "I'm here but I can't be here but I have to be here because I'm good enough to be here."'

He was later told that the federation had mapped out his career almost from the moment he'd turned professional. Carlos was taken to the World Cup in 1978 for experience with the intention that he should be the first-choice keeper in 1982. He might have been – in fact probably would have been, had he not been injured. After that, Carlos said, he felt he was always fighting 'resistance' within the federation, even after a move to Corinthians that guaranteed enhanced media coverage. Carlos Alberto Parreira didn't select him for the Copa América in 1983 and in the build-up to the 1986 World Cup Evaristo de Macedo made clear to him that his first choice was Paulo Vitor. But then Paulo Vitor was injured, and Carlos played superbly in defeats to Colombia and Chile. Telê Santana returned as coach and Carlos was number one again.

He had lost his place through injury and he regained it through injury; precisely the sort of uncertainty of which Turnbull spoke, that Taffarel was so proud to have conquered. Of course, players in other positions see their careers shaped by injuries, both to themselves and to others, but other positions always have more of a chance: they could come off the bench or replace a player being rested. Goalkeepers have, for those trying to take their place in the side, an irritating robustness, a tendency to play game after game. Once Carlos had lost his place, it took a major stroke of luck to get it back again.

His performances in the 1986 World Cup suggested he was worth his place. Having kept clean sheets in each of his first four games, Carlos was blameless for Michel Platini's goal in the quarter-final. But then came the moment that ensured his infamy. With three minutes of extra-time remaining, Platini slipped a pass through the Brazil back-line for Bellone. He ran on and, as Carlos came out of his box, knocked it past him on the goalkeeper's right. There seemed little doubt he would get to the ball, but Carlos grabbed at him, his hands making contact with the forward's chest. Bellone stayed on his feet but his run was undoubtedly impeded and the delay allowed Silas to get back to clear. The Romanian referee Ioan Igna, astonishingly, allowed play to go on. France were furious; not only had they been denied what would surely have been a goal, and probably a winning goal at that, but after what had happened in the semi-final four years earlier, when Harald Schumacher had taken out Patrick Battiston, it seemed a horrible case of history repeating itself.

'I don't feel guilt,' Carlos insisted. 'The forward was through against me alone. The player put the ball past me and I went to pull him down, but I didn't. I just slowed him down and a defender could get back. The referee didn't give the foul because he decided the forward had the advantage. It was lucky for me. In those days it wasn't a red card, so you did what you did. Now the rules are different so I would do something different.'

A form of justice was enacted almost immediately. Bellone took France's third penalty in the shoot-out. His shot hit the post, bounced back, hit Carlos on the back of the head and trickled over the line. It wasn't only desperate bad luck; the penalty shouldn't have counted. The rules state clearly that once the forward motion of the ball has ceased, the penalty is considered complete. Brazil's players knew that and surrounded Igna, but he ignored them – two wrongs, for once, making a right. Socrates had already seen his effort saved by the France goalkeeper Joel Bats and, although Platini fired his kick over the bar, Bats then saved from Júlio César to take France into the semi-final.

And so Carlos had his comeuppance, undone in the end by just the sort of cruel chance he had always feared. He played in the 1987 Copa América, when Brazil were shockingly thrashed 4–1 by Chile and so failed to make the quarter-final, but by 1989 he had been replaced in the national team by Taffarel. He drifted though Atlético Mineiro, Guarani, Palmeiras and the Turkish club Malatyaspor, but only found contentment late in his career with Portuguesa when, with the pressure off, he was able to relax. He had an excellent World Cup in 1986, but he is remembered now only for his foul and his misfortune. 'When somebody is unlucky in Brazil,' the journalist Paulo Guilherne said, 'we say they have cold feet. Carlos was a goalkeeper with cold feet.'

Goalkeepers may scoff at the title of Handke's book and Wenders' film but, amid all his anxieties, it turned out that the one thing Carlos did need to fear was penalties.

EPILOGUE

He should stand about six foot and no nonsense. Size gives one the impression of strength, and enables a goalkeeper to deal with high and wide shots with comparative ease, where a smaller or shorter man would be handicapped. On the other hand, a tall and ponderous goalkeeper is at a disadvantage with the smaller and more agile rival when required to get down to swift ground or low shots. To the agility of youth should be coupled the sagacity of veterancy.

That was Leigh Richmond Roose writing in *The Times* in 1906, so perhaps not so much has changed. Maybe we'd add three or four inches to his measure of six foot, but that aside it seems the essentials are the same. Certainly Peter Shilton – himself a straight six foot – is not taken by the modern obsession with height. 'There is a thing that you have to be six foot four but personally I don't think so,' he said. 'Just because you're six foot five it doesn't mean you're going to be agile and use your feet as well as somebody who's just under six foot. If you're very small it's very difficult, but you don't have to be six foot five. Look at Fabien Barthez – there are exceptions.'

He could equally have named Iker Casillas. It wouldn't entirely be true to say that the age of the gym-honed keeper has passed, but there does seem a greater diversity of size and shape than there was, say, a decade ago. There are still reactive goalkeepers and proactive goalkeepers, those who mop up behind their defence and those who prefer the sanctuary of their line, but it's rare now to find goalkeepers at the highest level who don't both command their box and feel comfortable with the ball at their feet as well as having a basic competence at saving shots. When a weakness is apparent, modern means of statistical analysis make it immediately clear, as for instance when Paul Robinson, then at Tottenham, was prove to be susceptible to long-range shots, seemingly because of a sluggishness in his footwork. When David De Gea conceded a long-range drive to Manchester City's Edin Džeko on his Manchester United debut in the Community Shield in 2011, it was immediately pointed out that, while playing for Atlético Madrid the previous season, he'd conceded more long-range shots than any other goalkeeper in La Liga. He clearly worked on his footwork over the season and, although he continued to have occasional problems dealing with crosses, his supposed vulnerability to long-range shots had almost been forgotten by the end of his first term in England.

The modern ball moves more in the air than the old ball did, at times swerving and dipping alarmingly, but before modern goalkeepers moan too much about that, they may consider how technology has aided them with ever improving gloves. Modern latex palms not merely take the sting out of shots, but make holding the ball much easier than it was. And, of course, modern goalkeepers are far better protected than they once were; not only is charging a thing of the past but any contact on them when they challenge for a cross now tends to be considered a foul.

It's ball-playing ability, though, that really marks out the goalkeeper of today from his counterpart of even twenty years ago. When the backpass law was introduced in 1992, it caused panic. On the opening day of the 1992–93 Premier League season, the first round of matches played under the new legislation in England, Lee Chapman scored for Leeds against Wimbledon after eight minutes, capitalising as the defender Roger Joseph dithered over whether to give the ball back to his goalkeeper Hans Segers. Later in the same game, the Leeds keeper John Lukic conceded an indirect free-kick by picking up a Chris Whyte backpass (an incident remembered largely because, after Steve Hodge had been booked for encroachment, his manager Howard Wilkinson tried to defend him using Pythagorean theory to prove that, if the centre of the wall was ten yards back, the ends of the wall were necessarily further from the ball). Back then, any backpass drew an intake of breath, largely brought on by how uncomfortable most keepers looked with the ball trickling towards them and no option but to kick: would he slice it, would he whack it into the forward, would he miss it altogether? Now, although there is the occasional pratfall (such as the luckless Robinson's when a Gary Neville backpass bobbled over his boot in England's defeat to Croatia in a Euro 2008 qualifier in Zagreb), most keepers look as natural on the ball as a centre-back, usually able to use both feet and so secure that forwards often don't bother closing them down.

This is a major step in the development of the goalkeeper for his history is a classic story of an exile trying to find his way home. It's one of the most pervasive myths there is, Odysseus trying to find his way back to Ithaca after the fall of Troy, Nala seeking Damayanti in Hindu mythology, the hobbits making their way back to the Shire after their adventures with the ring, Maximus achieving through death his reunion with his wife and son in *Gladiator*. The trope informs the Lacanian branch of post-Freudian psychoanalysis and the endless search for a wholeness the ego last enjoyed in the womb. It even forms the basis of the Abrahamic religions, the quest for redemption and a return to paradise after Adam and Eve's expulsion from Eden. Exile and return, questing and redemption, are fundamental.

In the mid-to-late nineteenth century, the goalkeeper was cast out of the rest of the team, given a specific role with specific duties and then a specific shirt. He was different from the other ten, an outcast. Since then, the process has been one of gradual reintegration. There have been setbacks, but generally speaking the last 140 years have seen the goalkeeper becoming increasingly another member of the team. Even the difference of his shirt, once the thing that seemed to mark him out as a pariah, is now celebrated with teams releasing new kits boasting of their new goalkeeper's shirt (home and away).

The goalkeeper was a specific type of exile – a scapegoat, always handily there to take the blame for the rest of the team.

As Charlie Campbell points out in his history of the scapegoat, the urge to blame has been there from the beginning of time: 'In the beginning there was blame,' he wrote. 'Adam blamed Eve, Eve blamed the serpent and we've been hard at it ever since.' He goes on, in his second paragraph, to point out that all the most influential opinion-formers have found a scapegoat: Marx blamed the capitalist system, Freud blamed sex, Dawkins blamed religion, Larkin blamed his parents and Dr Atkins blamed the potato. Footballers tended to blame the goalkeeper. The case of Moacyr Barbosa may have been extreme, but the habit of pointing the finger at the one marked out as different is well established.

The scapegoat originally formed part of Jewish ritual on the Day of Atonement, a literal goat which, from the period of the Tabernacle in Exodus through to the time of the temples in Jerusalem, would be cast out into the desert metaphorically loaded with the sins of the Israelites. It thus had a cleansing role. To Christians, of course, Christ is the scapegoat in human form, wandering in the wilderness for forty days before being slaughtered to redeem the sins of the world. To quote Sylvia Brinton Perera, writing in *Scapegoat Complex: Toward a Mythology of Shadow and Guilt*, 'Exiled scapegoats can return to serve the collective as agents of its deepest and most difficult needs.' There is, thus, something noble about the figure of the exile, standing alone as potential saviour. In that context, it's perhaps not surprising that so many goalkeepers were so opposed to the backpass law. Most hated it, of course, simply because it meant they had to learn a new skill, to play with their feet, their reluctance to do so perhaps precisely the reason they went in goal in the first place. But for others, Francis Hodgson in *Only the Goalkeeper to Beat*, for instance, opposition to the new regulation seemed rooted in anger that one of the things that made the goalkeeper different was being removed. At times, goalkeepers seem so dedicated to the protection of their difference that you wonder whether, like Camus's Meursault, they seek a crowd to ward off their loneliness with 'cries of hatred'.

Some, of course, enjoy the sense of standing apart: that seems to have informed the Soviet love of goalkeeping and it also perhaps explains why so many artists and intellectuals have been drawn to the position. Others maybe are inspired by that sense of being both exile and scapegoat, of being some sort of reflection of the Christlike redeemer; and of course, that chimes with the inate streak of existentialism that seems to run through goalkeeping for, as Sartre, following Nietzsche, pointed out, the process of devising a code by which to live in a world without a god is itself godlike. And in that context, it seems appropriate that the 'holy goalie' is such an archetype, from Pope John Paul II to Leonard Small, who played in goal for the Scotland amateur side before becoming Moderator of the General Assembly of the Church of Scotland and chaplain to the Queen; from Igor Akinfeev, with his profound Orthodox faith, to David Icke, who went from playing in goal for Coventry via a stint as a *Grandstand* presenter to declaring himself the Son of God.

The goalkeeper, then, is beset by a major inherent tension. How can he take on these godlike redemptive qualities if he is, by the logic of football as fertility rite, the one who prevents the soil being fertilised, if he is the one who spoils the harvest? Resolving that seeming contradiction requires philosophical twists worthy of the gnostics. And that is why, however heroic the likes of Iker Casillas, Manuel Neuer and Gianluigi Buffon may seem by comparison with the funk-sticks of the Victorian public schools, however many people walk round in shirts with 'Hart 1' printed on the back, there will always be a paradox at the heart of goalkeeping. He is doomed always to be an outsider.

BIBLIOGRAPHY

Agnew, Paddy, *Forza Italia: A Journey to the Heart of Italy and its Football* (Ebury, 2006)

Angrisani, Biagio and Luca De Prá, Luca: *Il destino nelle mani* (Fondazione Genoa 1893, 2008)

Antônio João and Bulhões Antônio (eds), *O moderno conto brasileiro: Antologia escolar* (Civilização Brasileira, 1978)

Arlott, John (ed), *The Great Ones: Studies of Eight Great Football Players* (Pelham, 1968)

Ball, Phil, *Morbo: The Story of Spanish Football* (WSC Books, 2001) *White Storm: 100 Years of Real Madrid* (Mainstream, 2002)

Banks, Gordon, *Banks of England* (Sportsmedia, 1980)

Barend, Frits and Hen van Dorp, *Ajax, Barcelona, Cruyff: The ABC of an Obstinate Maestro* (Bloomsbury, 1999)

Bartram, Sam, *By Himself* (Burke, 1956)

Bausenwein, Christoph, Siegler Bernd and Kaiser Harald, *Die Legende vom Club: Die Geschichte des 1. FC Nürnberg* (Werkstatt, 2008)

Bellos, Alex, *Futebol: The Brazilian Way of Life* (Bloomsbury, 2002)

Biermann, Christoph, *Die Fußball-Matrix: Auf der Suche nach dem perfekten Spee* (Kiepenheuer & Witsch, 2009)

Brera, Gianni, *Storia critica del calcio Italiano* (Tascaballi Bompiani, 1978)

Buffon, Gianluigi and Roberto Perrone: *Numero Uno* (Rizzoli, 2008)

Calirman, Claudia, *Brazilian Art under Dictatorship,* (Duke University Press, 2012)

Catton, JAH, *Wickets and Goals: Stories of Play* (Chapman and Hall, 1926)

Chambers, EK, *The Medieval Stage* (1903)

Chapman, Peter, *The Goalkeepers History of Britain* (Fourth Estate, 1999)

Cohen, Morton (ed), *Rudyard Kipling to Rider Haggard: the Record of a Friendship* (Rutherford, 1965)

Cosgrove, Stuart, *Hampden Babylon* (Canongate, 1991)

Creek, FNS, *A History of the Corinthian Football Club* (Longmans, 1933)

Csanádi, Árpád, *Soccer* (Athenaeum, 1978), first published in Hungarian as *Labdarúgás* by Medicina Könyviadó, 1963)

Delaney, Terence, *Century of Soccer* (Sportsman's Book Club, 1963)

Dryden, Ken, *The Game* (Macmillan, 1983)

Dunphy, Eamonn, *A Strange Kind of Glory* (Aurum, 2007)

Ferguson, Alex and Meek David, *Six Years at United* (Mainstream, 1992)

Filho, Mário, *O Negro no Futebol Brasileiro* (second edition) (Civilizaçao Brasiliera, 1964)

Finn, Ralph L, *My Greatest Game* (Saturn, 1951)

Foot, John, *Calcio: A History of Italian Football* (Fourth Estate, 2006)

Galeano, Eduardo, *Football in Sun and Shadow* (Fourth Estate, 1997)

Gibson, Alfred and William Pickford (eds), *Association Football and the Men who Made It* (Caxton, 1905)

Goldblatt, David, *The Ball is Round: A Global History of Football* (Viking, 2006)

Goram, Andy with Gallacher Ken, *Andy Goram: My Life* (Virgin, 1997)

Gregg, Harry, *Wild About Football: His Own Story* (Souvenir Press, 1961)

Guilherne, Paulo, *Goleiros: Heróis e Anti-Heróis da Camisa 1* (Alameda, 2006)

Hamilton, Aidan, *An Entirely Different Game: The British Influence on Brazilian Football* (Mainstream, 1998)

Hardcastle, Michael, *Soccer Special* (Mammoth, 1990)

Harris, Nick, *England, Their England* (Pitch, 2003)

Hazlewood, Nick, *In the Way! Goalkeepers: A Breed Apart?* (Mainstream, 1996)

Hodgson, Francis, *Only the Goalkeeper to Beat* (Macmillan, 1998)

Hagopian, Frances, *Traditional Politics and Regime Change in Brazil* (Cambridge University Press, 1996)

Hopcraft, Arthur and McIlvanney, Hugh, *World Cup 70* (Eyre and Spottiswood, 1970)

Inglis, Simon, *League Football and the Men who Made It* (Collins Willow, 1988)

Jenkins, Garry, *The Beautiful Team* (Simon & Schuster, 1998)

Jennings, Pat, *An Autobiography* (HarperCollins, 1983)

Johnson, WB, 'Football a Survival of Magic', *Contemporary Review*, CXXXV (1929), 225–31

Kavanagh, Dan, *Putting the Boot In* (Jonathan Cape, 1985)

Keith, John, *Dixie Dean: The Inside Story of a Football Legend* (Robson, 2001)

Kuper, Simon, *The Football Men: Up Close with the Giants of the Modern Game* (Simon & Schuster, 2011)

Kurt, Richard, *United We Stood, 1975–94: The Unofficial Account of the Ferguson Years* (Sigma 1994)

Leving, Yuri (ed), *The Goalkeeper: the Nabokov Almanac* (Academic Studies, 2010)

Livers, Keith A, 'The Soccer Match as Stalinist Ritual: Constructing the Body Social in Lev Kassil's *The Goalkeeper of the Republic*' in *The Russian Review* LX (Oct 2001) 592–613

Macadam, John, *The Macadam Road*, (Jarrolds, 1955)

Manfridi, Giuseppe, *Fra i legni. I voli taciturni di Dino Zoff* (Limina, 2011)

Marindin, GE, 'The Game of Harpastum or Pheninda', *Classical Review*, April 1890, 145-80

Marples, Morris, *A History of Football* (Secker and Warburg, 1954)

Martin, Simon, *Football and Fascism: The National Game under Mussolini* (Berg, 2004)

McCarra, Kevin, *Scottish Football: A Pictorial History* (Polygon, 1984)

McWeeney, JA (ed), *Football Guide, or How to Play Soccer* (British Sports Publishing, 1920)

Merrick, Gil, *I See It All* (Museum Press, 1954)

Mezarobba, Glenda, 'Between Reparations, Half Truths and Impunity: The Difficult Break with the Legacy of the Dictatorship in Brazil', *International Journal of Human Rights*, XIII (2010), 7-15

Michels, Rinus, *Teambuilding: the Road to Success* (Reedswain, 2001)

Mulqueen, Timothy and Woitalla, Michael, *The Complete Soccer Goalkeeper* (Human Kinetics, 2010)

Nabokov, Vladimir, *Speak, Memory* (Weidenfeld and Nicolson, 1966)

Naughton, Bill, *The Goalkeeper's Revenge* (Heinemann, 1961)

Olesha, Yury, *Envy* (Ardis, 2004; first published in Russian in *Red Virgin Soil*, 1927)

Pastorin, Darwin, *I Portieri del Sogno – Storie di Numeri 1* (Einaudi, 2009)

Pennacchia, Mario, *La vita disperata del portiere Moro* (Isbn Edizioni, 2011)

Rafferty, John, *One Hundred Years of Scottish Football* (Pan, 1973)

Reis, Daniel Aarão, Ridenti, Marcelo, and Patto Sá Motta Rodrigo, (eds), *O Golpe e a ditadura militar: quarenta anos depois (1964–2004)* (EDUSC, 2004)

Reng, Ronald, *A Life Too Short: The Tragedy of Robert Enke* (Yellow Jersey, 2011)

Riches, Adam, Parker, Tim, and Frankland, Robert, *Football's Comic Book Heroes: Celebrating the Greatest British Football Comics of the Twentieth Century* (Mainstream, 2009)

Robinson, FK, *Glossary of Words used in the Neighbourhood of Whitby*, Pt II (E. Dial. Soc., Ser. C, Vol IX, 1876)

Ross, Gordon (ed), *The Gillette Book of Cricket and Football* (Frederick Muller, 1963)

Rosselli, Sandro, *The Torino FC Legend: An Italian Fairy Tale* (Mirco Occhetti, 2007)

Sanders, Richard, *Beastly Fury* (Transworld, 2009)

Sant'Anna, Sérgio, 'No último minuto' in João Antônio and Antônio Bulhões (eds), *O moderno conto brasileiro: Antologia escolar* (Civilização Brasileira, 1978)

Sconcerti, Mario: *Storia delle idee del calcio – Uomini, schemi e imprese di un'avventura infinita* (Baldini & Castoldi, 2009)

Shearman, Montague, *Athletics and Football* (Badminton Library, 1887)

Skidmore, Thomas E, *Brazil: Five centuries of Change* (Oxford University Press, 1999)

Smith, Stratton (ed), *The Brazil Book of Football* (Souvenir Press, 1963)

Taylor, Hugh, *The Masters of Scottish Football* (Stanley Paul, 1967)

Thubron, Colin, *Among the Russians: From the Baltic to the Caucasus* (Heinemann, 1983)

Turnbull, John. "Alone in the Woods: The Literary Landscape of Soccer's 'Last Defender.'" *World Literature Today*, July–August 2010, 19–22

Vasili, Phil, *The First Black Footballer: Arthur Wharton – An Absence of Memory* (Sport in Global Society, 1998)

Vialli, Gianluca and Marcotti, Gabriele, *The Italian Job: A Journey to the Heart of Two Great Footballing Cultures* (Bantam, 2006)

Waddell, Sid, *Jossy's Giants* (Penguin, 1986)

Warsop, Keith, *The Early FA Cup Finals and the Southern Amateurs* (Soccerdata, 2004)

Whitcher, Alec E, *The Ace of Games* (Southern Publishing, 1944)

Wilson, Jonathan, *The Anatomy of England: A History in Ten Matches* (Orion, 2010)
Behind the Curtain (Orion, 2006)
Inverting the Pyramid: A History of Football Tactics (Orion, 2008)
Brian Clough: Nobody Ever Says Thank You (Orion, 2011)

Young, Percy M, *A History of British Football* (Stanley Paul, 1968)

Zoff, Dino and De Ponti, Roberto, *Dino Zoff. Campioni del Mondo* (Aliberti, 2006)

INDEX